Liddypool
Birthplace
of The Beatles

Liddypool

Birthplace
of The Beatles

by David Bedford
Foreword by Beatles drummer Pete Best

This book is dedicated to my wife, Alix, and daughters, Philippa, Lauren and Ashleigh and to the memory of my sister, Judy (1967-2007) and my father, Colin (1935-2009)

Liddypool: Birthplace of The Beatles

David Bedford

Published 2011
2nd Edition

© Dalton Watson Fine Books Limited

ISBN 978-1-85443-248-3

Printed and bound in
Singapore by Star Standard

for the publisher

Dalton Watson Fine Books
1730 Christopher Drive,
Deerfield, IL 60015,
U.S.A

www.daltonwatson.com

Apple

Q. What was the forbidden fruit that Eve gave to Adam in the Garden of Eden?

A. Simple. An apple.

How do we know? It has been mentioned in church, in books, in cartoons and has been repeated in many ways. So, we accept it as true.

But, there is one small problem with this. The Bible never mentions the forbidden fruit was an apple.

The Bible refers to the fruit of the tree of knowledge, not necessarily a piece of edible fruit. So why do we accept it? Because that is what we have been told many times.

Realising that there are too many readily-accepted but inaccurate facts about The Beatles, this book was undertaken. So follow me on a journey to the very 'genesis' of The Beatles' story, and revisit the birth of the greatest band the world has ever known.

LEFT: *The Beatles pose on the Victoria Monument in Derby Square, Liverpool, in February 1963*

Contents

Contents

The Beatles at the press conference held at Liverpool Airport on 10 July 1964

Cast of Characters

Neil Aspinall
Beatles roadie and school friend of Paul McCartney. He was the father of Roag, Pete Best's youngest brother. Neil went on to become Chief Executive of Apple, the company set up to run the business side of The Beatles empire. He died in 2008.

Julia Baird
Daughter of Julia Lennon and John Dykins, half-sister to John Lennon.

Tony Barrow
Beatles Public Relations Manager employed by Brian Epstein. Wrote The Beatles' record sleeve notes.

Sid Bernstein
U.S. promoter of the Shea Stadium concert and many more.

John Best
Father of Beatles drummer Pete Best.

Mona Best
Mother of Pete Best, founder of The Casbah Coffee Club and manager of The Beatles in 1961 before Brian Epstein took over.

Pete Best
Beatles drummer from August 1960 to August 1962 when he was replaced by Ringo Starr.

Roag Best
Pete Best's youngest brother, born in 1962.

Rory Best
Pete Best's younger brother.

Norman Birch
Married to John Lennon's mother's sister, Harriet, and guardian of John Lennon's half-sisters Julia and Jackie.

Tony Booth
Local promoter around Liverpool and Merseyside who painted the first picture of John, Paul, George and Ringo.

Tony Bramwell
School friend of George and Paul who later worked with The Beatles.

Ken Brown
Member of the re-formed Quarrymen who opened The Casbah Club in August 1959.

Norman Chapman
The Silver Beatles' drummer for a short period in 1960.

Bill Covington
Member of The Rustiks, managed by Brian Epstein.

Maureen Cox
Girlfriend and first wife of Ringo Starr.

Ian Crabtree
Beatles historian, plus owner and guide for Liverpool Beatles Tours.

Hunter Davies
Official Beatles biographer.

Rod Davis
Quarrymen banjo player and founder member: 1956–1957.

Paddy Delaney
Doorman at The Cavern.

Lonnie Donegan
Musician who started the skiffle craze in Britain.

John Duff Lowe
Occasional Quarrymen piano player during 1958.

John 'Bobby' Dykins
Partner of Julia Lennon, John's mother, and father of Julia and Jackie, John's half-sisters.

Peter Eckhorn
Owner of the Top Ten Club in Hamburg.

Brian Epstein
Beatles' manager from November 1961: arranged the record contract and made them famous. Died in August 1967.

Harry Epstein
Father of Brian.

Malka 'Queenie' Epstein
Mother of Brian.

Michael Fishwick
Medical student and lodger at Mendips who had a relationship with John's Aunt Mimi.

Joe Flannery
Liverpool promoter and friend of Brian Epstein.

Billy Fury
Ronnie Wycherley became 'Billy Fury', Britain's first rock 'n' roll star and answer to Elvis. The Silver Beatles auditioned to back him.

Len Garry
Quarrymen tea-chest bass player: 1956–1958.

Johnny Gentle
Singer for whom The Silver Beatles acted as backing band.

Harry Graves
Married Ringo's mother Elsie and became Ringo's stepfather.

Eric Griffiths
Quarrymen guitar player and founder member: 1956–1958.

Margaret Grose
Friend of Elsie Starkey, Ringo's mother. Current occupier of Ringo's childhood home in Admiral Grove.

Colin Hanton
Quarrymen drummer: 1956–1958.

Harold Harrison
George Harrison's father.

Louise Harrison
George Harrison's mother.

Olivia Harrison
Olivia Arias became George's second wife. They had a son, Dhani.

Bill Harry
Art College student friend of John Lennon and Stuart Sutcliffe who founded the Mersey Beat newspaper.

Leila Harvey
Cousin of John Lennon.

Harry Holmes
John Lennon's teacher at Dovedale School.

Tim Holmes
Friend of John Lennon from Dovedale School.

Johnny Hutchinson
Johnny 'Hutch' was considered the best drummer in Liverpool, and sat in with The Beatles occasionally.

Astrid Kirchherr
Fiancée of Stuart Sutcliffe from Hamburg.

Allen Klein
American businessman and record promoter brought into Apple by John, George and Ringo.

Bruno Koschmider
Hamburg club promoter who booked The Beatles to appear in Hamburg in arrangement with Allan Williams.

Sam Leach
Music promoter who organised the 'Operation Big Beat' concerts and booked The Beatles many times.

Spencer Leigh
Liverpool author, broadcaster and expert on The Beatles.

Alfred 'Freddie' Lennon
John Lennon's father.

Charlie Lennon
John Lennon's uncle.

Cynthia Lennon
Cynthia Powell married John Lennon in August 1962. Mother to Julian.

Julia Lennon
Mother of John, Julia Stanley married Alf Lennon. She then lived with John 'Bobby' Dykins and had two daughters with him: Julia and Jackie. Julia's family nickname was 'Judy'.

Julian Lennon
Son of John and Cynthia Lennon.

Pauline Lennon
Pauline Jones married Alf Lennon in the summer of 1968. He was fifty-six, she was twenty-years old. They had two sons, David and Robin.

Victoria Lennon
Daughter of Julia Lennon and Taffy Williams, put up for adoption. Her name was changed to Ingrid.

Annie Maguire
Best friend of Elsie Starkey, Ringo's mother.

Marie Maguire
Childhood friend of Ringo Starr.

Maharishi Mahesh Yogi
Founder and developer of the Transcendental Meditation technique whom The Beatles visited in India. He died in 2008.

Albert Marrion
Photographer employed by Brian Epstein to capture the Fab Four on film.

Gerry Marsden
Leader of Merseybeat band Gerry and The Pacemakers, managed by Brian Epstein.

George Martin
The Beatles' record producer at EMI who worked closely with them and sometimes referred to as the 'Fifth Beatle'.

Angela McCartney
Angela Williams married Jim McCartney in 1964. She was only thirty-four and had a five-year-old daughter, Ruth.

Jim McCartney
Paul McCartney's father.

Mary McCartney
Paul McCartney's mother, whose maiden name was Mohin.

Mike McCartney
Brother of Paul McCartney, and member of '60s group The Scaffold, using the name Mike McGear.

Ray McFall
Accountant who became The Cavern owner after Alan Sytner. Booked The Beatles for their debut.

Eddie Miles
Ringo's friend and neighbour with whom he formed the Eddie Clayton Skiffle Group.

Irene Milson
Second cousin of George Harrison.

Tommy Moore
Drummer for The Silver Beatles in Scotland with Johnny Gentle.

Ruth Morrison
George Harrison's first girlfriend who introduced him to Mona Best.

Pete Nash
Sub-editor, historian and photographic researcher. Author and editor of the magazine for the British Beatles Fan Club.

Chas Newby
Member of The Black Jacks and played bass guitar for The Beatles over Christmas 1960.

Ray O'Brien
Beatles historian and author.

Yoko Ono
John Lennon's second wife and mother to Sean.

Sean Ono Lennon
Son of John Lennon and Yoko Ono.

Larry Parnes
British music promoter who looked after Billy Fury and Johnny Gentle.

Dave Peacock
Member of '60s band the Night Boppers.

Percy Phillips
Owned a home studio in Kensington where The Quarrymen made their first record.

Geoff Rhind
Photographed The Quarrymen at St. Peter's Church on 6 July 1957.

Dot Rhone
Girlfriend of Paul McCartney and friend of Cynthia Powell.

Mike Rice
Drummer with Liverpool '60s band The Senators.

Ron Richards
EMI producer who worked with George Martin.

Dick Rowe
Decca Recording Manager who turned The Beatles down.

Faron Ruffley
Leader of Merseybeat band Farons Flamingos and friend of The Beatles.

Tony Sheridan
British rock 'n' roll musician who became an inspiration to The Beatles and recorded "My Bonnie" with them as Tony Sheridan and The Beat Brothers.

Pete Shotton
Quarrymen washboard player and founder member: 1956–1957. John Lennon's best friend.

George Smith
John Lennon's uncle and husband of Aunt Mimi.

Mike Smith
Artists & Repertoire (A&R) man from Decca Records.

Mimi Smith
Sister to John Lennon's mother Julia. Married George Smith and lived at Mendips.

Norman Smith
Engineer at EMI.

Annie Stanley
John Lennon's maternal grandmother.

George 'Pop' Stanley
John Lennon's maternal grandfather.

Elsie Starkey
Married to Richard Starkey and mother of Ritchie Starkey—Ringo Starr. She divorced her husband when Ringo was only three, and later married Harry Graves.

Richard Starkey
Ringo Starr's father.

Les Stewart
Leader of the Les Stewart Quartet whose guitarist was George Harrison.

Rory Storm
Alan Caldwell became better known as Rory Storm and with his group the Hurricanes established themselves as one of the first professional bands in Liverpool, with Ringo Starr on drums.

Stuart Sutcliffe
Art College friend of John Lennon who became the bass player for The Beatles. Died in Hamburg aged twenty-one.

Pauline Sutcliffe
Sister of Stuart Sutcliffe.

Alan Sytner
Founder of The Cavern in 1957. Sold it to Ray McFall.

Alistair Taylor
Assistant to Brian Epstein and Beatles' 'Mr. Fixit'.

Ted 'Kingsize' Taylor
Merseybeat band leader.

Ken Townsend
Engineer at EMI.

Steve Turner
Author of books on The Beatles and many other musical legends.

Ivan Vaughan
Quarrymen member, John's neighbour and the boy who introduced Paul McCartney to John Lennon.

Nigel Walley
Quarrymen member and manager.

Andy White
Session drummer who played with The Beatles at Abbey Road in September 1962.

Allan Williams
The Silver Beatles first manager from May 1960 who took them to Hamburg.

Stan Williams
Childhood friend of John Lennon and Ivan Vaughan.

Bob Wooler
Cavern DJ, promoter and music 'guru' to the Merseybeat bands.

I'm Partly Dave
"Paperback Writer"

> "There once upon a time was a man who was partly Dave—
> he had a mission in life. I'm partly Dave…"
> John Lennon, *In His Own Write*
>
> "Dear Sir or Madam, will you read my book?
> It took me years to write, will you take a look?"
> "Paperback Writer", John Lennon/ Paul McCartney

I'm 'Partly Dave' or wholly Dave Bedford, though probably not all there.

Why write another book on The Beatles to add to the many hundreds that have been written over the years?

Because not many Beatles books have been written by people from Liverpool. This is the city where I grew up; the city that influenced me. What do you know about the places you've read about in other Beatles books? Where did The Beatles grow up? Where did they live? What were their musical influences?

To understand The Beatles, you have to understand Liverpool. To understand Liverpool, you have to live here.

So, what about 'Partly Dave' then?

I grew up in The Dingle by the bottom of Madryn Street, where Ringo was born. In 1969, at the age of four, I started my education at St. Silas School, which Ringo had attended years before. My dad came to Liverpool as vicar of St. Philemon's Church, which was incorporated in the parish of St. Silas Church. St. Silas is the same church where Ringo sang in the choir and where his parents were married. My house was two doors away from the Men's Club, regularly attended by John Lennon's uncles.

I lived in The Dingle until I was twenty-four, having lived in Teilo Street after I was married. Our home was two streets away from Admiral Grove where Ringo lived from the age of five. Ringo once stated, "When you lived in The Dingle, you aspired to have a semi in the suburbs of Mossley Hill or Woolton".

My wife Alix and I decided to move out to Mossley Hill when we were ready to start a family, to within half a mile of Penny Lane—yes, that Penny Lane. Our children—Philippa, Lauren and Ashleigh—have all attended Dovedale School where John Lennon, George Harrison and Ivan Vaughan received their early education.

The Beatles have been a part of my life for a long time. After picking up my first guitar at ten years old, a Beatles' song book was added so I could learn my favourite tunes. They have always accompanied me on my own long and winding road. As many fans can testify, it is more than just liking their music; the awesome foursome has a profound influence on your life.

OPPOSITE TOP: *Bill Harry with the author in 2005*
OPPOSITE BOTTOM: *The Penny Lane roundabout from St. Barnabas' Church*
TOP: *The author with The Quarrymen at Dovedale School in May 2005.*
From left to right: Len Garry, Eric Griffiths, David, Colin Hanton and Rod Davis
ABOVE: *Madryn Street sign, Dingle*
RIGHT: *The view from the author's childhood house over Madryn Street*
and The Dingle, with the Anglican Cathedral to the left and the
Metropolitan Cathedral to the right on the horizon

In the summer of 2000 my doctor told me to take time off work because I was diagnosed with fibromyalgia, for which there is no cure. Suddenly I had time on my hands, though my health restricted my activities. I was forced to give up playing football and golf, and walking became more difficult. I had never been much of a reader, but I came across the *John Lennon Encyclopedia* by Bill Harry. It was a thick book, so I thought it would keep me going for a while. I read it with utter fascination because it brought home how much history there was in my own backyard.

As a form of therapy and to keep my brain active, I thought I'd find out more and use my other hobby—photography. One symptom of my illness is short-term memory loss, which is frustrating. By the time I had read twenty pages, I had forgotten what I had just read. The solution was to jot down little notes about the locations I wanted to visit. I then found these locations and photographed them.

Next, I read more books, which meant more paper notes. But I had a major problem. One set of notes didn't agree with another set, but they were supposedly about the same place. Which was right? Some of the addresses given were inaccurate and many conflicted with one another. I cross-checked with other sources and still had no definitive answers.

Why were there three different dates given for the day John met Paul? Why was The Cavern proclaimed the "Birthplace of The Beatles" when The Casbah Coffee Club and Percy Phillips' studio made the same claim too? Which was correct? There were many myths that had sprung out of Beatlemania that just didn't seem right. It has been said that Pete Best was dismissed because he wasn't a good drummer. Another account had it that he was dismissed because his mum Mona didn't get on with Brian Epstein. The dismissal of Pete Best has probably created more disagreements among fans and authors than any other topic from the early days of The Beatles. Then there is the claim that John Lennon was a "working class hero" and yet he grew up in middle-class Woolton.

I discussed my findings with Stan Williams and friends I had made through the British Beatles Fan Club. I then met Ray O'Brien who went to school with Paul McCartney and George Harrison. He is also the author of an excellent book, *There Are Places I'll Remember*, which details every venue The Quarrymen and Beatles had played in and around Merseyside. I now had more places to research. Ray's knowledge and expertise as a Beatles historian has been much appreciated.

In the summer of 2000, my wife Alix organized a school reunion at Dovedale School, which drew nearly 600 ex-pupils. Through this event, I met friends of John Lennon and George Harrison, particularly Stan Williams and Tim Holmes, who have now become my friends and they have some great stories for this book.

During my research, the biggest surprise came when I discovered a little club in the heart of suburban West Derby called The Casbah Coffee Club (also referred to as The Casbah or The Casbah Club).

I knew it was a venue but little did I know its importance in the history of The Beatles. The Casbah is a gem and a place every Beatles fan should visit. It is, in my humble opinion, more important to the history of The Beatles than The Cavern Club (also referred to as The Cavern). I don't write these words glibly and will later fully explain why.

I have since come to know the Best brothers—Pete, Rory and Roag—and they have given me much support, and many stories and photos over the years. I also conducted an interview with Pete Best, who was the original Beatles drummer before he was replaced by Ringo Starr.

Reading, talking to and meeting friends and family members of The Beatles, I realised how much knowledge I had acquired through my new-found hobby. I also collected many stories from those who were there at the time, not having to just rely on other books and articles. I wanted, as much as possible, to go back to the source of the story and not rely on second-hand versions. I have spent years tracking down eyewitnesses and am grateful to so many people for their generosity, especially with their time.

Someone then suggested that I detail my journey, and I jumped at the chance of something to keep my sanity and stay focused through my ill health. Thus began a seven-year quest (which I naively thought would last three months) to find out about the true early history of The Beatles. Through the British Beatles Fan Club, I met Rod Davis and Colin Hanton from The Quarrymen who answered many questions. This book contains their stories.

Pete Best wrote the foreword, without any editorial control over the content of the book. Everyone who has given an interview has been open and honest and trusted me. All I wanted to know was the truth. I just didn't realise how long it would take.

On page 22 and 23, I have tried to list everyone who has given me valuable help. They include Beatles drummer Pete Best, Beatles manager Allan Williams, Quarrymen members Rod Davis, Eric Griffiths and Colin Hanton, founder of *Mersey Beat* Bill Harry, John's half-sister Julia Baird, Brian Epstein's right-hand man and Beatles' "Mr. Fixit" Alistair Taylor, Beatles Press Officer Tony Barrow, Ringo's childhood friend Marie Maguire, Shea Stadium promoter Sid Bernstein, Quarrymen member Ken Brown, Beatles bass guitarist Chas Newby, George Harrison's cousin Irene, Stuart Sutcliffe's sister Pauline, Merseybeat legend Faron and John's teacher Harry Holmes and also to Ian Crabtree from Liverpool Beatles Tours for sharing his knowledge and contacts. I hope I haven't missed anyone off the list, but if I have, my apologies for the omission and my thanks for your help.

A special thank you to Marshall Terrill for his fantastic work in organizing, shaping and editing this book. His guidance and advice have been invaluable, and it would not have been the same without him. He also believed in the book and my writing and was a great source of encouragement. Thank you also to Glyn Morris for his support in publishing the book and for his advice, knowledge and expertise in making this dream come true for me. An extra thanks to the British Beatles Fan Club Editor Pete Nash, who has contributed to this book and his knowledge and support has been greatly appreciated.

Finally, a thank you to my understanding wife, Alix, who has continually supported me through this project. I have made full use of her typing skills, plus a little mention of some very patient speech-recognition software. This has been my hobby and therapy for the last few years and I hope you enjoy Liddypool. More important, I hope you learn more about the real story of the early Beatles and their proud roots.

I'm 'Partly Dave'.

David Bedford

My friend nearly knew The Beatles

This poem sums up the problems of trying to find out what exactly happened. In Liverpool, everyone has their own story of The Beatles.

My friend nearly knew The Beatles
He really nearly did
He nearly knew The Beatles
He really, really did

He saw them at a party
At someone else's house
He saw them really closely
And heard them speak by mouth

He touched one with his elbow
And smiled at one as well
He picked John Lennon's coat up
And laughed as Pete's joke fell

He saw two in the kitchen
He passed one on the stairs
He saw them in the hallway
And saw them sit on chairs

He found them on the toilet
He saw them do a wee
He watched them do their zip up
The same as you and me

He heard them talking pop talk
He watched them wash their hands
He watched them use the roller towel
And talk of other lands

He saw them drinking vodka
He passed them sausage sticks
He touched Paul's velvet jacket
And nearly lit his cig

He smiled at George's girlfriend
He brushed right past Pete's back
He stood right by McCartney
And gave his back a pat

He got behind John Lennon
And saw things Beatles do
And Lennon turned to face him
And said F*** off!

Anon

The Beatles were photographed by Michael Ward, February 1963 in The Cavern

Foreword

When the author, Dave Bedford, asked me to write the foreword to his book I was quite surprised and flattered, so I agreed to do it. Then the reality of the situation hit me and I thought, *what am I going to write that hasn't been said before about The Beatles?* I had no answer, so my first mission was to read *Liddypool* from start to finish.

As I was reading and turning the pages I suddenly realised and said to myself, *Hey, I'm enjoying this!* The reasons why, you may ask?

Without going into too much detail because that would spoil it for when you read the book, I found it to be different in layout, ideas and topics, and done in such a way that it was easy to remember the vast amount of detail that was revealed to the reader. Oh yes, and before I forget, here was an author that wasn't afraid to express his own views and theories and blow some fresh air into early Beatles history.

The icing on the cake for me was the guide to Liverpool and Beatle folklore with an explanation about each location.

Having been a Beatle for two years and not professing to be a Beatle historian, for me this was totally enlightening. To those who read this book, I hope that you find it the same.

The author refers to himself as 'I'm Partly Dave'. As far as I am concerned, he is 'A Whole Dave'.

Pete Best

LEFT: *Paul McCartney's homecoming concert at Anfield Football Stadium, Liverpool, on 1 June 2008*

Do you need another Beatles book?

"Do You Want To Know A Secret?"

If you can answer all these questions correctly, you probably don't need this book. If you can't, read on.

1. Which club is rightly called the 'Birthplace of The Beatles'?

2. When Stuart Sutcliffe stayed in Hamburg with Astrid Kirchherr, who became The Beatles' left-handed bass guitar player?

3. Who re-formed The Quarrymen in the summer of 1959 after the group hadn't played together for seven months, and what was the new line-up?

4. What was the name of the Liverpool foursome that blazed the trail for the Merseybeat bands in Hamburg?

5. Who was the common link, without whom Paul McCartney and John Lennon would never have met?

6. Whose surname should have been Parkin?

7. Which Beatle admitted that he wanted to be a hairdresser?

8. Which Beatle was voluntarily excluded from religious instruction by his parents when he started primary school?

9. Which members of The Beatles sang in a church choir?

10 Who was the pretty nurse in "Penny Lane"?

How did you do? All the answers are in this book, plus many more stories from the famous, and not so-famous people who came across The Beatles in their lifetime. There are stories you'll never have heard before: stories that seem familiar, and stories that have grown to myth, which can now be corrected.

TOP: *The Quarrymen played on this stage, and The Beatles were born. But where is it?*
BOTTOM: *St. Gabriel's Church, Huyton, where one of The Beatles sang in a choir*

Listen, do you want to know the answers?

Well done if you have all 10 correct!

Here are the answers.

1. If you said The Cavern, you are wrong. The answer is on page 119.

2. If you said Paul McCartney, have a look at page 145 to meet Chas Newby.

3. It wasn't John or Paul, but George was involved. But who else? It was Ken Brown. Read page 130 about Ken Brown.

4. If you said The Beatles, you'd be wrong. It wasn't Gerry and The Pacemakers, Rory Storm and the Hurricanes, or Derry and the Seniors (who were the first rock 'n' roll band to go to Hamburg). Read the interview with The Beatles' manager Allan Williams on page 136 to find out.

5. Not sure? Read about The Quarrymen on page 99 to find the answer.

6. It was Ringo—read about him on page 91.

7. Who do you reckon? It was Paul McCartney, whose brother Michael was a hairdresser, and Ringo wanted to open a chain of hairdressers too.

8. It was George Harrison when he started at Dovedale School. You can read more about George on page 83.

9. Church choirs—a great attraction, as you were paid. The choirboys were John, Paul, Stuart and Ringo.

10. The pretty nurse—if you don't know who she is, read about her on page 258.

How did you do?

If you scored less than 10, this is the book for you. You can go and test your friends.

TOP: *The pretty nurse stood here behind the shelter in the middle of the roundabout*
BOTTOM: *Who sang in this church's choir?*

Acknowledgements

Liverpool Records Office	Photos of old Liverpool
Salvation Army	Archive information and images of Strawberry Field
Chazz Avery	www.beatlesource.com
Ann Bagnall	School friend of John Lennon
Julia Baird	John Lennon's half-sister
Steve Barnes	A Beatles fan
Tony Barrow	The Beatles Press Officer from December 1961
Sid Bernstein	The Beatles promoter for Shea stadium
Pete Best	The Beatles drummer
Roag Best	Pete's brother and son of Neil Aspinall
Rory Best	Pete's brother and personal tour guide at The Casbah
Tony Booth	Artist commissioned by Brian Epstein to paint The Beatles
Ken Brown	Member of The Quarrymen at The Casbah and formed The Black Jacks, Pete Best's first band
Billy Butler	Bob Wooler's protégé and Cavern MC. Radio presenter in Merseyside
John and Flora Clucas	www.merseycats.com
Louise Collier	The Beatles Story visitor experience
Bill Covington	Member of The Rustiks, managed by Brian Epstein
Ian Crabtree	Liverpool Beatles Tours and Beatles historian
Marie Crawford	Childhood friend of Ringo
Rod Davis	The Quarrymen's banjo player
Don Dorsey	Music producer
Steve Dutton	Medical research on the death of Stuart Sutcliffe
Ged Fagan	Liverpool historian and author of the book *In a City Living*
Len Garry	The Quarrymen's tea-chest bass player
Phil Gresty	Liverpool historian
Eric Griffiths	The Quarrymen's guitarist
Margaret Grose	Friend of Ringo's mum and current occupier of Ringo's house at 10, Admiral Grove
Colin Hanton	The Quarrymen's drummer
Bill Harry	Founder of *Mersey Beat* and friend of John Lennon and Stuart Sutcliffe
Harry Holmes	John's schoolteacher
Jackie Holmes	Beatles expert
Tim Holmes	School friend of John Lennon
Ian Howe	Del Renas' drummer
Robin Howe	A Beatles fan
Adolfo Iglesias	Spanish journalist
Mal Jefferson	Friend of George Harrison
Paul Kilbride	Liverpool expert on music venues
Sam Leach	The Beatles friend and promoter in Liverpool
Spencer Leigh	A Beatles expert, author and broadcaster
Monty Lister	First radio interviewer of The Beatles
Adam Mannix	Proofreader

Beatlemania is sketched on the young faces of fans in Liverpool in 1964

Chris Mannix	A Beatles fan
Robert Marsden	Skiffle Band member
Craig McIntosh	Liverpool Stadium website
Irene Milson	George Harrison's second cousin
Pete Nash	*Liddypool* contributor and photo researcher. Editor of the British Beatles Fan Club magazine.
Chas Newby	The Beatles' bass player in 1960
Ray O'Brien	A Beatles historian and writer
Simon Osbourne	National Trust manager, Liverpool
Graham Paisley	Verger of St. Peter's Church, Woolton
Billy Parr	Friend of The Beatles in Rushworths music shop
Dave Peacock	Member of the Night Boppers
Mike Rice	Merseybeat drummer
Kevin Roach	Local historian and author of *The McCartneys*
Janine Ross	The Beatles Story
Faron Ruffley	Merseybeat star and friend of The Beatles
Wally & Kay Shepard	From Merseycats—the rock 'n' roll children's charity
Bill Shipton	School friend of John Lennon
Pauline Sutcliffe	Sister of The Beatles bass player Stuart Sutcliffe
Alistair Taylor	Brian Epstein's P.A. and Beatles' 'Mr. Fixit'
Ted "Kingsize" Taylor	Merseybeat band leader
Keith Turner	Member of Merseybeat band The Blues Angels
Steve Turner	Author of many music books, including books on The Beatles
Allan Williams	The Beatles' first manager
Stan Williams	School friend of John Lennon, George Harrison and Ivan Vaughan

The Beatles arrive at Liverpool
Airport on 10 July 1964

Liddypool
The History

Liddypool ⑤ The History
"In the town where I was born"

When most people think of Liverpool, they imagine a dark and grimy industrial metropolis that should be viewed in black-and-white only. Some historians would have you believe that nothing important could come out of the city. Before The Beatles, it seemed as if Liverpool never existed in any important way. What was it like before The Beatles emerged as world-famous figures? Many people who come to visit the famous Beatles sites are amazed at how beautiful and wonderful the city of Liverpool is.

So, before we venture on a 'Magical Mystery Tour' around Liverpool, let me tell you about the town where they were born.

Liverpool—The History

A settlement called 'Lytherpool', a little fishing village sited on the banks of the River Mersey in North-West England, is mentioned in the *Domesday Book*, compiled by William the Conqueror in 1086. After occupying England, William instigated a fact-finding mission in his newly conquered land. He sent out clerks and scribes to every town, conducted a population count and occupations and tax levels were recorded. This became the *Domesday Book* and is seen as a vital historical portrait of England in the 11th Century. In 1193, Prince John of Lancaster sought the Lordship of Liverpul. In 1207, King John needed a port outside the power of the Earl of Chester to station his army, as both the King and the Earl wanted to plunder Ireland. King John was not to be outdone. The charter was created in 1207 and the town of Liverpool was born.

Liverpool remained a small town for the next 500 years without much expansion or growth. However, with the advent of licensed pirates, Liverpool, with its excellent harbour, dominated the Atlantic Ocean, and press-gangs gathered local men to ride the high seas. Piracy gave way to an even more profitable commercial activity in the form of the slave-trade. The route was from America to Liverpool to West Africa, and then back across the Atlantic to the West Indies and the southern states of America. The first slaves were white rural Europeans who were sold in exchange for tobacco. However, Africans became an easy alternative as the tribal leaders would capture their rival tribe members and sell them to the slave traders. By 1825, over two million Africans had been transported on Liverpool-based ships from Africa to the West Indies and the American south, of which approximately 750,000 survived, so poor were the conditions on the ships.

Meanwhile, Ireland grew in importance to the King with English landowners, loyal to the monarch, taking the produce of the lands and taxes from the Irish people. Liverpool was the natural port from which to travel to reach Ireland. From 1741, Liverpool became the first modern dock in the world built specifically for the navy's frigates.

TOP: *Liverpool's World Heritage site of the Pier Head, from the Albert Dock* MIDDLE: *The Mersey Estuary, with Liverpool on the left and the Wirral on the right* BOTTOM: *Liverpool's Coat of Arms in St. George's Hall* OPPOSITE: *The Royal Liver Building at the Pier Head*

Liverpool soon became the second largest port in Britain after London. It was the world's leading market for cotton and grain, and controlled trade in sugar, soap and salt, and insurance underwriting became a significant commercial activity. The city's skyline began filling out with some of the finest Georgian buildings, including warehouses, civic buildings and churches. The Bluecoat Chambers, one of the earliest of these buildings, was founded as a Christian school and funded from slave trade profits. The building still survives as an arts centre, though the school moved to Wavertree.

The first custom-designed passenger railway in the world was constructed between Liverpool and Manchester in 1829 by George Stephenson. His famous engine, The Rocket, easily won a competition to haul a carriage full of passengers over a set length of track at Rainhill. Canals also flowed from Liverpool to all over the north of England and down to the Midlands.

Crowned heads of Europe and further afield visited. Nathaniel Hawthorne, who was American Consul between 1853 and 1857, wrote that Liverpool was "the greatest commercial city in the world". By 1850, Liverpool's reputation was gilded when its trade doubled that of London. More foreign and overseas trade was conducted there than any other city in the world, and in the latter part of the 19th Century, Liverpool was often at the forefront of educational, social and medical advances.

All this commercial activity required workers, and many of the less fortunate from across Europe settled around the city. Unfortunately, wealth for some tends to bring poverty for others. In 1830, the first German community was established in South Liverpool, predominantly around Mill Street in The Dingle. They were mostly sailors

ABOVE LEFT: *Bluecoat Chambers, the former school that is now an arts centre*
ABOVE RIGHT: *The Albert Dock, the work of the Civil Engineer, Jesse Hartley*
BOTTOM LEFT: *Ships on the River Mersey* BOTTOM RIGHT: *Liverpool's docks*
OPPOSITE: *Sunset on the River Mersey*

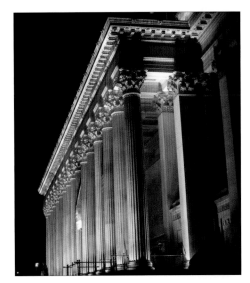

from Hamburg, a German port that 130 years later welcomed a little-known band from Liverpool to play in their rock 'n' roll clubs. That band was The Beatles.

Thousands came from Ireland following the infamous potato famine of the 1840s. The era's average life expectancy among the poor was only thirty-two years. In a three-month period, 90,000 Irish people arrived in Liverpool, the figure increased to 300,000 within a year. Many emigrated across the Atlantic to the United States and Canada, but about 80,000 stayed, and the numbers of families in poverty swelled. Liverpool had become the leading city for unemployment and crime.

By the early 20th Century, Liverpool's commercial power had waned and social conditions barely improved. In both World War I and World War II, the city became the headquarters for the 'Battle of the Atlantic' operations, keeping the trade routes with the United States and Canada open for the vital supplies. In World War II, Liverpool, along with the city of Coventry, suffered more bomb damage than any other British city outside London.

Liverpool in the 1940s was the birthplace for four boys: Richard Starkey, John Winston Lennon, James Paul McCartney and George Harrison. Growing up, they played music with other Liverpool-born boys, and were early Beatles with one lad born in India and one in Scotland: Pete Best and Stuart Sutcliffe. Eventually, the Fab Four would write their own piece of Liverpool history.

The post-war years saw the centre of commerce move towards London and southeast England. With the emergence of the European Common Market and no need for labour-intensive docks and ship-building, Liverpool declined for decades. Yet with the award of the 'European Capital of Culture' for 2008, and the waterfront and other great buildings receiving UNESCO 'World Heritage Site' status, Liverpool is back, with The Beatles contributing to its new global image.

TOP LEFT AND RIGHT:
St. George's Hall
MIDDLE: *The Albert Dock by the River Mersey*
RIGHT: *Liverpool in 1949, showing the damage suffered by the city centre during the war. The partially completed Anglican Cathedral is in the background*

Liverpool, The Beatles and Religion

At the mouth of the River Mersey, near where the Albert Dock now stands, was a large inlet that in the early days sheltered the ships from the open water. It started near St. Georges' Hall by the entrance to the Mersey Tunnel, but has since been filled in to become an integral part of the city centre of Liverpool. Around this pool and along the shore of the river grew a type of seaweed called 'laver'. When the two words are put together, it becomes 'laverpool', which was probably the derivation of Liverpool. There have been over forty different variations and spellings for the town before 'Liverpool' was accepted as the name of the city.

The mythical liver bird (pronounced ly-ver) has become the symbol of Liverpool, though its derivation is obscure. It was most probably a badly drawn recreation of the original seal of King John, which was an eagle. Other early historical documents suggest that the cormorant sea bird was incorporated into Liverpool's coat of arms. The cormorant is still found on the shores of the Mersey.

Liverpool has always been cosmopolitan. Being a port city, many nationalities have gathered here, and many of those have remained. Liverpool has the oldest Chinese community in Europe along with African, Greek, German, Scandinavian, Italian, Jewish, Irish, Scottish and Welsh communities.

Cormorant on the Mersey shore

Part of understanding Liverpool and The Beatles is understanding the religious traditions of the city. All religious denominations are represented. There are two Christian cathedrals: one is Anglican and was designed by a Catholic, the other is Catholic and was designed by an Anglican. These two cathedrals are connected by Hope Street. Liverpool housed one of the first mosques in Britain, and many local businessmen supported the Mormon Church, both in Britain and America.

After King Henry VIII founded the Church of England, Queen Elizabeth I formalized the split with the Roman Catholic Church by an Act of Parliament in 1559. The act embraced Roman Catholicism and Protestantism and established the monarch as the supreme head of the Anglican Communion. The Catholic Church and the authority of the Pope was superseded by this new form of worship. Catholic Mass celebrants were fined. Local rich landowners like the Norris family who owned Speke Hall offered to pay the fines for the poorer families. Catholics were considered social pariahs. It wasn't until the 1829 Catholic Emancipation Act that Catholics could worship openly or even vote or study at Oxford University. Liverpool's Catholics built St. Peter's Church in 1788 and designed it to look like a Methodist church so that Catholics could worship in secret. It was an open secret but Protestants were content to let them worship in peace. Religious tolerance and understanding were bywords for Liverpool life.

TOP: *Liverpool's famous waterfront*
ABOVE: *Liverpool's Chinatown, the oldest Chinese community in Europe*

All that changed in May 1909. Anti-Irish and anti-Catholic riots took place in Liverpool with Pastor George Wise preaching on behalf of the Protestant Reformers. Because of this week of madness, Catholics and Protestants physically separated from each other. The Catholics established themselves in the north of the city, with many Protestants moving to the south. Until a few decades ago, you could almost split Liverpool in two in this way. This is somewhat of a generalization, but it indicates the importance of religion in the local community. Until the 1980s when Anglican Bishop David Sheppard and Roman Catholic Archbishop Derek Worlock started working together to heal the divide, the Protestants and Catholics passionately hated each other. Some still do.

Years ago, the parish priests held positions of great prestige and power. They traded on guilt and kept their churches and bellies full. Once a week the priest would call round to see his parishioners. The housewife reserved her best china for the visit,

TOP: *Liverpool's two Cathedrals: The Anglican Cathedral in the background with the Catholic Cathedral in front, separated only by Hope Street*
ABOVE: *Princes Road Synagogue, one of the finest in Europe*

and any luxuries like biscuits were kept back from the children. If there was a small amount of alcohol in the house, the priest was offered the last drop. He then collected a donation from them, whether they could afford it or not.

Families like the McCartneys and Harrisons rejected a Catholic education, and moved away from the constraints of the church. This is particularly true of George, and his attitude was reflected in his song writing and statements right up to his death. Religion had a lot to answer for; religion, not faith. This is the difference which was George's driving force. He believed that faith was personal, between a human and God. Religion, he felt, was a man-made organisation and prone to failure.

Years ago, the worst social offence one could commit in Liverpool was to change one's religious affiliation upon marriage. When a Protestant married a Catholic, the Protestant was expected to change his or her religion and this person was then excommunicated from the family and never spoken to again. This still occurs and is commonly referred to as a 'mixed-marriage'; a mixture of religion, not race.

Ringo Starr was quoted as saying that if you met a girl and you loved each other, it shouldn't matter what your religion was. "The problem was", Ringo said, "if you were a Protestant and you married a Catholic, it was fine, but it was the families who would then ask 'What are you going to do about the kids? Where will they be christened—Catholic or Protestant?'—they pick on you, saying, 'Are you going to change your religion, or you'll never have any luck marrying a Catholic'. If you were just left alone there would be a lot more 'mixed-marriages'. If you love the girl and you love each other that should be enough". It obviously caused him some problems in his first marriage. Everyone, regardless of who they were or how much money they had, was under the same pressure. Even if you were a Beatle.

What then is a Scouser?

This term seems to have derived from the Scandinavians. One of their popular food dishes was known as 'lob-scouse', a stew combining some of the fattier pieces of meat with vegetables. This meal was introduced to Liverpool and was particularly popular with low-income families because it was nutritious and cheap. For those who couldn't even afford to buy the cheaper pieces of meat, they made this stew with vegetables only. It became known as 'blind scouse'. Therefore, the people who ate this meal became known as 'Scousers'. The city continues to host an International Scouse day, when Liverpudlians worldwide traditionally all make a bowl of Scouse.

Famous Liverpudlians

The Beatles were not the first Scousers to have an impact in America. In 1635, Dr. Richard Mather, once a preacher in The Dingle, emigrated to America with about fifty members of his congregation. His son, Increase, helped establish Harvard University and was its first president, and grandson, Cotton Mather founded Yale University. They were both involved in the Salem witch trials.

Robert Morris, who was born near Dale Street in Liverpool, emigrated to the States and in 1776 signed the U.S. Declaration of Independence.

One Scouser who profoundly altered the course of events in America was John Wilkes Booth, the Liverpool-born son of local Theatre Royal-actor, Junius Brutus Booth. John emigrated to America in 1821 and is forever remembered for the assassination of President Abraham Lincoln in Ford's Theatre in Washington, DC in 1865.

Liverpool has produced many famous and important people and milestones over the last three centuries.

- Mary Robinson of Liverpool devised the first district nursing service in Britain under the sponsorship of the wealthy Rathbone family. The service was overseen and assisted by the famous Florence Nightingale.

- Ronald Ross set up the World's first School of Tropical Medicine in Liverpool in 1898. Ross was awarded the Nobel Prize in 1902 after he discovered that malaria was transmitted by the mosquito.

- Liverpool born Felicia Dorothea Hemans wrote a poem titled *Casablanca*, with the famous line "the boy stood on the burning deck". She also wrote a poem titled *The Landing of the Pilgrim Fathers*, which was traditionally recited at early Thanksgivings in America.

- William Gladstone, the only British Prime Minister to serve four times (between 1868 and 1894) hailed from Liverpool.

- Kitty Wilkinson pioneered the first public washhouses to help stem the spread of cholera. When she employed a teacher to educate orphaned children how to read and write, she set up what was probably the country's first public infant school.

- The Boy Scout movement was started in Birkenhead on the Wirral after a visit by Lord Baden Powell. Paul McCartney, George Harrison and John Lennon were all Boy Scouts in their youth. The first Boy Scouts International Jamboree was held in Arrowe Park on the Wirral.

- The world's first crossword appeared in the *New York Sunday World* in December 1913. It was devised by Arthur Wynne, who had emigrated from Liverpool to America.

- Jeremiah Horrocks, the father of British astronomy, was born in Liverpool and buried in the Ancient Chapel of Toxteth in The Dingle. He investigated the transit of the planet Venus across the face of the sun and discovered how to measure the distance of the Earth from the sun. He also studied the motion of the moon and how it affects tides. Sadly, he died at the age of twenty-three.

- Most people would say that Marconi invented the radio. However, the radio was pioneered by Sir Oliver Lodge while he was the professor of physics at Liverpool University. His first transmission was in Oxford, but his subsequent transmissions were in Liverpool city centre from the top of Brownlow Hill to the top of the Lewis's store. Marconi then took Lodge's work and carried out the first signal from ship to shore. Being much better at public relations, he then went on to make his name in the manufacture of radios, and is usually credited with the invention.

- The first transatlantic cable was financed and made in Liverpool, and was laid by the Great Eastern steamship in 1866.

- The ship *Alabama* that sank so many ships in the U.S. Civil War was built and paid for in Liverpool by local sympathisers with the southern states. Two other famous ships, the *Titanic* and the *Lusitania*, were registered in Liverpool.

- The frigate Birkenhead was built by Cammell Laird on the Mersey. The boat inspired the Birkenhead Drill, known for its saying "women and children first".

- The world's first lifeboat station was established in Formby to the north of Liverpool in 1776.

- The overhead railway, which became known as the docker's umbrella, was the first elevated electric railway in the world with automatic electric signaling when it opened in 1893.

- When the first Mersey Tunnel was opened in 1934, it was the longest underwater road tunnel in the world.

- Liverpool had the world's first medical officer of health when Dr. William Henry Duncan was appointed in 1847.

- Liverpool's Frank Hornby gave the world Dinky Toys, Meccano and Hornby train sets.

- With its growth as a port in the 19th Century, Liverpool had the world's first tidal dock and the world's first enclosed dock system, the Albert Dock.

- Dr. Matthew Dobson, a Liverpool physician, discovered sugar diabetes.

- Britain's first school for the blind opened in Liverpool in 1791, and Britain's first Guide Dog for the Blind Training Centre opened in Wallasey, Wirral, in 1931.

- Alder Hey is the largest children's hospital in Europe. Liverpool also created the first children's ward in a hospital in Britain.

- Liverpudlians demonstrated a great social conscience in setting up the Liverpool Society for the Prevention of Cruelty to Children. It went on to become the National Society for the Prevention of Cruelty to Children (NSPCC).

- Britain's first animal welfare organisation was formed as the Liverpool Society for the Suppression of Wanton Cruelty to Brute Animals. This later became the Royal Society for the Prevention of Cruelty to Animals, better known as the RSPCA.

This just gives you a flavour of what Liverpool has done for Great Britain and the world. Is it any surprise, that the city was able to produce the greatest musical entity of all time?

Liddypool: The Poem

What, or where, is "Liddypool"? Well, it doesn't take a great leap of imagination to realise this is Liverpool, but it is written in the language from the strange world of John Lennon. I asked Bill Harry about John Lennon's poem, *Liddypool*. "I commissioned John to write for me and I dubbed his columns 'Beatcomber'. In a piece I published on 14 September 1961, John's column was entitled 'Around And About by Beatcomber' and he began: "Reviving the old tradition of Judro Bathing is slowly but slowly dancing in Liddypool once more."

Liddypool is a wonderful piece of prose for those Scousers who could understand—in the main—what he was talking about.

Liddypool

"Reviving the old tradition of Judro Bathing is slowly but slowly dancing in Liddypool once more. Had you remembering the owld custard of Boldy Street blowing. The Peer Hat is very populace for sun eating and Boots for Nude Brighter is handys when sailing. We are not happy with Queen Victorious Monologue, but Walky Through Gallery is goodly when the rain and Sit Georgie House is black and (white from the little pilgrims flying from Hellsy College). Talk Hall is very hysterical with old things wot are fakes and King Anne never slept there I tell you. Shout Airborne is handly for planes if you like (no longer government patrolled) and the L.C.C.C. (Liddypool Cha Cha Cha) are doing a great thing. The Mersey Boat is selling another three copies to some go home foreigners who went home. There is a lot to do in Liddypool, but not all convenience".

Liddypool from *In His Own Write* by John Lennon, published in 1964 by Simon and Schuster.

ABOVE: **"The Boot" (Boat or Ferry) on the River Mersey**
TOP RIGHT: **"The Peer Hat" (The Pier Head)**
BOTTOM RIGHT: **"Sit Georgie House" (St. George's Hall)**
OPPOSITE PAGE: TOP: **"Nude Brighter" (New Brighton)**
MIDDLE: **"Walky Through Gallery" (The Walker Art Gallery)**
BOTTOM LEFT: **"Shout Airborne" (Speke Airport)**
BOTTOM RIGHT: **"Talk Hall" (Speke Hall)**

"Yesterday"—a brief history of The Beatles in Liverpool

1934	19 September	Brian Samuel Epstein is born in a private nursing home on Rodney Street, Liverpool.
1938	3 December	Julia Stanley and Alfred Lennon—John's parents—are married at Mount Pleasant Registry Office, where John married Cynthia in 1962.
	12 December	Quarrymen drummer Colin Hanton is born in Bootle.
1940	23 June	Stuart Ferguson Victor Sutcliffe is born in Edinburgh, Scotland.
	7 July	Richard Starkey is born in the front bedroom of 9, Madryn Street, in The Dingle.
	9 October	John Winston Lennon is born at Oxford Street Maternity Hospital, Liverpool.
	31 October	Quarrymen guitarist Eric Griffiths is born in North Wales.
1941	18 June	Temporary Beatle Chas Newby is born in Blackpool.
	4 August	John's best friend Pete Shotton is born.
	7 November	Quarrymen banjo player Rodney Verso Davis is born in Sefton General Hospital, Liverpool.
	24 November	Randolph Peter Best is born in Madras, India.
1942	6 January	Quarrymen tea-chest bass player Len Garry is born in Liverpool.
	18 June	James Paul McCartney is born at Walton Hospital, Liverpool. Quarrymen member Ivan Vaughan is born in Liverpool.
1943	25 February	George Harrison is born at 12, Arnold Grove.
1946	6 May	John is enrolled in Dovedale School.
1947	6 July	Richard Starkey is rushed by ambulance to the Royal Liverpool Children's Hospital with peritonitis after his appendix burst.
1950	10 September	Brian Epstein joins the family business.
1956		John forms The Quarrymen early in the summer of 1956 with schoolmates from Quarry Bank School. Lennon plays guitar and sings vocals; Bill Smith on tea-chest bass; Rod Davis on banjo; Colin Hanton on drums; Pete Shotton on washboard, and then Len Garry joins in September on tea-chest bass.
1957	16 January	Alan Sytner opens The Cavern, a former fruit and vegetable warehouse, turned jazz club.
	9 June	The Quarrymen's first recorded engagement takes place at a Carroll Levis talent show at the Empire Theatre.
	22 June	The Quarrymen perform on the back of a lorry at a street party in Rosebery Street. The gig is arranged through Colin Hanton's friend Charles Roberts.
	July	George Harrison's first group, The Rebels, makes its debut in Speke.
	2 July	John Lennon and Nigel Walley attempt to join the Merchant Navy.
	6 July	Paul McCartney is introduced to John Lennon at the St. Peter's Church fete.
	7 August	The Quarrymen debut at The Cavern.
	18 October	Paul McCartney makes his paid debut with The Quarrymen at the New Clubmoor Hall.
	September	John enrolls in Liverpool Art College where he meets Cynthia Powell and Stuart Sutcliffe.
1958	6 February	George Harrison meets The Quarrymen at Wilson Hall.
	14 July	The Quarrymen record at Percy Phillips' studio at 38, Kensington, Liverpool.
	15 July	John's mother, Julia Lennon, is struck down and killed by off-duty policeman Eric Clague.
	20 December	The Quarrymen, now comprising John Lennon, Paul McCartney and George Harrison, play their final booking of 1958 at 25, Upton Green for Harry Harrison's (George's brother) wedding reception.
1959	24 January	The Quarrymen play in Woolton. This was their last known booking and they effectively disband after this gig.
	January	George Harrison joins the Les Stewart Quartet.
	July	The Les Stewart Quartet turn down The Casbah residency. Ken Brown and George Harrison decide to leave the group.
	29 August	The Casbah Club opens to the new resident band, The Quarrymen, re-formed by George Harrison and Ken Brown, with John Lennon and Paul McCartney rejoining.
	October	Ken Brown leaves The Quarrymen over an argument about money. The Quarrymen—John, Paul and George—walk out of The Casbah.
	October	The Empire Theatre is the setting for the Carroll Levis talent show. John, Paul and George enter as Johnny and the Moondogs, and were placed third.

1960 January — Stuart Sutcliffe is persuaded by John and Paul to buy a bass guitar and join The College Band. The group changes its name to The Beatals.

1 May — The Beatals soon become The Silver Beetles and add Tommy Moore as drummer.

5 May — Allan Williams becomes the manager of the group.

10 May — At the Wyvern Club, John, Paul, Stuart, George and Tommy Moore audition for the Larry Parnes' star, Liverpool's Billy Fury.

20 May — The Silver Beatles leave Liverpool for a tour of Scotland with Johnny Gentle. For the next eight days, The Silver Beatles used the name "His Group" in the band, Johnny Gentle and His Group.

June — Drummer Norman Chapman joins The Silver Beatles after Tommy Moore quits the group. Chapman leaves soon after when he is called for National Service.

24 June — Royston Ellis performs at Liverpool University before introducing The Silver Beatles to their first experience with drugs.

12 August — Pete Best auditions at the Wyvern Club and is asked to join the group on their trip to Hamburg. They drop "Silver" and become The Beatles.

15 October — John, Paul, George and Ringo make a record together in Hamburg, supporting Lou Walters, Ringo's fellow band mate in Rory Storm and the Hurricanes.

21 November — George Harrison is forced to return to Liverpool after breaking curfew in Hamburg for being under age.

29 November — Paul McCartney and Pete Best are deported from Hamburg.

December — John Lennon returns from Hamburg.

Paul is employed for a short time winding electrical coils at Massey & Coggins in Liverpool.

17 December — The Beatles re-form at The Casbah with Chas Newby replacing Stuart on bass. It's their first gig since Hamburg.

27 December — Litherland Town Hall sees the beginning of a phenomenon—'Beatlemania'.

1961 9 February — The Beatles' lunchtime debut at The Cavern.

15 March — Stuart returns to Hamburg to be with his fiancée Astrid Kirchherr.

21 March — The Beatles play their first evening gig at The Cavern Club on the same bill as the Blue Genes.

22 June — Tony Sheridan and The Beat Brothers—John, Paul, George and Pete—record "My Bonnie" for Bert Kaempfert over a two-day period.

6 July — *Mersey Beat* newspaper is launched with John's humorous version of the birth of The Beatles. The paper was conceived and edited by Bill Harry.

3 August — Brian Epstein debuts his new weekly feature in *Mersey Beat*.

28 October — Raymond Jones walks into the NEMS record store in Whitechapel and asks for "My Bonnie", a new record by The Beatles.

9 November — Brian Epstein visits The Cavern to see The Beatles at a lunchtime gig.

3 December — The Beatles discuss Brian Epstein becoming their manager at his NEMS office.

6 December — Epstein offers to become The Beatles' manager and they accept.

10 December — The Beatles sign the contract with Epstein at The Casbah, albeit without Epstein's signature.

13 December — Mike Smith visits The Cavern to see The Beatles perform and sets up the New Year's Day audition.

1962 1 January — The Beatles audition at Decca Records.

24 January — The Beatles sign a slightly amended contract with Brian Epstein at NEMS.

1 February — The Beatles play Macdonna Hall in West Kirby. It was the first gig under Brian Epstein's management.

10 February — Decca officially turn down The Beatles and lose out on hundreds of millions of pounds. The same day The Beatles play at St. Paul's Birkenhead, and are filmed. It's the earliest known film of the group.

12 February — The Beatles audition for their first radio broadcast for 'Teenager's Turn—Here We Go' in Manchester.

7 March — The Beatles return to BBC Manchester to record for 'Teenager's Turn—Here We Go'. It was broadcast the next day at 5.00 p.m.

10 April — Stuart Sutcliffe dies in Hamburg aged twenty one.

9 May — Epstein secures the deal with Parlophone, part of EMI.

1962	4 June	The Beatles sign with EMI.
	6 June	The EMI session takes place.
	24 June	The Beatles close The Casbah Club.
	July	George Martin confirms the details of the EMI recording contract.
	16 August	Pete Best is dismissed from The Beatles.
	18 August	Ringo joins The Beatles and debuts at Hulme Hall in the Wirral's Port Sunlight.
	22 August	Granada TV films The Beatles at The Cavern amidst protests over Pete Best's sacking.
	23 August	John and Cynthia are married at Liverpool's Mount Pleasant Registry Office.
	4 September	"Love Me Do" is recorded at Abbey Road with Ringo Starr during a three-hour session. Recording manager Ron Richards decides to bring in Andy White on drums.
	11 September	The Beatles record "Love Me Do", "P.S. I Love You" and "Please Please Me" with Andy White on drums.
	5 October	"Love Me Do" is released with Ringo on drums.
	27 October	Monty Lister records an interview with The Beatles at Hulme Hall for his local Hospital Radio show.
1963	11 January	Their second single, "Please Please Me" is released.
	11 February	The Beatles' first LP *Please Please Me* is recorded in one day. The album is released on 22 March.
	22 February	Northern Songs is formed to manage the song writing for John Lennon and Paul McCartney.
	22 March	The *Please Please Me* LP is released in the United Kingdom and stays at the top of the charts for thirty weeks. The sleeve notes are written by publicist Tony Barrow.
	8 April	Julian Lennon is born at Sefton General Hospital in Liverpool.
	12 April	"From Me to You" is released and becomes their first U.K. number 1 hit in the major charts.
	28 April	John Lennon and Brian Epstein fly to Spain for a short break.
	18 June	Paul's 21st birthday party was at 147, Dinas Lane in Huyton, which was Paul's Auntie Jin's house. A drunken John Lennon beats up Cavern DJ Bob Wooler.

	20 June	Ringo Starr becomes a fully-fledged Beatle with an equal share of Beatles Ltd., which is set up to handle the profits. The split is four ways.
	3 August	The Beatles make their last appearance at The Cavern after nearly 300 shows in two-and-a-half years. Brian Epstein promised the group would return to the venue, but they never did.
1964	9 February	The Beatles appear on "The Ed Sullivan Show" at the start of their first U.S. tour in front of a record seventy-three million viewers.
	2 March	The Beatles begin filming *A Hard Day's Night*.
	10 July	The Beatles appear at Liverpool Town Hall for a civic reception in front of approximately 200,000 fans.

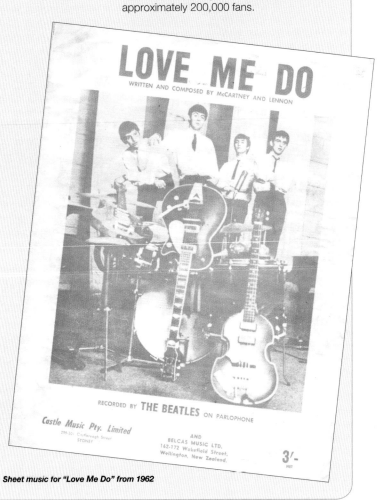

Sheet music for "Love Me Do" from 1962

From The Black Jacks to The Beatles:
The story of the "Fab 27"

"With A Little Help From My Friends"

To many people The Beatles are John Lennon, Paul McCartney, George Harrison and Ringo Starr—that's it, period, end of story. However, along the way they had the help of many friends without whom the Fab Four would have never existed.

How the group went from being The Black Jacks and The Quarrymen to The Beatles isn't a simple story. A table on page 43 shows the contributions made by many musicians on their long and winding road to fame and fortune, and the following will attempt to flesh out the details.

John, Pete, Eric, Rod, Ivan, Nigel or Bill

John Lennon (guitar), Pete Shotton (washboard) and Eric Griffiths (guitar) formed a skiffle group at Quarry Bank School around June 1956. They quickly recruited Rod Davis, who had just acquired a banjo. For a couple of weeks they used the name The Black Jacks but this didn't stick. They decided to call themselves The Quarrymen after the name of their school and the quarry in Woolton.

They had friends who played with them from time to time. There was Bill Smith, who frequently failed to turn up for practises and was quickly shown the door. Ivan Vaughan and Nigel Walley were John and Pete's friends and occasionally played the tea-chest bass, but didn't have the tenacity to stick it out.

The Quarrymen in Rosebery Street, 22 June 1957

TOP LEFT: *Quarrymen pianist John Duff Lowe* ABOVE: *Colin Hanton's drum kit*
BOTTOM LEFT: *The Quarrymen: George Harrison, Paul McCartney, Ken Brown and John Lennon at The Casbah's opening night on 29 August 1959*

John, Pete, Eric, Rod and Len
Ivan attended the Liverpool Institute and befriended Len Garry. Ivan introduced him to the group to take on the role of tea-chest bass player.

John, Pete, Eric, Rod, Len and Colin
One of Eric's neighbours was Colin Hanton. When Eric discovered Colin owned a set of drums, he was tapped as the next Quarryman.

By the end of 1956, The Quarrymen were:

John, Pete, Eric, Rod, Len and Colin
The Quarrymen played at Rosebery Street on 22 June 1957 and Julia Baird recalled that they called themselves "Johnny and the Rainbows" because of their shirts, though The Quarrymen have no recollection of this. The next recruit was another school friend of Ivan's, a lad named Paul McCartney, whom he introduced to John at St. Peter's Church fete on 6 July 1957. Paul played with The Quarrymen at the church's youth club for a few weeks before making his official debut in October 1957.

John, Eric, Len, Colin and Paul
Things started to move quickly for the group after Paul joined. Rod was more into folk music than rock 'n' roll and left after a few weeks. Pete also left after Rod's departure because he wasn't musically inclined and was only there because he was John's best friend.

John, Len, Colin, Paul and George
By the end of 1957, Paul had become friendly with George Harrison and wanted him to join the group. George had briefly appeared with his brother Pete and friend Arthur Kelly in a group they called The Rebels. George joined The Quarrymen around the beginning of 1958, replacing Eric Griffiths, as they didn't need four guitars. Eric was given the option of buying a bass guitar, or leaving. Eric left and joined the Merchant Navy.

John, Len, Colin, Paul, George and John Duff Lowe
John Duff Lowe joined them on occasion when they had a piano at a venue.

John, Colin, Paul and George
Len developed tubercular meningitis in August 1958 and spent several weeks in hospital, plus recuperation afterwards. By the time Len was back on his feet the band had moved on.

John, Paul and George
Colin then had a row with Paul after John, Paul and George became drunk at an audition. He was older than the others and had already started work. Colin didn't want to jeopardise his new career and decided he had had enough, so he quit.

By the end of 1958, the bookings for The Quarrymen had dried up. Skiffle had gone and rock 'n' roll was here to stay. Nobody wanted to book a group with only three guitars. Around this time, John drank heavily to cope with his mother's death in a tragic accident. He temporarily lost interest in music and the group. The Quarrymen eventually split up after a Woolton gig in January 1959.

Les, Geoff, George and Ken
Soon after, George joined the Les Stewart Quartet that included Ken Brown.

George and Ken
They walked out on the group after an argument about The Casbah, and began playing as a duo.

George, Ken, John and Paul
George brought John and Paul back to re-form The Quarrymen to open The Casbah on 29 August 1959.

John, Paul and George
After an argument over money, John, Paul and George walked out of The Casbah in October 1959, and the name, The Quarrymen, was never used again. Ken formed a new band with Pete Best, Chas Newby and Bill Barlow called The Black Jacks.

John, Paul, George and Stuart
The group changed its name to Johnny and the Moondogs in October 1959. George recalled how John stood at the front with just a microphone, and he and Paul were behind him on guitar. They recruited John's art college friend, Stuart Sutcliffe. They now appeared as The College Band at Liverpool Art College dances. In January 1960 they became The Beatals.

There are different theories about who gave the group its name. John wrote a piece for the *Mersey Beat* paper in July 1961 under the heading: "Being a Short Diversion on the Origins of Beatles". Lennon claimed: "It came in a vision—a man appeared on a Flaming Pie and said unto them 'From this day on you are Beatles with an A'. 'Thank you, Mister Man,' they said, thanking him". It was a wonderful piece of prose from Lennon, but it was pure fable. The more likely origin was Stuart's suggestion, in honour of Buddy Holly and the Crickets. It's an insect thing: crickets and beetles.

One thing's for certain: the name was not inspired by the film *The Wild One*, which was banned in England until 1968.

John, Paul, George, Stuart and Mike
At this point, an interesting temporary insertion to the list was Mike McCartney, Paul's younger brother. He has intimated that he drummed for both The Quarrymen and for The Beatles. Mike with The Quarrymen? There is a photo of Mike playing on The Quarrymen's drums. However, Colin Hanton doesn't remember Mike being involved with The Quarrymen at all while he was with them. Colin had joined The Quarrymen months before John and Paul met in July 1957. Also, while at scout camp, Mike had broken his arm in several places, damaging nerves and stayed in the hospital for several weeks, followed by months of physiotherapy. By his own admission any hope of playing drums had vanished. Colin and Mike have conversed on the subject and they have agreed that most likely Mike stood in as drummer for The Beatals on a couple of occasions in April 1960.

John and Paul
During the Easter school holidays in April 1960, Lennon and McCartney visited Paul's cousin Bett Robbins and her husband Mike who were tenants at the Fox and Hounds pub in Caversham. Lennon and McCartney worked behind the bar for the week, but appeared on the Saturday night as the Nerk Twins, performing a few songs. They never used the name again.

John, Paul, George, Stuart and Tommy
After Allan Williams became the group's manager, Brian Casser (also known as Cass) from Cass and the Cassanovas, suggested a new name: Long John and The Silver Beetles. They settled on The Silver Beetles and then The Silver Beatles. They did this because Casser helped them find a drummer through Williams' intervention. At Brian Casser's suggestion, they recruited Tommy Moore and soon were off for the Johnny Gentle tour of Scotland on 20 May 1960.

John, Paul, George, Stuart and Cliff
Appearing as The Silver Beats—the only time they used this name—they played at Lathom Hall on 14 May. The group was drummer-less for the night and they asked Cliff Roberts to fill in for the drummer. His band, Cliff Roberts and the Rockers, also appeared on the bill.

John as Johnny Lennon, Paul as Paul Ramon, George as Carl Harrison, Stuart as Stu De Stael, Tommy Moore and Johnny Gentle
The Silver Beatles temporarily became known as "His Group" when they set off for Scotland for their first appearance on 20 May backing local singer Johnny Gentle. Johnny Gentle appeared in the newspaper adverts and posters as "ITV Star of 'Oh Boy' and 'Wham'". John, Paul, George and Stuart even used pseudonyms for the short tour.

John, Paul, George, Stuart and Ron
When they returned, Tommy quit to take up a proper job at the Garston Bottle Works. On 14 June 1960 at The Grosvenor Ballroom, they had no drummer. When John asked if there were any drummers in the room, "Ron the Teddy Boy" stepped up and bashed away at the drums. It turned out that Lennon and The Silver Beatles were too scared to challenge this scary fellow. So for one night only, Ron the Ted was the group's drummer.

John, Paul, George, Stuart and Norman
They recruited accomplished drummer Norman Chapman in June 1960. However, Norman's time was cut short when he was called up for National Service after only a few weeks. Norman proved to be unlucky since National Service was abolished at the

TOP: *Roy Young (left) playing with The Beatles in April 1962 at the Star Club, Hamburg*
ABOVE RIGHT: *The Beatles' advert in the local newspaper for their performance at the YMCA, Birkenhead, shortly after Ringo Starr joined the group*
ABOVE LEFT: *An advertisement in the Scottish paper for Johnny Gentle and His Group*

end of December 1960. His fellow band members escaped having to undergo military training. Otherwise, history as we know it might have been dramatically different.

John, Paul, George, Stuart and Pete
The group returned to The Casbah where Ken Brown had formed a new group called The Black Jacks with Mona Best's son, Pete. They needed a drummer to accompany them in Hamburg, and knowing that Pete was a decent musician, recruited him and changed their name to The Beatles.

John, Paul, George, Pete and Chas
When they returned from Hamburg in December 1960 without Stuart, former Black Jack Chas Newby joined the group for four gigs. They first appeared as The Beatles at The Casbah over the Christmas holiday.

John, Paul, George, Pete and Stuart
Newby returned to college and Stuart returned from Hamburg to take up his place with the group again.

John, Paul, George, Pete and Tony
Stuart quit the group in Hamburg. In April 1961, The Beatles backed Tony Sheridan at the Top Ten Club in Hamburg.

John, Paul, George, Pete and Tony
The group signed a contract with producer Bert Kaempfert in June 1961 and recorded "My Bonnie" under the name of Tony Sheridan and The Beat Brothers. Tony was invited by The Beatles to join the group and come to Liverpool with them, but he was content in Hamburg.

John, Paul, George, Pete, Gerry Marsden, Karl Terry, Fred Marsden, Les Chadwick and Les Maguire
The Beatles and Gerry and The Pacemakers joined forces with Karl Terry at Litherland Town Hall on 19 October 1961 to perform as the Beatmakers. There was George on lead guitar, Paul playing rhythm, and the drumming duties being split between Pete Best and Freddie Marsden. Les Chadwick played bass guitar and John Lennon played piano with Karl Terry joining in the vocals. Finally, Gerry Marsden played guitar and sang, while Les Maguire played the saxophone.

Rory, Paul, George and Pete
Brian Epstein became the group's manager in November 1961 after hearing them play at The Cavern. On the first night under Epstein's management at Macdonna Hall, Wirral on 1 February 1962, John contracted laryngitis and Rory Storm stepped in for him at the last minute.

John, Paul, George and Pete
The Beatles became the best rock 'n' roll group in Liverpool and Hamburg and, with Brian Epstein's management, they secured a record deal with George Martin at Parlophone Records.

John, Paul, George, Pete and Roy
In April and May 1962 while at the Star Club, Hamburg, boogie-woogie piano player Roy Young joined The Beatles on stage. Also adding back-up vocals, Young recorded "Sweet Georgia Brown" and "Swanee River" with The Beatles on 24 May 1962.

John, Paul, George and Johnny
They were scheduled to record in early September, but on 16 August 1962, Pete Best was sacked. After initially agreeing to play for the interim bookings, drummer Johnny Hutchinson sat in with The Beatles.

John, Paul, George and Ringo
Ringo Starr made his debut with The Beatles on 18 August 1962 as a replacement for Pete Best.

That makes twenty-seven band members between June 1956 and August 1962 before the group's final line-up of John, Paul, George and Ringo although there were numerous other musicians and singers who made guest appearances, like Horst and Fred Fascher at Christmas 1962 in the Star Club.

Now the Fab Four were ready to conquer the world.

From The Black Jacks to The Beatles

Date	Band	John Lennon	Pete Shotton	Eric Griffiths	Rod Davis	Len Garry	Colin Hanton	Bill Smith	Nigel Walley	Ivan Vaughan	Paul McCartney	John Duff Lowe	George Harrison	Ken Brown	Les Stewart	Geoff Skinner	Stuart Sutcliffe	Mike McCartney	Tommy Moore	Cliff Roberts	Johnny Gentle	Ron the Ted	Norman Chapman	Pete Best	Chas Newby	Tony Sheridan	Rory Storm	Johnny Hutchinson	Ringo Starr	Roy Young
June '56	The Black Jacks	X	X	X	X																									
July '56	The Quarrymen	X	X	X	X			X	X	X																				
Dec. '56	The Quarrymen	X	X	X	X	X	X																							
6 July '57	The Quarrymen	X	X	X	X	X	X				X																			
Oct. '57	The Quarrymen	X		X		X	X				X																			
6 Feb. '58	The Quarrymen	X				X	X				X	X	X																	
Aug. '58	The Quarrymen	X					X				X	X	X																	
Dec. '58	The Quarrymen	X									X		X																	
Feb. '59	Les Stewart Quartet												X	X	X	X														
July '59	George and Ken												X	X																
29 Aug. '59	The Quarrymen	X									X		X	X																
Oct. '59	Johnny and the Moondogs	X									X		X																	
Nov. '59	The College Band	X									X		X				X													
Jan. '60	The Beatals	X									X		X				X													
April '60	The Beatals	X									X		X				X	X												
23-24 Apr. '60	The Nerk Twins	X									X																			
May '60	The Silver Beetles	X									X		X				X		X											
14 May '60	The Silver Beats	X									X		X				X			X										
20-28 May '60	Johnny Gentle and His Group	X									X		X				X		X		X									
14 June '60	The Silver Beatles	X									X		X				X					X								
June '60	The Silver Beatles	X									X		X				X						X							
July '60	The Silver Beatles	X									X		X				X													
Aug. '60	The Beatles	X									X		X				X							X						
17-31 Dec. '60	The Beatles	X									X		X											X	X					
Jan. '61	The Beatles	X									X		X											X						
Mar. '61	The Beatles	X									X		X				X							X						
April '61	Tony Sheridan and The Beatles	X									X		X											X		X				
22-23 June '61	Tony Sheridan and The Beat Brothers	X									X		X											X		X				
1st Feb. '62	The Beatles	X									X		X				X							X				X		
Apr.-May '62	The Beatles	X									X		X											X						X
16-17 Aug. '62	The Beatles	X									X		X															X		
18 Aug. '62	The Beatles	X									X		X																X	

One-off performance, recording date, or brief name-change only

10th July 1964. The Beatles answer questions at the press conference at the airport

Liddypool
The Stories

Liddypool 🔵 The Stories

In making this journey from the fledgling Black Jacks and Quarrymen to the Fab Four, there were many significant events in Liverpool, without which The Beatles phenomenon would not have happened. The key moments are selected—their births, families, schools as well as their musical history—so that you can better understand how the stars aligned in order to launch the group to worldwide fame.

With so many published books on The Beatles, there are many discrepancies, and so, whenever possible, original sources were used and the people who were present have been interviewed.

LEFT: *Promotional poster for The Beatles appearance at the Tower Ballroom, New Brighton, on 6 April 1962. Note the spelling error of the name "Beetles"*
OPPOSITE: *Fans welcome The Beatles back to 'Liddypool'*

3 December 1938—**Alf Lennon marries Julia Stanley**

9 October 1940—**John Winston Lennon is born**

18 June 1942—**Paul McCartney is born**

25 February 1943—**George Harrison is born**

7 July 1940—**Ringo Starr is born**

1956—**The Quarrymen are formed**

22 June 1957—**The Quarrymen perform in Rosebery Street**

6 July 1957—**Paul meets John at St. Peter's Church**

14 July 1958—**The Quarrymen record at Percy Phillips' studio**

15 July 1958—**Julia Lennon is struck down and killed by a car**

29 August 1959—**The Casbah Coffee Club opens**

29 August 1959—**Ken Brown joins The Quarrymen**

January 1960—**Stuart Sutcliffe joins The College Band**

5 May 1960—**Allan Williams becomes The Silver Beatles' manager**

12 August 1960—**Pete Best joins The Beatles**

17 December 1960—**Chas Newby joins The Beatles**

27 December 1960—**Faron witnesses Beatlemania**

9 February 1961—**The Beatles' debut at The Cavern**

6 July 1961—**Bill Harry launches** *Mersey Beat*

28 October 1961—**Raymond Jones asks for the record, "My Bonnie", by The Beatles**

9 November 1961—**Brian Epstein watches The Beatles at The Cavern**

10 November 1961—**The Beatles appear at Sam Leach's first 'Operation Big Beat'**

December 1961—**Tony Barrow and The Beatles**

1 January 1962—**The Beatles at Decca audition**

10 April 1962—**Stuart Sutcliffe's death**

6 June 1962—**The Beatles at EMI**

16 August 1962—**Pete Best is dismissed**

23 August 1962—**Cynthia Powell marries John Lennon**

September 1962—**Tony Booth's paintings of The Beatles**

4 September 1962—**The Beatles record at EMI Studios**

27 October 1962—**Monty Lister records The Beatles for radio**

19 February 1963—**Michael Ward photographs The Beatles in Liverpool**

18 June 1963—**Paul's 21st birthday party: John Lennon beats up Bob Wooler**

9 October 1963—**The Mersey Sound**

7 December 1963—**The Beatles answer a call for help!**

9 February 1964—**The Ed Sullivan Show**

10 July 1964—**The Beatles come home to Liverpool**

11 July 1964—**Leaving Liverpool**

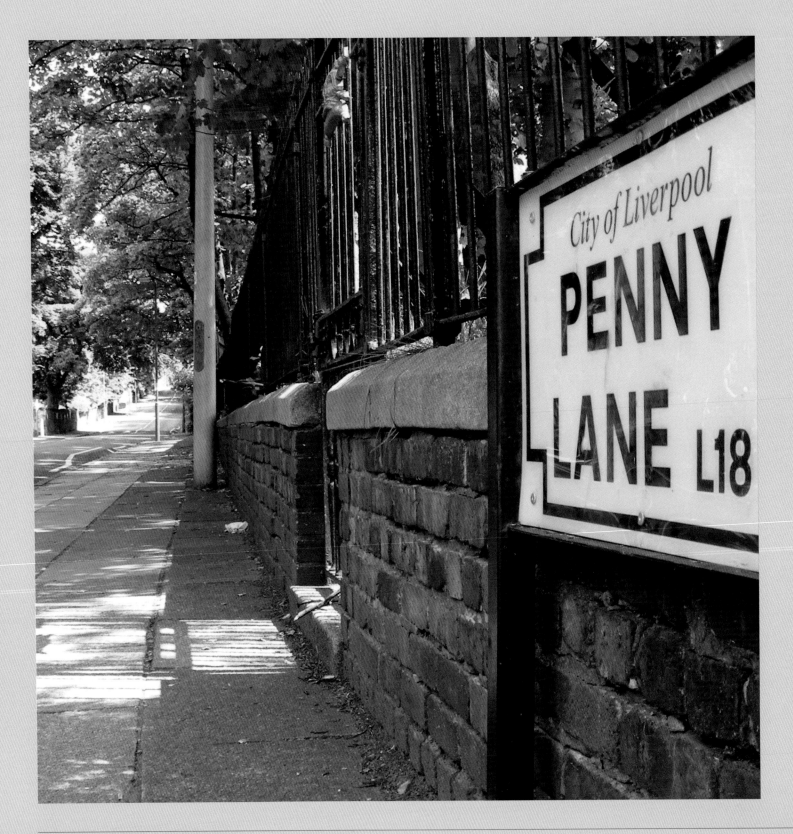

3 December 1938
Alf Lennon marries Julia Stanley
"Imagine"

LEFT: *The Penny Lane area where Julia Lennon's family, the Stanleys, settled*
ABOVE: *John Lennon's half-sister Julia Baird in 2006*

Julia Lennon's short life reads like a tragic novel. The song, "My Son John" by David Whitfield, was Julia's favourite that kept her going through the years when she was denied access to her son. She gave birth to John in October 1940, and he was stripped away from her by her sister Mimi. She also had a daughter, Victoria, who was taken away from her and given up for adoption. Seventeen years later Julia's life was taken at a tragically young age.

I spoke to Julia Baird, Julia Lennon's daughter and John's half-sister, in order to find out more about her family history. In February 2007, she published her book, *Imagine This—Growing up with my Brother John Lennon*.

During my research, it soon became clear that much has been written and said about Julia Lennon that is not accurate. Julia Baird's first memoir, *John Lennon, My Brother*, indicates the stories that Julia Lennon's sister, Mimi Smith, had been telling willing listeners were not quite the truth. At that stage, many statements Mimi made had been readily accepted as fact because there was no proof otherwise, and no one was prepared to contradict her.

John's mother was born Julia Stanley on 12 March 1914, the fourth of five sisters. They grew up in a lower middle-class family and Julia was both the rebel and the black sheep of the family.

The Stanleys were class-conscious. Annie 'Mama' Stanley (née Millward) was from a middle-class Methodist Church family and married George 'Pop' Stanley. Annie was a devout churchgoer. Julia was Pop's favourite, though she did try his patience at times.

The sisters were:
Mary Elizabeth—known as Mimi, born in 1906
Elizabeth Jane—known as Betty, Liz or Mater, born in 1908
Anne Georgina—known as Nanny, born in 1911
Julia—known as Judy, born in 1914
Harriet—known as Harrie, born in 1916

George and Annie were keen for their daughters to marry well. When Betty married the wealthy and respectable Captain Charles Parkes, they were delighted. Mimi had been engaged to a young doctor, but sadly, he died before the wedding. In September 1939, Mimi married George Smith, a 43 year-old dairy farmer from Woolton who

LEFT: *9, Newcastle Road, where John lived with his mum, Julia, until he was five-years old* RIGHT: *Julia Lennon with her daughter, Jackie Dykins, John's half-sister*

was ten years her senior. They had no children and Mimi devoted much of her time helping the other sisters with their babies. How disappointed the parents were when Julia began dating Alfred Lennon, a merchant seaman. Julia was a red-headed beauty who was musically inclined and played the piano, piano accordion, banjo and ukulele. She has often been incorrectly portrayed as a fun-loving, good-time girl who gave away her son.

Julia and Alf were married in December 1938, a decision not welcomed by Julia's family. With the outbreak of war imminent, the Stanley family had moved from their Berkley Street residence to a rented home at 9, Newcastle Road. Pop and Annie lived there with their daughters Mimi, Nanny and Julia. Julia and Alf did not own a house, and Alf was often away at sea. John was born in October 1940 while Alf was away.

When Annie Stanley died in 1941, Mimi assumed the role of the matriarch of the family—the moral voice. Liverpool has historically been a matriarchal society. For generations while the men were away at sea, it was left to the wives to run the home, bring up the children and handle the household budget. Mimi was now responsible for the entire Stanley family.

On his return, Alf stayed with the family at Newcastle Road. However, Julia was able to collect Alf's wages at the Seamen's Mission every two weeks. One payday she discovered that Alf had gone Absent Without Leave (AWOL) and that she was out of luck. For the next eighteen months, she had no financial support or contact from Alf.

Mimi was also hit by hard times—her husband had lost his dairy farm. It was requisitioned by the government for the war effort, and a factory to make barrage balloons was built on its site. There wasn't

much money from this deal, and George was left with a small cottage on Allerton Road in Woolton. Mimi and George were bitter about this setback for years.

Julia and John were allowed to move into the dairy farm cottage and for a short time, Alf, Julia and John lived together as a family. Alf soon returned to sea despite Julia's protests, and she moved back to Newcastle Road with John to live with Pop again.

To earn money, Julia worked at a local cinema as an usherette. She met a soldier known as 'Taffy' Williams (Taffy is a nickname for a Welshman) and became pregnant after a brief affair. Pop was insistent that the baby be put up for adoption. Julia gave birth to a daughter named Victoria in 1945. The child stayed with Julia for six weeks before being adopted by a Norwegian man and his Liverpool-born wife. Unknown to Julia and the family, Victoria lived in Liverpool for a while before they moved to Hampshire. The adoptive family named her Ingrid, and Julia would sadly never see her again.

John started his education in November 1945 at Mosspits Primary School on Woolton Road. Julia took a job at a café near the school, working around school times, so she could take John to and from school. A regular visitor to this café was John Albert Dykins, a salesman who still lived at home with his parents. They embarked on an affair which turned into a long-term relationship. The Stanley family did not accept this, and had nothing to do with Dykins. Julia had told him about John and her baby Victoria. This only attracted him more, for John Dykins was her 'knight in shining armour'.

Julia called John Dykins 'Bobby'—there could only be one John in her life. It was her term of affection, and for a while, their daughter Julia thought that this was his name. Bobby had moved to a small flat in Gateacre, which was attached to a large home.

Mimi had social services remove John from Julia in May 1946 so that he could live with her. There wasn't much Julia could do because she wasn't married to Bobby, nor was he John's father. Their situation was socially unacceptable at the time.

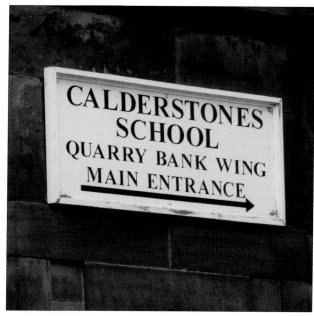

ABOVE AND RIGHT: *The original Quarry Bank School building which, since 1985, has become a wing of Calderstones Comprehensive School*

Between 1946 and 1949, Pop demanded that John be brought by Mimi to see him regularly. This was the only time Julia had an opportunity to see her son since Mimi often refused to let Julia visit him at her home at 251, Menlove Avenue, known as Mendips.

Julia became pregnant with Bobby Dykins child and, on 5 March 1947 she gave birth to a daughter, also named Julia. Her other daughter, Jackie, was born on 26 October 1949 two months premature. Pop died in 1949, and the owner of the Newcastle Road home offered it to Julia and Bobby. However, they could not afford the asking price, and were forced to leave quickly, so in August 1949, Bobby moved them to a new three-bedroom home in Blomfield Road, Springwood.

Mimi told John that his mother had gone to live with 'that Bobby' somewhere, and that she didn't know where Julia was. It was a long time before John discovered that Julia lived about a mile away.

John's cousin, Stanley, visited Liverpool from Scotland on holiday. He was only sixteen, but in time became a hero to Julia, Jackie and John. He asked Mimi if he could take John to see his mother, but Mimi vetoed the idea. Next, Stan suggested that he would take John to the dairy cottage to see their Aunt Harriet. Mimi was happy with that arrangement, and so the two of them left the house, but instead, they went straight to Julia's home and spent time with his mother, 'Bobby' and his step-sisters. John called Stan his 'Prodigal Son', for taking him back to his mum. His Biblical metaphor was slightly mistaken, but the point was made.

The pattern was set: every holiday, Stan took John to see his family. John also visited Scotland many times where he stayed with his Aunt Elizabeth, known as 'Mater'. Julia was more determined than ever to get John back. She often cried, "They've taken my son from me. They won't let me have him. We have to get him back".

John enrolled in Quarry Bank Grammar School in September 1952. The location made it easy for John to visit his mother's home on Blomfield Road. By the time John was thirteen, he stayed with his mother on a regular basis. Somehow, Mimi and Julia came to an arrangement where Julia was allowed access to Mendips with the girls to see John, and John was also free to go to Blomfield Road whenever he wanted.

John's sister Julia remembers accompanying John to Allerton Golf Course to look for stray balls. The idea was to take them home and clean them before selling them back to the golfers for a profit.

Julia inspired John to play the banjo, and the first tune he learned was Buddy Holly's "That'll Be The Day". It was the first song The Quarrymen recorded at Percy Phillips' studio in Kensington. Julia also took John, Julia and Jackie to Garston Cinema to watch Elvis Presley's first film, *Loving You*. They saw it five times in two days. She bought American cowboy shirts at Garston Market, which John wore at The Quarrymen's first outdoor gig at Rosebery Street, and on the famous day when John first met Paul at St. Peter's Church fete. Julia was present at the front of the crowd to cheer on her son's group.

The Quarrymen were in full swing by 1957, often practising in Julia's house. John and Julia's relationship was blossoming until tragedy struck. On 15 July 1958, Julia Lennon was killed by a speeding car driven by an off-duty policeman on Menlove Avenue, just down the road from Mendips. The distress was compounded by the actions of the family. John's half-sisters Julia and Jackie were whisked off to Scotland to stay with their Aunt Mater, simply being told that their mummy had had an accident and was going to be in the hospital for a while. They never returned to their family home in Blomfield Road, and were brought back to Liverpool at the beginning of September after about two months away. Still without being told what had happened, they were taken to the dairy cottage to live with Norman and Harriet. Eventually, it was Uncle Norman who sat them down one morning and told them the grim news.

"Your mother has died and gone to heaven", Norman said. "You won't see her again".

I asked Julia Baird to tell me about her childhood and being part of John Lennon's family. What was her mother like?

"Wonderful—what would you expect me to say? I remember my mother going everyday to the hospital to see Jackie, who had been born prematurely. Looking back, I wonder how much the stress of not seeing John affected her. I've not put it in the book because it's a psychological or emotional question. She'd had John, she'd had a baby taken away, and then I arrived. She had all the problems arguing with Mimi and Pop and then moving house. Pop died and my father had to find a house, and then physically coping with the move. I remember my father and I carrying things out of the house. We moved all the furniture out and the baby was due at Christmas and maybe it was not a surprise that she was born two months early.

"My mother was a wordsmith extraordinaire. She would have you laughing and rolling in the aisles about anything: she was clever. She has been dismissed by so many writers as just a woman who gave her children away. She was a highly intelligent, articulate woman who was witty, dry, funny, everything".

The affection that the other lads in The Quarrymen had for her, and have been happy to retell isn't consistent with Aunt Mimi's stories. Why is that?

"Mimi lived eleven years after John had died. And in that time, Mimi reinvented herself. With John gone, she could say anything she liked, without anyone to contradict her. Thus, she was able to dismiss Jackie and me for years".

How did you first hear about Victoria, (later named Ingrid)?

"That was Bill Smithies from the *Liverpool Echo*, the features editor then. He was trying to set the story straight, and within a short time he mentioned about the four children, and I just looked at him, and straight away he said, "You don't know, do you?" I said "No, what are you talking about, are you saying there are four of us?" He said, "Julia, your mother had four children, and I can see you don't know. I'm going". He was a lovely man, and gave me his number to ring him when I was ready to talk. I went straight out of the house and drove to Nanny's house in Rock Ferry (Nanny was Mimi's sister, Anne). I said, 'Nanny, I'm going to come again and again until you tell me the truth. I've been told by a complete stranger'. It took three visits".

You met Ingrid, didn't you?

"It was so strange when she turned up. My cousin, Stan and I were at Mendips putting up the Blue Heritage plaque. It was a sunny day and he turned round and quietly spoke—we were concerned he was going to fall off the ladder—"I think I can see Ingrid". "What?" I said. "Ingrid, she's over there". Stan had seen her before, but I didn't know what my half-sister looked like. He went down the ladder and there she was walking up the road with a friend. The first thing I did was look at her. John and I look alike, my sister

LEFT: *John's Aunt Mimi Smith* RIGHT: *Mimi, John, and lodger, Michael Fishwick* OPPOSITE: *Mendips*

and I look alike—some people even think we're twins—so the genes are strong. My mother had brown eyes—I don't know about Alf—and we're a red-headed family, and we also look like John. I thoroughly and absolutely expected Ingrid to look like me, John and Jackie, but that wasn't the case. She had pale blue eyes and fair hair, and I found this quite a shock. I had built up a mental image, because, despite the fact that John is our half-brother, Jackie, John and I all look alike. There is a common, strong gene. Obviously, Ingrid must favour her father more. Our father was dark, so different. We went for a short walk and talked for a few minutes. I invited her to a reception being given in John's honour, but she declined. Despite several invitations, I haven't seen her from that day".

Julia, tell me about John's childhood.

"One of my older cousins says, 'John was as happy as the day is long'. According to his own testimony, that was not true. John once called himself a 'social and psychological cripple' because he was torn away from his mother to live with Mimi. When I heard that I was in tears.

"The family is in denial about how all that to-ing and fro-ing can affect a child's life. It is unimaginable to the adults because it didn't happen to them. You can't go through all that and not be affected. All those things that he wasn't supposed to know or notice, or remember. Children do not talk to the oppressor. I know that from my own history and children I have worked with. If you tell the oppressor how unhappy you are, then they oppress you even more. You tell anybody that's not close".

The steps Mimi took to get John are almost beyond belief.

"She saw a window of opportunity, and if she'd have let that go, there wouldn't be another chance. She was like a bulldog, wasn't she? Like a mastiff or a rottweiler? The first time she came round, to collect John, my father put her out. The second time she came with a social worker who said or rather, told Mimi that she could find nothing wrong with John's staying with his mother. Mimi then probably appealed to the Director of Public Services. She was determined. He asked where John slept. There was only one bedroom and my parents weren't married. He agreed with Pop and Mimi that John should go and live with George and Mimi at Mendips.

"My 'family' say that Mimi loved Judy. I call it jealousy, spite and opportunism. I don't call that love, when you take them at their weakest point. Talk about kicking a dog when it's down. Mimi changed John's school to Dovedale from Mosspits, and took over running his life, or should that be ruining his life? It was obvious that Julia and Bobby needed a bigger place, where John would have his own bedroom. Julia and Bobby moved back with Pop at Newcastle Road, where John could have his own room. That would solve the problem, so Julia went to Mimi to get John back. Mimi turned her away at the door".

How would you describe Mimi?

"Hypocrite. To the core, flawed. Unbelievable what she put my mother through. I mention in the book that she had set her heart on having John, no matter what the price to pay, no matter what my mother thought, Mimi just battled away. This was her opportunity to have a child".

Mimi's story was about to take an unusual turn. She and her husband George had started to take in lodgers at Mendips. After George died in 1955, the student's rent became invaluable, with Mimi even giving up her bedroom to sleep downstairs in the dining room to accommodate as many students as possible. One of those students, Michael Fishwick, was about to become a more significant player than anyone realised.

Tell me about Michael Fishwick and his story.

"The hypocrisy is too big to take on board, and I've known now since 2005 and am still shocked by it. I had it in my head that Mimi had had an affair after what Nanny had suggested. She thought it was 'George' and 'New Zealand', but that's all I had to go on. She'd picked up that something was going on and only started to tell me about it in her last 18 months up to 1997. She knew that Mimi had talked about going to New Zealand and she thought it was with George. This was only partly correct.

"When I was getting in touch with Michael Fishwick, it was to find out what he knew and saw? On the other side of Mendips, where there had been waste ground, a bungalow had been built. It was occupied by Mr. and Mrs. Caplan. Mimi didn't like Mrs. Caplan, but Mimi was not a woman's woman, she was a man's woman. She didn't like the female race. You see, Mimi didn't go out; she never went anywhere, so it had to be close to home because you could go round, any day or evening and she was there. The only place she went to regularly was Woolton Village to shop. So if Mimi was having a relationship, it had to be within walking distance.

"Michael Fishwick didn't have to tell me anything; it was his decision. I tracked him down, hoping that he could unlock the secrets of life inside Mendips. Mimi's boyfriend would have had to have been one of the students who were there through thick and thin. That's why I set out to contact him, never imagining for a split second, about his involvement with my aunt.

The morning room and kitchen at Mendips, and the back garden where John used to cut the grass

"When I spoke to Michael Fishwick, I just said, 'Who was Mimi's boyfriend?' I didn't ask did she have one. If he'd have said to me, 'Good grief, Mimi didn't have a boyfriend, what are you talking about?' I would have thought, 'Nanny was wrong on that one'. She wasn't wrong on much: she'd picked up some feelings but that was all. I would have left it.

"He said, 'What made you think Mimi had a boyfriend?' Perhaps Nanny was right, as it wasn't a denial. We met again the next week and he told me about his improbable relationship with Mimi, given his much younger age.

"The relationship started in 1956. Michael had lived at Mendips as a student since September 1951 and finally left in 1960. George had died in 1955. Mimi at this point was over fifty years of age, although she told Michael that she was forty-six — Michael was twenty-seven. During Christmas of 1956, Mimi had taken John with her to Scotland to see her sister's family and to keep him away from his mother. Michael telephoned to say that he was ill, and was confined to his bed at Mendips. Mimi left Scotland the next day, without John and went straight back to Mendips to be with Michael.

"Michael was offered the chance to go to New Zealand on a project to complete his Ph.D. and he and Mimi considered leaving Liverpool and moving to New Zealand, with marriage a possibility. However, the funding for the doctorate fell through, and Michael had to stay in Liverpool. He was soon called up for national service and in 1960 the relationship was at an end. Michael later married someone else".

This helps to understand Mimi more. Tell me about 'The House of Correction'.

"Mimi called Mendips, 'The House of Correction' and when John was going back there he said, 'I have to go back to the House of Correction' and we were the 'House of Sin'. Society has changed a lot since then, but the hypocrisy hasn't. Mimi destroyed my mother's life, and the rest of our family, just to get the child that she never had. Here was a ready-made child. I can only think that she was an opportunist. I don't think that she had planned it, but as it became more obvious, it was an opportunity not to be missed. As I have already mentioned, Leila Harvey, my cousin, told me that when they (John's mother Julia and 'Bobby' Dykins) had moved back to the Penny Lane area — 9, Newcastle Road — Julia went to Mimi to ask to take John home. Mimi flung John behind her and said to my mother, 'Get out'. It's a lot stronger than I put in the book — 'Get out of here, you're not having him, you're not fit to have him, get out of my house'. Leila was at the back of the room and witnessed it all.

Menlove Avenue in 1960. Mendips is the first house on the left

"When I think of Mendips, I always think of it as an unhappy house, and people go round there on the tour and say, 'Isn't this wonderful, isn't this lovely,' but it was not a happy house. After Ernest died—the owner of Mendips who was a lovely man—Cynthia Lennon, John's first wife said, 'Do you want to buy it?' I said, 'No Cynthia, what are you suggesting?' Cynthia said she would speak to Julian—John and Cynthia's son—and did Jackie and I want the house?' I said, 'Cyn, thank you, but no thank you'.

"Cynthia knew what type of house it was, and I understood, even before I knew the whole story, that John was living in that house as a child because he had to live there, not by choice or that my mother had given him away. It was the house where my mother was turned away".

Your mother must have been distraught?

"We now know she had post-natal depression. Mimi couldn't have children for whatever reason, but I've tried not to surmise anything in the book. We always knew that there was something wrong about Mimi; I've never tried to write about it before because I couldn't

prove it. Once I knew about the student, everything fell into place. That was the final piece of the jigsaw. When I looked at everything Mimi had done, I realised that she had ruined my mother's life".

May Pang, John Lennon's former personal assistant-turned-lover in the 1970s said recently that she had a sense that John had been told that Julia was dead, when clearly she was living close by. Do you know anything about that?

"I don't know that, but it's entirely possible. I know that Mimi said to John that she didn't know where his mother was, because Nanny told me this and John told me in his conversations. He said, 'I didn't know where you were, I was told that mummy had gone away with Bobby, and Mimi didn't know where'. At the same time, Mimi told my mother, 'You keep away, he is unhappy and unsettled after he sees you, and he has to settle into his new life'.

"Mimi lived for eleven years after John and she continued to rewrite her story. She said, 'I knew I wanted John from the moment I first saw him'. We all like our sister's children, but she made all that up. Give her another fifty years and she'd have claimed she had John herself. There had always been an atmosphere between us that never ever went away. Bizarrely though, it was me that she sent for at the end of her life".

Why did she ask for you?

"I don't know, but I always went. When she came out of hospital, she was told that someone from the family had to be there, in her house, before they would let her go home, so she phoned me. Why me? I wonder did Mimi want to talk to me? I am surmising here because she never said anything".

Mimi died in December 1992. Her last words were, "I'm terrified of dying, I've been so wicked". Did she want to apologise and heal the wounds?

"I wish she would have done it years ago because I would have said to her, 'It's all right Mimi, I don't think you're going to be judged anywhere and I'm not going to judge you. Be happy. It's totally forgiven'. Do I have the right to forgive on behalf of my mother? Maybe I do. I would have told her, 'It's fine; no one is going to judge you, be happy, and be peaceful now'. I would have said it to her without a shadow of a doubt, but she didn't give me the opportunity to, and we were too frightened of her, even at this stage, to say anything. She was an absolute figure of fear to me".

What happened after your mother was killed?

"Jackie and I were nuisances, to be coped with as a matter of family duty. We were packed off to Scotland the next day and were told that mummy was unwell in hospital"

How long were they planning to keep your mother's death a secret?

"I imagine that if they could, it would have been forever. We came back to Liverpool, the first week in September. My mother died on 15 July, and we were sent away on the 16 July, so we were away for about eight weeks. Even when we came back they still didn't tell us. Were we not to ever mention our mother again? They were mad if they thought that we were never going to talk about her. They were mad, empty-headed, self-obsessed adults".

Mimi's sister Harriet, and her husband Norman, assumed responsibility for the girls and took them to live in the dairy cottage, not far from Mendips.

It's like there is a conspiracy between Mimi's whole family because your mum and dad weren't married, you and Jackie were not considered to be part of Mimi's family.

"We heard that forever. If they were alive we'd still be hearing it now".

It must have deeply affected you and Jackie?

"It still affects us. They didn't care, that is the truth. It was a duty to look after us. There was talk of an orphanage but my father went crazy. My father maintained us the whole time. I don't know what the agreement was, but he kept the family, as he should have done. It wasn't a duty; he paid for everything and more for us and in fact, for the household. He bought the beds, the washing machine, and the school shoes: he bought everything. He was never a father who decided not to pay. There was money going into the house all the time for us, but we never knew it then".

You were made wards of court, weren't you?

"We knew nothing about this until later. When I was 21, I just received a letter, which had been opened already, and I said, 'What's this?' I was told to go down to this place in Water Street (Liverpool City Centre) and they'll explain it to you. So I went down and I said, 'What's this?' My mother apparently had an insurance policy that was bought from the man at the door, and it was worth £300 when she died, to be paid out when we were twenty-one, split between her three children. John received £100 when he was twenty-one, though he was never told that it was from his mother. John always believed it was a gift from his auntie. He and Paul went to Paris with the money.

"When I was twenty-one, I went and I received £200, and when Jackie went it was about £320, because of the interest that had built up. I just said, 'What is this about the ward of court, I don't know anything about this'. I was told, 'Sign this, and you're not a ward of court any more'. But I said, 'What does it mean?' 'It means that your uncle and aunt became your guardians'. But my father was keeping us. We knew nothing about it".

It was something else from your childhood that's been taken away from you.

"Exactly. When we had our school reports, my uncle always signed them as guardian. My father could have done that. Why did they do that? We were raging inside but we never dared ask any questions".

Norman and Harriet Birch became their guardians. Since the girl's father, 'Bobby' Dykins, had not been married to Julia, he had little or no rights. Some books have portrayed Dykins as a drunk, an incompetent father incapable of looking after his daughters. This was not true. He was not allowed to look after his daughters, and legally could do nothing about it. He was allowed to visit them once or twice a week. Bobby couldn't cope with living in Springwood, and so he found a new house near Woolton Woods, close to the cottage. Unbeknown to Harrie and Mimi, Julia and Jackie found the house and would go to see their father for quick visits in secret.

How did your father cope?

"He was weak in the opposition of the family, caught in the teeth of the tiger. There was no respect for his feelings. Because they couldn't marry—Alf wouldn't give Julia a divorce—Bobby had no rights. They didn't have the right to do what they did, but they did it. They were like bulldozers. We lost our mother, and they took us away from our father and our grandmother because she was too 'common' to be allowed to visit".

In the summer of 1959, Julia and Jackie were told they could go and spend a week with their father, whose mother had come to live with him too. 'Nana' was able to take care of them when their father had to go to work. The week became two weeks and then the whole of the summer holiday. Bobby had a new job in the New Bears Paw pub in town, and arranged a part-time job for John there with him. It was all going well, when, in the summer of 1960, Nana became ill. It became clear that she couldn't continue to look after the girls, and they moved back in with their Aunt Harrie.

In January 1966, further tragedy struck when their father, Bobby, was killed in a car crash at the bottom of Penny Lane. John didn't know for months: he didn't need to be told, as it was nothing to do with 'the family'.

John Lennon by now was a Beatle and the contact between him and his two half-sisters became less frequent, and they rarely heard from him. They made contact again in the 1970s, and had many conversations. Julia talked to John about their mum and their emotions ran the gamut. John remarked to Julia, 'You had her, I didn't,' a lyric reflected in his song "Mother". He became nostalgic, and asked Julia to send over lots of his old things to America. Julia sent photos, and at the same time, Mimi mailed his Quarry Bank school tie and sent his Uncle George's hallway clock at Mendips.

Lennon spoke of visiting Liverpool to see everyone. He surprised Nanny by ringing her up on her birthday and told her of his impending visit in the New Year. Unfortunately, a crazed assassin stopped his long-overdue homecoming from happening in December 1980.

Before then, John had purchased a three-bedroom house in Gateacre Park Drive, which was intended for his two half-sisters, Julia and Jackie. John's Aunt Harriet and Uncle Norman had moved there from the dairy cottage where they had looked after Julia and Jackie. Harriet died in 1972 and after John died in 1980, Norman was still living there. Yoko wrote to offer Norman first refusal on the sale of the house, 'at a mutually agreeable price'. Norman lived on a fixed income from a pension and was unable to afford it. However, following a protest, Yoko allowed Norman to stay.

After a flurry of letters and phone calls between Julia Baird and Yoko, it became clear that Yoko was not giving the house to Julia and Jackie. Yoko, however, did offer the two money if they were in need. The house was handed over to the Salvation Army on 2 November 1993 as a gift from Yoko. After sitting empty for several years, the Salvation Army has put it to use as a retirement home for their officers.

This house in Gateacre Park Drive became important to you, didn't it?

"That house is a symbol of John's love and care for Jackie and me, and it was taken away from us. It is just more of the same treatment that has been meted out to us since our mother's death. When Norman died after being knocked down by a car in October 1991—a horrible reoccurring theme with car accidents—his son David was asked by Yoko's lawyers, to clear the house within weeks. He emptied it in a weekend. It was special to us. Yoko then donated it to the Salvation Army, so it was never ours.

"Mimi also subsequently found that the house John had bought for her in Poole, Dorset, was not hers, but owned by Apple.

"But Yoko helped her by paying for private nursing care. When she died, Cynthia came with me to the funeral. Yoko and Sean (John and Yoko's son) came too, but not Julian who was John and Cynthia's son. Cynthia spoke to Yoko about Mimi's house, as apparently John had intended for it to be used as a family retreat too, as well as being Mimi's home. However, the house had already been sold".

People keep repeating untruths, don't they?

"Why didn't Hunter Davies (The Beatles official biographer) come and see me? I was an adult and I could have told him that Springwood (where Julia and her family lived) was where it all happened. Why wasn't that in?"

All these books with myths and stories must hurt you?

"I've been quoted as contributing to books, such as Albert Goldman's, when I never gave interviews. I could have sued, but I don't let it bother me because I know it's rubbish. That's why I say at the beginning of my book that these so-called 'experts' are someone who knew someone who knew someone else or maybe they didn't, so here's the truth. A newspaper article was one of the reasons I started my book. I challenged Philip Norman over what he had written in an article. He contacted me and, after initially denying it, he rang back and to his credit apologised. That particular article had hurt me, but I knew that because it was written by the well-respected author, people would accept it. When he admitted that the article was wrong, he invited me to correct the story of John's childhood in his forthcoming biography. My reply was that I would write it myself".

It must be so strange, directly or indirectly, to have people writing about you and your family constantly?

"All the time. When the 'family' don't gainsay it, that's almost a taciturn acknowledgment that it is true. When I speak to my cousin Leila she says, 'You know it's not true'. That is not good enough. When we go, it will become the truth".

Julia Lennon's grave in Allerton Cemetery, Liverpool

Your mother has been described as this happy-go-lucky girl who gave John away and it didn't matter to her.

"That's why I've written this book, to put my mother back where she belongs. One of my cousins said that it's an assassination of Mimi, but believe me it could have been a lot worse. I've done the bare minimum because there is enough in there".

It could have been a tabloid-style sensationalist book, couldn't it?

"It was never my intention to do that, even though there was enough scandal to do that. It's a serious book about serious matters. People have written these accounts without speaking to me or to Jackie and

then new researchers just look at the research done before and refer to that without doing their own investigation. As an academic I know that won't do. Go back to the source. You wouldn't get away with it in school. I've been to see the house where my mother was born, the plot at 8, Head Street—the houses have been demolished. I've seen them all with Stan, and I've been to see the farm in North Wales.

"My mother's house has been demolished to make way for new developments. I don't know if I'm pleased about that because I'd have to buy it and live in it as a tangible association with her".

You mention your mother's grave.

"I've been looking to do something about my mum's grave for some time, and it turned out that my Uncle Norman had paid about thirteen shillings (65 pence) for the plot. I don't know where the money came from or whether they clubbed together or how it happened, but he paid for it. Therefore, my mother's plot belonged to him. It's just that they didn't care, and what did it matter to us? After all, she wasn't alive and we weren't at the funeral and were never told where she was buried. So that passed, when Norman died, to my cousin David. He has been great in going through the paperwork and probate, so soon we can look at a proper headstone. It will be for us, and not the public and I hope it never will be". In 2009, a new gravestone was placed on Julia's grave, to "Mummy", from her children John, Victoria, Julia and Jackie.

How do you deal with it?

"Since 2004, I have been consumed with the book, and it has been a cathartic exercise for me. I will be promoting the book in the near future to get the truth out there. After that, I don't know. I'm thinking of putting my book into poems. The book is about in the tenth draft (the book is since published in 2007, *Imagine This - Growing up with my brother John Lennon*). When I started writing it, I thought that Hodder, the publisher, might not be interested. It was an affair of the heart, I was researching and making notes and it came out more like modern poetry than prose. One example is called 'John'. My mother wanted John to know that he was the only John, and why she called my father 'Bobby'".

For a short time, A very short time,
My parents lived together with John.
My mother called John Albert by 'Bobby', as did John.
My mother wanted John to know that he was John.
The one John. The number one John. Her John.

Julia Baird is an extraordinary woman who has faced unbelievable treatment from her own family. On account of Mimi's scheming, Julia and Jackie were virtually disowned and ignored. They were not considered part of the family. More recently, Julia has found out that Mimi, the 'moral' voice of the Stanley family who destroyed her sister, Julia's life, who forcibly took John away from his mother out of some misplaced moral crusade, was herself later having a relationship with a student half her age in her 'House of Correction'. You can understand why Julia feels that Mimi was a hypocrite.

What makes it worse still is that her life has been constantly paraded in the public eye for the last four decades, and misrepresented. Her mother, who was not alive to defend herself, has been reviled and ridiculed for too long.

It is no wonder John had so many demons, and it is easier to understand the man more than ever before. Julia Lennon was an inspiration to her son and daughters, and should now be given the credit for what she was able to achieve, in spite of Mimi's actions which tore the family apart.

9 OCTOBER 1940
John Winston Lennon is born
"Working Class Hero"

"A working class hero is something to be" sang John Lennon on his 1970 solo album, *Plastic Ono Band*. It was a wonderful sentiment, but working class? Not a chance.

Homes

John was born in Oxford Street Maternity Hospital (Liverpool) on 9 October 1940, and brought home to 9, Newcastle Road (Wavertree) in the Penny Lane area. He was raised from the age of five in his Aunt Mimi Smith's house at Mendips in Woolton, a middle-class area. It is a common English middle-class custom to name a house, and in this case it refers to a range of hills in the prosperous south of England.

John was determined to leave his mark on Woolton, and engraved his initials on a tree near Mendips. It could safely be stated that Lennon not only left his mark on Liverpool but on the world.

Education

John first attended Mosspits School (Wavertree) before Mimi moved him to Dovedale School (Mossley Hill). At the age of eleven, he transferred to Quarry Bank Grammar School (Allerton) where The Quarrymen were formed. After Quarry Bank School he enrolled in the Liverpool Art College (Liverpool) where he met Cynthia Powell and Stuart Sutcliffe.

Music

The first group he formed was briefly called The Black Jacks (See Dingle - Pavilion Theatre on page 287) before becoming The Quarrymen. The first photograph taken of The Quarrymen is at the Rosebery Street (Dingle) performance in June 1957. Only a few weeks later, he performed at St. Peter's (Woolton) where he met Paul McCartney. They often practiced at his mother Julia's house at 1, Blomfield Road (Allerton), and occasionally at Mendips.

John started his musical journey on a guitar which his mother bought for him. Julia taught John to play, but only banjo chords—the instrument she played. The other instrument he became famous for was the harmonica or mouth organ. I always wondered why he chose that instrument. Part of it was because he was given one, though there are various stories about who gave it to him. Over the years it has been suggested his Uncle George, a student or a bus driver. Either way it doesn't matter. He used it to great effect on "Love Me Do" and other early Beatles tunes. One possible reason for his interest in the harmonica could be traced to "*The Goons*", one of his favourite radio shows. Every show had two musical interludes. One of them was Max Geldray who would play a different song on the harmonica every week accompanied by his band. He was a versatile performer and could play almost anything. It's quite possible that he inspired a young John Lennon to take to the instrument.

TOP: *John on the top row, centre, at Dovedale School, 1951*
LEFT: *John's initials carved into a tree, still just perceptible in black at the centre of the picture*
RIGHT: *John on the Isle of Man school trip*
OPPOSITE: *John Lennon, The Beatle, pictured in 1963*

The gates of Strawberry Field, Woolton

He recalled his childhood in the songs "Strawberry Fields Forever", "Penny Lane" and his original draft lyrics of "In My Life". However, one of Lennon's most famous solo songs was "Working Class Hero", but was he reflecting on his working class childhood in Liverpool? When Mimi asked John why he talked like a Scouser when he'd been brought up to speak correctly, he responded: "It's about money. The fans expect me to talk like this". Aunt Mimi revealed when she was asked by a publisher to write her memoirs: "Take the money, Mimi", John told her. "Tell them I was a juvenile delinquent who used to knock down old ladies".

The two prominent women in his young life were his mum Julia and his Aunt Mimi, who were different individuals. Colin Hanton came

to know both of them while he was playing with The Quarrymen. Colin had his own reasons for understanding John's loss when Julia was killed. "My mum died when I was about ten, and The Quarrymen came to rehearse at my house, and I said, 'This is my mum'. She was only about ten years older than them—she was my second mum, only about twenty-six. It wasn't like meeting the other mothers who were quite old. They were shocked. I had lost my mum, like John and Paul did. I remember when I saw John after his mum died and he had his guitar—he always had his guitar with him—and we just stared at each other. I knew what he was thinking, he knew what I was thinking, and we never said anything, and that was it. We never mentioned it again; it's a man thing—no hugging and stuff".

Regarding Julia, Hanton recalled, "She was like a big sister, not anything like any mother I'd ever seen. You could go to her house when you should be in school and

LEFT: *John Lennon's piano in The Beatles Story* RIGHT: *John Lennon's glasses in The Beatles Story*

she wouldn't mind. I remember once we were at Mendips and John said, 'I'm going to my mum's, do you want to come?' So we walked down to Springwood and we just sat on the settee and she took her banjo out and she showed John some banjo chords. She was like no one I'd ever seen.

"She was different to Aunt Mimi. Oh, Mimi could freeze you to the spot with one stare. I don't remember going in the kitchen door like Pete does; I went to the front door. We were all Woolton boys, and well brought up—we weren't scallies. Paul talks about being a 'scruff from Speke'—he was never a scruff. Even our language was different, it wasn't that deep guttural language like George or Ringo—we were brought up with good manners and you respected other adults. You were on your best behaviour when you were there, but you just applied what you learnt at home.

"I have mixed memories about us practising at Mendips. Mimi wasn't one for excess noise. I was there in 2005 and we went to John's bedroom, and I was asked, 'Do you remember being in this room?' and I don't know why I didn't say no. I remember John's bedroom being downstairs in the front room. I remember sitting in there with my back to the coloured, patterned windows and John was facing me and so was Paul. I remember Paul saying to John, 'Is that where you sleep?' Behind me in the window was what looked like a long flat thing with a pink cover over it—no headboard. It was disguised as a bench so you wouldn't know it was a bed. I reckon that with all of those lodgers there, Mimi was sleeping downstairs in the back room and John was sleeping in the front room. I must have had my drums there with John and Paul but it was one of the rare occasions.

"Because Mimi's lodgers were medical students, one of them taught us a filthy alphabet: A is for arsehole, B is for bastard…….. etc. right through the alphabet. It was absolutely disgusting, but a medical mind could remember it all. I told this recently and Pete Shotton said 'Oh yes, I'd forgotten about that'.

"I heard a story recently that Mimi was sleeping with one of the lodgers—one of the vets told his story and he admitted he had slept with her: it has destroyed my image of Mimi".

Alf Lennon

When it comes to the parents of The Beatles, none have been so controversial or discussed as John's mum and dad. The reasons are numerous.

Alf and Julia split up when John was young, but Alf came back into his life in the sixties in a public way, appearing in the newspapers and releasing a single called "It's My Life". He and John played out their relationship publicly for a while.

Was Alfred Lennon a rogue? Most of the early books were written with Mimi Smith as the main source of information, even having some editorial control. It wasn't in her interest to paint Alfred in a good light or Julia in too bad a light. Julia didn't meet any of Alf's family until after John was born, when she met his mother. Alf would occasionally meet Julia at her home in Berkley Street, but on one occasion, Pop Stanley demanded that Alf leave his daughter alone.

Pauline Lennon, who married Alfred in the sixties, has published a book, *Daddy Come Home*, which is based on the manuscript that Alf wrote to be passed on to John. When John read it after Alf had died, he realised that he had not known the whole story about his mum and dad. The following is a synopsis of the various accounts of Alf and Julia's life, according to Alf Lennon's memoirs.

Alf's life had started at 57, Copperfield Street in The Dingle in 1912. Alf's mum, Mary, known as Polly, was his father Jack's second wife. She brought up the six children. However, when Jack—who was older than her—died, she couldn't afford to bring up all six children, so she accepted the offer of two places for her eldest children—including Alf—at the Bluecoat School in the Penny Lane area of Liverpool. It was an orphanage, and offered a great education. And so, at the age of seven, Alf left home for the Bluecoat. He suffered badly from rickets, which gave him weak legs, and he didn't grow as tall as he should have, reaching just 5-feet-4-inches.

Alf (or 'Freddie' as he was often called) befriended Jackie Bond, who became a teacher at Quarry Bank School. He later taught Alf's son, John. Alf was interested in the sea, and joined the Merchant Navy when he came of age. Shortly before his first voyage, he met a young girl in Sefton Park named Julia Stanley. They hit it off. He was sixteen and she was a year younger. Julia had beautiful long red hair, and a gorgeous figure. Her only fault was poor eyesight, something she would pass on to John.

Alf's first voyage was on the *SS Montrose* which was owned by the Cunard Shipping Line. While away he thought constantly of Julia, and couldn't wait to see her again.

He visited the Stanley's family home in Berkley Street, but tensions grew when Pop Stanley told him to stay away from his precious daughter.

This only served to push Julia into Alf's arms and so they decided to get married. They exchanged vows in the Mount Pleasant Registry office (where John and Cynthia were married) and crossed the street and entered the Big House pub for a meal and drinks supplied by his brother Sydney. Julia jokingly listed her occupation on the marriage certificate as 'Cinema Usherette' because of her love of the movies. Their 'honeymoon', of sorts, was in the Forum Cinema on Lime Street. They then went home to their separate houses.

Alf had made an honest woman of Julia and so Pop Stanley agreed to help them. On return from his latest trip, Julia met him at the ship and took him to 9, Newcastle Road—their new home, which they shared with Julia's parents. Pop and Anne Stanley greeted him warmly, much to his surprise.

Away at sea on the *Empress of Canada* when John was born, Alf didn't see him for a few weeks. His frequent trips to sea started a rift between Julia and Alf. Julia commented that Alf was married to the sea. It wasn't an exaggeration. Between 1 August 1940 and 13 January 1944, he spent three months at home in total. Julia was fed up and told Alf it was a choice between her and the sea: the sea won. This could be considered unfair of Julia since this was in the middle of World War II and every man had to do his duty.

The rank of Saloon Steward on the *Moreton Bay* was gained, which showed he had good prospects. Even Pop and Mimi were impressed—maybe they could make a decent man out of him yet. After John was born, Julia and Alf moved with their son to the Dairy Cottage in Woolton. While he was home, Alf was a firewatcher for the war effort. Even when he was on leave, he wasn't in the house much.

Alf then set off on the *SS Berengaria* and promised everything would be better when the war was over, and he would be home soon. The *Berengaria* was bound for New York. Alf had been promoted to Chief Steward and Mimi was even more impressed. Alf, Julia and Mimi celebrated before he set sail for New York, a city he dearly loved. However, it was eighteen months before Alf and Julia saw each other again. Alf constantly entertained people whether on the ships or in the bars of New York. He sang songs and did a hilarious send-up of Adolf Hitler, which was his party piece and something that John performed as well.

For the return voyage, Alf was offered a ship, not as Chief Steward but as assistant. Since he did not want to lose his higher rating, his options were to wait until he returned home and complain—which could take months—or miss his ship, which was risky. He decided to miss his ship with dire consequences. He went the next day to the British Consul to explain, but when he arrived there he was arrested and held in Ellis Island for two miserable weeks. By this time, he had already been away for months, and there had been no contact with Julia, nor had he sent her any money. Finally, he was ordered to take a position on the *Sammex*, which was bound for the Far East,

carrying whisky and cigarettes. Alf soon discovered that the voyage was not altogether legal, and when they reached Bone, in North Africa, military policemen boarded the ship and everyone was arrested and sentenced to three months in an army prison. Alf went to the Consul and he was permitted to board the *Monarch of Bermuda* as a Distressed British Seaman. By the time Alf made it back home, he had been away for eighteen months, and Julia suspected he might be dead.

Alf returned to sea at the end of 1945, and didn't come back until March of the next year. When he arrived at the house, he found Julia outside talking to a man. He went inside to be greeted by Pop Stanley, whose tone of voice was completely different, and Julia walked in with John 'Bobby' Dykins. Alf had to report for another voyage, but on his return, he went straight to Mimi's house, as John was now living there. Mimi told him how Julia and John Dykins were 'living in sin' at Newcastle Road, and added that she was disgusted with her. Alf took his son—after giving Mimi the £20 she asked for to cover expenses for John—to his friend's house in Blackpool. It was there that Alf discussed his plan to emigrate with John to New Zealand.

They had been living in Blackpool for a short time, when on 22 June 1946, Julia turned up at the house. She had found them by contacting the Merchant Navy Pool. A heated discussion over custody ensued and they agreed to let their child make an adult decision. The two turned to John and unfairly asked him what he wanted to do. John sat on his dad's knee, and Julia realised the decision was made. As she walked away, John let go of his dad and ran after her with those haunting words he later reproduced in the song "Mother": "Momma don't go; Daddy come home". John wanted to live with both of his parents in peace and harmony. Unfortunately, that was not an option.

Julia returned to Liverpool with John in tow and returned him to Mimi at Mendips. Heartbroken, Alf considered emigrating, and nearly did, but at the last moment changed his mind.

After getting into a fight in London, Alf spent four months in prison. When he returned home to Copperfield Street, he was greeted by his brother Charlie with the news that they had been trying to reach him. Two months previously his mum had died. Alf was distraught. The Merchant Navy wouldn't take him on again, and he had no job, no home and no money. He eventually washed dishes for a living.

Julia was killed on Menlove Avenue in July 1958, but again Alf didn't know. He only found out later when his brother Charlie sent him a newspaper clipping with the news about the accident.

When John first became famous, Alf didn't pay much attention. However, people started to recognize him, so he kept moving jobs. Eventually stories appeared in the press, but giving Mimi's version of John's life, and Alf was convinced by a reporter at *The Sketch* newspaper to discuss the story. They arranged a meeting with John in London. Alf went to see him, first seeing Brian Epstein, and then Paul, George and Ringo in the hallway. John and he talked for a while and Alf convinced him he didn't want to cash in on his son's fame. They laughed and joked for a time.

He later had a change of heart and sold his story to the magazine, *TitBits*. Alf was approached by fellow Liverpudlian Tony Cartwright who was managing an up-and-coming Welsh singer named Tom Jones. Tony convinced Alf to make a record called "It's My Life", which was sold around the world. However, it disappeared overnight in the United Kingdom. It was suggested that Brian Epstein was responsible for putting pressure on the record companies and shops to withdraw the record from sale, as John was horrified when he discovered that Alf was making a record. Alf and Tony went to John's house, but John told him forcefully to leave. Alf gave up his brief recording career and returned to his unremarkable life.

9, Newcastle Road, where John lived with his mum, Julia, until he was five

After John's trip to see the Maharishi Mahesh Yogi in London in the summer of 1967, John began meditating. The first step to discipleship, according to the Maharishi's teaching, is to forgive your parents. At the same time, Uncle Charlie wrote to John and told him blankly what had happened, and not to believe everything Mimi told him. John discovered that Julia had been pregnant with another man's child, and confronted Mimi with this information. Naturally, the subject matter was not up for conversation.

Six days after Brian Epstein died, John wrote to Alf out of the blue. He started his letter with "Dear Alf, Fred, dad, Pater whatever", and wrote "there's hope for us yet". He finished the letter by telling Alf not to say anything to the press because he didn't want Mimi 'cracking up'. Interestingly, John signed off all of his subsequent letters with the phrase 'write if you feel like,' a classic sign of being insecure and fearing rejection.

John later sent official Beatles biographer Hunter Davies to meet Alf to get his father's side of the story of his childhood. Alf was delighted to share the truth with Davies. However, when the book eventually

came out, Alf was dismayed to see that his side had been left out. John later admitted that he had allowed Mimi to check the manuscript first.

John and Alf met up once again, and John asked his father to live with him, Cynthia and Julian. This worked within reason, but John was never home and Alf was soon bored. It was decided that he should move into a flat of his own. John set him up and gave him an allowance of £10 a week, through Peter Brown at Apple. Then things changed dramatically. Alf met nineteen-year-old Pauline Jones, and against her family's wishes, she agreed to marry Alf in the summer of 1968. Alf was fifty-four, a good thirty-five years her senior. John was pleased for them and even took Pauline on as a secretary and to help Cynthia with Julian. John also paid for their flat in Brighton, and soon she was pregnant again after a previous miscarriage. They had a son called David. Not wanting to miss out on fatherhood a second time, Alf became a house-husband while Pauline went to work (exactly as John would later do for his second son, Sean).

John started Primal Scream Therapy in 1970 and his years of pent up anger and the bitterness of his childhood came to the forefront. The trauma of being asked to choose between his mum and his dad came back to him, and broke him. Once again, this led to anger and resentment against his father. On John's thirtieth birthday, Alf, Pauline and David were invited for a visit. When the family arrived, John screamed at his father for ruining his life and for abandoning him. John finished his vitriolic rant by telling Alf that he wished he were dead. Alf panicked and left with Pauline and David in tow. Soon after, John had them thrown out of the Brighton flat, and they set up home in a little cottage in Blisworth, near Brighton and didn't see or hear from John for five years. Pauline became pregnant again and gave birth to Robin in October 1973.

Alf, Pauline, David and Robin shared a peaceful existence until Alf was diagnosed with terminal stomach cancer. When Alf was admitted into hospital, he knew it was the end. Pauline contacted John through the Apple offices. It seemed that John had tried to find them, but without success. John sent a massive bouquet of flowers to Alf's room and telephoned him. The two shared a laugh and John promised to get together when Alf was discharged from hospital (John didn't know how ill Alf was). They parted with a typical Scouse phrase—'see you la'. According to Pauline, Alf was remarkably changed after that phone call—he had reconciled with his son. Alf passed away shortly afterwards on 1 April 1976. John sent a wreath but he did not attend the funeral as he could not leave the U.S. at the time because of his long-running immigration case.

Pauline promised Alf that she would send John a copy of his autobiography. The book had not been published, but Alf was more concerned that John should read it. John was so grateful to Alf for putting pen to paper that he determined to do the same for his first son, Julian, and he started keeping a journal in 1975 and did so right up to his death.

John at Dovedale School
Harry Holmes was John Lennon's teacher when he attended Dovedale School. Holmes spoke in 2006 of the young John Lennon—with some surprises. Harry had quite specific recollections of Lennon's time at Dovedale.

"Dovedale had a reputation for the eleven-plus exam. Some critics dubbed it an 'eleven-plus factory' and there was some justification for the description. John was in C1, the top stream for his age-group".

The majority of children in England had to take the eleven-plus exam in their last year at junior school, when they would reach the age of eleven. If the exam was passed, they progressed to a grammar school such as Quarry Bank and the Liverpool Institute. If you failed the exam, they went to a secondary modern school.

Family of John Winston Lennon

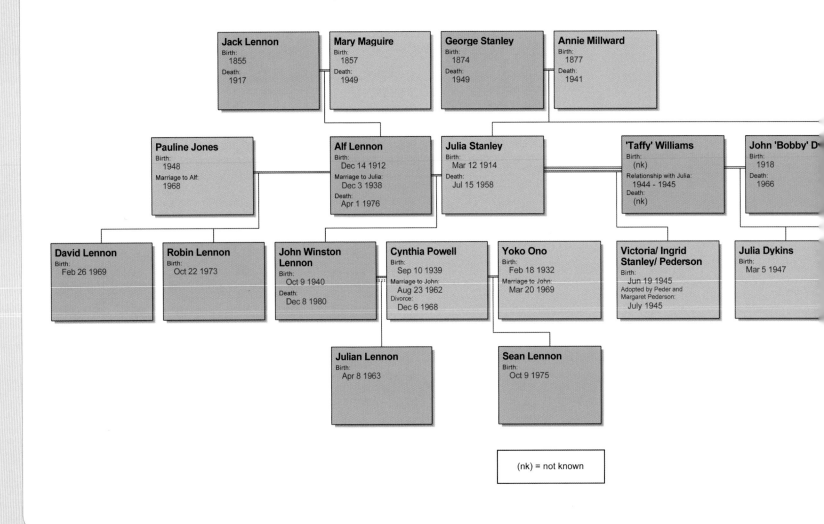

Jack Lennon
Birth:
1855
Death:
1917

Mary Maguire
Birth:
1857
Death:
1949

George Stanley
Birth:
1874
Death:
1949

Annie Millward
Birth:
1877
Death:
1941

Pauline Jones
Birth:
1948
Marriage to Alf:
1968

Alf Lennon
Birth:
Dec 14 1912
Marriage to Julia:
Dec 3 1938
Death:
Apr 1 1976

Julia Stanley
Birth:
Mar 12 1914
Death:
Jul 15 1958

'Taffy' Williams
Birth:
(nk)
Relationship with Julia:
1944 - 1945
Death:
(nk)

John 'Bobby' D
Birth:
1918
Death:
1966

David Lennon
Birth:
Feb 26 1969

Robin Lennon
Birth:
Oct 22 1973

John Winston Lennon
Birth:
Oct 9 1940
Death:
Dec 8 1980

Cynthia Powell
Birth:
Sep 10 1939
Marriage to John:
Aug 23 1962
Divorce:
Dec 6 1968

Yoko Ono
Birth:
Feb 18 1932
Marriage to John:
Mar 20 1969

Victoria/ Ingrid Stanley/ Pederson
Birth:
Jun 19 1945
Adopted by Peder and Margaret Pederson:
July 1945

Julia Dykins
Birth:
Mar 5 1947

Julian Lennon
Birth:
Apr 8 1963

Sean Lennon
Birth:
Oct 9 1975

(nk) = not known

Michael Fishwick
Birth:
1929
Relationship with Mimi:
1956 - 1960

George Smith
Birth:
1903
Marriage to Mimi:
Sep 15 1939
Death:
Jun 5 1955

Mimi Stanley
Birth:
1906
Death:
Dec 6 1991

Elizabeth Stanley
Birth:
1908
Death:
1976

Anne Stanley
Birth:
1911
Death:
1988

Harriet Stanley
Birth:
1916
Death:
1972

queline Dykins
26 1949

*The cousins: John and Leila Harvey at the back, with Michael Cadwallader,
David Birch and Julia Dykins at the front*

The front room at Aunt Mimi's home, Mendips, the house where John Lennon lived from the age of five

What was school like in John's day—how is it different to now?

"In direct convocation with the staff, the female members were given the appropriate prefix Mrs. or Miss, while the male members were Sir, but informally the males were called Pop, like Head Master Pop Evans, his Deputy Pop Williams and Pop Holmes. The exception to this rule was the uniformed caretaker (who lived across the road from the school) who was Mr. Aspinall. Many of the younger children in both the Infant and Junior departments firmly believed he owned the school".

How did you end up teaching John?

"My first class in 1950 contained forty boys—one of whom was John Lennon. He was a pleasant boy, with only a trace of a Scouse accent. I believe he cultivated a lapse in this respect later in his professional life for reasons unknown to me. I saw no evidence of musical ability—but there was not the opportunity to display such ability at Dovedale, if it existed. He was, however, very well-spoken, polite, self-confident with a twinkle in his eye and an unusual, mature sense of humour. His academic rating would be 'good average'."

How about Ivan Vaughan?

"Oh, Ivan Vaughan was a different boy to John: what I would call a 'rough diamond'".

John appeared in a play at school too didn't he?

"Yes, I produced a school play—*Treasure Island*—and cast John as Squire Trelawney. His qualities, previously listed, shone in the part, which he played with self-assurance and aplomb. He carried it off well. He had a good speaking accent—which was his naturally, not a broad Scouse accent he became famous for. He was a good performer, and ideal for the role of the well-spoken squire with his manners and voice".

How interesting when you think that, in 1960 when they were looking for a new name, Brian Casser suggested Long John and The Silver Beatles—which they shortened to The Silver Beatles. He can't have known that John had appeared in the play featuring Long John Silver.

"Of course, I followed the progress of this class throughout the years at Dovedale, and remember giving them a pep-talk prior to their eleven-plus examination. In the hopes of easing stress (which was considerable—from school and eager parents alike) I told them they could only do their best and if we could re-assemble in twenty years who would be the happiest or wealthiest—not necessarily the cleverest today. How right was I?"

So how was Lennon's behaviour at school?

"I have been questioned many times about John. Indeed, a reporter from the *Liverpool Echo*, together with her photographer, travelled from Merseyside to Hemel Hempstead—in the south of England—to interview me. But, like many other questioners, her interest faded when she found I had no scandal to reveal: no dirt to dish and no fabricated stories to tell. He was simply a happy member of a happy class, well-mannered and reasonably hard-working. He certainly lived up to the Dovedale motto of the time—Kindness, Courtesy and Consideration for others".

Is this the John Lennon who became famous?
How different he was back then?

"He attended the summer camp we held in the Isle of Man and enjoyed it. In fact, I took the much-published snap of him and British comedian Jimmy Tarbuck in the sea at Port Erin as the official camp photographer. Now, Jimmy Tarbuck: he was the only boy in eight years who ran away from camp. He used to 'buy' his popularity by bringing in sweets for everyone when his father had a success.

"Over the years we had selected various 'photo shoot' sites and Fred Bolt (the camp's organiser) had most of my snaps made into slides, which were shown at a P.T.A. meeting during the following autumn term. Of course, neither of us knew the fame which was to come John's way—or how many more pictures of him may have been taken".

John's primary school, Dovedale, taken from the top of St. Barnabas' Church, Penny Lane

Tell us about your taste and experience of Beatlemania.

"By 1964, I had reached the dizzy heights of Deputy Head Master at a large modern junior mixed and infant school in St. Albans. The eleven-plus examination was still playing a large part in children's lives. Pupils at private schools were not allowed to sit the examination in their own premises (for obvious reasons). My school had been detailed to look after a group of about twenty-five girls on two consecutive mornings for their examination. The Head Master in a welcome speech designed to put them at their ease in their new surroundings concluded by introducing me with something like—'This is Mr. Holmes who will be your invigilator. Mr. Holmes comes from Liverpool and once taught John Lennon of Beatle fame'. The school hall immediately became an unbelievable scene of mass hysteria with those prim and proper young ladies screaming and having left their desks, surrounding me to touch me and ask endless questions. I eventually restored some order by promising to bring my class photo with John in it the following morning for them to see. This I duly did and the eager group passed it around—kissing and cuddling it. Many asked me to sell it—'Daddy will pay and buy it for me'—and it took quite a while before the group were convinced that it was not for sale—and made a start on the second part of their examination. I still have no idea how their results matched up to their ability. Such is the price of fame".

Harry died peacefully in February 2007.

Stan Williams attended Dovedale with George Harrison and Ivan Vaughan, as well as John. Here are Stan's thoughts on '*that* Lennon', as he was often referred to.

"What of Lennon? Although I grew up with him, went to Dovedale with him, regularly saw him in the Liverpool 18 neighbourhood, and was in his company often enough to make a judgment about the type of person he was, I was not a friend and, therefore, did not see him as his close friends saw him. I was an onlooker, but a keen observer... and John was someone who you could not fail to take notice of. He made sure of that. 'I'm John Lennon... People notice me... Have you noticed that?' Why I should have found him quite so riveting that I began to make mental notes, I do not know... Even then, did I sense being privy to a piece of social and cultural history? Who knows?

ABOVE: *John Lennon (circled left) and Jimmy Tarbuck (right), who became a popular comedian, on a school trip on the Isle of Man*
BELOW RIGHT: *John at Quarry Bank in July 1955, third row from the back, third from the left*

"I was no sappy Norman, but Lennon had a hardness of spirit about him, both as a young boy and teenager, which frightened me. At Dovedale he was in the year above me, but I noticed him all right. He had a small group of camp followers, even then, and I saw him use the power of his personality over his cronies to bully others. They ganged up on me once for bringing a toy replica of a Colt 45—sent to me from America by an aunt—into the school playground. One of his deputy dogs rode out and kicked me in the balls for possessing something he would have loved to own. He was a sly bugger, who would get others to do his dirty work. John had self-belief; a rare confidence in himself, which allowed him to take a leading role in Dovedale School's 1952 school production of *Treasure Island*. I went to see the play and can remember Lennon strutting about brandishing flintlock pistols in one of the main parts. Years before skiffle and rock 'n' roll, there was, clearly, a relish he derived from being on stage. His Squire Trelawney was much more of a performance than a piece of acting.

"As a young teenager, I remember competing with his first skiffle group, The Black Jacks, in a talent contest at The Pivvy Theatre in Lodge Lane. This was the first time Lennon had ever taken part in any public performance as an embryo musician. He had no guitar then, but had the bravado, nevertheless, to sing and play a tea-chest bass wearing a natty pair of black gloves. In the words of skiffle king Lonnie Donegan, "He took centre-stage with a pair of leather gloves he'd borrowed from his dad".

"Like us, they chose to sing "Maggie May"".

Oh dirty Maggie May
They have taken her away
And she'll never walk down Lime Stre......

"Thank you boys... that's enough...we'll ring you, don't you ring us."

"A couple of months later and John could play well enough to front his new group, The Quarrymen. The rest is history. I was always wary of him. Being that one year older than me gave him the edge, but his personality had a razor-sharp, cutting-edge to it which was too cynical and intimidating for me to handle. I watched him head-butt someone in a pavement skirmish outside Capaldi's ice cream parlour on Smithdown Road in 1956. Likewise, I will never forget him tossing a flick-knife between my open legs as I sat on the grass with Beth in Calderstones Park. He was telling me to go away...and I did.

"I was there, in Penny Lane, in 'the shelter in the middle of a roundabout' the day John came over from Woolies with his gang to speak to Beth. Dressed the part, in her cadet nurses uniform, she was selling red poppies in a tray suspended from her neck for the Earl Haig Remembrance Day Fund. The image of 'Beth the pretty nurse' burnt itself not only into my memory, but deep into John's too. Later it would be incorporated into the unforgettable lyrics for "Penny Lane".

"Beth was Pete Shotton's girl and they saw the other face of John Lennon. Pete was his loyal, best friend for years and Beth was always telling me tales about the funny and daring things John did. To her he was kind, thoughtful and entertaining. Such people would not have been so fond of John had he not shown them the sweeter side to his nature. Likewise, if you wanted a teenage life with excitement and improvisation, then you could have no better friend than John. Beth had been my pal since our infant days and John never laid into me, verbally, the way he could have done. I was too nice and too well brought up for him. I also had a strong personality and once I realised John had to be the main man, I knew it could be dangerous even to compete. The best thing was to sit back and watch.

QUARRY BANK HIGH SCHOOL FOR BOYS,
CALDERSTONES, LIVERPOOL.
July 1955.

"Quick-minded, quick-witted and crushingly cruel with an amazing economy of words, on the occasions when he was holding court, I said nothing…or very little. I hoped that his generosity towards a close friend of Beth would save me from either ridicule or confrontation. With the exception of Pete Shotton, who I liked, I saw more than enough of King John and his travelling court of advisers, jesters and bully boys to want to keep this rather threatening fellow at arm's length.

"I was brought up by a loving guardian uncle, who was not only a fine Christian man, but also an ex-Fleet Air Arm war hero, as well as being a local sporting personality. John, however, had no male role model in the home to help shape his actions and ideas. At fourteen he was becoming his own man, free to roam and imitate the adult world, whereas I was still a boy more interested in playing football and reading comics. John was from another planet in his desire to assimilate adult behaviour and in his disregard for rules. He said and did things I would not dare. Occasionally, as with getting into the Pivvy to see the nude shows, I wished I had possessed the bottle to sneak into places like that years before I did.

"I am no Beatles expert, although I think the music is wonderful. The musical genius locked up in Lennon springs in part, perhaps, from the spiritual and emotional tension in his young life. It was an

anger and aggression, which made him such an unusual and disturbing person to those who did not know him well enough. Beth gave me the chance to meet him when he had become famous, but I backed out, fearing the same old tension. I regret it now, for even today, when he is glorified, I will not worship at the shrine of someone, who as a young man was too unpleasant, too provocative, far too often.

"Now, just as I am about to draw my old age pension, my stories have appeared in *The British Beatles Fan Club Magazine* since 2000 and my book of childhood memoirs was published in 2008. I am someone whom my intrigued friends and long-suffering family have learned to live with, all because of the chance juxtaposition of time and place in my accidental journey with such a gene pool. All of this took place in a remarkable, post-war, Liverpool childhood".

Ann Bagnall attended Dovedale School from 1945 to 1948. "I used to sit next to John Lennon in class. I remember being at my boyfriend's birthday party when John Lennon slid down the banister, kicked me in the mouth and knocked out my front teeth. He certainly left an impression on me".

TOP: *John, centre back row with his classmate Ann Bagnall in front of him to the left, with ribbons in her hair*
ABOVE: *John, back row, fifth from the left, with his class at Dovedale School in 1951. Tim Holmes is on the far right, second row up*

Tim Holmes is another classmate of Lennon's. I had the pleasure of meeting him at the Dovedale School reunion in 2000, and he had some great stories to tell. These are related in his own style.

"It occurred to me recently that there must have been at least 10,000 children attending Dovedale School when I was a kid in the '40s and '50s. Everybody you speak to was at school with John Lennon.

"Well, so was I. A check on a school photograph that shows the class of 1951 will confirm that John and I were both there when it was taken. We were eleven at the time, and just about to move schools—he to Quarry Bank and then on to fame and fortune, and I to St. Margaret's, Anfield and on to poverty and obscurity. My memories of John sometimes don't seem to match those of other anecdote tellers. I remember him as just another kid in the class. He never bullied me or was nasty to me in any way. We hit it off right away.

"We used to go to each other's birthday parties. He came to my house in Calton Avenue, just off Penny Lane with all the other children. I went to his house in Menlove Avenue with, probably, the same kids. At one particular party of mine, I recall him sitting astride a little pushcart that belonged to my younger brother. He was pretending to be a duck. He was making quacking noises and shouting something like, 'Watch out, I'm going to lay an egg'. Well, it was funny at the time. In 1951 the Head Master of the school, Pop Evans, decided that boxing would be a good way to toughen up us children. A boxing ring was set up in the school hall, and children were invited to put on boxing gloves, get into the ring and knock the blazes out of each other. My opponent was John Lennon.

"We were about the same height and weight, but he obviously had more courage than me. I managed to keep out of John's way for much of the time, poking out the odd tentative fist in a flurry now and again, hoping to hit him. At some stage in the bout, he caught me a blow on my nose that instantly brought tears to my eyes. I cannot recall three minutes ever going more slowly in my life. It was endless. I couldn't wait to get out of the ring and put an end to the madness.

"I suppose I must have managed to hit him at some stage in the bout, but nothing seemed to slow him down. Any punishment I may have handed out to him obviously had no effect. I can't remember the announced result, but I am certain it wasn't me who won on points. Lennon 1—Holmes nil. That was the only time I ever donned boxing gloves and stepped into a boxing ring. And, not surprisingly, I have never had much interest in the sport since that day.

"Another fond memory of John was when we both appeared in the school production of *Treasure Island*. A teacher namesake of mine, Mr. Holmes, produced it in about 1950. While John and the other members of the cast were out on stage, strutting their stuff to good effect, I was lying concealed in the huge wicker basket that sat at the front of the stage. On top of the basket was a large birdcage that contained a live parrot. When the story called for the parrot to shout out 'Pieces of Eight', the bird could not be relied on to deliver the words. That was where my great acting skills came in to play. There I was inside the dark basket with a torch and the script,

Dovedale School which John Lennon attended from May 1946, at the age of five

delivering the line at the appropriate moment. It obviously was not a well trained parrot. But it was my first acting job. John had the opening lines in the play, so as well as always wanting the last word, it seems he had the first ones too.

"Living close to John for many years we would see each other often either at the shops in Allerton Road or at the Plaza cinema, or on a Sunday afternoon in Calderstones Park, eyeing up the girls. The last time I spoke to him was around 1959. I worked at Clarke Bros. (Liverpool) Ltd. in Speke Hall Road (the company manufactured leather watch straps). One day I came out of work at five o'clock, and there was John standing waiting for a bus. We had a chat and he told me all that was going on with this group of his, where they had been, where they were going, and how exciting it all was. I moved to London in 1961 and lived in the south until I came back to this area in 1988".

Bill Shipton was also a fellow pupil of John Lennon's at Dovedale School. I spoke to him about his memories of John.

"I remember meeting John aged six. We were all standing in a ring holding hands (boy, girl, boy, girl etc.). John was on the opposite side of the ring to me—though I didn't know him by name then—holding hands with a girl named Jean. At that moment I just had to hold Jean's hand, so I walked across the ring and hit John, and took hold of her hand. The next second I felt a ruler across the back of my legs, and so both John and I were sitting on the floor crying. I was taken to the front of the class and told to sit there until my mum came for me.

"Another time I remember going up to John's house at Mendips and playing football with him for a couple of hours. This was a rare occasion for John to be playing football, as he was not known for his sporting prowess—apart from swimming—mainly because of his poor eyesight. I didn't see John a lot as we had gone to different schools. We would occasionally meet on the bus and talk for a while, or at St. Barnabas' Church Hall on Penny Lane where they had a regular Saturday night dance—though it usually resulted in there being more fighting than dancing".

Bill also recalls seeing John in the late 1950s in the Liverpool town centre. "We went into NEMS and down into the basement. John persuaded me to ask for a particular record, and to have it played into hood four—the small booths for listening to records. I went to the counter, and there was a 'puff' (slang for homosexual) there who asked me what record I wanted. I gave him a dirty look, and went down the counter as there was a pretty young girl serving there. The other man was Brian Epstein and we knew he was gay. John called me a lucky bastard, as I was served by the pretty girl".

Statue of John Lennon, at Liverpool John Lennon Airport

This apparently was John's attempt to get back at Bill who had barracked him from the balcony at a poetry reading—he thinks at Blackburne House in Hope Street, opposite the Art College—to the extent that John started to stutter. John swore he would get his revenge.

In 1952, John left Dovedale School for Quarry Bank Grammar School where, with friends Pete Shotton, Rod Davis and Eric Griffiths, he formed The Quarrymen.

To find out more about John, I wanted to speak to someone who knew him as an adult. I met May Pang, who was John's former personal assistant-turned-lover in the 1970s. They stayed in touch and remained friends until his death. May Pang is a name many people will know in connection with John Lennon. She was the lady who was famously paired with John, by Yoko, when they separated in the autumn of 1973.

In March 2005, May visited Liverpool for a couple of days. I took her round some of the famous places where John grew up.

May Pang

A native of New York's Spanish Harlem, May Pang grew up with music all around her. From street-corner 'do-wop' groups like Dion and The Belmonts to the British Invasion of 1964, rock 'n' roll became May's passion. It was no surprise that when she left college in 1970, she was determined to land a job in the music world. Only a New York girl would attempt to start at the top, so she marched into the offices of The Beatles' management company, ABKCO Industries, and a career in music was launched.

"While I was working at ABKCO, John and Yoko decided to move to New York City and chose me to be their personal assistant", May recalled. "It was excitement beyond belief. Not only did I have a key role in the records and films of John and Yoko, but I was meeting everyone I'd read about in fanzines since I was a kid".

As exciting as this was, little did she know what fate had in store. "One day in June 1973, Yoko approached me in my office at the Dakota. She explained that she and John needed a break from each other, which was obvious to everyone around them. Yoko also decided that I would be his 'companion'—effective immediately. By now, nothing could come as a shock in the zany world of John and Yoko. But this? This was beyond the pale, even for them".

This eighteen-month relationship has become known misleadingly as Lennon's "Lost Weekend". During this period, John was the most productive and successful in his post-Beatles career. He achieved his first No. 1 single, "Whatever Gets You Thru the Night", his first No. 1 album, *Walls and Bridges*, and collaborated with Elton John ("Lucy in the Sky with Diamonds"), David Bowie ("Fame"), Harry Nilsson *(Pussycats)*, Ringo Starr *(Goodnight Vienna)*, and Mick Jagger ("Too Many Cooks"). During their relationship, May continued as John's production assistant and coordinator. Her efforts were rewarded with an RIAA Gold Record Award for *Walls and Bridges*.

In February of 1975, John and Yoko reunited and May began the next phase of her life (though she secretly saw John until 1978). She worked for Island Records and coordinated the release of albums by Bob Marley and The Wailers, Robert Palmer and Third World. She then switched to United Artists Music where she worked with unknown songwriters, successfully having their songs recorded by Diana Ross, the Four Tops, Air Supply and Judas Priest.

After John Lennon's tragic death in 1980, many myths and misconceptions began surfacing about John and May's time together. In 1983, she decided to set the record straight by publishing her memoirs, *Loving John* (Warner Brothers), an insightful look into John's world and his complex relationships with Paul, George, Ringo, his oldest son Julian and, of course, Yoko. May is a full-time single mum, but her heart's still in rock 'n' roll. She recently released a photo book, *Instamatic Karma,* and is putting together an international exhibition of her photos and memories of John Lennon.

But is that all of the story? I wanted to find out more.

May's eyes light up whenever John's name is mentioned. Why? Because it has always been reported that she had an eighteen-month affair with John, and then he went back to Yoko when she called him. That was it, and she disappeared into the background. However, that is not the entire truth.

"When we were first put together by Yoko, I wasn't interested in John in a physical sense. He was married, and he was my boss. However, I eventually gave in to him and accepted his assurance that 'everything would be OK'. I did fall in love with him and this love has never died. During this eighteen-month period John was healthy and stimulated—without narcotic assistance. He was writing and recording. Plus he was full of life. John was making long-term plans with me, and even toyed with rekindling his songwriting partnership with Paul McCartney. At this point, fate stepped in, with a little help from Yoko.

"When Yoko called John, she told him to come and see a hypnotherapist about helping him to quit smoking. I wasn't stupid. I knew this therapy would last for months and that he would be leaving me to go back to Yoko. John was maybe more naive. One hypnotherapy session would not be enough, and so it was that John went back to Yoko.

"However, John and I stayed in touch until he died. The eighteen-month affair became a love story of several years, which only ended when he was killed. Yoko had John back but he was still in touch with me. The last time we spoke was in 1980, when he called me from South Africa out of the blue".

I wanted to know from May what John told her about Liverpool.

"He didn't often talk about specific places in Liverpool, but he did have fond memories", May said. So, we headed off around Liverpool. We visited Mendips and spent time talking about some of her memories of him. While we were there, I asked her how it felt to be in John's childhood home.

"I feel comfortable and peaceful. I met Mimi and talked to her and in a way, I feel that I have her permission to be here". Suddenly, stories came flooding back.

"I remember a story he told me about his first job. John says he found a job at a local petrol station to earn some money. However, on his first day he overfilled the tank, leaving the petrol to spill everywhere. He was sacked on his first day!

"John always said that he was inherently lazy. I remember him saying that his job was to mow the lawns at Mendips, for which he received pocket money. He would pay someone else to do it for him, and then pay him part of his pocket money".

We ventured to Liverpool John Lennon Airport where May spent time perusing the statue of John there, for which she gave a hearty approval. It reminded her of more stories about John.

"I remember a time in New York, not long after George had met Olivia Arias, who became George's second wife. They came round for the evening and there was an underlying tension. George and John hadn't seen each other for a while and I could tell George had something on his mind. Before long, George was face to face with John, their noses almost touching. He stared in John's eyes and shouted 'Where were you when I needed you?' I remember

May Pang at Liverpool John Lennon Airport

thinking that this could get nasty. John was not averse to using violence if necessary. However, John said calmly, 'I'm here now, what do you need?' Luckily, John diffused the situation and we went on to have a good evening. Afterwards, John explained to me that he knew George had something to get off his chest, so it was better to let him say his piece than bottle it up. As I saw it, it was a brotherly thing. The four were so close and they could call each other anything they wanted, whether to each other's faces or in song".

When we arrived at Strawberry Field, it was another surreal experience for her. I was able to tell her what I had learned about the history of the place and why it was special to John. May asked me questions about John's childhood from the research I had done.

May continues to have a great love for John and has a unique insight into the last decade of his life, including a chapter that has been airbrushed out of Lennon's history.

In memory of

JOHN LENNON

Attended Dovedale Infant School

May 1946 - July 1948

& with many thanks to

YOKO ONO LENNON

for her generous support

This plaque was erected on the school hall of Dovedale Infant School to the memory of John Lennon, and to thank Yoko Ono for her support

May Pang visits Strawberry Field on her pilgrimage to Liverpool

18 JUNE 1942
Paul McCartney is born

"Mother Nature's Son"

James Paul McCartney was born in Walton Hospital on 18 June 1942 where his mum was a nurse. Although he was named James, his parents added Paul as a middle name. It stuck, and that's what his parents, Jim and Mary, called him from when he came home. He was baptised at Our Lady and St. Philomena's Catholic Church on Sparrow Hall Road, Fazakerley, on 12 July 1943.

Homes

The McCartney family lived at several different addresses during Paul's formative years in Liverpool. Their first home was in 10, Sunbury Road (Anfield), near to Walton Hospital where Mary worked. They moved in 1942 to 92, Broadway Avenue, Wallasey (Wirral) as Jim was given a wartime job in an armaments factory there. After a short stay and too many bombs falling close to their home, they moved back across the River Mersey to the outskirts of Liverpool into a temporary house in Roach Avenue, Knowsley, before returning to the Everton district of Liverpool, near Jim's family.

LEFT: *Sir Thomas White Gardens, Everton, where Paul lived when he was aged one*
ABOVE: *Paul's bedroom at 20, Forthlin Road* OPPOSITE: *Paul McCartney, photographed in 1963*

They lived in a flat in Sir Thomas White Gardens in 1943. Mary needed to return to work after Paul's younger brother Mike was born, but instead of resuming her nursing duties in a hospital, she was promoted to district nurse, becoming responsible for patient care outside a hospital environment, within the area she lived. She took a job in the far south of Liverpool, in a new housing estate in Speke. A house came with the job. The McCartneys first settled in 72, Western Avenue in 1947 before moving across the estate in 1950 to 12, Ardwick Road, close to where George Harrison lived. Their final move was in 1955 to 20, Forthlin Road (Allerton), where Mary became the resident district nurse and midwife. Allerton was considered a better area than Speke, and was a step up the social ladder for the family. When stardom hit, Paul moved his father in 1964 from Forthlin Road to a house he bought in Heswall. The residence, "Rembrandt", was in Baskervyle Road (Wirral).

Education

Paul was enrolled in Stockton Wood Primary School (Speke) in 1946 at the age of four, but was moved to Joseph Williams School (Netherley) after Stockton Wood Primary became overcrowded. Paul was a good pupil and one of only a few who passed the eleven-plus exam. He progressed to the Liverpool Institute Grammar School in 1953,

Family of James Paul McCartney

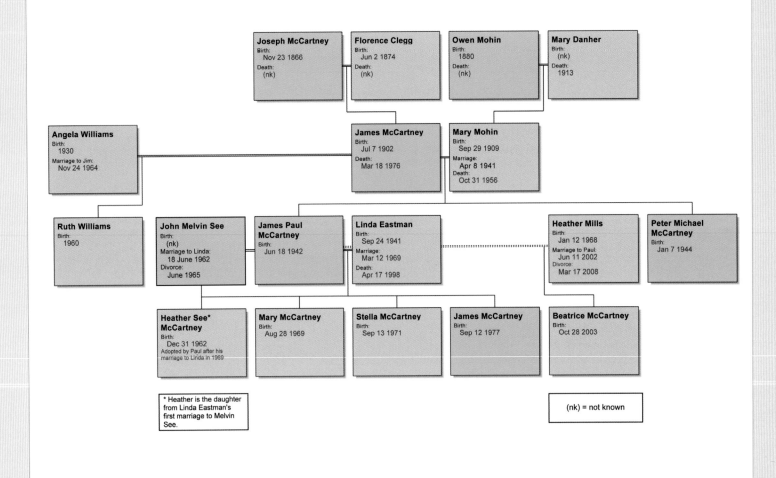

Joseph McCartney
Birth:
Nov 23 1866
Death:
(nk)

Florence Clegg
Birth:
Jun 2 1874
Death:
(nk)

Owen Mohin
Birth:
1880
Death:
(nk)

Mary Danher
Birth:
(nk)
Death:
1913

Angela Williams
Birth:
1930
Marriage to Jim:
Nov 24 1964

James McCartney
Birth:
Jul 7 1902
Death:
Mar 18 1976

Mary Mohin
Birth:
Sep 29 1909
Marriage:
Apr 8 1941
Death:
Oct 31 1956

Ruth Williams
Birth:
1960

John Melvin See
Birth:
(nk)
Marriage to Linda:
18 June 1962
Divorce:
June 1965

James Paul McCartney
Birth:
Jun 18 1942

Linda Eastman
Birth:
Sep 24 1941
Marriage:
Mar 12 1969
Death:
Apr 17 1998

Heather Mills
Birth:
Jan 12 1968
Marriage to Paul:
Jun 11 2002
Divorce:
Mar 17 2008

Peter Michael McCartney
Birth:
Jan 7 1944

Heather See* McCartney
Birth:
Dec 31 1962
Adopted by Paul after his marriage to Linda in 1969

Mary McCartney
Birth:
Aug 28 1969

Stella McCartney
Birth:
Sep 13 1971

James McCartney
Birth:
Sep 12 1977

Beatrice McCartney
Birth:
Oct 28 2003

* Heather is the daughter from Linda Eastman's first marriage to Melvin See.

(nk) = not known

Paul McCartney, left, standing alongside his father, Jim, and brother Mike, in their garden at 20, Forthlin Road

where he met George Harrison. After the school closed down in the 1990s, it was earmarked for demolition. Paul, together with local businessmen, saved the school building and created the Liverpool Institute for Performing Arts, also known as LIPA.

Religion

Jim and Mary McCartney's union was considered a 'religious mixed marriage' in Liverpool since Jim was linked to the Church of England while Mary was Catholic. The McCartneys decided against enrolling their boys in the Catholic school system because they concentrated too much on religion. As a compromise, Paul and Mike were baptized Catholic but sent to non-Catholic schools.

Paul sang in a Church of England choir at St. Barnabas' on Penny Lane, and was a member of the Boy Scouts. He admits some of his songs are semi-religious, like "Lady Madonna" and "Let it Be". The phrase, 'let it be', is in common use throughout the major religions of Judaism, Islam and Christianity in its Hebrew form: "Amen". "There will be an answer, amen".

Paul reckons he developed much of his religious philosophy at the speaker's corner at the Pier Head. The Catholics and Protestants constantly argued and bickered, providing hours of free entertainment. From these great debates, Paul developed a simple philosophy: God was good without an 'O' and the Devil was evil with a 'D' added. This arguing between the denominations was a classic case of religion getting in the way of faith.

Musical Influences

Paul's musical education was forged at Forthlin Road, where his father Jim, an accomplished musician, constantly had music playing in the house. Jim imparted a wonderful piece of Irish-Liverpool wisdom to his son, "If you learn to play the piano, you'll get invited to lots of parties". Jim and his band, Jim Mac's Jazz Band, filled the house with music, and before long Paul had progressed from the trumpet to guitar, piano and the drums.

Jim often set Paul down and put a record on, and then explained how the song was constructed. He went over the melody, the harmony, the bass line, the strings and the brass. The Beatles, in the latter phase of their career, started adding strings, horns and classical influences to their songs, thanks to Jim's great education. That however was just the foundation: Paul still couldn't read or write music. That is why record producer George Martin, often referred to as the fifth Beatle, became such a vital part of The Beatles song writing success. He could interpret what Paul wanted and produce the orchestral arrangement that would underline so many of The Beatles' songs.

Liverpool inspired Paul in his music with "Penny Lane", and his mum was commemorated in "Lady Madonna" and "Let It Be" amongst others. He also took the inspiration for "Mother Nature's Son" from his childhood visits through the countryside to the nearby village of Hale.

Paul's debut with The Quarrymen has been recorded as being at New Clubmoor Hall. However, Colin Hanton remembers playing with the group, including Paul, at St. Peter's Church Hall. They then played without being paid at Wilson Hall in Garston. The promoter at Wilson Hall was Charlie McBain and he liked what he saw and heard, so he booked them at his other club, the New Clubmoor Hall. This last event was the first paid appearance Paul made with The Quarrymen.

Jim and Mary McCartney

Paul's parents were very influential during his childhood. Jim was born on 7 July 1902 and baptised at St. Benedict's Church of England Chapel on Heyworth Street, Everton. He was educated at Steers Street School and, as a boy, was a program seller and limelight boy in the Theatre Royal, Breck Road. Jim was a cotton salesman, and his strength of character came to the fore when his wife died prematurely of breast cancer. He kept working, while bringing up Paul and Mike, no small feat for a widower.

Mary was different. She was the strong, silent type. The quiet matriarch didn't need to shout because her presence was enough to make the boys obedient. She was determined that her sons grew up with a strong education and aspire to be professionals. Mary was born in 1909 at 2, Third Avenue, Walton, and baptised at the Blessed Sacrament Roman Catholic Church in Walton Vale. Mary even enrolled them in private elocution lessons to lose their Liverpool accents. Mary died on 31 October 1956 when Paul was only fourteen, something that would bring him and John Lennon closer. Mary's requiem mass was held at St. Bernadette's Roman Catholic Church in Allerton on 3 November 1956. Paul's way of dealing with his bereavement was to lose himself in his music.

In November 1964, Jim remarried to a thirty-four-year-old widow, Angela Williams. Angela was considerably younger than Jim and had a five-year-old daughter, Ruth, whom Paul was happy to call his sister. His song "Golden Slumbers" was inspired by Ruth's piano book.

Ray O'Brien

Ray O'Brien attended the Liverpool Institute with Paul and Mike McCartney, as well as George Harrison and Neil Aspinall (who went on to become the Chief Executive of Apple) among others.

"I don't have many memories of Paul, who was a couple of years ahead of me, but the one vivid memory is of seeing him walking across the yard with his guitar over his shoulder, heading for the Art College for a practice with John. Paul was a model pupil, never in trouble and academically good. I remember him from the morning assemblies, and how Paul was always immaculately turned out. He even won an art prize at school".

Paul settled in well at the Liverpool Institute. He befriended two key people at the school: George Harrison and Ivan Vaughan. Vaughan was in The Quarrymen with his friend, John Lennon.

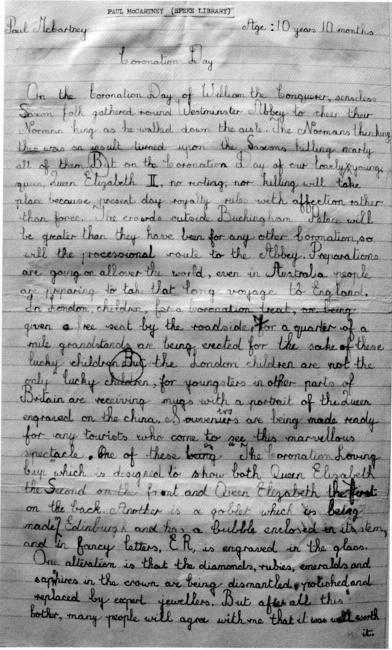

LEFT: *Paul makes his paid debut with The Quarrymen on 18 October 1957 at New Clubmoor Hall. From left to right: Colin Hanton, Paul, Len Garry, John, Eric Griffiths*
ABOVE: *Paul's prize-winning essay about the Queen's Coronation, written in 1953*

25 FEBRUARY 1943
George Harrison is born
"I, Me, Mine"

George Harrison was born on 25 February 1943, though he often told people he was born on 24 February.

Homes
Harrison was born at 12, Arnold Grove (Wavertree) where he lived until he was nearly seven-years old. He was the youngest of four children born to Harold and Louise Harrison, with the eldest child the only girl, named Louise after her mother. George's two older brothers were called Harold and Peter. The family moved to 25, Upton Green (Speke) in January 1950. They lived there until 1962 when they moved again, to 174, Macketts Lane (Woolton), but they soon became overrun with a new phenomenon, Beatlemania which meant that the house was soon besieged. Acting swiftly, George moved his family out of Liverpool to a bungalow, 'Sevenoaks', in Appleton, near Warrington, in 1965.

Education
His schooling began in April 1948 at Dovedale School (Allerton) where he attended the same school as John Lennon (though they didn't know each other at the time).

At the age of eleven, George passed his eleven-plus exam and moved on to the Liverpool Institute (Liverpool) where he befriended a lad who rode the same bus to school: his name was Paul McCartney.

Religion
George Harrison's father, Harold, described himself as a 'lapsed Anglican' while his mum, Louise, was Catholic. George was christened into the Roman Catholic Church at Our Lady of Good Help, Wavertree, and was a Cub in the Boy Scouts at St. Anthony of Padua Catholic Church in Mossley Hill. Interestingly, the Harrisons excluded four-year-old George from daily religious instruction when he started at Dovedale School.

George's fascination with Eastern religions was sparked by a 1966 trip to India but this interest was possibly started by Pete Best's mum Mona, who regaled him with stories of her native country. Mo spent hours talking about her life in India and experiences of the Indian religions and beliefs. George thanked Mo by bringing her back many necklaces and trinkets from India after he had met the Maharishi Mahesh Yogi.

Mo had an Eastern outlook but was married to her Western upbringing. She was Church of England, though not a churchgoer. She had statues of Jesus and of Mary, but also had a giant Buddha in the hallway. She was spiritual, not religious. Mona believed in karma and reincarnation and prayed every night. She believed that despite the different religions, every road leads you back to the one divine being.

TOP LEFT: *George outside his home at 25, Upton Green, Speke*
TOP RIGHT: *George at Dovedale, second from left bottom row in about 1953*
LEFT: *George playing his guitar at Upton Green*
RIGHT: *George at Dovedale School, second from left, back row, in about 1951*
OPPOSITE: *George concentrates while his guitar gently weeps in 1963*

Family of George Harrison

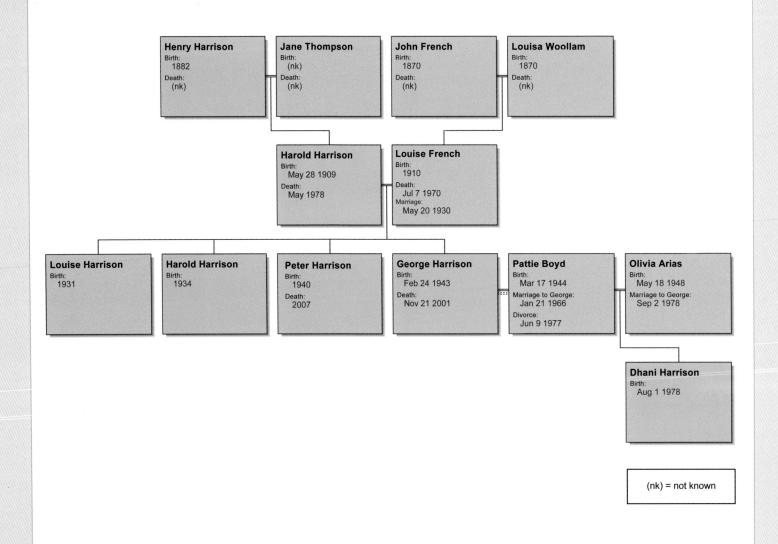

Henry Harrison
Birth:
1882
Death:
(nk)

Jane Thompson
Birth:
(nk)
Death:
(nk)

John French
Birth:
1870
Death:
(nk)

Louisa Woollam
Birth:
1870
Death:
(nk)

Harold Harrison
Birth:
May 28 1909
Death:
May 1978

Louise French
Birth:
1910
Death:
Jul 7 1970
Marriage:
May 20 1930

Louise Harrison
Birth:
1931

Harold Harrison
Birth:
1934

Peter Harrison
Birth:
1940
Death:
2007

George Harrison
Birth:
Feb 24 1943
Death:
Nov 21 2001

Pattie Boyd
Birth:
Mar 17 1944
Marriage to George:
Jan 21 1966
Divorce:
Jun 9 1977

Olivia Arias
Birth:
May 18 1948
Marriage to George:
Sep 2 1978

Dhani Harrison
Birth:
Aug 1 1978

(nk) = not known

TOP LEFT: *Harold and Louise Harrison's home, "Sevenoaks", which George bought for them in 1965*
BOTTOM LEFT: *Our Lady of Good Help Catholic Church, Wavertree, where George was Christened in 1943*
ABOVE: *Louise and Harold Harrison*
PREVIOUS PAGE: *George pictured in 1963*

a lie, and he rejected them. He often poured scorn on them, particularly if you read the lyrics of his posthumous album *Brainwashed*. The most 'spiritual' of The Beatles, he was content with life and thought that it was all part of a spiritual journey that included reincarnation. When George knew that the end was near he was not afraid of death.

Musical Influences

After receiving a guitar as a gift and learning to play until his fingers bled, George formed a group with his friend Arthur Kelly. They appeared as The Rebels at the British Legion, Dam Wood Road (Speke).

Early into his apprenticeship, he and Paul learned the guitar together. Soon it was Paul who introduced him to John Lennon. George joined The Quarrymen after playing a guitar riff of "Raunchy" for John and The Quarrymen at a gig at Wilson Hall (Garston) on 6 February 1958.

He left The Quarrymen after their appearances dried up, and joined another band called the "Les Stewart Quartet", who appeared at Lowlands (West Derby). After a band argument, George and Ken Brown left the Les Stewart Quartet and re-formed The Quarrymen adding John and Paul again to open The Casbah Coffee Club (West Derby) in August 1959.

Harold and Louise Harrison

When George was born, his father Harold commented, "I remember tiptoeing up the stairs to see him. All I could think of was that he looked remarkably like me".

Harold had left school at fourteen to become a delivery boy and then three years later went to sea. He joined the White Star Line, working his way up to a first-class steward by the age of twenty-one. On one of his trips home he met his wife-to-be, Louise, who was working in a greengrocer's shop at the time. They exchanged letters, married a year later and Harold gave up the sea in 1936. After spending a year looking for work, he became a bus conductor. Harold was later a bus driver, a union official and the master of ceremonies at the Speke bus depot social club. For over ten years,

How interesting that George had similar religious beliefs. When The Beatles went to India in 1968, it wasn't a complete culture shock. Mo had taken them there in their minds with her tales years before. George eventually believed that organized religions were all continuing

Harold and Louise ran ballroom dancing classes. Harold booked The Quarrymen for a Christmas party at Wilson Hall in Garston in January 1959. Louise encouraged George's musical talents and gladly let The Quarrymen and Beatles practice in their home. Louise and Harold often invited fans into their home, and faithfully answered George's fan mail.

All About George

To find out more about George Harrison, I spoke to one of his second cousins, Irene Milson. George had twenty-five cousins and second cousins in total. She talked about her family.

George (circled) at the Liverpool Institute in 1956

"The Harrison family was Lizzy, Janey, Harry, Jimmy, Harold, Teddy and Billy. Harold was George's father—but Harold had a brother called Harry too.

"The family originally came from Ash Grove, off Picton Road in Wavertree. They were a wealthy family and always had money. My grandmother, Lizzy, was a real lady. They were all little, about five feet four at the most, which is why George was not that tall. This was the house where George's dad and his brothers and sisters lived. The house was damaged during the war and the family were evacuated to North Wales. The house was then demolished.

"Uncle Harold liked a joke and was funny. Auntie Louise was not too bad, but then she was an in-law, not a Harrison. Uncle Harold was a gambler, and he went on to work for a bookmaker. Did you know that Uncle Harold appeared on TV? Harold used to visit the U.S. quite often, and even appeared in a TV commercial for Jaffa Oranges. He appeared in an advert with Dan Blocker from the hit TV show 'Bonanza', and Harold appeared as the caveman, because of his long hair.

"When he went to America, Uncle Harold promised to get me something from Elvis, because he knew how to get to him. Elvis was my hero. Uncle Harold always had long hair, something that George also had from a young age. I never much liked The Beatles and I was so excited at getting something, anything, from Elvis—even a toenail clipping would have done. And you know what? Harold died over there. I never forgave him for that. He promised me.

"We know that while George was in the Liverpool Institute, his hair was long as a rebellion, though also to hide his ears, which always stuck out. Hair is important in the Harrison family too, because there is a family secret. All the Harrisons, apart from my Uncle Harry, had a hereditary condition that made our hair turn grey or white at a young age. Uncle Harry was the only one who had a full head of brown hair when he died at seventy. Everyone else in the family went grey early, including George. George's dad, Uncle Harold went grey quite young, so George will have done the same as well. I went white by the age of seventeen, and my dad by twenty-one, so we were all affected".

Stan Williams attended Dovedale School with John Lennon, Ivan Vaughan and George Harrison, and is in a unique position to recall some of his childhood memories. "I possess a photo of a Dovedale School sports occasion with George standing next to our shared pal, Ashley Thom. George sat with Ashley in the year below me and Ashley used to go out to George's house on the new Speke council estate. At Mrs. Harrison's, Ashley would be guaranteed the tea of egg and chips his own mum couldn't be bothered to cook for him. I saw George at school, of course, but he was a quiet boy and it was through Ashley that I found out more about him. He and Ashley would go out into the Cheshire countryside around the Speke housing estate or down to Oglet Shore, where they would walk and talk amongst the driftwood and debris washed up from the Mersey. George liked one-to-one relationships and quiet conversation Ashley told me.

"When George started to play the guitar, I must have been one of the first to know about it, as Ash used to bring me updated reports on his gradual mastery of his first, crap guitar and then the Hofner, bought from a shop. I think it was Hessy's, in town. He must only have been in the second year at the Liverpool Institute, but Lonnie Donegan had taken possession of our young lives and skiffle groups were being set up by teenagers all over Liverpool in 1956. We had a group called "The Satellites" and we boasted an accomplished guitarist with his own amplified Hofner. His name was Brian and he was in the sixth year at Old Swan Tech, while Ashley was raving about the bludgeoning skills of a fourteen-year old.

"Ashley visited George down in London when he became famous. I can't remember when and where he obtained 'an audience,' but he was let into a big house and met George for an hour. Fame had not made a bit of difference to George's manner and his gentle spirit had prevailed. I remember Ashley remarking that George was a spiritual person. He was gentle natured, thoughtful, and he seemed so genuinely glad to see friends from the past who mattered".

George, centre of the top row, at Dovedale School in about 1951

Ray O'Brien attended the Liverpool Institute with George Harrison and Paul. He too has fond memories of George.

"George's taste in dress code was unique, particularly his range of waistcoats that stood out from the uniform. He was a rebel and obviously never happy at the Liverpool Institute, as George has stated. One of my clearest memories is of George standing at the bus stop in his uniform, but he didn't have a school badge on his blazer. This was a standard rule for every boy, who had to buy a black blazer and have the badge sewn on to the jacket. I was curious as to how he had managed to achieve this. It turned out that George had never had his badge sewn on, and managed to keep it temporarily pinned on by using a pen top or the like so that it appeared to be attached. This was just one of his rebellions, each one a little victory.

"One of the other ways of standing out from the crowd was morning religious assembly. Every morning on the dot of nine o'clock, all the boys would gather in the hall for assembly. If you were late, then at the end of the assembly, you were paraded down the middle of the hall to the front and made to stand in front of the whole school: being named and shamed. This was supposed to be a deterrent, which worked for many boys. George would often be in this group.

"As well as the latecomers, there were the boys excused from the religious service. This group included those boys who were from either Jewish or Catholic families, and George was often with them".

Mal Jefferson was also a fellow pupil of Paul and George at the Liverpool Institute. I spoke to him about his recollections of the former Beatle.

"George was in the year above me. I remember George as a good-looking lad with a strong square jaw and a great smile—though his sticking out ears were more prominent with his teddy-boy quiff. George and Paul would lean against the bike sheds, out of sight of the teachers, smoking their Woodbines and talking about music. George was a friend of my older brother, and so I was used to him coming to the house and talking about music—something he would still do if we met years after we had left school.

"I remember one day—probably in 1958—when Paul and George brought their guitars into school with an amplifier and played in their classroom for an hour. I remember George singing "Earth Angel" amongst others, and I was impressed by their harmonies, as well as their presentation and professionalism—that Beatle harmony sound with George doing John's part. George had been intrigued by how great guitarists like Scotty Moore could play so accurately and so quickly, a skill he tried to emulate all his life".

Mal himself went on to form The Mastersounds who played regularly at The Cavern, and to form his own recording company Mastersound after an apprenticeship in London working with legends like Marvin Gaye.

"I met up again with George in the mid-eighties at the Winter Gardens in Blackpool for the quarterly George Formby Society concerts". Formby was a famous Lancashire ukulele player and also sang in many black and white movies.

"Every member had to get up and sing, and play his or her favourite Formby song: George was no exception. George sold me an original George Formby ukulele, which he owned, pleading poverty after losing so much money with *Handmade Films*. He asked me for £2000. I pretended to feel sorry for him, and gave him a cheque for £2001 and told him not to go mad with the extra pound. He pocketed the cheque without so much as a smile—he seemed to have lost his sense of humour. Apparently, it also didn't help that a nine-year-old boy came on after us and produced a blistering double-speed solo which neither George nor I could manage.

"George redeemed himself a year later when he had a beautiful eight-foot colour portrait of George Formby commissioned for his lounge. George sent me a photograph of it for me to use exclusively on the covers of Mastersound's series of George Formby tapes and videos. That was a kind gesture and the last thing I remember of him".

George made many friends at the Liverpool Institute, especially Paul McCartney. It was those long bus rides to school each day with Paul that cemented their relationship. They would meet at each other's homes to practice guitar. Paul realised how good George was, and when The Quarrymen needed a lead guitarist, Paul knew who it should be.

ABOVE: *George, photographed in 1963*
OPPOSITE: *George waves as he leaves Liverpool Town Hall after the civic reception in 1964*

7 JULY 1940
Ringo Starr is born
"I Wanna Be Your Man"

Ringo Starr was once described as the luckiest man on the planet. It was a spot-on assessment as he joined The Beatles just two weeks before they began recording their first single, "Love Me Do", and their debut album *Please Please Me* at Abbey Road Studios. However, it needed more than just luck to be a Beatle.

Homes
Richard Starkey was born on 7 July 1940 at 9, Madryn Street (Dingle). His mum and dad divorced when he was three, with Richard Sr. moving out of the house and back in with his parents at 59, Madryn Street. His paternal grandparents, John and Annie Starkey often baby-sat young Ritchie, but the relationship between his parents was strained, and living in the same street was awkward. A bigger problem for his mother Elsie was meeting the high rent as a single parent. In order to make ends meet, she moved to 10, Admiral Grove, (Dingle) in 1945 when Ritchie was only five. Elsie worked two jobs as a barmaid at the Wellington pub (Garston) and Yates' in Liverpool, and not in The Empress (Dingle) as has been often reported. Elsie married again when Ritchie was thirteen, to Harry Graves. Ritchie's last name should have been Parkin, not Starkey, but his great-grandfather changed his name to Starkey after his mother remarried.

When the tidal wave of Beatlemania hit, Ringo moved Elsie and his stepfather Harry to a new house in Gateacre at Heath Hey in Woolton. Elsie often returned to visit her friends in The Dingle as she missed them.

Education
Ritchie attended St. Silas School (Dingle) on High Park Street, just a few minutes from his house. When he was nearly seven, Ritchie was rushed to the Royal Liverpool Children's Hospital on Myrtle Street, Liverpool, after his appendix burst. He eventually recovered from his life-threatening illness, earning the nickname of 'Lazarus' given by his paternal grandfather for his miraculous recovery.

Despite his illness, he moved on to Dingle Vale Secondary Modern School at the age of eleven. However, he suffered another setback two years later when he contracted tuberculosis, and this time he missed more than a year of schooling. He was moved to the Royal Liverpool Children's Hospital in Heswall (Wirral), where his love for drumming was stimulated by childhood friend Marie Maguire.

Ritchie worked for a short time for the railways and was sent to Riversdale College (Aigburth) for training. After a period working on a ferry boat, he became an apprentice at Henry Hunt & Sons Ltd. near to his home in The Dingle.

TOP: *Ringo and neighbour Eddie Miles outside their homes in Admiral Grove*
ABOVE: *Ringo with Rory Storm and the Hurricanes, the Tower Ballroom, New Brighton, 10 November 1961*
OPPOSITE: *Ringo arrives on a 'Starways' plane*

Family of Ringo Starr

Richard Starkey, Ringo's father

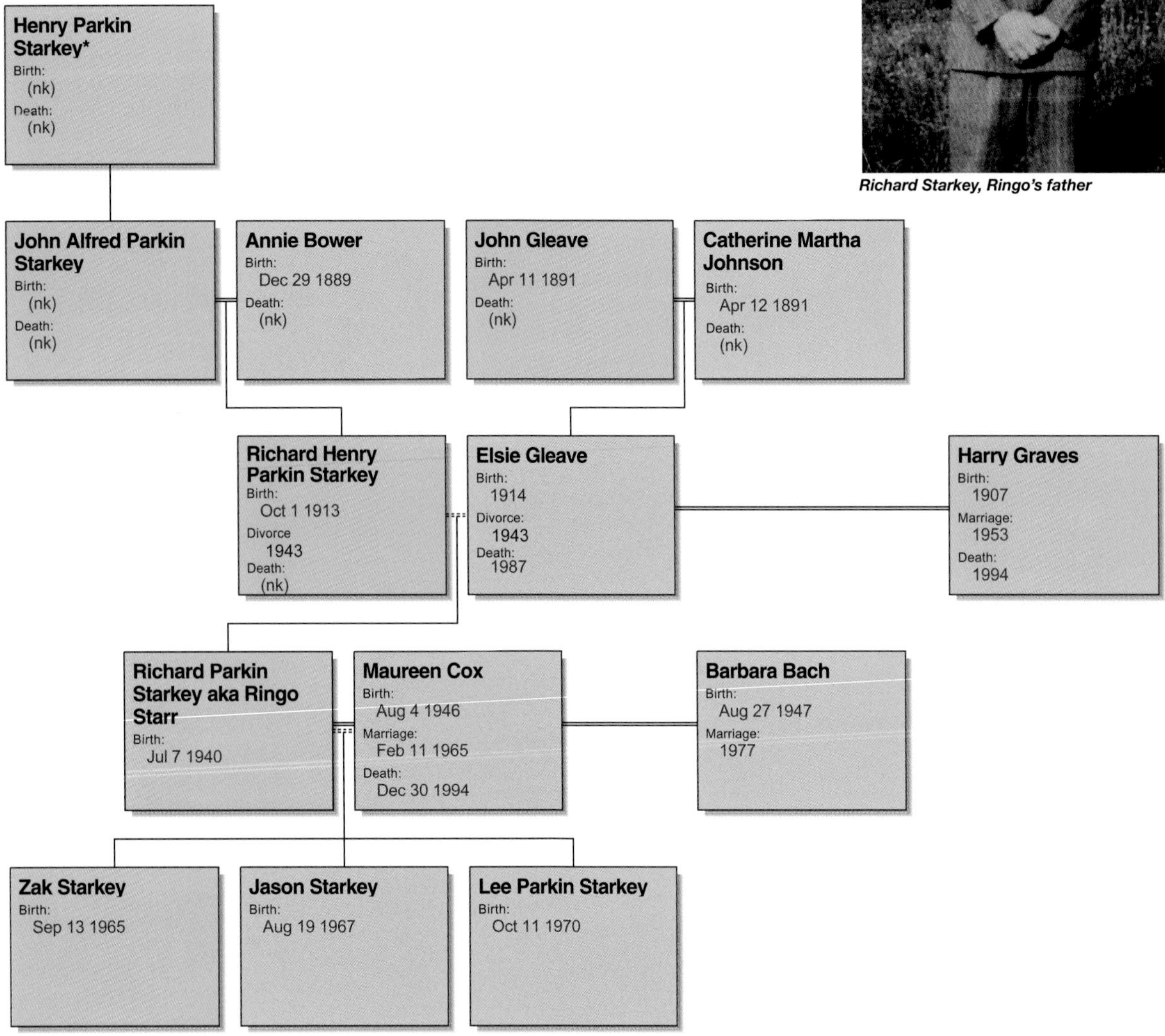

Henry Parkin Starkey*
Birth:
(nk)
Death:
(nk)

John Alfred Parkin Starkey
Birth:
(nk)
Death:
(nk)

Annie Bower
Birth:
Dec 29 1889
Death:
(nk)

John Gleave
Birth:
Apr 11 1891
Death:
(nk)

Catherine Martha Johnson
Birth:
Apr 12 1891
Death:
(nk)

Richard Henry Parkin Starkey
Birth:
Oct 1 1913
Divorce
1943
Death:
(nk)

Elsie Gleave
Birth:
1914
Divorce:
1943
Death:
1987

Harry Graves
Birth:
1907
Marriage:
1953
Death:
1994

Richard Parkin Starkey aka Ringo Starr
Birth:
Jul 7 1940

Maureen Cox
Birth:
Aug 4 1946
Marriage:
Feb 11 1965
Death:
Dec 30 1994

Barbara Bach
Birth:
Aug 27 1947
Marriage:
1977

Zak Starkey
Birth:
Sep 13 1965

Jason Starkey
Birth:
Aug 19 1967

Lee Parkin Starkey
Birth:
Oct 11 1970

* Henry Parkin changed his surname to Starkey when his mother remarried.

(nk) = not known

LEFT: *Ringo (left) with Rory Storm (in blue) and the Hurricanes in their new pink suits outside Eric's on London Road, Liverpool*
RIGHT: *Mike Rice, drummer with a popular Merseybeat band, The Senators, in 1962*

Religion

Ringo's parents were Protestants and members of the Orange Lodge, an organisation formed in 1795 by supporters of King William III (known as William of Orange) of Britain who defeated the Catholic army of King James II at the Battle of the Boyne in 1690. Every year on 12 July, the Orange Lodge parade as a celebration of this event. It attracts a lot of criticism as it is anti-Catholic. Richard and Elsie were married in St. Silas Church. Ringo sang in the choir, attended Sunday School and sometimes accompanied his mum on marches with the Orange Lodge band.

Marie Maguire said her family, who were Catholic, had no problems getting along with the Starkeys. The two families made a conscious choice not to let religious bigotry spoil a friendship and so they joined in each other's religious celebrations. It was forward thinking for its time.

When The Beatles visited India, he was not as enthusiastic about the Maharishi Mahesh Yogi as the others and didn't take to meditation in the same way. However, he says that he has learned a lot from meditation, and often speaks of love and peace. In 2010, Ringo announced that "after a winding life of enlightenment, for me, God is in my life. I don't hide from that: I think the search has been on since the '60s."

Musical Influences

As an incentive for coming home from hospital, Ritchie's step-father Harry promised to buy him a drum kit and he travelled to London and returned with a small drum kit, for which he paid £10. Ritchie's musical career started with his friends from work, including Eddie Miles, his next-door neighbour from 11, Admiral Grove (Dingle). They formed the Eddie Clayton Skiffle Group and first played at Peel Hall (Dingle). Soon they were given the spot as the resident band at the Florence Institute on Mill Street (Dingle). When Miles married in 1958, it signalled the end of the Eddie Clayton Skiffle Group.

Ritchie was offered the position of drummer in a few local groups, but decided to join the Darktown Skiffle Group. He met Alan Caldwell—who had changed his name to 'Rory Storm'—at a talent contest. Rory's group were playing rock 'n' roll, not the primitive skiffle music that had been played on tea-chest basses and washboards. That is what ultimately persuaded Ritchie to join Storm's group. On 25 March 1959, Ritchie made his debut in Rory's band, Al Caldwell's Texans. The band later changed its name to The Raving Texans and eventually to Rory Storm and the Hurricanes. They even took on cowboy personas and Ritchie became 'Rings' because of the number of rings he wore. His first name evolved into 'Ringo' and Starkey became 'Starr'. (At one point George Harrison wanted to join Rory Storm and the Hurricanes but was turned down because he was too young).

When Derry and the Seniors—the first Merseybeat band who went to Hamburg—returned to Liverpool from Hamburg in October 1960, they were replaced by Rory Storm and the Hurricanes at the Kaiserkeller. The Hurricanes played split shifts with The Beatles, where the friendship between Ringo and John, Paul and George was forged and cemented. On 15 October 1960, Hurricanes band-member Lou Walters decided to make an amateur record. He needed a band and so he asked John, Paul and George to join him, together with Ringo. They recorded Gershwin's "Summertime" and "Fever". And so for the first time, John, Paul, George and Ringo appeared together.

Ringo eventually became disillusioned with Rory Storm and the Hurricanes because he didn't see them progressing beyond summer seasons at Butlin's holiday camps in Britain. At the end of 1961, Hamburg club owner Peter Eckhorn came to Liverpool to book The Beatles to back Tony Sheridan for his Top Ten Club, but Brian Epstein priced them out of that deal. Eckhorn went in another direction and recruited Ringo after seeing him perform. Eckhorn offered him £30 a week, plus a flat and a car if he would travel to Germany. After a few weeks in Hamburg, Ringo became frustrated and disillusioned with the erratic Sheridan and returned to Liverpool. Sheridan was a great influence on the Liverpool bands, but on stage he would change the songs he wanted to perform or the key he was playing it in, and this made him unpopular with some musicians. Many believe Tony Sheridan could have had a greater recording career. Unfortunately, he was unreliable and not motivated to progress beyond Hamburg and his association with The Beatles.

When Ringo returned to Liverpool, he hooked up with Rory Storm once again. His reasoning was that his worst day drumming was better than returning to work at the factory of Henry Hunt and Son Ltd., making school equipment. Seeking a life away from England, he applied to the Chamber of Commerce in Houston, Texas. However, when he saw the complexity of the application forms, he gave up on that idea. Shortly after, Ringo received a phone call from Brian Epstein that changed his life. He later recalled, "I'd played with them so many times anyway down The Cavern. We were at Butlin's again and Epstein phoned through saying 'Oh, I'd like you to join The Beatles,' and I said 'Oh great, when?' and he said 'Tonight' and I said 'No I can't join tonight because we have a gig here, so I'll come on Saturday,' that was our day off. Liverpool went mad but they were soon over it".

Ringo Starr joined The Beatles on 18 August 1962 as replacement for Pete Best, making his debut at Hulme Hall in Port Sunlight (Wirral).

The Beatles returned to Hamburg in December 1962. Their first trip to Hamburg had solidified them as a group with Pete Best; on their fourth trip, they had the same experience with Ringo.

Mike Rice, the Liverpool born drummer in Merseybeat band The Senators, met Ringo when he first joined The Beatles. The two shared a love of drumming and conversation came easily, recalled Rice.

"My wife Doreen and I used to go on the Rockin' River Cruises on the Royal Iris. There was a great atmosphere and good music. One day, we'd arrived there handy, and The Beatles were setting up their equipment. The others had finished, except for Ringo. So I went over for a chat. Behind him, lounging on the seats was John Lennon, laid out flat with his eyes shut. What a sight. If only I'd had my camera.

"I said 'Hello' and we started to talk about drums, as I'm a drummer. We were talking for a little while, when I asked him about the set-up of his hi-hat cymbals. I told him that I knew he used a hi-hat a lot and asked him what adjustments he used. He replied with a quizzical look on his face, 'I don't know what you mean?' 'Well,' I responded, 'the screw under the hi-hat, what angle do you have it at?' Again he looked puzzled, so I reached for it to show him the adjusting screw.

Where the screw should have been, there was just a little hole. He just looked at me and I wonder if at that point he didn't know what an adjustment screw was.

"It was a nice memory. Ringo was a great fella, down-to-earth and easy to talk to. There was no ego or a big head about him, considering they became so famous. Plus, how often after that did Ringo set his own kit up? Not long, I reckon. He had someone to do it for him".

Elsie and Richard Starkey
Ringo's parents met at Cooper's Bakery where they worked, and married at St. Silas Church where four years later, young Ritchie was christened. They loved the high life and danced at places like Reece's in town. That all changed when Elsie gave birth to Ritchie. She could no longer go dancing, but Richard wanted to, so he did.

When Ritchie turned three, his parents divorced and his dad moved out of their home at 9, Madryn Street. Ritchie's dad moved back in with his parents who lived down the road at 59. After a few months, Richard's financial help ceased and Elsie had to go to work as a barmaid. When Ritchie was about thirteen, Elsie asked him for approval to marry Harry Graves. She was a lovely lady who was popular with her neighbours, like Margaret Grose who currently lives in Ringo's Admiral Grove home.

Elsie worked so much that she enlisted help from her friend's daughter, Marie Maguire, who was four years older than Ritchie. As well as helping him to read and write, Marie took on the role of bigger sister and brought young Ritchie everywhere. They took tram rides, played in Princes Park, visited cinema houses like the Gaumont, or the Mayfair and Rivoli on Aigburth Road. It's almost certain that Elsie was forever in her debt.

Harry Graves
Harry Graves was Ringo's stepfather, though Ritchie would refer to Harry as his 'step-ladder'. Harry worked at the American Burtonwood Air Base, near Warrington, and it was he who travelled to London and bought Ringo a second-hand set of drums after he had been so ill. When Harry died, Ringo and his wife Barbara Bach attended the funeral at Huyton Cemetery, which took place on 1 September 1994.

Marie Maguire
Born in The Dingle, Marie Crawford, nee Maguire remembers the young Ritchie Starkey well. Her family moved into 10, Madryn Street in June 1943, immediately opposite Elsie and Ritchie's house.

Recently interviewed, she was asked:
What do you remember about The Dingle?

"It was a lovely place to grow up: not the squalid slums that some writers portray it as, especially when they've never been near the place. I remember that you could walk in and out of each other's houses, with your door being open all the time. Everyone knew everybody else. You knew who your neighbours were and we helped each other out. That was what it was like, and why I was happy to help out. Ritchie's dad had moved out when Ritchie was only three, and so Elsie had to work to pay the rent.

"When our family moved to Madryn Street, we lived opposite the Starkeys who lived at number 9. Mum became good friends with Elsie Starkey, and I was regularly called in, and trusted, to baby-sit young Ritchie. This would often entail going to Ritchie's grandparents' house at the bottom of Madryn Street where I would collect him—often fast asleep. I would carry him home and put him to bed.

LEFT: *Ringo's mum Elsie, with his stepfather Harry Graves, pictured in the '60s* RIGHT: *Elsie and Harry at home in 10, Admiral Grove, in 1963* BELOW: *Elsie in Admiral Grove*

"Mum and Elsie became good friends and I spent a lot of time with young Ritchie. When he was near his seventh birthday, his appendix burst and he contracted peritonitis and was very ill. On 7 July 1947, Elsie was called into the hospital, as they weren't sure if he was going to make it. I remember that day, because it was the day my father died. But mum still went with Elsie and sat with her through the night, even though she had lost her husband that same day: she wanted to stay with her in her time of need".

If you want to know what growing up in a community like The Dingle was like, then this selfless act sums it up. For those who don't know the area, then it is hard to describe. Those who do understand Liverpool will not be surprised.

Ritchie went to St. Silas School but Marie went to Mount Carmel, the local Roman Catholic School. However, this brought up an interesting point about the clash of religion.

"I was brought up a Catholic by my mum, and Elsie was a member of the Orange Lodge—staunch Protestants who normally hate the Catholics. However, mum and Elsie celebrated the 12 July (Orange Lodge celebration) and 17 March (St. Patrick's Day for the Irish Catholics). They would sing the songs together and enjoy the day, and proved that not all Protestants and Catholics had to hate each other".

Ritchie became ill again and most books say it was pleurisy. Marie disputes that long-held belief. "Ritchie contracted tuberculosis (TB) which of course was serious. At the time, there was a terrible stigma attached to having TB, and so the family said it was pleurisy.

TOP: *The Fab Four arrive in Liverpool for their civic reception on 10 July 1964*
ABOVE: *Ringo Starr launching the European Capital of Culture celebrations in Liverpool, January 2008.*

He was at the convalescent home in Heswall on the Wirral. That is when I took him Eric Delaney's record, 'Bedtime for Drums', which he loved".

While convalescing, children with TB would spend a lot of time in bed, often outside in the sunshine and fresh air. Part of the therapy to relieve boredom was to give the boys some 'noise time'. This consisted of giving them a toy drum or tambourine to bang and crash while sitting on their beds. It was here that Ritchie developed his love for drumming, helped along by Marie's simple but memorable gift.

The other Beatles moved their parents out of Liverpool when they became famous. John moved Mimi to Poole in Dorset; Paul moved Jim to Heswall and George moved Harry and Louise to Appleton near Warrington. Elsie didn't want to move too far, so Marie helped Ringo to find a house for his mum and stepfather.

"Elsie wanted to be close enough to come back to see her friends. Admiral Grove was surrounded by fans twenty-four hours a day, which was awkward, particularly as the toilet was still in the yard. So I went and found three houses which I thought could be acceptable. She and Harry chose the bungalow in Heath Hey in Woolton, which was a lovely house".

Marie and Ritchie moved on in their adult lives. Marie has been a leading tour guide in Liverpool for many years. She has fond memories of the young boy who went on to become one of the most famous men on this planet. Her viewpoint is refreshing: no dirt, no scandal, just great memories of a special area that produced a famous son— a lad who grew up to become Ringo Starr. But to Marie he will always be Ritchie.

1956
The Quarrymen are formed
"In Spite Of All The Danger"

The Quarrymen (or Quarry Men)

The Quarry Bank School song contained the words "Quarrymen, strong before our birth", which probably gave John Lennon and Pete Shotton the idea for the group's name. The Quarry Bank motto was "Out of this rock, you will find truth", which was ultimately what Lennon filtered through his music.

You will often see their name split as Quarry Men—this is how it appeared on Colin's drum. If you ask Nigel Walley, he would be adamant that it is Quarry Men, as two separate words. However, speaking to the original group members who were still performing— Rod Davis, Colin Hanton, Eric Griffiths, Len Garry and John Duff Lowe—they have always used Quarrymen, one word. "It was only split to fit on the drum head and the tea-chest bass", Rod Davis said.

Skiffle

Lonnie Donegan was responsible for the introduction of skiffle music in Britain when his record, "Rock Island Line" hit the U.K. in 1956, and made it to No.1 in the U.S. chart. Skiffle groups started springing from nowhere because performers did not need technology or musical expertise. The basic line-up for a group was a guitar, banjo, washboard, tea-chest bass and if fortunate, a drummer. The music was quite straightforward, and didn't need much musical tuition or know-how. Guitar sales surged, and an estimated 5,000 skiffle groups formed in England around this time.

The tea-chest bass has been described in various books, but rarely accurately. It was a square packing case that used to contain the tea being imported to the United Kingdom, hence tea-chest. It was upturned, painted, and then a brush handle was strung to the box, and as it was pulled tight, the player would twang the string, making the sound reverberate in the sound box at the bottom.

Paul McCartney remembered the numerous skiffle contests The Quarrymen entered and once commented that they "were always beaten by the girl who played the spoons". Her name was Marie and she was part of a skiffle group called the "Broadway Skiffle Kids" that appeared on the 'Carroll Levis Junior Discoveries Show'. The group appeared three times—the only ones with a spoon player.

The skiffle craze didn't last long as "Rock Island Line" was knocked off the top of the U.S. charts by Elvis Presley's "Heartbreak Hotel". Rock 'n' roll was here to stay and by the end of 1957 skiffle was already on its way out.

TOP: *The Quarrymen's skiffle instruments: banjo, guitars and washboard*
ABOVE: *Robert Marsden, playing the guitar, with Marie on the spoons (left) with The Broadway Skiffle Kids*
OPPOSITE PAGE: *The Quarrymen parading in Woolton. From left to right: Pete, Eric, Len, John, Colin and Rod. Note the sign using 'Quarrymen' as one word*

ABOVE: *A tea-chest bass*
RIGHT: *Quarrymen Colin Hanton, Len Garry, Rod Davis and Eric Griffiths outside The Beatles Story*

Quarrymen line-up

The Quarrymen were formed in the middle of 1956, though no precise date is available. Many books suggest it was 1957, but not according to Len Garry, The Quarrymen's one-time tea-chest bass player. Len remembers joining the band around September 1956.

Eric Griffiths recalled a schoolmate named George Lee who initially suggested a skiffle group, but nobody knows what happened to him. To be formed at Quarry Bank, the time frame had to be before mid-July when school finished for the summer break.

John Lennon was the instigator with his Quarry Bank schoolmates—Pete Shotton Eric Griffiths and Rod Davis. The initial line-up was John on guitar and vocals, with Pete Shotton on washboard (who also helped John make the first tea-chest bass). They enlisted Bill Smith to play tea-chest bass, and practiced in Shotton's air raid shelter in the garden. They sought out the only person they knew at school who had a guitar—Eric Griffiths. He couldn't play either, so he and John learned together from John's mum, Julia. They took a few guitar lessons in Hunts Cross, but they couldn't be bothered with all that theory rubbish. Another Quarry Bank pupil and friend, Rod Davis, had acquired a banjo around this time. Because he had an instrument, he was in.

Pete's shelter was a good place to practise, as was Julia's house. Eric and Rod's home also provided musical refuge at times. Eric suggested one afternoon that his friend Colin Hanton play drums with the group. Drummers were a rarity in the 1950s and worth their weight in gold. He was duly invited to join them.

After toying with the name Black Jacks for a couple of weeks, they settled on The Quarrymen. Pete Shotton claimed it fell to him to name the group. The main reason for choosing the name has been well-documented and the lyrics of the school song back that account. Shotton said another reason they chose The Quarrymen was because of the massive stone quarry in Woolton, off Quarry Street. Pete said, "Since our native Woolton was pocked with sandstone quarries, and most of us attended Quarry Bank School, The Quarrymen seemed as good a choice as any". So in that sense, living in the shadow of the quarry, they were also 'Quarrymen'.

Colin Hanton concurs with Pete. "Many years ago, because I didn't know about The Quarrymen name being associated with the school song, I always linked it with Woolton Quarry. There was a public footpath just past the church, which took you through the middle of the quarry (it is still there) and this was the route to John's house for me, Eric and Rod. Therefore, we were all familiar with the quarry. The others lived by it, and we walked through it. I went to St. Mary's School which was right next to the quarry, and when they were dynamiting they used to do three blasts on this horn, so if you heard that you ducked, so it was still an active quarry when I was at school, which was 1949".

ABOVE: *Woolton Quarry* RIGHT: *Ivan Vaughan with Pete Shotton*

So that was it; they were The Quarrymen.

When Paul met John at the Woolton fete, The Quarrymen were playing at St. Peter's Church, built from the local quarry, and the field where they played is right on the top edge of the quarry.

Not long after they were formed, another friend, Bill Smith, proved unreliable as a tea-chest bass player. He was replaced by Ivan Vaughan, or sometimes Nigel Walley.

A permanent tea-chest bass player was required and another of Ivan's mates from the Liverpool Institute, Len Garry, was asked by John and Pete to join. Len was also a good singer and shared the vocals with John.

And so, by the end of 1956, The Quarrymen Skiffle Group had a settled line-up in place. They were: John, Pete, Eric, Rod, Colin and Len. Three years later when they finished using The Quarrymen name, they had added other musicians such as John Duff Lowe and Ken Brown as well as future Beatles Paul and George.

Pete Shotton

Pete Shotton was born on 4 August 1941. His parents hailed from the North East of England, and moved to Liverpool after his father, George, left the Merchant Navy and landed a job in Tate & Lyle as a draughtsman. His mother Bessie owned and ran a number of small shops around Woolton Village, including one in Quarry Street. He had an older sister, Joan, an older brother Ernest and a younger brother, David. Pete and John Lennon attended Sunday School together and often spent their collection money on sweets;

a suggestion from John who couldn't believe they took the money to church and put it in the offering plate.

Discovering John's middle name was Winston, Pete taunted him by calling him 'Winnie'. Pete went to Mosspits School where John initially attended. They both eventually progressed to Quarry Bank School, and became the dreaded duo, terrorizing Quarry Bank and Woolton. They were lifelong friends and John helped to set Pete up in business, eventually recruiting him into Apple in the late '60s.

Pete wasn't musical and was only in the group because he was John's best mate. Pete wanted to leave, but didn't have the heart to tell John. John wanted him out, but couldn't sack his best mate. It all happened one day in August 1957 at a wedding reception in Toxteth. They were both drunk and were sitting on the floor laughing and joking. Intoxicated, Pete plucked up the courage to tell John he wanted to leave. With that, Lennon picked up Pete's washboard and smashed it over his friend's head. "That takes care of that problem, doesn't it?" laughed John. That was it—no one lost face, although Pete nearly lost half his head.

Eric Griffiths

Eric was born in North Wales and his parents were both Welsh. Eric's father was a male nurse before World War II and was later called up for duty as a pilot. He was killed in 1941 over the North Sea. At the age of three, Eric moved to his grandparent's house in Bootle.

When Eric turned ten, he moved into a semi-detached house in Halewood Drive in Woolton, where he lived until he was eighteen. He attended Belle Vale Primary School, and was one of only two students who passed the eleven-plus exam. He attended Quarry Bank. On 4 September 1952, he was placed in the same form as John Lennon and Pete Shotton. Eric was a founding member of The Quarrymen and performed with them on guitar, but was eventually eased out when George appeared.

ABOVE: *John Lennon, with Eric Griffiths, at New Clubmoor Hall on 18 October 1957*
RIGHT: *Eric Griffiths playing guitar with The Quarrymen at Dovedale School in 2004*

Eric remembered an interesting story that could have changed the history of the group. "Not long after Paul joined, I remember walking down the road with John, with Paul talking to Pete behind us. John, feeling perhaps that Paul was starting to dominate a bit, or even take over, suggested to me that maybe they should split the group, and he and I start again together. I told John that we needed Paul as he was so good and contributed a lot to the group. John agreed, and the subject was never mentioned again". That, says Eric, was his contribution to The Beatles—not letting John get rid of Paul. Thank you, Eric.

Paul was looking to get George into the group, and so someone had to go: that one was Eric. Opinions differ on who made the call. Colin remembers it was he who spoke to Eric, who had rung Paul's house at Forthlin Road during a Quarrymen rehearsal that he hadn't been invited to.

Eric was given what is commonly referred to as 'Hobson's choice'. Buy a bass guitar or leave the group. Eric was angry and wanted to speak to John, but was told he wasn't there. Eric was convinced John was lurking in the background. Eric couldn't afford a bass guitar and amplifier—not many people his age could—and so he was left with no option. Eric took the decision to join the Merchant Navy, and reported for duty in January '58, joining his first ship on 11 February '58.

Eric died at the beginning of 2005 after a short battle with cancer. A gentleman, and a gentle man, I met him at the concert The Quarrymen performed at Dovedale School for me in 2004, and it was through Eric that I made the final arrangements for the concert. Like the other Quarrymen, he was great fun with no pretensions, for which he could have been excused having been an integral part of the story.

LEFT: *Quarrymen banjo player Rod Davis on 6 July 2007 at the 50th anniversary of John meeting Paul at St. Peter's Church, Woolton* RIGHT: *Quarrymen drummer Colin Hanton*

Rod Davis

Rodney Verso Davis was born in Sefton General Hospital on 7 November 1941. His father was a clerk at Tate & Lyle's sugar refinery in Liverpool. They owned their house at 129, King's Drive in Woolton, which they bought in 1939. The Davis family were also one of the first families to have a car in the area, which they occasionally used to travel to gigs when Rod's father could take them. Rod attended Sunday School with John, Pete, Nigel and Ivan at St. Peter's.

He was given piano lessons, but didn't keep up with them. When he purchased a banjo from a relative, he was added to The Quarrymen line-up. But soon after the famous summer fete, he left the group to pursue his love of folk music. After John had played his copy of "Rock Island Line" to death on his record player, Rod bought it from him for half-a-crown.

Colin Hanton

Colin was born in Bootle, but his father's family was from County Wexford and his mother's family from Dublin, Ireland. His father,

John, was a fireman in the Bootle Fire Brigade in Liverpool. During the war, he saw action as Bootle suffered in the May Blitz when the Luftwaffe tried to attack the great Liverpool docks, gateway to America. Colin remembers Liverpool practically being on fire. In 1942, his father's fire crew received a direct hit. John was the only one to survive and spent many months in hospital. In 1945, the family moved to a rented house in Woolton—swapping houses with family members who wanted to return to Bootle. Colin then returned to Bootle after his mum died when he was only nine-years old. The family then moved again to 4, Heyscroft Road in Woolton. This time he attended St. Mary's Catholic primary school in Woolton and then senior school in Horrock's Avenue, Garston. He met Eric on the bus, and Eric soon discovered he had a set of drums, and quickly recruited Colin into the group. He was the last of the original Quarrymen to leave, following a row with Paul after a gig in Norris Green.

Colin told me:

"We were at the Finch Lane Busmen's Sports & Social Club. We all turned up and George's dad was there. I didn't know why we were there, as I didn't spend much time with John and Paul, I just received a call to say we were playing somewhere.

"There was a manager from the Pivvy in Lodge Lane there, as they had started bingo and wanted a resident group for thirty minutes in between houses. He came along to see us perform. We were in the dressing room, which was nice, and they had pictures of famous people who played there. We even had proper curtains on the stage. As the curtains opened, John started straight into the songs, and then he would introduce us. After our last song—we did about five songs—the curtains were due to close, but they were stuck, so John joked, 'While they get the curtains fixed we'll play another song'. We did "Lost John" and then the curtains did close this time. We went backstage and the manager came to see us and said 'That was an excellent show lads, so there's a pint at the bar for you', which was a mistake. We didn't just stop at one, and then me, Paul and John were drunk, and there was only poor George who wasn't drunk. I don't remember much, but we went back on stage for the second half, and at one point I said to John, 'What are we doing?' and Paul laughed and John said, 'See, he doesn't even know what we're doing,'—if you weren't drunk you'd be embarrassed.

"We finished our set and went into the dressing room, then the manager came in and said, 'You've blown it lads, that was a disaster'. The man from the Pivvy then came in and he had obviously just come off stage as he still had his stage make-up with plenty of rouge, eye make-up and stuff. John was slouched in the corner and he ribbed the poor man unmercifully, as only John could. He was telling us about being professional and how to treat your audience and I was suddenly sobering up quickly as I didn't know it was an audition. I remember standing on the tables and singing, and I was wondering what was happening, and then things didn't seem that funny anymore.

"We jumped on the bus, and I don't normally tell this part of the story, but Paul had started to do this funny voice. I had some deaf friends, and you know how a deaf person speaks, well he was doing this voice. I'm sure he wasn't insulting deaf people, as that wasn't his way, but I was in this drunken state sobering up. Paul kept making these noises and talking in this stupid voice, and I just rounded on him and verbally attacked him. I don't think it would have come to anything, but Pete Shotton was with us and he shouted, 'This is our stop Colin'. So we ran down the stairs, I grabbed my drums and we jumped off. Of course, it wasn't our stop; we were in the middle of Old Swan or somewhere, so I think that was his way of diffusing things.

"And that was that. So we had to get the bus back to Woolton. I just went back to my house and put my drums away and that was me, finished. I never told them I was quitting but they never contacted me again. I thought *I don't need this*. We just had the row, I told Paul to shut up and I think he was shocked. They probably didn't want me and I didn't want them so that was it.

"No regrets. You can't have regrets. You just have the life you've been given. I could have given up my trade, gone to Hamburg and been sent back with nothing, so I didn't, and I'm still working now. Of course, I've had a bit of a life again recently with The Quarrymen, which is great".

Ivan Vaughan at Dovedale School, second from right in the second row, in 1950

Ivan Vaughan:

Ivan attended Dovedale School with John Lennon, and was John's neighbour: their gardens backed on to each other. When John attended Quarry Bank, Ivan went to the Liverpool Institute where he met a lad born on the same day as him: Paul McCartney. The two became friends, which enabled Ivan to take Paul to meet his old friend John at St. Peter's Church fete on 6 July 1957. If it hadn't been for Ivan, there is a good chance that John and Paul would not have formed their great partnership. In fact, they probably would never have met, as they lived in different areas and attended different schools. Ivan was their only common link.

Ivan was drafted by The Beatles in the late sixties to set up a private school for Apple, but this never materialized. He died prematurely from Parkinson's Disease in 1994 at the age of fifty-two. His death prompted Paul to start writing poetry again.

I spoke to a school friend of Ivan's, Stan Williams, who also attended Dovedale School with John Lennon and George Harrison, for his memories of Ivan.

"Along with the glittering names like John Lennon, George Harrison, and Ivan Vaughan, I attended Dovedale in the Golden Years of the school's history between 1947 and 1953. I had known Ivan before we arrived at Dovedale because we spent three years together at Lidderdale Road Infants. We were part of the first post-war intake of five-year-olds to toddle through its gates in 1946. He was a big, strong lad and much more confident than me—always in the thick of harmless mischief which, nevertheless, in those days spelled big trouble if you were caught by one of the strict, spinster schoolmistresses.

"Ivan and I loved Dovedale School. We sat alongside one another in the top sets of Pop Bell's eleven-plus class and played together in all the school football, baseball and cricket teams. Ivan was not the most skilful sportsman, but he was fearless. Once or twice in an emergency he was put in goal by Pop Bell, who knew a brave bugger when he saw one. Ivan was afraid of nothing and this quality endeared him to John Lennon, I'm certain of that.

"That he was dearly loved by John there can be no doubt. Have a look through Lennon's book of poems, *In His Own Write*. Sprinkled throughout the verses can be found references to his pal, such as, "My Ivan's are getting cold"… "We must strike the Ivan while it is hot"…and "Treasure Ivan". Clearly 'Ivy' as John and Paul liked to call him, is very much a part of the Lennon psyche.

"My last memory of Ivan was sad and tragic. It was Christmas 1984, and I happened to switch on to a controversial BBC 2 'Horizon' programme about Parkinson's. It was simply called 'Ivan'. I had no idea that the university lecturer, engaged in a brave, moral and scientific struggle to find out more about the illness that was ravaging both his mind and body, was the Ivan of my childhood. I wrote to him and he typed a letter back, although his illness must have made the task difficult. He invited me to visit him, but he was gone soon afterwards and the world was a poorer place for his passing.

"I know that he will always be remembered in Beatles folklore as the person who got the Lennon-McCartney partnership going, when he introduced John to Paul at the Woolton Parish Church garden fete. He was, however, someone far more significant than that to his close family, and those he taught and influenced, as well as the extended family group known as The Beatles. Paul was so affected by Ivan's death that he was inspired to write poetry. To me he was a smashing school pal; a sympathetic, lion-hearted boy, who grew into a man of great moral fortitude. In the end that counts for more than anything else".

Nigel Walley

Nigel lived in a house near to Ivan called 'Leosdene' in Vale Road, where both Pete Shotton and Ivan Vaughan resided. John referred to him as 'Wallogs'. After occasionally playing tea-chest bass he became The Quarrymen's first manager, placing a card in a local Woolton Sweet Shop window. It read:

> **Country. Western. Rock 'n' roll. Skiffle**
> **The Quarry Men. Open for engagements.**

It was Nigel's contact through Lee Park Golf Club where he worked that he met Dr. Sytner, whose son Alan ran The Cavern Club. The group performed at Lee Park as an audition, and were subsequently booked. They appeared at The Cavern on 7 August 1957. Even though Paul had met John a month earlier, he did not appear with them at The Cavern.

According to Bill Harry's *Encyclopedia of Beatles People*, Nigel was squeezed out of The Quarrymen after Paul allegedly complained that they weren't earning enough to allow Nigel to take his ten per cent commission, so he was asked to leave.

Len Garry

Len was born in Liverpool on 6 January 1942. His father Harry was a printer with the *Liverpool Echo*. His mother Phyllis was a hairdresser, and continued to work at home. Len had an older brother Walter.

TOP LEFT: *Nigel Walley (left) with John Lennon in 1958*
TOP RIGHT: *Nigel Walley (forefront) with John Lennon and Pete Shotton with their wives Cynthia and Beth*
LEFT: *Len Garry with The Quarrymen at New Clubmoor Hall on 18 October 1957*
RIGHT: *Len Garry with The Quarrymen in 2007*

They lived at 77, Lance Lane, just off Woolton Road. Len went to Mosspits Primary School, where Pete Shotton had attended the year before (though they didn't know each other at the time). Len took piano lessons, but soon gave up. He often visited his grandparent's baby wear shop on Woolton Road to listen to records in the flat above the shop.

Len passed the exam for the Liverpool Institute, where he soon made friends with a lad from Woolton named Ivan Vaughan. Ivan introduced him to John, and they became friends. Len joined The Quarrymen on the tea-chest bass and played with them until he contracted tubercular meningitis, which meant a long stay in hospital. The Quarrymen carried on playing without him.

Ken Brown

Ken Brown was born in Enfield, North London, and moved to Liverpool when he was only nine-months old. His father was a civil servant who worked at The Royal Ordinance Factory at Enfield Lock in Middlesex. The factory manufactured firearms and ammunition and he was offered the opportunity of relocating to another part of the country. The family was transferred to Liverpool early in 1941.

Ken lived at 149, Storrington Avenue, Norris Green, a suburb close to West Derby on the outskirts of Liverpool, and attended Wellsbourne Road Primary School. Ken started piano lessons when he was ten, but skiffle excited him more, so he learned the guitar and joined a group called The Lowlanders, which was the resident band at Lowlands in Haymans Green, West Derby.

TOP: *The Quarrymen in 2007: John Duff Lowe, Len Garry, Rod Davis and Colin Hanton*
RIGHT: *Percy Phillips' studio was in the back room of his house at 38, Kensington*

The group leader, Les Stewart, agreed that a young lad with his guitar could join the group, which had been renamed the Les Stewart Quartet. The young lad, who had left his other group, as he wanted to play live, was George Harrison.

Through George's first girlfriend Ruth Morrison, Ken met Mona Best at The Casbah and arranged for the Les Stewart Quartet to play there. That never transpired.

Ken became a member of The Quarrymen when he and George re-formed them for The Casbah residency. His time with them, however, only lasted a few weeks before he was sacked after a dispute over money with Paul, John and George. Ken then formed The Black Jacks—which had the same name as John Lennon's first group, but the name was just coincidental—with friends Chas Newby, Bill Barlow and a novice drummer by the name of Pete Best.

Ken was important in the evolution of The Quarrymen, but isn't often mentioned. He deserves his place in Beatles folklore.

John Duff Lowe

John was in the same year at school as Paul and Len at the Liverpool Institute, and was drafted in whenever there was an opportunity to add piano. They would have to rely on the venue providing one, so his appearances were sporadic.

He had known Paul since they were about ten and sang in the choir at St. Barnabas' Church on Penny Lane. They auditioned together for the cathedral choir and failed. John reckons had they passed their audition, Paul would have been singing in the cathedral choir on 6 July 1957 and wouldn't have been able to watch The Quarrymen. John's parents insisted that he give the choir another go and six months later he was accepted. He believes Paul didn't want to join the choir and deliberately failed. John never told his parents he was in a group, and didn't even own a pair of jeans. How could he survive?

John was one of The Quarrymen when they recorded their first disc together, "In Spite Of All The Danger" and "That'll Be the Day" in the studio in Kensington. He had the only disc in his possession, which he realised many years later. That disc was eventually purchased in 1981 by Paul McCartney and used in The Beatles' *Anthology* project.

He returned to Percy Phillip's Kensington house with Colin Hanton to unveil a plaque on 1 August 2005.

John rejoined The Quarrymen in 2006.

ABOVE LEFT: *The author, Rod Davis, Head Teacher Wen Williams and Colin Hanton at Dovedale School in 2004*
ABOVE RIGHT: *Len Garry, Eric Griffiths, Colin Hanton and Rod Davis with the author's daughter, Lauren*

The Quarrymen at Dovedale School

Q: What do John Lennon, George Harrison, Paul McCartney and the author have in common?

A: We've all played with The Quarrymen.

Yes, I have played, on stage, "live" with The Quarrymen during a concert at Dovedale School—as a washboard player. It was a privilege, and one of the greatest moments of my life.

As a Beatles fan, being a parent-governor at Dovedale School has an extra privilege. Dovedale School, near Penny Lane in Liverpool was the primary school for not only John Lennon, but George Harrison and Ivan Vaughan as well.

Knowing this, I approached Rod Davis of The Quarrymen to see if they would come to the school for a fund-raiser and a chance to celebrate the lives of three ex-pupils who were 'instrumental' in the legend that is The Beatles. Rod came back with some proposed dates and that they would play for expenses only. Rod Davis, Colin Hanton, Eric Griffiths and Len Garry were delighted to play at the school.

Once we agreed on the date of Saturday 8 May 2004, I set about trying to build a great day's entertainment. In the afternoon, Rod and Colin did an interactive story of skiffle and The Quarrymen, which kept the audience enthralled for an hour. This was also my debut on the washboard—with Head Teacher Miss Wen Williams on tea-chest bass. Eric Woolley, who had played with Len Garry before brought his band, The Clayton Squares, to play either side of Rod and Colin and were superb.

The Blue Meanies appeared that evening along with The Prellies, who drove all the way up from Birmingham for the fun of it. The concert was promoted as "The Beatles' Musical History"—albeit in reverse. The Blue Meanies gave great renditions of The Beatles hits. The Prellies relived Hamburg, and then, where it all started—The Quarrymen.

The group members showed that they hadn't lost their ability or sense of humour, and the stories and anecdotes in between songs were great, as was Lennon's classmate, Tim Holmes, on the piano.

Rod, Eric, Len and Colin were four "superstars" whose place in Beatles history is important, but whose humility is remarkable.

22 JUNE 1957
The Quarrymen perform in Rosebery Street
"I Don't Want To Spoil The Party"

One of the first known gigs that The Quarrymen played was on the back of a lorry at a street party on Rosebery Street in Toxteth. The event took place on Saturday 22 June 1957, arranged through Colin Hanton's friend Charles Roberts.

I asked Colin what he remembered about the gig.

"Charlie Roberts was one of my friends, and it was the 750th Anniversary of Liverpool, though we didn't know it at the time. I didn't hang around with John and the other Quarrymen members. I knew Eric well, but I was a bit older than the others, so I was off drinking in town with my friends. Unless we were rehearsing, I was drinking with Charlie and Kevin Hansen, who was my closest mate for a long time.

"Charlie Roberts' parents had something to do with the committee. There was a competition to have the best-decorated street and they thought about booking The Quarrymen for the street party. "We played the gig in the afternoon on the back of a coal wagon and then I went to the pub. During the second performance at teatime, I knew some of the other lads in the crowd, and heard that they were planning to grab John as he got off the wagon, because he had been making eyes at the girls in the crowd, and the lads weren't happy. I was on the end of the wagon with my drums, so I called John over and told him, so we jumped off quickly, and headed for Charlie Robert's house, which was the only one we could get in to. The lads chased us, but we just made it into the house in time.

"We had to finish early because of the trouble, so the police were called and this bobby came and walked the other band members down to the bus stop. I had met this girl in the pub so I later walked her back to her house in Rosebery Street. I think it was the drums that did it!

"As to the suggestion that we played as Johnny and the Rainbows, I have no recollection of playing under any name other than The Quarrymen", confirmed Colin.

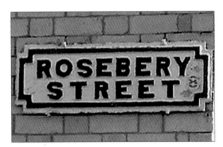

TOP: *The Quarrymen at Rosebery Street on 22 June 1957: Colin (hidden), Eric, Len, John, Rod and Pete*
LEFT AND RIGHT: *Rosebery Street in 2002 before the houses were demolished*

6 JULY 1957
Paul meets John at St. Peter's Church
"Two Of Us"

Saturday, 6 July 1957 has to be the most historic day in popular music. It was the day that John Lennon's group, The Quarrymen, performed at St. Peter's Church annual summer fete.

That morning, John had spent hours arranging his hair just right, and squeezing into his skin-tight, leg-hugging drainpipe trousers. This was the prelude to a row with Mimi who didn't know what he was up to. John stormed out of the house. This was his day and Mimi wasn't going to ruin it for him.

Every year the church celebrated on the first Saturday on or after 29 June, which is the Feast of St. Peter. This was the highlight of the calendar for the village of Woolton. The festivities included a parade around the village on the back of lorries. There were usually five vehicles and in 1957, the last of these carried The Quarrymen. The parade also included children's organizations like Brownies and Scouts, Sunday school and Youth Club members. In between there were Morris Dancers and the highlight for one young lady, in this case, thirteen-year-old Sally Wright, who was crowned as the Rose Queen.

At exactly 2 p.m., the bells of St. Peter's Church chimed. The parade route headed down Church Road, left on to Allerton Road, right on to Woolton Street, and left down King's Drive toward where Rod Davis, Colin Hanton and Eric Griffiths lived. It snaked along Hunts Cross Avenue and up Manor Road, turning right on to Speke Road and back along Woolton Street, turning left into Allerton Road and right up Church Road back to the church.

Everyone paraded into the field at the rear of the church, where a small stage had been erected for the event. The Scout hut, which housed The Quarrymen's instruments, was up the hill where the school currently sits. There were tents for refreshments and first aid facilities.

The Rose Queen was crowned, and, following a fancy-dress parade for the children, the Rector formally opened the summer fete. He introduced The Quarrymen and John took over on the microphone. He introduced himself and the band members and then performed "Be-Bop-A-Lula". In the audience were his mum Julia and her two daughters Julia and Jackie, plus his good friend Ivan Vaughan. Ivan was standing next to someone John didn't know: Paul McCartney, whom Ivan had invited there to see this group.

Ivan was the only common link between John and Paul. Ivan had to convince Paul to come and see The Quarrymen—Ivan's clinching argument was that it was "a good place to meet girls". With best jacket on, Paul set off with Ivan for what turned out to be a momentous day.

I asked The Quarrymen's banjo player Rod Davis what he remembered.

"We were on the back of a lorry for the parade around Woolton, much to John's disgust—how could we play and sing while moving? The acoustics were appalling. All John remembered was thrashing his guitar as loudly as possible as there were no amplifiers. Thrashing the guitars was the only way; some skiffle groups had four guitarists. As a rule, we had to keep telling Colin to play the drums with his brushes so he didn't drown us out, now we have to urge him to 'give it some welly'".

Len remembers they entered the Scout hut with their equipment, and then walked around the stalls. John smashed a few plates at one of the game stalls (after putting his glasses on) and that made him feel better. When they heard the brass band finishing, they made their way to the stage and set up. They played at 4.15 p.m. after the Police Dog display team, which was the main attraction.

"John Lennon was at the microphone", Len said. "He was centre stage and positioned in the front, saying before we started, 'Len, get a bit closer'. I replied, 'I can't. Not with this thing,' referring to the tea-chest with frustration".

Standing in the crowd was one of their friends, Geoff Rhind, who had the foresight to bring his camera with him. He stood by the stage and took the famous photo of the young group of upstarts.

Rod Davis showed me, based on details in the image that a church lady had pointed out, the exact spot from where the photo was taken.

John then introduced the group. Nervously, he asked, "Is this thing on?" When the crowd replied yes, he decided against a long introduction and launched into "All Shook Up" followed by "Blue Suede Shoes".

When Mimi saw John on stage, he started changing the words to the song he was singing, and instead sang "Mimi's coming". John was happy with the show because this was the first time he had performed Gene Vincent's "Be-Bop-A-Lula".

John then smiled as he said, "This next song is dedicated to Prycey", referring to Reverend Pryce Jones, vicar of St. Peter's.

GARDEN FETE
ST. PETER'S CHURCH FIELD

WOOLTON PARISH CHURCH   Rector: M. Pryce Jones.

Saturday, 6th July, 1957
at 3 p.m.

ADMISSION BY PROGRAMME:
CHILDREN 3d.

PROCEEDS IN AID OF CHURCH FUNDS.

The program from St. Peter's Garden Fete

John launched into "Maggie May", the famous song about a Liverpool prostitute. They played many popular skiffle numbers like "Cumberland Gap" and "Railroad Bill", plus The Del-Vikings' number "Come Go With Me". Many books quote Paul McCartney saying how impressed he was that John was making up the words like "going down to the penitentiary" because they sounded right.

Rod Davis disputes that claim and said John wasn't making up the words. "They were the words that we always sang, as the only way we could learn words was by listening to the records—often in the NEMS record shop near to Penny Lane—or on Radio Luxembourg, and scribbling down the words we thought we were listening to. So when we performed these songs, these were the words we sang. What we couldn't recognize we improvised, and penitentiary sounded bluesy so it went in. The problem was", explained Rod, "that we couldn't afford to buy all the records we wanted, so you had to get the words off the radio or in record booths". However it happened, Paul was impressed by John's performance, though he noticed John was playing some strange looking guitar chords. I also spoke to Quarrymen drummer Colin Hanton about his memories of that day.

"Pete's mum was on the church committee I think, so she got us the gig. It was a brave decision by the church committee, because of course we were the first generation of teenagers, and skiffle was just in, and it was the early days of rock 'n' roll, and the music was frowned upon as the devil's music. It was like a grey world before and suddenly it was Technicolour. I remember being bold and going down to town and buying two pairs of luminous socks: shocking green and orange. Such was rock 'n' roll.

It was my little rebellion. The church took a gamble and it paid off. Everyone in the village came, as there was no sitting in watching the television as not many people had one.

"Back in 1957, Woolton was out in 'the sticks'. The trams used to stop at the top of Kings Drive and the conductor would unhook the wiring and then go back to town. After that you had to walk. Woolton was an isolated village and it has still maintained a village mentality. A lot of building went on, but back then, below the bottom of Kings Drive where I lived was all fields.

"If anything big was coming up in the village, everyone turned out to march or to watch. The summer fete was the biggest event of the year. There was a marching band and everyone would be marching along with them. The local coal wagons and potato wagons were dressed up and decorated with banners and streamers. It was an important day for Woolton.

"People say we played two sets in the afternoon, but I don't remember playing two sets. The way these events go we were programmed to go on twice, but things overrun and it knocks everything out, so I only remember playing once in the afternoon.

"At some time in the afternoon after playing, we had stored our equipment in the big Scout hut. We went in, and I was messing with my drums and there was a lad on his trumpet and then there was John and Ivan and this other lad, who of course turned out to be Paul McCartney.

"Now, everyone says that the meeting of John and Paul took place in the church hall later on that day, but I wasn't in the hall then, so it must have been in the Scout hut. I couldn't confuse the two. I reckon the first introduction happened in the Scout hut in the afternoon".

This makes sense to me, as you obviously saw it happen, and you can't have mixed them up, as you weren't present in the church hall later. Plus, I've always thought, why wait until the evening? Paul watched you play, so why wait another few hours before being introduced?

"I am adamant that the introduction took place in the afternoon in that hut. Paul suggested John was drunk, but you couldn't get hold of booze, there were no off-licences (shops where you could purchase alcohol) or places to buy booze, and if you looked under eighteen there was no chance at all, so he couldn't have been drunk. He maybe had obtained a bottle off someone, but that would have been all".

"Bishop Martin School has been built on the site of the Scout hut. As you go through the main gate, the stage was on the left, and I was watching hordes of people leaving the field for home. The hut was close to the edge of the quarry, right near the wall.

"The evening performance was The Grand Dance in the Church Hall across the road at 8.00 p.m., with the George Edwards Band and us—we were an interlude. For the meeting with Paul in the evening I wasn't there, as the hall was on my side of the village.

ABOVE: *The Quarrymen appearing at St. Peter's Church fete on 6 July 1957*

I had probably gone home for some tea, while the others hung around until the evening performance".

At the end of the afternoon performance, Len recalls a conversation between Ivan and John, where Ivan mentioned that Paul had promised to bring his guitar. John suggested to Paul that he go home and bring it back. Len is the only one to mention this, and recalls Paul cycling home and returning later with his guitar over his shoulder.

Ivan and Paul discussed times and agreed to meet in the hall about teatime where food was being served. Paul mentioned that he couldn't stay for the evening performance.

So, what did happen when Paul met John?

There were six members of The Quarrymen, plus Ivan and Paul. That is eight of them, and yet, if you ask any of the guys who were there that day they will all have a slightly different version of what happened. We have to read all the different accounts from each person present and take the bits they agree on, and come up with the best guesstimate. Rod seems to think he was in the toilet for half of it. Colin had gone home. Len was convinced Paul went home for his guitar and returned with it in hand.

What we can deduce is that the meeting lasted for about twenty minutes by the steps of the stage in the church hall. Ivan introduced Paul to John, who nodded an acknowledgement, probably without lifting his head, and grunted as teenage boys do. Paul didn't stay long as he had to leave early, and was planning his dad's birthday party for the next day. The problem is that those present were teenagers, preparing for a gig, and didn't realise what they had witnessed was the most important meeting in music history.

John was sitting on the steps by the stage, next to the radiator, strumming his guitar, looking like he knew what he was doing. Rod explains what happened next.

"We had been playing together for something like a year and we could play the correct chords for all the tunes in our repertoire, except that Eric and John had their guitars

LEFT: *St. Peter's Church Hall where The Quarrymen played in the evening, and where Paul first performed with The Quarrymen*
RIGHT: *Site of the Scout hut in St. Peter's field, now a school, and a view over Woolton and Allerton from St. Peter's Church*

tuned like banjos and played banjo chords, as opposed to tuning their guitars normally and using guitar chords. Funnily enough, Lonnie Donegan did the opposite and played guitar chords on a banjo. Banjo tuning is an open G chord and lots of guitarists nowadays experiment with open tunings. We could tune our guitars like banjos, as we hadn't learnt guitar chords and there was no point in learning to tune them like a guitar. I played a banjo anyway, so I had no problems.

At that time, John tuned the top four strings of his guitar like a banjo. I asked Rod Davis about John's prowess on the guitar.

"John and Eric went to a guitar teacher in Hunts Cross to learn the guitar; this was before the group even started, according to Eric. After two lessons or so they realised that it would take forever as he was trying to teach them from the music and all they wanted was a few chords to accompany songs. So John's mother, Julia, offered to teach them some banjo chords. This involved tuning their guitars to four-string banjo tuning—I can't remember what they did with the fifth and sixth string. I asked Eric some time ago and I think he said that they just tuned them to the G chord. As I recall we played almost everything in C or G".

It has also been suggested that John and Eric paid someone to tune their guitars for them. What did Rod think?

"This business about taking them to a man in Kings Drive, Woolton for him to tune them I have read, but it does not make sense to me. I lived all my life in Kings Drive and didn't know anyone who lived there who could play the guitar. As far as I remember we must have used a pitch pipe. It is however true that John could tune it like a banjo.

When Paul McCartney met The Quarrymen at St. Peter's, he had to re-tune John's guitar from banjo tuning to guitar tuning".

So, Paul offered to show John how to tune it, which was a good start, and certainly impressed John. At Ivan's prompting, Paul then showed John that he could play, by singing "Twenty Flight Rock" by Eddie Cochran.

Paul played John's guitar upside-down, a feat he had conquered, as the world wasn't prepared for a left-handed guitarist. This looked even more impressive. As an aside, apparently years later, while on tour in Paris, John and Paul were observed playing each other's guitars upside down—John had to attempt it, didn't he? As a guitarist who has been playing for three decades, if I had seen someone at fifteen playing my guitar upside down, I would have been impressed.

Paul not only knew all the words, but he could play all the proper guitar chords too, as well as tuning a guitar. Paul remembered the advice of his father Jim not to be too pushy. John Lennon was most impressed. No wonder.

As if that was not enough, on prompting from John, and at Ivan's suggestion, Paul sang "Long Tall Sally". Paul had a greater vocal range than John, and could do an excellent Little Richard impression. Paul also performed Gene Vincent's "Be-Bop-A-Lula". Paul then went home and all that was left to John was the big decision. Could he, as the group's leader, welcome another person who was a better guitarist, musician and a good singer? Thankfully, John allowed his brain and not his ego make the decision and he invited Paul to join. That is where, as the plaque on St. Peter's Church Hall says, "it all started moving". In later interviews, John recalled that he asked Paul that day to join the group. However, Paul McCartney and Pete Shotton remember it happening later, which is more likely.

The plaque that was erected on the wall of St. Peter's Church Hall in 1997 was unveiled on the occasion of the fortieth anniversary of this event, attended by the

ABOVE: *St. Peter's stage in the church hall, with the steps on the left where John Lennon sat when Ivan Vaughan introduced Lennon to McCartney*
RIGHT: *The view from the stage of St. Peter's Church Hall in 1957*

St. Peter's Church magazine from August 1957 recorded this momentous day:

In most of us, the sights and sounds of early spring will inspire thoughts of golden summer days ahead, and we allow ourselves a little luxurious day-dreaming of blissful holidays of ease and pleasure. Not so the Garden Fete committee. For them, the stern reality of organizing the most important social event of Woolton must be faced. The outstanding success of the Garden Fete was largely because of the enthusiasm and enterprise of this hardworking team.

We were blessed with a fine warm day, and the decorated lorries bearing their colourful loads presented a gay sight as they proceeded along the "lower route". Murmurs of appreciation greeted the charming queens and their retinues as they took up their positions on the stage. Against a leafy background, Miss Sally Wright, Rose Queen for 1957, was crowned by Mrs. Thelwell Jones; after which Mr. Thelwell Jones declared the Garden Fete open. The Fancy Dress Competitions were judged by Mr. and Mrs. Thelwell Jones. Not only were there stalls and sideshows to suit all ages and tastes, but the musical accompaniments were lively and varied. The folks who favour martial airs enjoyed the selections played by the Band of The Cheshire (Earl of Chester) Yeomanry, while the rock 'n' roll fans appreciated the vigorous numbers given by The Quarrymen's Skiffle Group.

The display of obedience training by the dogs of the Liverpool City Police was a popular item on the programme. Meanwhile, amidst the friendliest atmosphere, the stalls and sideshows did good business. Hot and thirsty folk sought refreshment and a willing spirit of co-operation was found everywhere.

The final proceeds of £400 was a result worthy of all the efforts and hard work put into a great day.

ABOVE: *The original stage steps from St. Peter's Church Hall where John and Paul met in 1957, on display in the museum, Liverpool*
RIGHT: *The plaque on St. Peter's Church Hall, unveiled in 1997*

IN THIS HALL ON
6TH JULY 1957
JOHN & PAUL
FIRST MET

The Quarry Men featuring, Eric Griffiths, Colin Hanton, Rod Davies, John Lennon, Pete Shotton and Len Garry performed on the afternoon of 6th July 1957 at St Peters Church Fete. In the evening before their performance in this hall Ivan Vaughan, who sometimes played in the group, introduced his friend Paul McCartney to John Lennon. As John recalled ......

" that was the day, the day that I met Paul, that it started moving. "

original Quarrymen. Cut from the local quarry stone and based on the silhouette of the one famous photograph, it is an excellent plaque showing the line-up for the day. From left to right is Eric Griffiths, guitar; Colin Hanton on drums; Rod Davis on banjo; John at the front on guitar; Pete Shotton on the washboard at the back and Len Garry on the right with his tea-chest bass.

Bob Molyneux was at the summer fete in July 1957 and recorded The Quarrymen performing on his recently purchased portable tape-recorder. Unfortunately, he later erased most of this and only one tape containing two songs was preserved. He rediscovered it in 1994 and at auction it fetched £78,500.

And that was it. What a day; an ordinary day at a little summer festival in a small suburb in Liverpool. It was there that a simple introduction by a friend of both Paul and John led to the greatest musical partnership is music history.

It must be fate.

The Quarrymen: Len Garry, Colin Hanton, Rod Davis and John Duff Lowe at St. Peter's Church, Woolton in 2007

The Quarrymen Anniversary

On 6 July 2007, it was the fiftieth anniversary of that famous meeting and St. Peter's became the focus once again. There were many events over the weekend, culminating on 8 July with a summer fete in the grounds of Bishop Martin School, which was built on the site of St. Peter's field.

Messages were sent from Paul McCartney, Ringo Starr, Yoko Ono and Her Majesty The Queen.

Paul wrote:
It was a very special day in my life when my friend Ivan (Ive the Jive, the Ace of the Bass) took me to the Woolton church fete to see John play and to meet him later that evening. Thank you to everyone for helping me to celebrate this special day.

Ringo wrote:
Hi everyone at The Quarrymen Anniversary Party. It gives me great pleasure to join Bob and everyone in celebrating the grand meeting of John and Paul. Have a great day. Peace and Love.

Yoko wrote:
When John and Paul met on this day fifty years ago, it not only changed their lives but changed our world as well. It was a momentous day indeed.

Her Majesty The Queen wrote:
I send my sincere thanks to all those assembled at St. Peter's in Woolton, Liverpool, for the kind message of loyal greetings on the occasion of the celebrations to mark the 50th anniversary of "The Birth of The Beatles", the first meeting between John Lennon and Paul McCartney, which led to the formation of The Beatles. I received this message with much pleasure and send my best wishes to all concerned for a most enjoyable and successful occasion.

The surviving members of The Quarrymen, except for Pete Shotton, were there—Rod Davis, Len Garry, Colin Hanton and John Duff Lowe—amusing the crowd with their music and stories. They discovered that they still enjoyed entertaining everyone, even if they were nervous. When the call went up from the band that they needed a volunteer to play washboard with them, I trampled over children and pensioners to make it to the front of the queue. I then found myself on stage with The Quarrymen, playing washboard on the Lonnie Donegan song, "Putting on the Style". As ever it was great fun and an honour to be on stage with them at such a historic event.

12 July 1958
The Quarrymen record at Percy Phillips' studio
"That'll Be The Day"

LEFT TO RIGHT: *Percy Phillips' house, John Duff Lowe with The Quarrymen's record, and 38, Kensington, 'Birthplace of The Beatles'*

This small studio tucked inside a Victorian terraced house at number 38, Kensington is where The Quarrymen made their first and only demo record. It was a disc that eventually became one of the most historic recordings in popular music. John, Paul, George, Colin Hanton and John Duff Lowe paid seventeen shillings and sixpence (87.5 pence) and cut a two-sided disk made of shellac. They couldn't afford to pay for a tape and so the recording was made straight to disk. The five-piece ensemble recorded Buddy Holly's "That'll Be The Day" and "In Spite Of All The Danger", an original McCartney-Harrison tune. It was seen as Paul's song with George providing the guitar solo.

Percy Phillips owned the studio, which was on the ground floor. His clients waited in the front parlour and recorded in the back room studio. The studio consisted of two tape-recorders, a microphone hanging from the ceiling, a piano and disc-cutter, which produced these shellac discs.

Colin Hanton spoke about that famous first recording.

"We met at a theatre and walked up there. All I remember was this back room with electronic equipment in the corner. We set up our equipment with me in the corner and the lads with their guitars: there were no amps, it was all-acoustic. John Lowe was over by the wall on the piano. I was hitting the drums and he said that they were too loud, so I tried again but there was still the same problem which was finally fixed by putting a scarf over the snare to soften it and keep it as quiet as possible.

"John Duff Lowe reckons there was one microphone hanging down from the ceiling, which picked everything up. He was complaining because he said we should get the tape, which was a pound, but we just had enough each—three shillings and sixpence (17.5 pence). I always felt that was one of the reasons to invite John Lowe along to split it five ways. John and Paul went white at the thought of a pound.

"Percy was fed up because we were taking too much time, and starting to look at the clock. 'In Spite Of All The Danger' was quite long, and he said to chop a verse off. John said no. John Lowe could see Phillips from where he was sitting and he was apparently telling John to finish. We kept going, so the record ended with the song going almost to the centre of the disc, right to the hole in the middle.

"He gave us the disc and off we went. It was a big thing. How many people had records like popular crooner, Matt Monro? So we had a record too, and could listen to ourselves. We had heard our group before because the girl who lived next door to me, Geraldine Davies, had a Grundig tape recorder. She'd record us and then we'd all sit down and listen to it. It was a momentous day for us. I can still remember it so clearly".

In August 2005, Hanton returned to Kensington for the unveiling of a plaque to commemorate this first recording. John Duff Lowe was in attendance, as well as Julia Baird, John's half-sister. Radio presenter Billy Butler was also on hand for the festivities.

As for the claim above the door to be the "Birthplace of The Beatles", well I'm sorry, but no. The first record The Quarrymen made was a significant step on the road to fame, but the real birthplace was in the basement of a house owned by a female entrepreneur named Mona Best.

15 July 1958
Julia Lennon is struck down and killed by a car
"My Mummy's Dead"

From the high of the recording session, John Lennon could not have envisioned what unfolded next. Where three days ago he had sung, "That'll be the day, when you say goodbye, that'll be the day, when I die", little did he know how prophetic this lyric would be.

The events of 15 July 1958 would forever remain in John's memory, and caused irreparable emotional damage.

John's relationship with Julia was back on track after years of enforced separation. It just so happened that Julia went to see Mimi at Mendips that fateful day. When Julia decided it was time to return home, instead of Mimi walking her to the bus stop, Julia spotted John's friend Nigel Walley. In Julia Baird's book, *Imagine This, Growing up with my Brother John Lennon,* Walley recalled her last moments. "Mimi and Julia were chatting at the gate; Julia saw me and said, 'John isn't in, so you can escort me to the bus stop'".

Menlove Avenue hasn't changed much since John lived there apart from the central reservation, or median. Originally this was where the tram tracks ran along Menlove Avenue. At either side of the track was a small hedge. Walley walked Julia to the corner of Vale Road and the two chatted for a few minutes. They bid each other farewell and Walley walked along Vale Road towards his home. Julia walked across the road, and stepped across the tram track and through the hedge, and into the path of an oncoming car. Walley was traumatized by this tragic event for years, often blaming himself.

He remembered, "I heard a car being driven at high speed and braking very hard. I heard a real thump. I turned round and to my horror, saw Julia flying through the air before landing with a sickening thud in the road". If only he had said one more thing, asked her one more question, then she wouldn't have been killed Nigel told himself. If only they had talked for another twenty seconds. If only.

Menlove Avenue in 1958, where Julia crossed the hedge and tram track

Julia was struck and killed by a Standard Vanguard car driven by an off-duty constable, PC Eric Clague, who was a learner-driver. Clague later said: "Mrs. Lennon just ran straight out in front of me. I just couldn't avoid her. I was not speeding, I swear it. It was just one of those terrible things that happen". A post-mortem later revealed that she had died of massive brain injuries caused by skull fractures.

When the doorbell rang at 1, Blomfield Road, John Lennon opened the door of his mother's house and was confronted by a policeman standing on the step. John was virtually unapproachable in his sorrow. His half-sister Julia Baird said, "It was many years before he could bring himself to talk about that night. What John finally said was, 'An hour or so after it happened a copper came to the door to let us know about the accident. It was awful, like some dreadful film, when they ask you if you are the victim's son and all that. Well I was, and I can tell you it was absolutely the worst night of my entire life'".

John was unable to look at his mother's body when he was taken to view Julia at Sefton General Hospital. At the funeral he was inconsolable; so devastated that throughout the service he lay with his head on Aunt Mimi's lap, seemingly oblivious to everything.

An inquest into the accident a month later recorded a verdict of misadventure. The coroner said that Mrs. Lennon "did not appear to look either way before she walked into the road". But it was more complicated than that. Clague was an unaccompanied L-driver, and it was rumoured that he was drunk too. That meant the twenty-four-year old should not have been driving the car alone. He was later reprimanded by his superiors and suspended from duty for a short time. Soon afterwards he left the police department and took a job as a postman.

"Like everyone else I started reading in the papers about them (The Beatles) and they were never off the TV", Clague said years later. "I read that John Lennon's mother was dead and that he used to live in Menlove Avenue. I realized that it was his mum that I had killed. Everything came back to me and I felt absolutely terrible. It had the most awful effect on me. The Beatles were everywhere, especially in Liverpool, and I couldn't get away from them".

Reminders of the accident came back to Clague in an even more astonishing way. "My postman's round took in Forthlin Road, where Paul McCartney used to live. At the height of The Beatles' fame I used to deliver hundreds of cards and letters to the house. I remember struggling up the path with them all. But of course they just reminded me of John Lennon and his mother".

Clague was not identified for approximately forty years. That is until *Sunday Mirror* reporter Alan Rimmer tracked him down in 1998. He admitted to Rimmer that he had kept it a secret from his family for more than four decades. "It is something I have always kept deep inside", Clague said. "I haven't even told my wife and children. I suppose I will have to now". Clague also admitted it was an incident that had haunted him for years.

For the young John Lennon, the accidental death changed him from a happy-go-lucky lad to a hardened young man. A young cynic with a chip on his shoulder; the bitterness and anguish surfaced in his songs and changed the face of popular music.

29 AUGUST 1959
The Casbah Coffee Club opens
"Come Together"

Much has been written about The Cavern and its place in Beatles history. However, there is a large chunk of Beatles history that has been overlooked for many years. While The Cavern was entertaining jazz fans, The Casbah became the place to be.

Roag, Rory and Pete Best's book, *The Beatles—The True Beginnings,* opens with this quote:

I think it's a good idea to let people know about The Casbah. They know about The Cavern, they know about some of those things, but The Casbah was the place where all that started. We helped paint it and stuff. We looked upon it as our personal club. Sir Paul McCartney

If Paul says it, it must be true.

You may have heard about The Casbah as a club at which The Quarrymen played, but not much else.

Any place with all that history should be the focus for all Beatles fans across the world. When fans visit The Casbah they are surprised that such an important place has remained hidden for all these years. The whole story of The Casbah is amazing, yet I was stunned when I realised that I wasn't aware of it—and I live in Liverpool. I had to find out more.

Most fans will know of Hunter Davies' 'definitive book' *The Beatles— The Authorised Biography* (written in 1968) and will notice The Casbah hardly gets a mention. Even years later when he had the chance to correct things in his book *The Quarrymen*, The Casbah's only real mention is, "In August 1959, they had a bit of luck— The Casbah opened. It provided them with regular bookings and their next drummer, Pete Best".

If you have only read the early editions of Davies' book then you will have missed out. When Davies later updated his book, he rectified the original omission after meeting Pete and wisely inserted a chapter giving it its rightful place. So, as Mo would say, "Come with me to The Casbah".

Let's start at the beginning.

Our story begins in India, where Pete's dad John Best was stationed in the Army during World War II as a fitness instructor. John trained the Gurkhas in unarmed combat and the martial arts, plus he was a good boxer.

There he met Mona Shaw, whose father was a Major in the British Army and had been stationed there during the days of the Empire. She was blessed with an exotic olive complexion and was multi-

ABOVE: *The Quarrymen open The Casbah on 29 August 1959*
OPPOSITE: *The Fab Four pictured in 1963, just over four years after The Quarrymen had opened The Casbah Club*

talented. She had a beautiful singing voice and had attended dance school, and later taught many of The Casbah members to dance. They married in India, and Mona gave birth to Pete in 1941, and then to Rory in 1944.

After the end of the war, the Best family came to Liverpool on the last troop ship out of India, landing at Christmas 1945. John Best, Sr., Pete's grandfather, had helped set up the Boxing Board of Control and promoted many great fights at the Liverpool Stadium. After the young family returned from India, John Best, Pete's dad, took over the mantle of running the boxing fights at the stadium.

John and Mona lived in several different homes, but Mona never felt settled. She wanted a big home, similar to the one she had enjoyed in India and she spent a lot of time looking for a large, permanent residence in Liverpool.

I asked Rory Best what he remembered.

"I attended the school at the bottom of Haymans Green called Marlborough College, and on my way home I saw a house that was for sale in the road. I went home and told Mo and she went to look at it. She only needed one look, and she knew she wanted it".

Consider some facts about The Casbah:

- The Casbah was the first 'Beat' club in Liverpool—all the others (like The Cavern) were still jazz clubs.

- This is where George Harrison and Ken Brown re-formed The Quarrymen after not playing together for months.

- The Casbah was hand-decorated by John Lennon, Paul McCartney, George Harrison, Pete Best, Ken Brown and Cynthia Powell. It is still there with all of their handiwork untouched, including John's name inscribed on the wall.

- It was here that John and Paul convinced Stuart to join the band and spend his money on the bass guitar—under duress—as remembered by Paul McCartney and witnessed by Rory Best.

- It was home to all the major Merseybeat bands to emerge in the '60s, like The Beatles, The Searchers, Gerry and The Pacemakers, Rory Storm and the Hurricanes, Derry and the Seniors, Billy J Kramer, The Big Three, Farons Flamingos, The Undertakers, and so the list goes on. This is why the musicians called Casbah owner Mo Best the 'Mother of Merseybeat'.

- This was the first place they played outside Hamburg as 'The Beatles'—they dropped the 'Silver' for Hamburg.

- Mona Best was the first to describe The Beatles as 'Fabulous'.

- The Beatles had to regroup at The Casbah after being thrown out of Hamburg, and came back together to perform. Paul had found a job and the others were disillusioned. It was Mo who managed to get them back together again and let them play at The Casbah. She also took a more proactive role in getting them bookings.

- The Beatles warmed up at The Casbah before going to Hamburg and immediately after they returned. They rehearsed there, often in the lounge.

- It was Mo who helped them to get back into Germany after they had been deported by the authorities.

- It was Mo who arranged for their first proper rock 'n' roll gig at The Cavern after convincing owner Ray McFall to book The Beatles.

- Mo purchased and allowed The Beatles to use the equipment she had bought for The Casbah, and they stored everything there. If The Beatles were playing elsewhere, she closed The Casbah. Even after her son Pete was dismissed from the band, they continued to visit and see Mo, though they didn't see Pete. In fact, The Beatles still stored their equipment at The Casbah until the summer of 1963—which shows the true character of Mo.

- On 10 December 1961, The Beatles, consisting of John, Paul, George and Pete, signed their management contract with Brian Epstein at The Casbah. An amended version was signed shortly after at NEMS.

The original radiogram on which The Beatles listened to their first radio broadcast on 7 March 1962

- The first radio broadcast The Beatles made was in Manchester on 7 March 1962 for a show called '*Teenager's Turn (Here We Go)*'. Pre-recorded, all but George came to The Casbah the next day to listen to it on the radiogram in the lounge.

- Just as John, Paul and George as The Quarrymen opened the club; it was The Beatles—John, Paul, George and Pete—who closed it on 24 June 1962.

- The Casbah marked the birth of The Beatles when they opened it on 29 August 1959, and The Beatles' last live concert was at Candlestick Park, San Francisco, exactly seven years later—29 August 1966.

TOP: *Pete and Rory Best* ABOVE: *John Best (centre), father of Pete and Rory at Liverpool Stadium*
RIGHT: *8, Haymans Green, soon to become the home of The Casbah Coffee Club in its basement*

But John wasn't keen to buy the house, or for that matter, any of the others she had seen. The house was owned by the local Conservative Party Association. Mo enquired about the house but without her husband's financial support, she had to find a way of paying for it. She had no income and no savings. Most people would simply give up. But not Mo. Married women didn't go about buying houses in 1950s Britain. But Mo was not like most married women.

She took her valuable Indian jewellery to the pawnshop and then took the cash to the betting shop. She placed a bet on a horse that was entered in the 1954 Derby, one of the most prominent horse races in Britain. She liked the sound of a horse named Never Say

Die, which was ridden by a young unknown jockey called Lester Piggott (who went on to become one of Britain's best-known jockeys). The horse was not a favourite and won at the juicy odds of 33–1, and the winnings enabled Mo to realize her dream of owning this house.

How much she won was never discussed, but she was able to retrieve her jewellery and buy the house with the proceeds, leaving her needing only a small mortgage of about £1,000, after clearing some of her husband's debts. But this too was extraordinary. When she had inquired about purchasing the house, the estate agent had to check if a married woman could buy a house without her husband's help; they had asked when her husband was coming to sign the papers. After checking if it was legal, Mo bought the house in 1957 and became one of the first married women in Britain to take out a mortgage in her own name.

The house had fifteen rooms, including a large underground basement and needed a lot of work. Mo began to renovate and when Pete started inviting his friends round, she suggested that they play in the basement.

One night, Pete's friends had gathered at Haymans Green to watch a television show. When Mona saw the famous London club, the 2i's Coffee Bar, featured on the television, she was thunderstruck and after the show ended, she decided that she should open a coffee club for young people. Rory remembers: "Mo stood up and declared: 'I'm going to turn the basement into a little coffee club'. My father turned round and said, 'Over my dead body'. John Best just kept repeating the phrase 'You're crazy' while shaking his head. What happened next and who said what has not been recorded, but we know they started clearing the basement the next day to prepare for a new coffee club".

And what about the name, Rory? Why The Casbah?

"Mo had remembered seeing the film *Algiers* with Charles Boyer, and recalled the line, 'Come with me to The Casbah' and so decided to call it 'The Casbah Coffee Club'".

The house had initially been nicknamed 'Dracula's Castle' by Pete and Rory, and was eventually renamed 'Shangri-La', and it was about to be transformed into a historic club. On 29 August 1959, The Casbah Coffee Club opened. However, The Casbah was more than just a club.

The Best family claims that The Casbah was the true 'Birthplace of The Beatles'—with some justification. There is a big chunk of Beatles' history that is simply either glossed over or given lip service. Part of this was because the club closed in June 1962, just before Pete was unceremoniously dumped by The Beatles. When the early Beatles books were being written, Mona Best wasn't receptive to any interviews, considering the way her son had been treated. Because of this, writers didn't discuss The Casbah in any depth. Therefore, the books that followed don't consider The Casbah as having much of a part in the whole scheme of things. They just mention it as a venue.

Why is The Casbah Coffee Club so important to the history of The Beatles?

By the beginning of 1959 The Quarrymen had effectively disbanded, as their last performance was on 24 January at a belated Christmas party at Woolton Village Hall. Although John and Paul were still writing together, the performances had dried up. John had lost some of his focus after his mum, Julia, had been killed, and was relying more on drink than music for his therapy.

Wanting to play again, George Harrison began performing with the Les Stewart Quartet at a community hall called Lowlands, also in Haymans Green. Lowlands was just down the road from where The Casbah would soon open. Regulars included Ruth Morrison and Pete Best. This new band had been going well for a few months. But then Ruth Morrison, George's girlfriend and a friend of the

Lester Piggott, on Never Say Die, the horse on which Mona Best had a winning bet in 1954

Best family, told George and fellow band-member Ken Brown about the new club opening soon in the basement of 8, Haymans Green.

When brainstorming for a name for the opening night, John suggested that as they used to play as The Quarrymen, they might as well use that name again. And so, with this act, George re-formed The Quarrymen to take up the residency at The Casbah Coffee Club. Would they have re-formed otherwise? Who knows? It's an interesting question to ponder. John, Paul, George and Ken Brown became the new Quarrymen and the foundations of The Beatles were laid.

The Quarrymen were effectively reborn on 29 August 1959 when they opened The Casbah. By the time The Beatles closed the club in June 1962, they had played there at least forty-four times.

As there was still a lot of work to do to get the club ready for opening, they were all asked to help out: John and his girlfriend Cynthia Powell, Paul, George, Ken, Pete and Rory Best. The Casbah is still untouched after more than almost five decades and you can see the work carried out by them all: a club that was hand painted by John Lennon, Paul McCartney, George Harrison, Pete Best and Cynthia Powell—not a bad firm of interior decorators.

I remember the first time I went into The Casbah, accompanied by Roag Best who explained all the history. It took my breath away, and no matter how many times I go there I am still amazed.

stripes for each colour. The two ceilings are interesting: Paul's is structured and organized, just as John's was free and abstract, according to their character. This was above the little space, about 5 x 6 feet where the bands played—surely the smallest stage they ever performed on. There was only room for the singer to stand by the one microphone, while the others sat around him. A bit claustrophobic, but as Roag says, "From here to Shea Stadium". In a recent interview with Roag, Paul McCartney asked if his ceiling was still there and was amazed to learn that it was.

Very soon, the Best family realized that this little room was inadequate for the bands to play there. Now all the top bands in Liverpool wanted to play and, unlike The Quarrymen, they had drums, and needed more space.

Rory recalled the club had to be closed down for alterations.

"We had to move the stage area into the back room. The end of the basement had once been divided into little compartments, separated by walls. We knocked them down to open up the room to give them more space to play. You can see the small section of the basement where they initially played—Ken Brown's piano that they all played is still there—later turned into a piano bar by Neil Aspinall, the former head of Apple. I prefer it as a bar", Rory says, with a grin on his face.

They also have a guitar played by all of The Beatles during rehearsals.

Rory remembers what it was like when The Casbah was filled to capacity. "It was so packed that the crowd would be almost face to face with the musicians—literally. The band would be pressed up against the wall, with a microphone in front of them and the crowd a matter of inches away.

"Above the band area is a hole in the ceiling where Rory Storm jumped too high and put his head through it, which wasn't unusual for Rory, 'Mr. Showmanship'. We decided to preserve it for posterity. Common sense prevailed and Mo erected a barrier in the form of iron railings to give the bands a little bit of space. On the wall behind the band area, there is a massive spider's web that Mo and Pete painted, but I don't know why, because Mo hated spiders".

You can even go into the little coffee bar. "This was my domain where I could not only serve the Coke and coffee, but chat up all of the beautiful girls", recalls Rory with a glint in his eye. "What a job—I had to be forced into it of course".

"John, Paul, George, Stuart, Pete and Ken all combined to paint the stars on the ceiling in the coffee bar. There are about 200 stars on the ceiling, all individually created and worth a fortune. This is one expensive ceiling; just don't ask me who painted which star".

Also in the coffee bar just above the fireplace, Cynthia painted a silhouette based on the poster designed by Mike McCartney. He had adapted a photo of The Silver Beatles taken at the audition to support Liverpool-born singer Billy Fury, who was seen as Britain's answer to Elvis. Cynthia painted him in silver as their very own 'silver Beatle'.

Mo never missed an opportunity to light a fire no matter what the weather. Rory complained about the heat, but Mo just responded that they would buy more Coke.

In the corner is a double-hinged American refrigerator, which opens to either side. "In the 1950s, not many people had a fridge, let alone a big fridge like this", Rory says, "but we needed it, because of course we could only sell Coca-Cola or coffee; no alcohol was permitted. The Casbah became the biggest retailer of Coke in the whole North-West of England, with deliveries every day".

Rory Best, with a copy of the Best brother's book, "The Beatles—The True Beginnings"

What can you see in The Casbah?

The first room you enter is the Aztec Room, painted by John. Rory remembers what happened. "Originally, John painted his now famous three-legged pot-bellied caricatures, but when Mo saw what he'd done she disliked it and told him to change it. John then painted over them with green gloss paint—he should have used matt emulsion but, not wearing his glasses, he used the wrong paint. Mo also hated the colour green, so she told him to get rid of it. He then produced something with a more Aztec feel, which is what Mo wanted.

"To leave his mark", Rory said, "Lennon started to engrave his name into the wooded wall panelling and got as far as 'John' before Mo caught him and stopped him. She slapped him across the back of the head and his glasses fell off. He then trod on his glasses and so had to borrow Mo's mother's glasses to finish the job—we still possess both pairs of glasses. The scratched name is still there, standing out in Mo's beautiful new woodwork".

This room became the area for dancing if you could find any space to move. You then go through the low archway and turn right. Rory continues: "Not to be outdone, Paul painted a rainbow ceiling, with

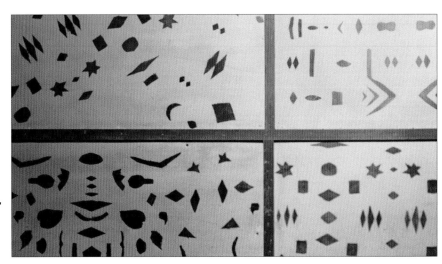

LEFT: *Performing with The Quarrymen, Paul McCartney with Cynthia Powell (seated), next to John in the rainbow room at The Casbah, 1959*
RIGHT: *John's hand-painted 'Aztec' ceiling*

One night, Rory witnessed Stuart Sutcliffe's entry into the group. Sitting in the corner of this coffee bar, up against the wall, was Stuart. Pinning him in were Paul McCartney and John Lennon, trying to convince Stuart to spend his art money on a bass guitar. Stuart wasn't keen on the idea as he wanted to buy art supplies. Paul McCartney remembered, "We were sitting with a cup of coffee; John, Stuart and I, the two of us trying to persuade Stuart that he should get this bass, and he said, 'No, this is a painting prize. I'm supposed to get canvases'. That was where we talked him into it, at The Casbah".

"Stuart was not keen. The club was closed and I was clearing up", says Rory, "waiting to go up to the party that was starting upstairs. These parties were the stuff of legends and everyone wanted to be there, though not everyone was allowed in. I saw what was happening, and that Stu was explaining that he and his dad were adamant he had to buy paints, brushes and canvases". Exasperated, Rory finally took action. "I went over to him and said, 'For God's sake, Stu, just buy the guitar and let's get up to the party'. And so he said, 'okay' and that was it".

The original Casbah entrance had a narrow corridor-like passage with a giant dragon painted on the wall by Mo. Being so heavily influenced by Eastern philosophy, she believed that a dragon facing the door would bring good luck and ward off evil spirits.

Mo also felt they needed a cloakroom. With no space downstairs, they had to ship the coats upstairs to the living room. Rory starts to laugh as he tells what happened. "One day, we heard this scream from Ken Brown and ran out of the coffee bar to see that he had put his legs through the wooden stairs and was left dangling. We had to call in Frank Garner, our trusty bouncer, who later set about building the brick staircase thats now there. He amazed everyone by taking the bricks and snapping them in two with his bare hands—he was a master of karate. He then passed the half-bricks to his son, who snapped them in half again with his hand. A 'handy' man to have around".

Stepping into The Casbah now is like taking a step back in time. Remarkably, as you pass through the door, you can still feel the atmosphere of those early days of rock 'n' roll. How great it must have been to stand there and listen to the music. Approximately 150 to 200 people crammed into this small basement. Mona, an astute businesswoman, moved her till from the door of the basement to the front gate, allowing more people to pay their entrance fee as they came in. Unless you were early, you had to be content with staying outside in the garden to listen.

Membership soon expanded to more than 3,000 young people. The Casbah wasn't advertised but word spread quickly and hundreds turned up at the club before it was opened so that they could join. After all, there wasn't another one in Liverpool—The Cavern, like most other clubs, was still a jazz club.

Mona Best was influenced by the mysticism of the East, years before The Beatles were. Mona probably influenced them all with her beliefs in karma and Feng Shui. They all looked up to Mo and respected her. Did they remember these discussions when they went to India to meet the Maharishi Mahesh Yogi? Was it all so new an experience or had Mo started their minds thinking years before? When they had returned from India after their time with the Maharishi, they all had something for Mo. George in particular bought her many gifts, especially bracelets and necklaces.

Very much in demand at The Casbah were the after-hours parties held upstairs, which only the chosen few were allowed to attend. If you had an invitation you were indeed privileged. This was where everyone wanted to be and where Mo held court, with her admiring young friends captivated by this beautiful, olive-skinned lady with an air of mystery. Here you can picture Mo talking about her life growing up in India and about her beliefs. "She was so different. She was strict, but I was one of her favourites, so I made it upstairs to those parties", said Casbah member John Miller. Gerry Marsden, from Gerry and The Pacemakers, recalls how many of them felt about Mo. "She was like our mum", Marsden recalled.

Considering West Derby is a suburb on the outskirts of Liverpool and the public transport would be limited, it says so much for Mona Best's ability to make a success of this new kind of club. On paper everything was against her and none more so than location. Add to this the fact that they never advertised and it was all down to word of mouth, which makes the story more remarkable.

ABOVE: *The 'Spider Room' where the bands performed*
RIGHT: *The 'Rainbow Room' where Paul painted the ceiling above The Casbah's first stage area*

At first, The Casbah was open three times a week, but it soon proved to be so successful, that it changed to every night. There was initially just one band night. Other nights teens listened to the jukebox. It was a place to listen to music and chat and dance with kids your own age.

The Quarrymen opened The Casbah as a four-piece guitar group, with John, Paul, George and Ken. John began by declaring: "Hi everyone, welcome to The Casbah. We're The Quarrymen and we are going to play you some rock 'n' roll". They did so well that on 18 September 1959, the local newspaper, *The West Derby Reporter*, covered the story in an article entitled: 'Dance Club in House Cellar'.

Four young men making a name for themselves in the world of skiffle and 'pop' music are The Quarrymen, who played for many teenagers to dance at the opening of West Derby's 'Kasbah' (sic) Club on Saturday evening. The club where teenagers can meet their friends, dance and drink coffee has been opened in the cellars of a house in Haymans Green, West Derby. The Quarrymen, complete with a varied repertoire and their electric guitars, will play at the club each Saturday in the future.

They are John Lennon, 251, Menlove Avenue, Woolton; Paul McCartney, 20, Forthlin Road, Allerton; George Harrison, 25, Upton Green, Speke; and Kenny Brown, 148, Storrington Avenue, Norris Green.

The Quarrymen headlined The Casbah for several weeks, before an unfortunate turn of events. Ken Brown had stomach cramps and couldn't play one evening. The other three agreed to play without him, and so Mona asked Ken to take the money on the door. At the end of the night, Mona came with the £3 fee to share out—four ways.

John led the argument that as Ken hadn't played, the fee should be split between the three that did play: him, Paul and George. Mo refused, stating they should get paid as a group even though Ken couldn't play that night. John didn't agree, and threatened to never play The Casbah again. Mo didn't back down. "Right, that's it then", said John and led the walkout.

They left, never to play there again as The Quarrymen. They were lucky Mona let John, Paul and George return since it was the best place to see live music. They were still members, as were their girlfriends Cynthia, Dot Rhone and Ruth Morrison.

John had regained his thirst for performing and, while not appearing at The Casbah, John, Paul and George spent some time playing as Johnny and the Moondogs. It was not long before Stuart was added—he'd bought his guitar—and they became The Beatals. When the opportunity to play in Hamburg arose, the group needed a drummer. Where should they go? Well, to The Casbah, as they had been watching Ken Brown's new group, coincidentally called The Black Jacks, though not connected to Lennon's first group, who had a drummer called Pete Best.

Pete was always tapping a rhythm on something as a boy, whether it was on a table or bottles, or a set of bongo drums. Pete with his new complete drum kit was the obvious choice and he was quickly enlisted by the group.

ABOVE LEFT: *Paul McCartney at The Casbah in 1962* ABOVE CENTRE, TOP: *The Silver Beatle that Cynthia painted*
ABOVE CENTRE, BOTTOM: *Stars on the coffee bar ceiling, painted by John, Paul, George, Ken, Stuart and Pete* ABOVE RIGHT: *Rory Best demonstrating where John and Paul cornered Stuart and persuaded him to buy a bass guitar to join the group* OPPOSITE PAGE: *The dragon, painted by Mona and Pete, by the entrance of the club*

After Allan Williams had gone to The Casbah to watch Pete, Paul approached Mo and then spoke to Pete, who checked with the other members of The Black Jacks. They said they were happy to let Pete join The Beatles. Pete recalls that when Paul spoke to him, he was asked to join The Beatles—not The Silver Beatles. They had already decided to change their name before they left for Hamburg. With the addition of Stuart Sutcliffe, and now Pete Best, the renamed Beatles left Liverpool for Hamburg in August 1960.

When they returned home that Christmas, dishevelled and distraught, it was Mo who kept them together and was partly responsible for stopping The Beatles from falling apart. Hamburg had been a disaster. George had been deported for being under eighteen and breaking the curfew. Pete and Paul had been arrested for allegedly trying to burn the Bambi Kino down and were returned to Liverpool. Back in Liverpool, they didn't contact each other. The future looked bleak. Before going to Hamburg, The Silver Beatles had a poor reputation, so there were no bookings back in Liverpool. Between 21 November and 10 December, The Beatles thought seriously about giving it all up. John admitted to his girlfriend Cynthia, as far as he knew, it was "the end of the road for The Beatles".

Paul's dad, Jim, had opposed Hamburg in the first place. He sent his son to the labour exchange to get a job. Paul found work with the Speedy Prompt delivery service around the docks, and then with Massey & Coggins engineering firm, where he was winding armature coils. Paul admitted that he wasn't sure if he wanted to make another go of The Beatles.

Even George thought they were about to split up. Just before they had left for Hamburg, George had broken the neck on his guitar and had to return it to be repaired. He asked if he could borrow Rory's guitar to tide him over and on his return, tried to sell it to another band member for £30. Thankfully, George was turned down.

"He had this great Futurama guitar which, when he opened it upstairs, was like looking at the Holy Grail", Rory recalled. "This was the closest you could get to the American Fenders. I liked it so much that I went out the next day and bought one. I couldn't play it but I had to have one. After George broke the neck on his, he came to me and said, 'Can I borrow your guitar, Rory?' so I said, 'Okay, as long as you teach me to play it'. He said okay, and eighteen months later I got it back, battered. And he didn't teach me to play either".

Most of their gear had remained in Hamburg, so Pete and Mo had to contact Peter Eckhorn the Hamburg club owner, to make arrangements the return of their drums and guitars. Mo persuaded The Beatles to return and when they did walk in that December night, The Casbah members thought it was a con. Mo had put up signs proclaiming 'The Fabulous Beatles, direct from Hamburg' and they all expected a German band. All they saw were John, Paul and George of the Quarrymen and Chas and Pete of The Black Jacks. But here they were, the newly christened Beatles, the best rock 'n' roll band they'd ever seen. For the Christmas gigs, the line-up included Chas Newby, a friend of Pete's who had been in The Black Jacks with him and Ken. Chas played the bass guitar for four gigs over that Christmas—two at The Casbah, one at The Grosvenor Ballroom, and the famous one at Litherland Town Hall. He was drafted in as Stuart had stayed in Hamburg with Astrid. Stuart, however, did play at The Casbah in January 1961 on a brief visit home.

Most people will agree that the concert at Litherland Town Hall on 27 December 1960 was the defining moment in the birth of the new phenomenon known as Beatlemania.

ABOVE: *John, George and Paul perform at The Casbah, 1962*

TOP: *Rory Best with the medals that John borrowed for the Sgt. Pepper album cover*
ABOVE: *Rory's Futurama guitar borrowed by George Harrison*

But that first night at The Casbah was a foretaste of what was to come just a few days later. Not much was expected of them. Rory Best was so unimpressed with The Beatles that after the first band, Gene Day and the Jango Beats appeared, he went with them to the pub and didn't wait to see them. I wanted to know why?

"I had been to the Wyvern with Pete for the audition before Hamburg, and they were alright, but not great. When they left Liverpool, The Silver Beatles had a poor reputation. So I went to the pub with the Jango Beats. They went down in their gold lamé suits, and Georgie Spruce—aka Gene Day—was wearing his pink suit. A girl came in shouting at us to come and see the group who were playing at The Casbah: they were brilliant. I thought, it's only our Pete and The Beatles, but they left their pints and went running back. I walked behind them. When I joined them there I couldn't believe how good they were. All I could hear was Pete's bass drum going 'boom, boom, boom' and bouncing off the walls.

"They were superb, and everyone was going wild. I couldn't believe the difference. They went out as a loose unit who could play some average rock 'n' roll, but when they came back from Hamburg they were a tight, fantastic band. No one had heard anything like them before, they just blew everyone away. And they looked so good in their black leather, because all the other bands were doing this synchronized walking up and down with their guitars like the Shadows did, dressed in their pink and gold suits. The Beatles just stood there, chewing gum, doing their own thing and playing their own arrangements of the songs, unlike the other bands who just covered the records as they sounded on vinyl".

That night The Casbah witnessed what was going to be revealed just a few days later when the rest of Liverpool heard about this new rock 'n' roll sensation. This alone makes The Casbah Coffee Club, in my humble opinion, of more significance than The Cavern. The Cavern became famous because it was the club they played the most, but more importantly, the club they were playing when they were discovered by Brian Epstein, who would make them world-famous.

As John Lennon said: "The Cavern didn't make The Beatles, The Beatles made The Cavern". By the time The Beatles were a worldwide phenomenon, The Casbah had closed down and Pete Best had been sacked. The Cavern was grateful for the publicity; The Casbah and Mona Best didn't want to know about The Beatles after what had happened to Pete. She wouldn't speak about it for years.

Ian Edwards, from Ian and the Zodiacs, remembers The Casbah well.

"You have to remember that in those days nobody had done The Casbah, nobody knew about clubs below street level. Everybody was doing dance halls like Litherland, St. Luke's, and all of a sudden you're in this place where the atmosphere's completely different and you're all on top of one another".

The Casbah was their musical home, not just a venue. However, by the middle of 1962, The Beatles were managed by Epstein and were playing further afield. Mo's mum died in early 1962, and she was due to give birth to her new baby boy, Roag, who appeared in July 1962 after Mo had begun a relationship with The Beatles' roadie Neil Aspinall. And so Mo took the decision to close the club. The Beatles performed on the last night on 24 June 1962. Two months later, Pete was back without the band, being sacked in August 1962.

Strangely enough, The Beatles did keep in touch with Mo, even after they had dismissed Pete and had become world-famous. They sent her presents from all over the world. John's way of saying thank you was to borrow Mo's dad's medals and he wore them on the cover of *Sgt. Pepper's Lonely Hearts Club Band*. When he returned the medals, he gave Mo the trophy that was also on the album cover.

When asked about Mo, Paul McCartney said, "Some grown-ups are different. Mo was one of them. John's mum Julia was another. You could go to Mo's place late at night when you'd finished a gig. She always understood what kids were going through".

So is The Casbah the 'Birthplace of The Beatles'? John McNally of The Searchers certainly believes so.

"The kudos of having The Beatles there, The Beatles rehearsal room, The Beatles' 'little venue' meant it became the embryo of sixties music. Because The Beatles started there and wherever something begins is the source", McNally said.

To underline its importance to music history, The Casbah Coffee Club was awarded English Heritage Grade 2 listed status, and so is now protected for future generations.

So when you are in Liverpool, visit The Casbah, the true 'Birthplace of The Beatles'.

ABOVE: *John Lennon at The Casbah in April 1962*

29 AUGUST 1959
Ken Brown joins The Quarrymen

"Don't Pass Me By"

Ken Brown's name occasionally pops up in Beatles history, but is often overlooked. He had an important role in the group and I spoke to him about his story.

Ken came into the picture in early 1959 when his band, the Les Stewart Quartet, was offered the residency at the soon-to-be opened Casbah Coffee Club. He had heard about the new club through his fellow band member George Harrison's girlfriend, Ruth Morrison. So Ruth took George and Ken along to meet Mrs. Best, though he was soon calling her Mo like everyone else.

"We hit it off straight away", recalls Ken, of his first meeting with a lady for whom he still holds great affection. "Mo was very warm and friendly, and took everyone as they were. She was shrewd, mind you, and she could read people well. Unlike the other mothers, she was so full of enthusiasm and had the energy of a teenager. I was so drawn in with the excitement that I would go to work, come home and go to The Casbah, and then work there until 3 a.m., when I'd slip home, go to bed, get up and do it all again. It was a special place".

This desire to be there and help get the club ready caused friction in the band. The Les Stewart Quartet had played at Lowlands at the bottom of Haymans Green, but was now without any gigs. They would still meet once a week or so to rehearse at Les' place, but there were no prospects on the horizon.

"I thought that if we worked with Mo to get the residency I was doing well for the group. So I worked hard there helping as much as I could so that our band would have a regular place to play, because there were so few opportunities to have a residency anywhere. Anyway, I started missing rehearsals because I was spending time at The Casbah getting it ready for the opening night. So one night at Les' place he tells us that we weren't going to play at The Casbah. In fact, Les was quiet, and it was his girlfriend Sheila who spoke up, telling me how I'd missed rehearsals and wasn't committed to the band. I thought, hang on, I'm doing this for the band. I said to Sheila, 'Why don't you let Les speak for himself?' But he didn't. She was adamant, so that was it. I said I'd very clearly promised Mrs. Best that if she would give us the residency, I would bring the band and I would help in whatever way I could. I couldn't go back on that. I promised I wouldn't let her down.

"They wouldn't change their minds, so I said, 'Right, I'm going, who's coming with me?' George stood up and out we went and left the group".

OPPOSITE: *Ken Brown, who, with George Harrison, re-formed The Quarrymen in 1959*
ABOVE: *Mona Best*

This was all a few weeks before the club was due to open, and so Ken was left with a dilemma.

"I had promised to have a band for the opening night, and here I was with only George. It's a start but we needed to do something. It wasn't unusual then to have a group and no drummer, so that was all right. It was then that George told me about his two friends who he had played with before, and gave them a ring. That, of course, was John Lennon and Paul McCartney. I went to see Mo and told her what had happened and that George had a couple of friends who could help us out. So they came down and we had a few practises in The Casbah to be ready to open in a couple of week's time".

On 29 August 1959, George, Ken, John and Paul opened the club as The Quarrymen.

"By that time", says Ken, "I was living and breathing The Casbah. Mo just had this way of attracting you in and making you feel welcome there, that this was a special place to be. Of course, we had no idea how important it would become, but it didn't matter. It was our personal club and it holds so many good memories".

The Quarrymen played for the next few weeks until one night when Ken wasn't well and couldn't play. He had stomach cramps and was desperate to play, but obviously couldn't in his state. John, Paul and George offered to play as a threesome, and did. Mo put Ken in charge of collecting the money. At the end of the night a row broke out over money. Mo would hand out the fee to them, splitting the £3 evenly: fifteen shillings (75 pence) each. After Mo had given John, Paul and George their fifteen shillings, they asked for Ken's share of the money, which they didn't get from Mo. She was adamant that

they were a group and were paid as a group. Mo wouldn't give them Ken's money. The others, led by John, protested.

"The first I knew was when George came up to me and told me what the others had told Mo", said Ken. "As far as I was concerned, if I didn't play, I didn't get paid. But then I wasn't the boss, Mo was, and so whatever she had decided was the most important. And so I told George what I thought and that they should speak to Mo about it. It was up to her. Anyway, George went back and there was a row with Mo, and they picked up their stuff and left. I didn't know what had happened as I was upstairs and didn't even know they'd left. I only found out later. They never said anything more to me".

"So there I was again, this time on my own. I thought, start again and get a group together. I asked Rory (Best), because he had a great personality and would have been ideal, but he said no. I then spoke to Pete and suggested we form a group—me on guitar and him on drums. 'Great,' he says, 'but I haven't got any drums'. So we saw Mo and she bought Pete his set of drums. We then added Pete's friends Chas Newby and Bill Barlow and The Black Jacks were formed".

John, Paul and George came back to the club after a few months, with Stuart Sutcliffe in tow. They approached Pete about joining them to go to Hamburg. Ken saw the others but they never broached the subject of the falling out or the money; they had all moved on.

"One day, Pete came to us and said he had this offer to go to Hamburg, but he didn't want to let us down. We said go, this is a once in a lifetime chance and you have to take it. You could tell they were going places. John and Paul were such great front men, they were all fired up and determined to succeed. They were showmen. We told him not to turn down this chance, and he didn't".

Ken's family was in the process of moving to Enfield in Middlesex, where all of Ken's family resided. His dad had gone ahead and found a house to live in, and so Ken, his brother and his mother all left Liverpool to join his dad. "I didn't want to go, but back then you moved with your parents, so I had no choice, but I was never happy there. I asked to delay the move until at least I had the chance to say goodbye to Pete and my friends. And so I only saw The Beatles once, their first gig back from Hamburg at The Casbah with Pete on drums and Chas on bass guitar, and then I left".

Ken obviously has much affection for Mo to this day. "Mo was forty years ahead of her time. Her boys had far more freedom than us. They had freedom of speech and actions but they never abused it or caused her any embarrassment. We all had such respect for her. She was a wonderful woman".

Ken came back to The Casbah for an important day in August 1999 which was the fortieth anniversary of its opening. "It was amazing that day. There were two recollections that stick in my mind. Firstly, the weather. It rained all the week before, and yet on the day it was non-stop sunshine, and a clear, bright moon at night. After that it returned to bad weather again. I also remember the little rose plant that stood near the front door of the house in a plant pot. It didn't grow well, but that day, the single bud opened and flowered. Now I'm not into superstitions but I think that was Mo looking down on us then".

Ken Brown's role was brief, but important. What if he hadn't possessed those strong principles and walked out on the Les Stewart Quartet? What if, after leaving The Quarrymen, he had decided to quit music and not form The Black Jacks, encouraging Pete to get drums? Or getting him to take the gig with The Beatles in Hamburg? Fate is a strange, strange thing. Sadly, Ken died suddenly in June 2010.

JANUARY 1960
Stuart Sutcliffe joins The College Band
"Love Me Tender"

Stuart Ferguson Victor Sutcliffe was vital to The Beatles for his influence on John Lennon and how he envisioned art. Even though he died at the age of twenty-one, the impact he had on the group was lasting.

Sutcliffe was born on 23 June 1940. His parents were Charles and Martha (known as Millie) Sutcliffe—he was a seaman and she a teacher. Millie was Charles' second wife, his first also being called Martha. Having briefly moved to England, they returned to Edinburgh, Scotland, for Stuart's birth. Charles worked in the Cammell Laird shipyard on the Mersey, which brought them to Liverpool. Stuart had two younger sisters: Joyce and Pauline.

Homes
When Stuart's family first moved to Liverpool from Edinburgh, they set up home at 17, Sedberg Grove (Huyton), where Stuart's sister Pauline was born in 1944. The Sutcliffes then moved to 43, St. Anne's Road (Huyton) in 1950. The family moved again to 22, Sandiway (Huyton) in 1953.

In 1956 when he enrolled at Liverpool Art College, Stuart's first flat was at 83, Canning Street (Liverpool), not far from the college. It was a flat he shared with friend Rod Murray. However, he was back home by the summer of 1957. Stuart decided again to get his own flat for his second year at Liverpool Art College, and he rented a small attic flat at 12, Canning Street (Liverpool).

He then moved into a flat at 9, Percy Street (Liverpool) with his friend Rod. Stuart and Rod then moved to Gambier Terrace (Liverpool), a building with a Georgian facade in the shadow of the Anglican Cathedral. John Lennon also lived there for a spell.

The Sutcliffe family moved from Huyton to 53, Ullet Road (Wavertree) on the edge of Sefton Park. It was to here that Stuart returned after being beaten up after a gig at Lathom Hall, Seaforth, in North Liverpool. The family then moved to 37, Aigburth Drive, (Aigburth), on the other side of Sefton Park.

Education
For his schooling, Stuart attended Parkview Primary School (Huyton) from 1946 to 1950 before moving on to Prescot Grammar School (Huyton) from 1950 to 1956. He left the grammar school with five 'O' levels, including art, for a place at the Liverpool Art College (Liverpool) where he met John Lennon in 1957.

Stuart's mother, Millie, was an active member of the Labour Party, taking the local Huyton district constituency minutes and successfully helping Huyton Member of Parliament (MP) Harold Wilson. After Millie had addressed the envelopes for the Labour Party, Stuart and a few neighbours delivered them. Later, Harold Wilson was the Prime Minister who recommended the M.B.E.s for The Beatles.

Religion
Stuart's dad was Protestant (Church of Scotland) and his mother was Catholic—a classic case of a "religious mixed marriage". To make matters worse, Charles was a divorced Protestant. Millie's parents were opposed to the union on both grounds. Charles and Millie had a civil ceremony and shortly after, Charles was shunned by the community, causing him to lose his job. Charles and Millie moved away from Scotland altogether.

Stuart sang weekly in the Protestant choir at St. Gabriel's in Huyton. He often led the procession in the church while carrying the cross.

After his untimely death at the age of twenty-one, he was buried in the Anglican cemetery in Huyton, Liverpool, where his father is also buried. When Millie died in 1983, Stuart's sisters secretly took her ashes and scattered them over Stuart's grave because as a Catholic, Millie couldn't be buried in the Anglican graveyard.

Musical Influences
Stuart took piano lessons when he was a child, and owned a Spanish guitar, a gift from his father, from the age of fourteen. Despite what has been written about him in the past, Stuart did have a musical background. His sister Pauline said, "He was in love with rock 'n' roll and loved being on stage. His stage presence was excellent and the female fans loved his 'James Dean' look".

The Beatles—John, George, Pete, Paul and Stuart—at the Indra Club, Hamburg, 1960

Stuart joined The College Band, before suggesting the name "Beetles" for the group.

Stuart was a very competent bassist and a lot better than he has been given credit for. He didn't need to know many chords to play most of the songs. He wrote down a list of their usual set which is reproduced as it was written, complete with spelling mistakes.

Rock 'n' roll set list from Stuart's notebook, 1960

Johnny B. Goode	Dance in the Streets
Gone, Gone, Gone	Upon Lazy River
Ain't She Sweet	Somebody help me
Halleluia (sic)	Home
Carol	Winston's Walk
Sweet Little Sixteen	Cats Walk
Milk Cow Blues	Rock–a–chicka
Move Over	Bebopalula (sic)
True Love	What'd I Say
Blue Suede Shoes	Move on down the Line
Honey Don't	I Don't Care (If The Sun)
Lend me your Comb	Whole Lotta Shakin'

Stuart joined John, Paul and George to form the Beatals after being coaxed and harassed by John and Paul at The Casbah. He had just had a painting exhibited at the Walker Art Gallery, sponsored by John Moores, one of the founders of Littlewoods Pools. The piece he submitted was in two parts, but the second was never taken to the gallery. It was purchased by John Moores and with this money, John and Paul convinced Stuart to buy a bass guitar. He also painted the cellars of Allan Williams' Jacaranda Club—only one small piece of the original remains as the rest fell off the wall or was removed because of the dampness.

On 27 March 1960, Stuart, in his new role as "manager", contacted as many venues as possible to arrange gigs for the group. This is a letter where he crosses out the start of Quarrymen and replaces it with "Beatals", the first time the name is mentioned.

Dear Sir,

As it is your policy to present entertainment to the habitués of your establishment, I would like to draw your attention to ~~a band to the Quar~~ "Beatals" This is a promising group of young musicians who play ~~all~~ music for all tastes, preferably rock and roll. They have won many competitions, including a Carroll Levis and auditions for A.T.V. Unfortunately pedagogical activities have ~~forced~~ hindered them from devoting ~~full~~ themselves full time to the world of entertainment.

~~Hope you find time~~ If necessary the ~~group will give you an~~ group is prepared for an audition. I hope you will be able to engage them.

Yours sincerely,
Stu Sutcliffe (Manager)

When Stuart stayed in Germany after the others were deported, George wrote to him telling him how crummy it would be without him in the band. Other bands let Stuart play with them when the others returned to Liverpool. Pete Best was happy with Stu because drummers work closely with the bass player to provide the rhythm. These were not the actions of a band that wanted to get rid of their bassist; a musician who stood with his back to the audience, a myth perpetuated to this day.

Stuart Sutcliffe wrote to his mother from Hamburg on 2 December 1960:

Dear Mum,

Just recently I have found the most wonderful friends, the most beautiful looking trio I have ever seen. I was completely captivated by their charm. The girl thought that I was the most handsome of the lot. Here was I, feeling the most insipid working member of the group, being told how much superior I looked—this alongside the great Romeo John Lennon and his two stalwarts Paul and George, The Casanovas of Hamburg. We have improved a thousand fold since our arrival and Allan Williams, who is here at the moment, tells us that there is no band in Liverpool to touch us.

We finished the Kaiserkeller last week. The police intervened because we had no work permits. Paul and Peter the drummer were deported yesterday and sent in handcuffs to the airport. I was innocent this time, accused of arson—that is, setting fire to the Kino where we sleep. I arrive at the club and am informed that the whole of the Hamburg police are looking for me. The rest of the band are already locked up, so smiling on the arm of Astrid, I proceed to give myself up. At this time, I'm not aware of the charges. All of my belongings, including my spectacles, are taken away and I'm led to a cell, where, without food or drink I sat for six hours on a very wooden bench, and the door shut very tight. I signed a confession in Deutsch that I knew nothing about a fire, and they let me go. The next day Paul and Pete were deported and sent home by plane, John and I were without money and job.

The police had forbidden us to work, as already we were liable to deportation for working there months in the country illegally. The next day, John went home. I stay till January at Astrid's house. At the moment she's washing all my muck and filth collected over the last few months. God I love her so much. One thing I'm sure about since I've been here, I hate brutality. There is so much in this area. Last night I heard that John and Paul have gone to Paris to play together—in other words, the band has broken up. It sounds mad to me: I don't believe it.

Stuart

Many historians have Stuart leaving The Beatles to pursue his art. But I am not so sure that is the entire truth.

My theory is that if you look at the picture of The Beatles in Hamburg, where is Paul? With his back to the audience on the piano. Paul's role in The Beatles at the time was "Jack-of-all-trades", master of none. He was the most talented musician, but his flexibility and talent nearly cost him his role in the band. Look at the rest of the band: a definite role for everyone that couldn't change. John was rhythm guitar and vocal. Pete was on drums. George was lead guitar and vocals. Stuart was bass. It's quite likely that none of those were going to do another job within the group. But Paul was a guitarist and singer stuck on piano. After all, they didn't need three guitars in the line-up. Out of the group, Stuart's role was the most attainable to him. Paul wasn't a good enough drummer to replace Pete. He wasn't a good enough lead guitarist to replace George. John was rhythm guitar and leader and wasn't going to change.

Paul viewed Stuart as the weakest link. He knew Stu wasn't a great bass player but was good enough for what they were doing at the time. So, did Paul see the bass guitar as his salvation as far as the band was concerned? He has admitted in the past that he was jealous of Stuart because he and John were so close. Paul went on to reinvent the role of the bass guitar within a band and was inventive with his playing, but did this almost not happen? Would Paul have left the group? I doubt it because of his talent, and the partnership that he and John were forging.

When The Beatles returned to Liverpool minus Stuart, guitarist Chas Newby sat in with The Beatles for four gigs over the Christmas period in 1960 as bass player. Paul stood on stage with a borrowed guitar, which wasn't plugged in.

Before Stuart arrived back in Liverpool, Paul had successfully taken up bass and was making a go of it. There was talk of asking Stuart to leave as they were doing so well without him but John wouldn't hear of it. Stuart then rejoined the group, but it wasn't long before Paul sensed the bass guitar job could be his. He harangued Stuart to the point where Stuart quit to concentrate on his art. With Stuart's departure Paul was finally installed as The Beatles' permanent bass player. By the time of The Beatles' second visit to Hamburg, Stuart had enrolled at the Hamburg State School of Art. For two years he studied in Eduardo Paolozzi's Art Master Class.

Stuart died in Hamburg on 10 April 1962 from a cerebral bleed in his brain. His funeral was at his home church of St. Gabriel (Huyton), where he had grown up. He was buried in Huyton Parish Cemetery (Huyton).

What did The Beatles think about Stuart?

"I looked up to Stu, I depended on him to tell me the truth. Stu would tell me if something was good, and I'd believe him". — John Lennon

"I felt I knew Stuart because hardly a day went by that John did not speak about him". — Yoko Ono

"He (Stuart) was a major attraction because of the James Dean thing, the dark, moody thing. I think a lot of people liked that". — Paul McCartney

"Stu was more than just the bass player—he was like our art director". — George Harrison

Stuart's sister Pauline has done so much to preserve the memory and talent of her brother, who could so easily have become just another discarded musician on the way to the fame and fortune that awaited The Beatles.

"It's an endless surprise and joy that interest in Stuart, as a painter of real talent is now more important than him having been an early Beatle. Not that this was insignificant— indeed once upon a time, that mattered more. It's also a constant revelation that each new generation of admirers of Stuart and his talents is now focused on some of the myths that have held fast for so long; examining them, and if found to be false, dispelling them.

"The technological age has made it possible to refine the search for a more coherent view or picture to emerge and of course provide universal access to Stuart's art, poetry, lyrics and essays, thus bringing with it more and more admirers".

Stuart, unfortunately, has suffered the same fate of those who have departed this earth too soon—he is appreciated more in death than he ever was in life.

ABOVE: *Klaus Voormann, Astrid Kirchherr and Stuart Sutcliffe in Hamburg, 1961*
BELOW: *Stuart, Paul on piano, George, Pete and John at the Indra Club, Hamburg in 1960*
OPPOSITE: *Stuart's painting from the John Moores exhibition in Liverpool, 1959*

5 MAY 1960
Allan Williams becomes The Silver Beatles' Manager
"The Fool On The Hill"

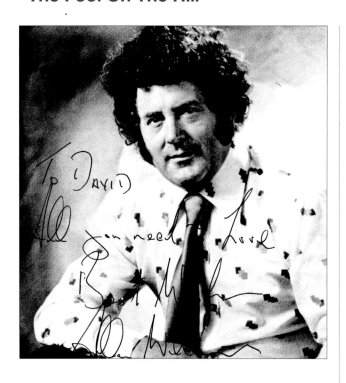

LEFT: *The Silver Beatles' manager, Allan Williams*
RIGHT: *The reproduced paintings in The Jacaranda basement*

Meet Allan Williams—"The Bootle Buck" and founder of The Jacaranda Club. What hasn't been written about Allan Williams, The Beatles' first manager? Williams has become known by the title of his first book: *The Man Who Gave The Beatles Away*.

Losing The Beatles has been recorded as one of the biggest business mistakes of the 20th Century. Is Williams a fool, unlucky, or misrepresented?

In *The Beatles Anthology*, Paul McCartney describes Williams as "the little Welsh manager (little in height that is)". This is important because many have tried to claim he wasn't their manager, so Allan was pleased with this quote.

To find out more, I met Allan in The Grapes, the historic pub in Mathew Street where The Beatles used to drink. I was determined to meet the man, not the myth. His sparring with friend and Cavern DJ Bob Wooler was infamous at Beatles conventions the world over, with Bob doubting the validity of some of Allan's stories.

The first surprising fact was that Allan was born in Bootle, North Liverpool, and not in Wales—a 'Bootle Buck' as he calls himself—though he did grow up in Wales and his family was Welsh.

You first made your mark on the Liverpool music scene by opening The Jacaranda Club in Slater Street. How did that come about?

"My wife Beryl and I used to love to travel around Europe, hitch-hiking and just enjoying ourselves. We stayed in the YHA (Youth Hostel Association) in Paris, and we loved to go to the St. Michel jazz clubs (like Alan Sytner, founder of The Cavern Club did) and see these youngsters in cellar clubs having fun. It was not possible in Liverpool then, but I thought it was a great idea.

"I had been to the famous 2i's Coffee Club in London and then others opened clubs too. So I said to Beryl, 'let's open one'. I was still a plumber and found an old clock repairer's building at 23, Slater Street and we bought it and did it all up—my mates and I did all the work. It cost us £300 for the lot and we had to borrow from the bank to get it finished.

"I went to a social club in Upper Parliament Street and heard this great Caribbean Steel Band. I thought, that would be a novelty and would maybe last for a week, but they lasted ten years. Half of them left and became the first Liverpool foursome to go to Hamburg, which opened the door for all the Merseybeat bands. The rest of the steel band went to London and found some new members, came back and performed with the new line-up of the Caribbean Steel Band.

"The 'Jac' took off straight away. We had art students hanging out there. This was because there was an art tutor called Don McKinley who did the original paintings on

The Silver Beatles audition for Larry Parnes at the Wyvern Club in 1960: Stuart Sutcliffe, John Lennon, Paul McCartney, Tommy Moore and George Harrison

walls, which in turn attracted the art students. We had to share the toilets with the sweet shop next door, which didn't go down well, as the girls used to leave obscene scribblings on the toilet walls. I had the lads (John, Paul and George) re-decorate them, which didn't take long. Stuart and his friend Rod Murray then painted murals on the walls in the basement, though most of that original artwork disappeared when the plaster fell off because of damp. There is only a small piece of Stuart's artwork left.

"There were few building regulations back then. Our only fire escape was just a step ladder where the coal was thrown in, and that was mainly for the band. But then everywhere was concrete, so there was not much chance of fires breaking out.

"It's funny. We made more money in the Jac than I did in the Angel—the Blue Angel, which Williams later opened on Seel Street—even though we didn't sell alcohol in the Jac. We used to sell Pepsi—I was a bigger seller than Lewis' department store in Pepsi—I didn't have Coca-Cola as Pepsi was a penny a crate cheaper and we sold gallons of it. The delivery guy was delighted. There was nothing else to drink.

"I do remember The Beatles, though. They were all bums, especially John who was the biggest bum of them all as he only received a small amount of pocket money from Mimi".

How did you go from managing a coffee club to being the manager of The Beatles?

"Music Promoter Larry Parnes decided to put on a show at the Liverpool Stadium, featuring Eddie Cochran and Gene Vincent. But Eddie Cochran was killed two weeks before and so Parnes said I could cancel and get a full refund. I said, 'It's a bit inconvenient Eddie dying, but ask Gene Vincent if he'll still do it'. Well, Gene said all right, as he wasn't too seriously injured in the crash.

"As we only had half a show, I suggested putting Liverpool groups on in the first half. So we put on Gerry and The Pacemakers, Rory Storm and the Hurricanes and Cass and the Cassanovas, who were the best bands around then. John, Paul, George and Stuart went

to watch, and then Stu and John came to me the next day and said, 'When are you going to do something for us?'

"I didn't know they had a proper band, as they only played in art school dances then. So I said, 'What do you mean? There's no more painting to do'. They then told me they had a group, though they had no drummer. What kind of group is that? 'We've managed so far' was their cry. Well, Cass from the Cassanovas was there and so I called him over. He asked what they called themselves and they said they were using The Beatals, and he suggested Long John and The Silver Beetles, which became The Silver Beatles—which they hated, by the way—but they kept it, as Cass gave them a drummer in Tommy Moore.

"Tommy was not too bright and so came under the unmerciful wit of John. Poor little Tommy, he was about ten years older than them, around my age. He was a very good drummer and I believe he eventually gave drumming lessons to kids. He left to go to work for the Garston Bottle Works to drive a forklift truck. His girlfriend said to him, 'It's either me and a proper job or them'. He chose to quit The Silver Beatles after their disastrous tour of Scotland with Johnny Gentle. I remember driving up to his work in Garston and asking him to reconsider, but his mind was made up for him. So again they had no drummer".

After Tommy, they recruited a guy called Norman Chapman. How did they find him?

"One night, we heard the sound of drums coming from the street, so we went outside to find out where it was coming from. There was a drummer rehearsing across the road from the 'Jac'—in what became the Bamboo Club—and the company repaired old cash registers. We shouted up to him and down he came. He just played there on his own after work. He came and joined them and he was a good drummer. But of course National Service took him away after only a few weeks. He would probably have still been with them, as he got on well with them. His original drum kit is above the bar in The Jacaranda. Norman died young and I went to his funeral. His mum thanked me for attending. I hardly knew him but he was a nice man".

Once they had the band together, how often did they play at the Jac?

"They used to play on Monday nights after the steel band left me in the lurch. I couldn't believe it when they came upstairs looking for brush handles. I wondered what they were up to, as they never cleaned up. I found out that because they had no microphone stands the girlfriends were sitting on the floor, holding the brushes for mic stands".

Before they went, did they look at other drummers or just Pete?

"They remembered Pete from The Casbah, and he was now playing on his new set of drums, which sealed it. They didn't ask anyone else. So I acted like a manager should and said he needed an audition, so Pete came down and played a few songs but he had the job anyway. Pete learned along with them out in Hamburg".

You were instrumental in getting the whole Hamburg scene off the ground for Liverpool groups. What happened?

"The Beatles almost didn't go to Hamburg. Everyone wanted to go as Derry and the Seniors was doing well. The Silver Beatles was regarded as a bum group, always scrounging. I'll give you an example. The staff at the Jac used to get a taxi home, and so these scroungers would hang around to bum a lift off the staff, which was a private taxi. They had no money. They'd only go out with girls who were local because they couldn't afford the bus fare.

At the Arnhem War Memorial in Oosterbeek, Holland (from left to right): Allan Williams, Beryl Williams, Lord Woodbine, Stuart, Paul, George and Pete

"The Silver Beatles didn't go to Hamburg the first time, as they weren't good enough. Promoter Larry Parnes had promised Liverpool band Derry and the Seniors a U.K. summer season at Yarmouth, and so they gave up their jobs, purchased suits, and then Parnes cancelled the tour. I was not even getting commission but they asked me for help, so I took them to the 2i's Club in London.

"I saw Tommy the owner who put them on. After all, he was not paying them, so he had a free group. A guy came over to me and asked if I was Herr Williams. He told me someone wanted to see me. I went over and who should it be but Herr Koschmider whom I'd met in Hamburg—it was like Stanley and Livingston, the chances are a million to one of it happening. I remember him saying, "Ah, Herr Williams". Koschmider had come to London before, looking for groups. I had told him in Hamburg that the best groups were in Liverpool—doing the bullshit job of the salesman again—and so when he came over he went to London, not Liverpool, and went to the '2i's'.

"Tony Sheridan was the first to go over but Herr Koschmider was a difficult person to get on with—an ex-circus cripple and gay—so Tony had a row and went to play at the Top Ten for Peter Eckhorn, who was young and a bit of a swinger. He had lost his artist, so he came over to London to find someone else. He needed a translator and so he arranged for a waiter from the Act One Scene One club to interpret. He was called Herr Steiner

and he impressed Herr Koschmider so much that he offered him a job in Hamburg. He came with us to Hamburg in the minibus".

Why did you send The Silver Beatles to Hamburg and not any other band, as The Silver Beatles' reputation wasn't that good?

"I was their manager and so I arranged the bookings at places like The Grosvenor Ballroom in Wallasey and a place in Neston—the violence there was so bad that someone was booted to death.

"So we set off for Hamburg in our little van with all the equipment on the roof. Dockers didn't want to load it on to the ship, so I had to plead with them. There were ten people in the van. There was me, my wife Beryl, Barry Chang, who was Beryl's brother, Lord Woodbine, John, Paul, George, Stuart, Pete and the translator Herr Steiner, who we picked up on the way. They didn't have money for the trip, so I lent them money for food and clothes, like black t-shirts, trousers and pumps. I still have an 'I.O.U'. from Paul for £15, which he hasn't paid. I had to feed them and pay for the ferry and for the minibus".

You must have seen something in them to invest the money, otherwise you wouldn't have done it?

"They were all right as musicians but nothing special at that stage. They were all witty, had a good education; they were brainy lads. But they had something special about them".

Tell me about the journey?

"We had trouble getting on to the ship as the famous photo shows, with all their gear on the roof. We landed at the Hook of Holland and took a wrong turning somewhere and we were lost. We had arrived about 7 a.m. and of course we were driving on the wrong side of the road. I remember it was like a sea of bikes. Lennon was telling them all to f**k off and to stop leaning on the van.

"We arrived at the Arnhem War Memorial and that famous photograph was taken, which was a bit prophetic: 'Their Name Liveth For Evermore' taken by my brother-in-law Barry Chang. John was not in it as he didn't want to be involved. I don't know if he was just being miserable, but seeing all of those little white crosses as far as the eye could see commemorating the hundreds of soldiers who lost their lives attempting to liberate Holland got to us all. It was sickening.

"We all then went into Arnhem. They went into a music shop and all came out laughing. I asked them why and they laughed again and John produced this mouth organ that he had stolen from the shop. I thought, we aren't even going to get to Hamburg at this rate. What if he'd have been caught?

"We had a real job getting through the customs. We had to say we were students on a holiday with all this equipment, and we were going to play in a coffee bar. We didn't have the visas. They had to itemize each piece of equipment we had. The lads were messing around and in the end the customs just said to go.

"We finally arrived in Hamburg about 1 a.m. and pulled up outside the Kaiserkeller and saw Derry and the Seniors. They all thought this was great. But Herr Koschmider came over and said, 'You don't play here, you play at the Indra'. We went over there and it had a striptease artist on. They said, 'We've not come to Hamburg to back a stripper'. Remember, they'd already done that in Liverpool.

"It was Koschmider's second rock 'n' roll club—he thought he could keep them both going. They played there for a couple of weeks and then there was trouble. A woman who lived above the club didn't mind the strip music, but when the loud rock 'n' roll music started she complained, so they had to stop. They went over to the Kaiserkeller. Herr Koschmider decided to use two bands and had one band on, one off, alternating in the evening.

"However, once Rory Storm and the Hurricanes arrived over there, the two groups plotted together to break the poor stage in the Kaiserkeller. But this was overheard by Herr Steiner (the translator working for Koschmider) and he told his boss what they were plotting. It was Rory Storm who eventually broke it, and he was sacked.

"Their accommodation, of course, was appalling. They were in the filthy dump in the Bambi Kino. The only water was in the toilet block of the cinema, so they had to wait until it was closed to get any water. The place was disgusting, the filth was thick on the walls, but they were young enough to cope".

How did you convince the parents, especially Mimi, to let them go to Hamburg?

"I told them it was a holiday resort like Southport – the usual sales job. I don't know what they thought afterwards, especially when they were expelled. I think Mimi expected John to come back a rich man but instead he returned malnourished and pale".

They came back early didn't they?

"They had gone for three months then extended it for another two months. Tony Sheridan was playing at the Top Ten and they admired him. They jumped up on the

The Jacaranda Club, Slater Street, Allan Williams' club where he managed The Silver Beatles before taking them to Hamburg, as The Beatles

stage with Tony, and Herr Steiner spotted them and he reported all this to Koschmider. That is when he went to the police and all the trouble over George and the curfew occurred. All the kids had identification cards. The police were ruthless. If you were under eighteen and still out after 10.30pm then they threw you out and the club could lose their licence. The police came in and there was George, only seventeen years old, on stage with a crate of ale. So that was George gone. Then of course there was the incident with Pete and Paul in the cinema, when they lit a condom and Koschmider had them arrested and thrown in jail. They were then deported. John eventually wandered home a couple of weeks later when his visa expired. In fact, the others hadn't realised he had come home for a couple of weeks, as nobody saw him. They were falling apart".

While they were out there you opened the Top Ten as well as the Blue Angel in Liverpool. What happened?

"I opened the Top Ten club and I modelled it on what I'd seen in Hamburg. I thought I'd alternate the groups like Herr Koschmider was trying to do between two clubs. I realised that the only places to play were little town halls and village halls or little clubs like The Casbah in the suburbs. I saw how it worked in Hamburg, so I knew it had to be in the city centre, not the suburbs like Bootle, Litherland and Aintree. I think I upset a lot of promoters locally who saw I was going to make money.

"The Top Ten—named after the one in Hamburg—was only open for six days and it burned down. Some have said it was for insurance, but you can't get loss-of-profit insurance when you've only been open for six days. You can't show profit and loss statements, so I only received a small payout, nowhere near enough to cover what I'd lost. Of course, Bob Wooler was going to be full time and suddenly he had no job. I don't think he ever forgave me for that, but it wasn't my fault".

When The Beatles returned from Hamburg, with the Top Ten gone, you arranged the booking at The Grosvenor for them, but the big one was at Litherland Town Hall wasn't it?

"We were in the Blue Angel and John and Pete were saying they had had all the trouble in Hamburg and had nowhere to play. I spoke to Bob and he fitted the group in at Litherland. They were so sensational that the bouncers thought there was a fight. Everyone froze and then ran to the stage. Brian Kelly had to stop the other promoters from getting to them, so the bouncers formed a barrier. He took his diary out and booked them for as many dates as possible. They were so different from the crap band that went out to Hamburg".

After The Beatles returned to Hamburg, they stopped paying you commission, didn't they?

"When they tried to get back into Germany, they couldn't. I had to sign a fidelity bond, as did Peter Eckhorn, to be responsible for any damage made by them or if they stole something. If they had have done anything wrong, the visa would have been cancelled again and they would have had to come home. They therefore went

ABOVE: *John Lennon looks on, left, as the van is loaded on to the ship*

over legitimately. I then received this letter from Stuart saying John was refusing to pay commission. Well, I hit the roof and sent them a letter".

This is an extract:

"May I remind you seeing that you are all appearing to get more than a little swollen-headed, that you would not even have smelled Hamburg if I had not made the contacts. Williams claims that under the terms of Koschmider's contract they could *"not play within thirty weeks of termination of the contract or play within twenty-five miles of the place of entertainment without his consent".* Williams then went on to threaten to have them thrown out of Hamburg within two weeks *"through several legal ways and don't you think I'm bluffing".*

"Basically, I told them The Blue Angel was singing, so I said you'll never ever f***ing work here again", Williams said.

At that time, you could have sued them for breach of contract but you let them go. Why didn't you pursue them?

"I had the Top Ten disaster and then I was opening the Blue Angel, so I was busy, which is why I had to let The Beatles go. I had the Blue Angel half-built when I ran out of money, so I was trying to get some money and had to go to the bank for a loan. In the end, Cain's Brewery backed me and I opened it: a club that could sell alcohol. I'd spent enough money on them and they threw it in my face, so I thought, fine, go and do your own thing because I have my own business to build here".

The Blue Angel was a great success, wasn't it, and you eventually made up with The Beatles?

"Yes, we eventually made it up as I cut off their social life because the Blue Angel had become the place to be, instead of The Cavern and the Jac. We had a licensed club and cabaret, plus alcohol. All the stars of stage and screen that played at the Empire came to the Angel, like Judy Garland and the Rolling Stones. It was the show business club; we didn't have many 'normal' clients. I barred The Beatles from the Angel and Epstein came begging and asked if they could come back. So I said, 'Come back tomorrow night' and he said, 'They're outside'. In they came like drowned rats and threw their arms around me. All was forgotten because life's too short.

"I was enjoying the Angel. I remember we got everyone to sign the grand piano lid. The piano was no longer any use, so I had the lid taken off and had it painted white. I put it on the wall and all the artists signed it, until idiots started signing it 'Joe Bloggs'. I took it down and put it in the attic. It was signed by Judy Garland and the Rolling Stones and all the showbiz people. A guy was doing some jobs for me and we needed a cupboard to keep the brushes and the mops in. The guy needed a door, so he told me he'd taken that old bit of white wood from the attic and cut it to size for the door. And that was that—it was Lord Woodbine but he blamed the joiner".

What about Brian Epstein? What did you think of him?

"He did his best. He was the classical story of the so-called 'fifth Beatle'—I always say it was Stuart. I had a lot of admiration for Epstein, as he was from the old school of behaviour. He dressed them up in suits, which they hated, but it was the right thing to do at that time.

"In the beginning there was no doubt there was a sexual attraction, the rough boys in black leather, but he was no different to a lot of the people involved in the music business then. A lot of them went into the business because they were homosexuals like Epstein, Joe Flannery, Bob Wooler, Bruno Koschmider and many more. John had the charisma that would attract homosexuals. But it was so much more than that, even if it was the initial attraction.

"I remember George saying to me, 'Look at this cake,' and then drew a thin slice and said, 'That was our cut'. It was unknown territory to Epstein. I said to George, 'Yes, but he got you where you are now'. Well he said, 'There's groups now—this was in the 1970s—who are making more than we ever made because of his lousy deals'. I did tell him, 'He made you famous, George'. All he said was, 'Yes, but we could have had ten times more'.

"I also remember Alun Owen telling me a story about the film *A Hard Day's Night* when he went to see them. They were going to pay anything to get the rights but, when they had the meeting, Epstein turned up and said, 'I know you are busy boys, so here's the deal for you' and turned and left. When they all read it they started laughing. They couldn't believe how little he had asked for.

"He was inexperienced. You can't bluff them. Epstein had no chance against these managers and entrepreneurs from America who just carved him up".

What about Pete Best and Ringo?

"There wouldn't have been The Beatles without Pete".

That's a big statement to make. Why do you say that?

"There wouldn't have been The Beatles, as there wouldn't have been Hamburg without a drummer. I couldn't work it out. If he had been a bad drummer I could have understood, but he was with them six and seven hours a night, seven nights a week in Hamburg. It was as if they smelt the whiff of success and they didn't want him on the trip with them.

"And then of course they knew that Ringo and George got on very well together. I used to think Pete was too good looking, and as for not getting his haircut, that was just nonsense. I just think socially he didn't fit in, and as they had to live in each other's pockets, maybe they thought with Ringo they could have a better time. I know that Johnny Hutch said, 'I'm not working with those maniacs' and he still says that today; he still hates them. He was a no-nonsense guy and rough and if Lennon had tried it on with him he'd have received a broken nose.

"Now they're talking about making a statue in Hamburg with John, Paul, George and Ringo, with Stuart looking on. They can't include Stuart and not Pete. Stuart was only there in sufferance before giving it up for his art. It was Hamburg that kicked them off, yet commercially people wouldn't even know who Pete was. Epstein didn't want people to know that Pete and Stuart existed in The Beatles before he found them".

You were especially close to the late Bob Wooler. What are your memories of him?

"I remember them playing at The Grosvenor and Bob was there. He didn't rate The Beatles—he was more or less managing Gerry Marsden, and I had them booked in. I asked him proudly what he thought of The Beatles and he said 'Not very encouraging', but of course after Hamburg he loved them and helped them. He arranged the gig for them at Litherland Town Hall and of course became the famous compere at The Cavern Club. We did lots of Beatles conventions around the world and he would tell his story and I would tell mine and we had a good argument on stage, but it was great theatre. It was good fun.

"I didn't go to The Cavern very often. Bob was the compere and then he brought The Beatles up to the Angel to socialise after playing The Cavern. They loved the atmosphere and had a few drinks and then they'd get up and perform for free. Ray McFall hated me because he was paying for them and then they were playing for me for free. I'm not sure if I was barred".

You've had an amazing life. Do you have any regrets?

"I did all the hard work in the early days, giving them work and getting them set up in Hamburg. There was always someone like me in the early days working for them, but they're ruthless. All groups are users, it's their living: everyone else is expendable. At the end, even Epstein was expendable. I remember he was in the studio with them and he suggested something and Lennon told him to go and count the f***ing money. When I heard that through the grapevine I thought, you're dead, they're going to get rid of you. His life had gone. His death was an accidental overdose but the rot had set in by then.

"I'm one of the last ones of those who were there. I've lost lots of friends and I miss them all. People say, 'You could have been a millionaire' and I say, 'I was a millionaire'. A millionaire couldn't have managed The Beatles in the early days. We were breaking the rules left right and centre". Allan is a survivor, a millionaire in memories that money can't buy. As with many in the story of The Beatles, he was discarded along the way once he had served his usefulness. But he just dusted himself down and got on with life, a life he is enjoying to this day.

Portrayed as 'The Fool on the Hill', he is sometimes overlooked because of this tag. In truth, he couldn't have done for The Beatles what Epstein did—he admits that. But without his input, they wouldn't have made it to Hamburg, which was what made them the greatest band ever. For that we should be thankful.

12 August 1960
Pete Best joins The Beatles
"My Bonnie"

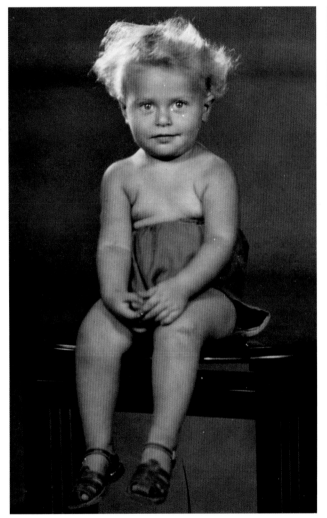

Pete Best as a baby

Randolph Peter Best was born in Madras, India on 24 November 1941 to John and Mona Best. Pete's brother, Rory Best, followed in 1944 and the family came to Liverpool at Christmas 1945.

They first lived with John Best's family at Ellerslie Manor (West Derby), but because of tension between Mona and the Bests, they eventually moved to a flat in Cases Street (Liverpool). Unfortunately, the family thought the place was haunted and

they relocated to a one-story brick and corrugated-iron house in Princess Drive (West Derby). These small quarters proved unsatisfactory, and they next settled in a three-bedroom, semi-detached house at 17, Queenscourt Road (West Derby).

When Mo's parents retired from India they lived with John, Mo, Pete and Rory, but the house was cramped. Mo wanted a big house and when Rory spotted a house for sale at 8, Haymans Green, Mo sprang in to action, bought it and turned the basement into The Casbah Coffee Club.

Pete attended Blackmoor Park School (West Derby) and then The Collegiate, (Kensington) where he made friends with Bill Barlow and Chas Newby, with whom he would later form The Black Jacks.

After Ken Brown left The Quarrymen over a money dispute, he asked Pete to start a band with him as its drummer. Pete agreed and after persuading Mo to buy him a drum set, Pete, Ken, Bill and Chas formed The Black Jacks. He was drumming with them at The Casbah when he was approached by Paul McCartney to join The Beatles when they were getting ready to travel to Hamburg in August 1960. After he parted ways with The Beatles, Pete joined Lee Curtis and the All Stars.

I met with Pete Best in the coffee bar of The Casbah in July 2005 where five decades previously he bashed away on the drums, the object of affection for many females. He also caught the eyes of John Lennon, Paul McCartney and George Harrison, who asked him to be their drummer.

My first question, Pete, is about The Casbah itself. Tell me about it, and its place in Beatles history, a place that has been often overlooked.

"It is like Tutankhamun's grave, a gem that has remained unchanged for nearly fifty years; a place that can only be conveyed in books to a certain degree. You have to stand here to feel the atmosphere. I have always seen it from this side as my home, but it is only when I see the faces of fans that I realise what we have here. It has its own special atmosphere that is unique in the world".

What was it like to have this great club in your house?

"You have to stand here and feel the buzz. This is where it started. We've grown up with it, so it is part of the family: it has always been here, and so for us it is home, but for visitors it's like stepping into history".

How do you feel about the fact that people are finally recognising the importance of The Casbah?

"The Best family have always told the true story, but now other people are saying it too, so a lot of these myths are being destroyed. We've not gone out in the documentary *Best of The Beatles* to say this is black, this is white; you were told this, but this is what happened or this is the truth. We are just presenting the facts and then it's up to you to piece it together. Others have written about it, often from their own slant and plagiarised other books.

LEFT: *Pete Best in the garden at Haymans Green* RIGHT: *Mona Best, Pete's mum and proprietor of The Casbah Coffee Club*

"Many researchers say it all started in 1962 with four Beatles; John, Paul, George and Ringo, but there were three years before that. Everyone has their own slant and reasons for writing their version. There are certain facts and stories, which they twist in order to sell books. Fans therefore read these books, and see it in black and white and assume it to be true. There are some ridiculous and made up stories, which are often sensationalism and just ways to make some dollars. They write garbage and people believe it—it's in a book, so it must be true".

One thing I have noticed in Pete, Rory and Roag is that at the slightest reference to Mo, there is a glint in their eye and smile on their face, and no wonder. "If Brian Epstein has been credited with polishing the rough diamond to create the biggest and best group of all time, then it is surely Mo who helped to produce the rough diamond in the first place", Pete declared.

I asked Pete to tell me about Mo—all three boys refer to her as Mo, a genuine term of endearment.

"I could sit here and talk for a year about her. She was our mother first, and then a mother to all the club members. We became like a family to all the members, and she would hand out advice when asked, even to some of the parents. She was a diplomat and a politician. She was the matriarch, who had a clear vision of what she wanted The Casbah to be. At the time, we didn't realise the ideas that she had.

"She saw the potential in The Beatles when we came back from Hamburg. Derry—from Derry and the Seniors, the first Merseybeat band to conquer Hamburg—had come back from Hamburg and told Mo how good The Beatles were. When we came back and played that Christmas at The Casbah, we were the best rock 'n' roll group around".

At this point, Pete typically apologizes for sounding big-headed, but this is what everyone else was saying. Let's review the facts: George was deported from Hamburg for being underage. Pete and Paul were then shown the door soon after for their alleged arson attempt at the Bambi Kino. They returned in disarray, and Paul admitted doubting whether they had a future, and his father made him go out and find a job. Stuart wrote home about John and Paul going to Paris and the group splitting up. Stuart stayed in

"My Bonnie", by Tony Sheridan and The Beat Brothers, signed by Pete Best

Hamburg with Astrid, so The Beatles could have called it a day at that point. Enter Mo. She knew they possessed something special. Mo arranged for them to play at The Casbah twice and, through local promoters, they also played Litherland Town Hall and The Grosvenor Ballroom, Wallasey, with Chas Newby on bass guitar.

"When Mo saw us she saw that we had something extra and was determined to do her best for us, not just because of me", Pete said. "She helped arrange bookings outside The Casbah—forming Casbah Promotions. It was Mo who rang Ray McFall at The Cavern to get us our first lunchtime appearance. The Casbah is Mo. Yes, we had our part to play, and it was a family thing, we all helped, but The Casbah is Mo's legacy. Maybe it's karma. I put it down to karma".

Mo was an amazing woman, wasn't she?

"That is the greatest understatement. Whatever evolved from The Casbah, whichever direction it went, emanated from her. She was the lady with the vision".

Pete and I then moved on to the change of manager, when Brian Epstein came on the scene. Some writers have suggested that after Allan Williams and The Beatles parted company in early 1961, they managed themselves until Epstein came along at the end of 1961. Mo has never been given the credit for managing them during 1961

and keeping them together. It has even been suggested that one of the reasons for Pete being dismissed from The Beatles was because Mo was a tough character who wanted to tell Epstein how to run the group, so Epstein had to get rid of Pete to get rid of Mo. Pete enlightened me.

"Epstein came to see Mo. They had a chat and Mo was happy to hand over the running to Epstein. By this time in her life, she had her mum living with her, who was seriously ill with cancer. She died in the spring of 1962.

"Then of course, Roag was on the way—he was born in July 1962—and the work at The Casbah was taking it out of her, so she was more than happy to pass on the responsibility to Epstein. He asked her if she had any reservations and she said no. 'Just promise me that you will do a damn good job of looking after them, as they deserve it'." They eventually signed their contract with Epstein at The Casbah.

Pete has released a DVD, *Pete Best of The Beatles*, about the story of The Casbah, and no account could be complete without mentioning Pete's dismissal. So I asked him how they handled it.

"I've nothing new to add to what I've said before, so there's no 'oh by the way, after forty years I've just remembered'. So, what we have done is interview different people who were around at the time, and create the atmosphere of what led up to it and let other people give their views. There are some giving their comments for the first time and putting a different perspective on it".

Tell me about Hamburg?

"They were good times, and that was where we became tighter as a band. You have to, playing all those hundreds of hours together. Instead of just singing and playing the songs as a straight copy from the record, we started to play around with them. We had to improvise, as we had a limited repertoire which had to last all night, so we started to put in lots of solos and stuff".

I've read that the others would walk off stage and leave you to do a drum solo for while and then come back on. Is that true?

"Oh yes, they would just put their guitars down and go off for a drink and a cigarette and stuff and then wander back on. But don't worry, I got my own back. I'd put my sticks down and go off, and they'd turn round and suddenly realise I wasn't there. That's how we survived".

That brings me to the subject of *Backbeat*. How accurate is the movie?

"It's a fanciful love story between Stuart and Astrid which has been fictionalised. As entertainment it is very good, but it isn't the story of us five in Hamburg. The soundtrack is great; it manages to capture the savageness and ferocity of the music we were playing. Don't look on it as 'it's on the screen, therefore it must be true'. Just look on it as entertainment".

In the end Pete, what is the message of your life?

"Regardless of what happened, Hamburg, The Casbah and Liverpool were two great years—plus they had the year before too as The Quarrymen before I joined. They were great times".

Pete summed up his life in a simple sentence. "There have been highs and lows, but Pete Best has a good family and a good life and he's happy".

17 December 1960
Chas Newby joins The Beatles
"I'm Happy Just To Dance With You"

Chas Newby in 1960, practising for his forthcoming debut as the first left-handed bass-player with The Beatles

Who was the left-handed bass-playing Beatle at Litherland Town Hall in December 1960? Before you blurt out Paul McCartney—think again. It was Chas Newby, friend and former band mate of Pete Best.

I tracked Chas down to ask him what he remembered of his brief flirtation with fame.

How did you come to play with The Beatles?

"Stuart Sutcliffe didn't return from Hamburg, and so The Beatles were in need of a bass player. As I was a friend of Pete's and we'd played together in The Black Jacks, he asked me to play with them over the Christmas holiday. Our first engagement was at The Casbah on 17 December 1960. There was confusion as Mo Best billed us as 'The Fabulous Beatles—Direct from Hamburg'. The crowd was expecting a German band, and when they saw us they realised they had seen us before in The Quarrymen and The Black Jacks. The screams were great and the applause was fantastic. The second appearance was at The Grosvenor Ballroom in Wallasey, where we appeared alongside Derry and the Seniors".

Where were you born and where did you go to school?

"I was born in Blackpool in 1941. Because of the continuing air raids in Liverpool, my mum was evacuated, as she was heavily pregnant. I grew up in Queens Road, Anfield, a street long since demolished.

"I went to Anfield Road Primary School and then on to The Collegiate from 1952–59, where I befriended Pete Best, Bill Barlow and Ken

Brown. We formed our own skiffle group—The Barmen. We even had a mention in the *Liverpool Echo*".

Where did you play?

"As with most skiffle groups, we entered local competitions, including an appearance at the Empire, playing alongside The Vipers and Jim Dale. We also appeared at The Cavern in 1957".

How did you get your start in music?

"I started playing acoustic guitar and then progressed to the bass guitar. I never wanted to be a professional musician—I had always longed to be a scientist. After Ken Brown left The Quarrymen, he and Pete asked Bill and me to form a new band, The Black Jacks. As The Black Jacks, we often played at The Casbah, which gave Pete his first taste of drumming with a band, and I became—and remain—good friends with Pete and the Best family".

What about after leaving school?

"After leaving school, I joined Pilkington's (the glass makers) and left for London. As a student, I would come home for the holidays. It was for this reason that I was home over the Christmas holidays in 1960".

Chas Newby (second left) with The Barmen

Plaque at The Grosvenor Ballroom, Wallasey, where Chas Newby played with The Beatles. The group played here as The Silver Beatles in June 1960 and returned from Hamburg as The Beatles for the gig in December 1960

The Beatles' most important gig—often seen as the pivotal moment in the start of Beatlemania—was at Litherland Town Hall, on 27 December 1960. Again, billed as "The Fabulous Beatles, Direct from Germany", this was one of their first adventures into North Liverpool. The local fans also assumed therefore that they were German.

What do you remember about that night?

"We were lined up on the stage, behind the curtain. As the curtains opened, Paul launched into 'Long Tall Sally'. The buzz in the atmosphere was incredible. In the main, bands played as the people in the hall danced. Part way through, the dancing stopped and the crowd came towards the stage and watched—we were performing to a crowd, like you would do now. They were shouting and screaming".

You had seen The Beatles before they went to Hamburg, and were now playing with them on their return. Did you notice any difference in them?

"The influence of Hamburg was obvious. They were different and had moved up a notch. I remember sitting in the dressing room afterwards with Bob Wooler. Bob was excited, as was promoter Brian Kelly. Beatlemania had begun. No one had witnessed scenes like this before—frenzied and screaming teenagers. We all knew something special had happened. Before we could leave, Brian Kelly had sealed off all the routes to the dressing rooms so that rival promoters couldn't get in. Kelly took his diary out and booked The Beatles then and there for thirty-six dances between January and March 1961".

Did you play with them again?

"I played one more time with them on 31 December 1960 at The Casbah, and my career with The Beatles was over".

What did you do after The Beatles?

"I happily returned to obscurity with Pilkington's and didn't pick up my guitar again for years. I left Liverpool permanently in 1972 for Alcester with my wife Margaret, who was also a Casbah member. I achieved a degree in Chemical Engineering and worked for Pilkington's for twenty years. In 1990, a career change beckoned and I decided I wanted to be a mathematics teacher. I went to university for one year, and then taught until retirement. I've been happily married for thirty-two years and have two children. My son John is a bass player in a band who is on the verge of the big time, and my daughter Jacqui is a successful accountant".

No regrets about not staying with The Beatles?

"I have no regrets about my temporary flirtation with fame, and I wouldn't have changed my plans for my career just for a shot at playing music professionally. I never wanted to be a full-time musician".

Are you still in touch with your old friends?

"Yes, I have remained in contact with my friends in The Black Jacks—Pete Best, Ken Brown and Bill Barlow".

Being a good friend of Pete's, do you have an opinion on his sacking?

"I just remember all the work that Pete and Mo put in to make sure The Beatles became famous. They would make the bookings, negotiate the fees, transport and store the equipment. I just wondered how they could do that to him after everything he had done.

"I remember seeing them on the Royal Iris on 10 August, just days before he was sacked, and everything seemed fine. I was as shocked as everyone else at the events that unfolded".

Are you playing again now?

"Yes. I've recently come out of musical retirement and picked up my bass guitar again. At the end of 2002 I joined a band called The Rackets. We play for fun and to raise money for charity".

And that is Chas Newby, a Beatle for a couple of weeks, at the start of an amazing phenomenon. He played his part and then left to continue a normal life with no regrets.

27 December 1960
Faron witnesses 'Beatlemania'
"Oh My Soul"

Written on the toilet wall of The Grapes in Mathew Street:
"Faron has the best rock 'n' roll voice on Merseyside after me"
signed John Lennon.

William Faron Ruffley is a Merseyside legend, but his stage presence stretched beyond this region. As Farons Flamingos, he and his group entertained audiences with their unique brand of rock 'n' roll. Their rendition of "Do You Love Me?" has been hailed by many as the best version of the song. Unfortunately, having told Brian Poole from The Tremeloes about the song, Poole quickly recorded it and made it a hit even though it was inferior to the Flamingos' version.

Faron is a natural performer and entertainer, loved by fans and music legends alike. He is known and respected by Paul McCartney, Little Richard, Willie Nelson and many others. Ray Davies of the Kinks said that Farons Flamingos was the one band they never wanted to follow on stage. That is some compliment.

Cavern DJ Bob Wooler nicknamed Faron "The Panda Footed Prince of Prance" for his energetic displays on stage.

Faron was close to John Lennon, but also befriended the rest of The Beatles, and his group often appeared on the same bill. Until recently he was still performing, an act I have witnessed at Merseycats and at The Cavern. It's easy to understand why he was such a favourite.

I spoke with him for nearly two hours, even though he was unwell. His health has deteriorated to the extent that he can no longer perform, which is a shame as he is an original, unique talent, recognised by many international stars and performers. But, as the show must go on, Faron still makes appearances at local fund-raising events for Merseycats, the rock 'n' roll children's charity.

Faron's storytelling is as colourful as his former stage act. He told me some great stories about the boys from Liverpool.

What is your recollection of John Lennon?

"We were great friends and he, like many others, would sleep over at my house, and my mum would look after us all. When I see things in books stating that John was a homosexual then I can say it's absolute rubbish. We once shared a bed with three girls and, believe me, there was not a gay bone in his body—I know.

"He was a great friend to me. One occasion I remember was us sitting in town and having a drink, and I mentioned I was after a leather jacket. He went over to the Army and Navy Stores and then he ran back and told me there were three left. We returned to the store but they were something like £8. I only had £5, so he gave me

the other £3 and said buy it; I could pay him back whenever. I never did and he never asked for it. That was the measure of John that not many people saw.

"Another time we were confronted by a gang whose leader was well known for beating up as many people as he could. I am not the tallest, but John just showed them his belt with this great big buckle on it and then proceeded to walk right through them. That was John looking out for me".

Tell me your memories of The Beatles' Litherland Town Hall appearance.

"The Beatles were added on as an afterthought by DJ Bob Wooler. Before going to Hamburg they were crap, but I'll never forget that night at Litherland after they returned. I was chatting to the girls at the back of the hall. Bob announces 'Direct from Hamburg, The Beatles' and they started with 'Long Tall Sally' which Paul sang. I'll never forget it, it was so loud and piercing, and then they belted the song out. The crowd went wild, and the girls ran from the back of the hall to the stage, leaving me on my own. They started screaming—I'd never seen it before; no one had.

"I had my trademark white suit and these lads were scruffy. Paul had a brown tweed jacket; they all had smelly leathers with fur trim and they did stink. John had ripped jeans. They were a right mess. Paul had a red guitar with three strings on it, and it wasn't even plugged in. John hit his amp with a hammer to get it going. What on earth was going on?

"They were different. Paul sang 'Oh My Soul' and 'Long Tall Sally', and then John would do Gene Vincent's 'Dance in the Street' and George would do 'Everybody's

Farons Flamingos

Trying To be My Baby' and then they would all do 'Searching' together. No other groups did this. There would be one singer and backing singers, but they had all three of them doing solos and then singing three-part harmonies together. However, I then made my famous quote: 'They'll never last'. How wrong was I? I say that the world never saw the real Beatles, the greatest rock 'n' roll band ever known".

What are your thoughts on The Casbah and Mona Best?

"Mona—what a lovely woman. I sang at The Casbah many times before The Cavern. I remember once taking Screaming Lord Sutch—who I was good friends with—to The Casbah and suddenly seeing him run in to the room and start writing in his book, looking guilty. Mo ran in screaming like a banshee, 'It was you, it was you, you're barred. And you (turning to me, who was non-plussed)—get out.

"Apparently, Sutch had gone into the garden and dug up worms and thrown them all over the girls' hair, which was full of sugary water lacquer. Mo wasn't impressed and you didn't cross her. What a wonderful woman. We all loved her".

Weren't you invited to play in a band with George and Pete at one time?

"When Paul and John went off to Paris hitch-hiking, George asked me to join him and Pete in a new band, obviously thinking John and Paul were going to do their own thing. I was with my own band and couldn't see it happening anyway, but it was an interesting proposition".

"One of their party tricks was to have a college scarf around their neck for whoever was singing the song. When Paul had finished, he took it off and passed the scarf to John, who would then sing his song. He would then pass it to George who would put it on and sing his song. It was a great piece of stage theatre, and was the cause of great fun wherever they went".

Tell me about George Harrison.

"One time, George—who was quite fashion conscious and a great dresser—had these fantastic cowboy boots. They were black with a white eagle on them. He was selling them, so I said I'd have them and gave him £4 one morning for them. That night, at a party, I see that Ringo has a pair exactly the same on, so I asked him where he bought them. He says, 'I bought them off George this morning and I gave him £5'. It was the same pair of boots.

"One other thing that I remember is that we would all finish our set with 'What'd I Say' by Ray Charles, because it was a great crowd song with its 'hey hey' and the crowds loved it. The Beatles wanted to do something different, so Bob Wooler suggested 'New Orleans' which still had the 'hey hey' singing, but it was a different song. They always wanted to be one step ahead. We all did".

There's a famous story regarding you and Paul McCartney's leather trousers. Can you tell us the story?

"We were in Joe's Café on Duke Street, and had all been upstairs—where the bands went—with 'Polythene Pat', and we'd all signed her leg. When I arrived downstairs I was the last one there, and saw McCartney running out the door, shouting 'You've got to pay the bill'. What? All I had was the £5 band money on me. The bill came to 4 pounds, 8 shillings and 9 pence (£4.44), so I was not happy with him. He'd left his leather trousers there, so I thought right, I'll take them in exchange. He asked me the next day if I had them and I said no, intent on teaching him a lesson. Well, they were forgotten about, and by the time I next came across them it was too late to give them back. I started wearing them in my new stage show with a leather jacket and told Allan Williams they were Paul's. He said we should make some money, and I was short, so I said okay. We went to the local paper and I was pictured in them, and we were going to auction them. It was suggested that they could fetch £30,000, so I was made up. Then, my brother rang me up and reminded me of something. I had sold them to him for £6, and when he had a bad motorcycle accident while wearing them, they were destroyed. What I had was a pair of his trousers. I wanted to call it off, but Allan reckoned we were too far down the line. So I rang Paul and told him what had happened, which is why Paul intervened. We didn't want any fans being ripped off".

Speaking of Paul, how did you two get on?

"I've always got on well with Paul, despite the bill at Joe's Café. He was always a great diplomat and thoughtful about the public relations side of things. There are occasions which I won't go into where Paul did well to make sure everything went smoothly; he was always good at that, and has kept in touch over the years. We were always close and I regard him as a friend. I remember I had been in France and returned with this suit with rounded collars. Paul asked me where I had bought it from, and so I told him from France. He obviously liked it, and not too long after, The Beatles were wearing them".

What do you remember about Stuart Sutcliffe?

"Stu looked great on stage and was a competent enough musician—not as bad as some people make out. One night, I was waiting to go on and I looked at his leather trousers, and it was something I hadn't seen before. He had his cowboy boots on, but he had split his trousers up the side so that they fitted over his boots, but looked almost like flares at the front. They were great.

"So I went home and told my mum, so she came down to see for herself. Of course, I walk in with my mum and they start singing 'Faron's with his mum, Faron's with his mum. He can't go anywhere without his mummy'. What else would you expect? But she took a look at them and said 'okay son,' and went home. She then altered mine for me. That's what it was like—we copied each other".

Didn't you, George, John and your father once hold a most unconventional concert?

"A lot of people called me a liar when I said that George played the ukulele. But it was my dad who taught him. We had a ukulele that George played, a piano accordion and guitars. This night my dad was complaining of toothache, and so John said he had some medicine that would help him. He gave him two purple hearts—most people only took one at most—and the toothache went away, but my dad was stoned. We were out in the field at the back of our house with George on the uke, me and John with guitars and this piano accordion, singing songs being followed around this field by cows. It was superb".

And, as Bob Wooler said, here's to "Faron, The Panda Footed Prince of Prance".

9 FEBRUARY 1961
The Beatles' debut at The Cavern
"Twist And Shout"

Much has been written about The Cavern, but written history and facts don't always agree. Such is the case with The Cavern Club.

Mathew Street is on the edge of Liverpool's city centre, away from the main shopping area. Originally there were warehouses to hold goods coming off the ships moored in Liverpool's inlet off the Mersey. Later, it became a dark back street in the city's commercial quarter.

Liverpudlian Alan Sytner, a big jazz fan, visited Paris in 1956. He ventured into the fashionable Left Bank area where he stumbled on a great jazz club—Le Caveau Francais Jazz Club, which later inspired the name, The Cavern. When Sytner discovered basement space available for rent at 8-10, Mathew Street, he decided to open a jazz club. The rest as they say is history, though not always retold accurately.

The Cavern opened on 16 January 1957 with a capacity of 650 customers. The Merseysippi Jazz Band was the opening night attraction, entertaining approximately 600 people. Sytner insisted that The Cavern was strictly a jazz club and refused to change over to rock 'n' roll.

The membership of the club had grown to over 25,000 in a short time, but the spectre of rock 'n' roll wouldn't go away. Out in the suburbs, The Casbah was building a membership of 3,000 and was open seven nights a week. Both were successful clubs, catering to different audiences.

Alan Sytner left Liverpool in 1959 and handed the club over to his father. But Dr. Joseph Sytner had his own business and so asked Alan's accountant, Ray McFall, to take over. McFall was a traditional jazz fan but saw the Liverpool music scene change before his eyes. When he took over, The Cavern was open from Thursday to Sunday with a mixture of traditional and modern jazz. He realised the possibility of the lunchtime trade with so many offices and businesses nearby, and incorporated midday gigs for two hours, from Monday to Friday.

The only problem with the gigs was the availability of bands. Most local musicians worked during the day and played during the evenings. McFall scrambled to find groups who could play to fill in the afternoon gaps.

Weekends were still reserved for jazz, but the rock 'n' roll lunchtimes were growing in reputation. Jazz audiences at The Cavern had dwindled by 1961 and the club was only pulling in about three dozen jazz fans. McFall had a simple choice: open the club up to rock 'n' roll or close the business. McFall had heard of The Casbah's

RIGHT: *The Cavern entrance on Mathew Street*

success and spoke to Mona Best about her burgeoning club. When Mona rang him to say she had a group who could fill the lunchtime slot, he was intrigued. She told him the name of this group—The Beatles.

After checking with Bob Wooler, Ray booked The Beatles for a lunchtime appearance.

Cavern doorman Paddy Delaney remembered this scruffy group of lads appeared one by one In ragged clothes and long hair. They certainly were not what the club was used to. But the numbers didn't lie. The Cavern was soon packed as news of The Beatles' appearance had spread quickly to their loyal fan base. With a few minutes to go before they took to the stage for their debut, Ray McFall walked into the dressing room and spoke to The Beatles. "Right lads", he said, "you have a few minutes to get changed before you're on".

The group was wearing their black leathers and didn't know what McFall was talking about. "We are changed", they exclaimed. "You're not appearing on my stage dressed like that", McFall said angrily. He had been used to smart suits. The Cavern had a strict dress code of suits and ties, not scruffy torn leather. Lennon, ever the diplomat, dressed down McFall and was prepared to leave. Bob Wooler wisely told McFall that if The Beatles walked out, there would be a riot. McFall relented and let them play that once, under duress and under dressed.

The Beatles came on and looked a mess. They turned their amps on full and let rip with a most horrendous noise that bounced off the walls. Loud but superb, the crowd went wild. The Beatles had arrived at The Cavern.

After they'd finished, McFall came into the room with diary in hand. "I'll take as many bookings as you have and you can wear what you want". He knew a good thing when he saw it.

This Beatles' lunchtime debut was Thursday, 9 February 1961—they received a fee of £5. Their first evening appearance was on Tuesday, 21 March 1961. The Quarrymen had first appeared at The Cavern on 7 August 1957 after Paul and John had met, though Paul didn't play.

It's lore that The Cavern made The Beatles successful. John Lennon, however, dispelled that notion with his trademark tongue. He was once quoted as saying: "The Cavern didn't make The Beatles, The Beatles made The Cavern".

What was The Cavern like in the late '50s and early '60s? Being a basement, it was dark and damp. It had previously been used for storing fruit and vegetables, so the rotting smell of decaying food was still ingrained in the walls. There were only the stone steps in and out, which would undoubtedly fail a plethora of today's health and safety laws. To improve visibility, the owners painted the walls white, giving rise to "Cavern dandruff", where the paint would flake off on to patron's clothes. With so many people crammed into a small place, sweat and condensation would pour off the walls.

ABOVE: *The Cavern crowd watch The Beatles, transfixed by seeing their heroes on stage*

Add this smell to the cigarette smoke (at least half of the people would be smoking) and a lack of ventilation and an unpleasant picture starts to emerge.

But, it was even worse than that say those who visited the club. Mike Rice remembers going into the gents toilets, which were constantly flooded. If you were sensible, you stood on the plank of wood provided, to stop your feet getting too wet. You would therefore have to add this horrendous smell from the toilets to the mix. Conscious of all the smells, The Cavern counteracted them with strong pine disinfectant.

When you put all of that together, the only conclusion is that the music must have been so incredible, as there was no sane reason to go there.

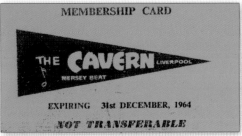

TOP: *John, Paul and Pete at The Cavern in 1961*
LEFT: *The Cavern Club card*
MIDDLE: *A Cavern Club membership card*
RIGHT: *Cavern Club promotion*

CAVERN

The walls are bare; the ceiling is low; arches dominate the scene in this old fruit-storage cellar.
In almost total darkness the groups beat out their rhythmic sound. Nearly all the Liverpool groups of any talent play here at some time or other. This is the heart of the Mersey beat.
Group with special connection: do we really have to tell you?

Minimum age: 17   *Membership*: 1/–
Closed: MONDAY & THURSDAY

EVENING SESSIONS			LUNCHTIME SESSIONS	
7.30 to 11.15			Noon to 2.15	
	members	guests	*members*: 1/–; *guests*: 1/6	
TUESDAY:	3/–	4/–		
WEDNESDAY:	3/6	4/6	SATURDAY TEENAGE	
FRIDAY:	4/6	5/6	SESSIONS	
SATURDAY:	5/–	6/–	13–16 YEAR OLDS ONLY	
SUNDAY:	5/–	6/–	1 p.m. to 4 p.m.	
No admittance after 9.30			*members*: 2/–; *guests*: 3/–	

where to find it: 10 Mathew Street (off North John Street)
telephone: CENtral 1591

ABOVE: *George, Pete, John and Paul outside The Cavern, Mathew Street, in 1961*
BELOW RIGHT: *The statuesque Lennon looks down Mathew Street*

The entrance to The Cavern was down the stone steps, leading to a vast cellar with the famous three long tunnels, separated by six-foot archways. These tunnels were only ten feet wide and, when packed with teenagers, the condensation and lack of air would cause many to faint. Lunchtime admission to The Cavern was one shilling (5 pence) for members and one shilling and sixpence (7.5 pence) for non-members. The Beatles received twenty-five shillings (£1.25) each per day for two forty-five minute spots.

It all started happening in a big way for The Beatles in late 1961. Brian Epstein and his assistant Alistair Taylor visited The Cavern on 9 November. Alistair recalled that their attendance was not announced and no special treatment had been requested. The two sat at the back and listened. It was a horrible noise in a smelly place, and they felt uncomfortable. Four scruffy lads in black leather appeared, drinking Coke and smoking on stage. Somehow, they couldn't help but admire the music.

But what it was that they had, they never knew. It was something intangible—the mysterious "X" factor. Alistair remembers them playing about five songs: "Money", "Twist and Shout", "A Taste of Honey" and "Till There Was You". The fifth song was probably what intrigued Epstein and Alistair the most. The Beatles played a song that they had written themselves, called "Hello Little Girl". The song was quite good, but it was so unusual for a group to have the confidence to perform their own tunes. Epstein and Alistair visited backstage to say "hello". Epstein told them he thought they were great, and they exchanged a few pleasant remarks and then left.

Epstein and Alistair then went for lunch at The Peacock Restaurant when Epstein stunned Alistair by declaring that he wanted to manage The Beatles. Epstein had no management experience but he knew that The Beatles had something special. The group were invited to Epstein's NEMS offices in Whitechapel on 3 December 1961 to discuss his proposal to become their manager. The contract was signed at The Casbah Club on 10 December 1961.

Ringo's Cavern debut with The Beatles was 22 August 1962, the same day that George received a black eye. There were protests from the fans who were angry over Pete Best's sacking. In the commotion, George took a hit in the eye over the sudden change in this personnel. The chant of "We want Pete!" reverberated around The Cavern throughout the whole gig. However, it was not long before Ringo's place was cemented in the band and in the affections of the fans.

The Beatles, with Ringo on drums, went on to make around sixty further appearances at The Cavern, though the majority of these were between September 1962 and February 1963, when, after the success of their debut single, "Love Me Do", they were travelling further away from home. They made their last appearance at The Cavern on 3 August 1963 after nearly 300 appearances. Brian Epstein promised they would return, but they never did.

The late Alan Sytner foolishly claimed the credit for making The Beatles. "Without me, no Cavern; without me, no Beatles; without me, none of the bloody things. I don't think any of this would have happened without me. Obviously, Lennon and McCartney were geniuses but would they have flourished without The Cavern?" Sytner was not known for his modesty. If The Casbah was the birthplace of The Beatles, and Hamburg was where they grew up, then The Cavern was where, after nearly 300 appearances, Brian Epstein's Fab Four matured into the finest pop group of all time.

The Cavern survived for many years, playing host to most of the biggest names in music. But like most clubs, it had a life span. Despite protests from Beatles fans, the buildings were demolished in 1973, the bricks being sold, to make way for a ventilation shaft for the underground railway. However, the shaft was never built and the lot eventually became a car park. The Cavern Club was filled in, making it easier to unearth in 1982 and rebuild for the current version of The Cavern.

The new Cavern was opened in 1984. The club is deeper underground with thirty steps now, and occupies about fifty per cent of the original site.

On the evening of 19 December 1999, Sir Paul McCartney was back performing in The Cavern Club, and the show was broadcast around the world on the Internet.

TOP: *The Fab Four perform at The Cavern in 1963* BOTTOM LEFT: *John Lennon in The Cavern with Pete Best on drums behind him in 1962* BOTTOM RIGHT: *Paul McCartney at The Cavern in 1999*

6 JULY 1961
Bill Harry launches *Mersey Beat*

"Don't Bother Me"

At Liverpool College of Art in 1958, Bill Harry introduced Stuart Sutcliffe to his new friend, Mr. John Lennon. That singular act led to Stuart joining The Beatles.

Bill was asked what first attracted him to Stuart and John at the Liverpool College of Art.

"I was in separate classes to Stuart and John, but people with extraordinary talent were talked about. I had heard all about Stu and so with him and his flat-mate Rod Murray, we would sit for hours in our local pub Ye Cracke and talk about culture, art, poetry, writing and films. For banned books, we had books sent from City Lights Bookshop in San Francisco and Olympic Press Books in Paris.

"I remember this guy walking into the canteen at the Art College and seeing his scruffy clothes and a smart DA (duck's arse) haircut and he really stood out. But then I looked around the room to see the rest of the students smartly dressed in their duffel coats and I realised they were all conforming to society's idea of a student. John was the rebel and I had to know more about him."

What was so special about Ye Cracke?

"We would sit for hours talking in Ye Cracke as it was so close to the ArtCollege. John really immersed himself in beat poetry and particularly Lawrence Ferlinghetti's *Crucifixion*. We discussed books like Colin Wilson's *The Outsider* and J.D. Salinger's *The Catcher in the Rye*. We talked about the things that interested us all and discussed the future and the depths of the soul and what inspired us. Stu was into the writings of Danish philosopher and theologian Soren Kierkegaard. So there we were, four friends determined to make ourselves and our city famous. We were into the American Beat poets. We went to hear British poet Royston Ellis in the University, and Ellis came back with us to Ye Cracke and then to Stu's flat at Gambier Terrace where we went through our first drug experience using Benzedrine in that room.

"When we were talking about beat poetry, we realised that what Ellis was doing was imitating the American style poets. We wanted an alternative—a poet based on the British experience. I had heard that John had written some poems and I asked him to let me read them. He was reluctant and felt that writing poems was not macho. But as the two of us sat there he produced a couple of poems from his pocket. John read them to me and I told him they were good. He was picking up influences from "*The Goons*" radio show and his favourite book, *Through the Looking Glass* by Lewis Carroll. We decided that you could only write from what you knew, not from what you had heard. Liverpool, like a lot of Britain, was facing a U.S. cultural domination of comics, films and music.

We believed that there was so much creativity in Liverpool 8 that we should buck the trend, which is why we called ourselves 'The Dissenters'. We decided that we would use our own talents to make Liverpool famous. I would for my writing, John for his music and Stuart and Rod for their painting".

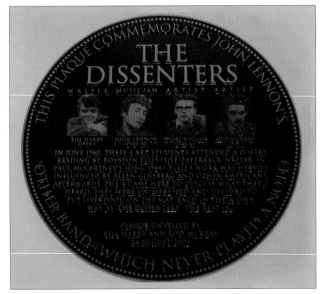

LEFT: *'The Dissenters' plaque in Ye Cracke* RIGHT: *Bill Harry holding a copy of Mersey Beat*

TOP: *Zbigniew Cybulski, Stuart's screen Idol*
ABOVE: *Cynthia and John in Liverpool in 1962*

When did you begin writing?

"I had started my own sci-fi publication at home called *Bi-Ped*, and then *Premier* as well as a fanzine *Jazz* for Liverpool Art College. Stu and I discussed doing a book together about Liverpool. I would write it and he would illustrate it. It never happened, sadly".

What was student life like?

"Student grants in those days were small. Stuart's mum, Millie, subsidized Stuart's tuition, which was about £24 per year, whereas I had to work through the holidays. I got a job on a building site and with the proceeds I bought a blue jacket. I went to Stu's flat in Percy Street wearing the jacket and Stuart offered to paint me

wearing it. He even asked me in which style I would like it. I chose Van Gogh. I still have the painting: I gave Stu the jacket in lieu of payment for the painting.

"The beatniks were the subject of discussion in the national press and Allan Williams was friendly with the local journalists. The Sunday People wanted to do an exposé on the beatnik generation, so Allan arranged for them to visit Stu's flat in Gambier Terrace. He had messed the whole flat up to make it look disgusting with these beatniks lying around doing nothing. The paper ran it on the front page, much to our disgust, as we had been duped into participating in a nasty story".

You were in a unique position to know what Stuart was like. Tell me about him?

"Stu was an introvert and easily hurt. John liked to have a go at him in front of his friends and he hated that. Sometimes if he had taken too much he would burst with anger. He had a tough exterior to many people, but only a few of us had the pleasure of knowing what he was really like. We discussed our inner feelings and thoughts and talked for hours about life. He loved his work and his painting. Initially he was influenced by famous artists like Van Gogh, but he started to develop his own style and became a talented artist. I ran a film society at the college and we watched films about Salvador Dali and continental films, especially from the Polish underground by Andrzej Wajda and others. Poland's leading actor was Zbigniew Cybulski. Stu copied Cybulski with the clothes and the dark sunglasses, and not James Dean as is commonly believed. We would go over to Wallasey to the Continental Cinema where we would watch French and Italian films".

What was Stuart like as a musician?

"All this nonsense about him standing with his back to the audience annoys me. The audition for Larry Parnes at the Wyvern Club was not a failure and he did not turn them down because of Stuart. Parnes wasn't happy with Tommy Moore, who looked a lot older than the rest of them and turned up late for the audition. No mention was made of Stuart's playing ability. In fact, if they were no good, why did Parnes book them to back Johnny Gentle? They didn't fail the audition; they just didn't get the number one slot to back Billy Fury.

"When Stuart stayed behind in Hamburg in 1960, he played with Howie Casey and The Seniors. Casey said that Stuart was a good bass guitarist. You can't hide the bass guitar in a band. If they are inadequate, then you soon know. Stuart's dad had purchased a guitar for him when he was younger and he sang in the choir and played piano too".

Harry spoke to Rick Hardy from the Jets, the first British rock group to appear in Hamburg, featuring Tony Sheridan. The Beatles played on some of the sessions with the Jets on their first trip. When I told him what Allan Williams had written in his book, he replied, "Stu never turned his back on stage. I remember him as he played the rock 'n' roll classic "Matchbox", appearing to be a lonely figure on stage. He certainly played to the audience and he definitely played bass. If you have someone who can't play the instrument properly, you have no bass sound. There were two rhythm guitarists with The Beatles and if one of them couldn't play, you wouldn't have noticed it—but it's different with a bass guitar. I was there and I can say quite definitely that Stuart never did a show in which he wasn't facing the audience".

Harry also spoke to Howie Casey, who topped the bill at the Kaiserkeller in Hamburg, while The Beatles played at the Indra Club.

"Promoter Bruno Koschmider decided to have another band at the Kaiserkeller so he separated The Beatles from the Seniors", Harry recalled. "Another outfit was

The beatniks: Allan Williams seated (with beard), and John Lennon sitting by Williams' feet, together with some of John's friends including Rod Murray and "Pete the Beat" on 24 July 1960, Gambier Terrace

formed with Casey on saxophone, Stan Foster on piano, Stuart on bass and a German modern jazz drummer. If Stu couldn't play, Casey certainly wouldn't have tolerated him in this outfit.

"Klaus Voormann, who befriended Stuart and The Beatles in Hamburg, became a famous bass player in his own right and backed each of the solo Beatles. He had his opinion too. Klaus said, 'He (Stu) was a good bass player, a basic bass player, completely different. So basic that you could say he was, at the time, my favourite bass player'. It was Stuart who helped Klaus learn the bass guitar.

"Nobody even mentioned this idea of Stuart being a bad bass player until Allan Williams wrote it in his book. If you repeat a story often enough, people believe you. If you throw enough mud, some of it sticks".

What about Stuart's death? There have been so many stories.

"So many writers have repeated the story that John Lennon kicked Stuart in the head during a fight in Hamburg, or following a fight outside Litherland Town Hall. Firstly, the fight was after a gig at Lathom Hall, when John and Pete came to Stu's rescue. Plus, the injury could not have killed Stuart that long afterwards. I kept in touch with Stuart's mum Millie every month and she told me how Stuart was doing in Hamburg. She told me that Stu had fallen down the stairs in Astrid's home. Stu had the attic flat at the top of the house where he painted. The stairs were steep and he fell down and banged his head. Millie was worried about him. Shortly after, Stu died".

Do you think any other city than Liverpool could have produced a band like The Beatles?

"Many people have stated that it was really a Hamburg sound, not a Mersey sound, but I disagree. In Hamburg, there were only two clubs where the bands played. Yes, they played long hours and this certainly improved their musicianship, but they didn't have to compete in the same way as in Liverpool. Back home there were hundreds of clubs all over Liverpool, each having two or three bands playing each night and the bands sometimes playing at two separate venues each night.

ABOVE: *The Fab Four pose for the cameras at Liverpool's Empire Theatre in November 1964*

"At one point, there were over 300 clubs affiliated with the Merseyside Clubs Association. All the clubs were competing with each other and every band was competing with each other. There were at least 350 bands in the Merseyside area and so you had to work hard just to get the best gigs".

Did The Beatles have an extra hunger for success?

"No, I wouldn't say they did. All the bands had to work hard just to survive. The dream of every band was to get a good residency at a club, but these were hard to come by. There were great bands in Liverpool like Rory Storm and the Hurricanes, The Big Three, Kingsize Taylor and the Dominoes and many more".

What did The Beatles have that was different?

"It is hard to describe. They weren't performing their own songs much, but when they returned from Hamburg with their black

ABOVE AND LEFT: *Inside Ye Cracke, where 'The Dissenters'—Bill Harry, John Lennon, Stuart Sutcliffe and Rod Murray—met*

"Love Me Do", the Fab Four's first hit single, released on 5 October 1962

leather and attitude, they knew they were good. John and Paul had a uniqueness about them, even before they introduced their own songs. They were already writing together, but they had that extra something that separates the great from the good".

Knowing John so well, how would you describe him?

"I was the first one to call John a genius and it was justified. He wanted to create so much all the time. Some people need a stimulant to get them going, and initially with John it was alcohol. A few beers would release his inner creativity and provoke him to create something new. He wasn't drunk, but he searched for that inner soul that held the secrets of his creativity. It started with alcohol in Liverpool, and then it was Preludin in Hamburg, marijuana, LSD, the Maharishi Mahesh Yogi and Primal Scream therapy. I believe John wasn't just abusing his body, he was seeking an altered state of consciousness to stimulate his inner creativity to find out more and more. He was the opposite to George, who believed in inner peace and that meditation would bring out his creative genius".

What was it like in the *Mersey Beat* office?

"It became the meeting place for bands, promoters and managers who wanted to advertise and discuss bookings. We would then head for the Roscoe Arms for a drink. John and Paul spent many lunchtimes sitting at the desk with my wife, Virginia, in the tiny office chatting away, answering phones and occasionally helping with the typing. John scraped together spare change to pay for funny ads in *Mersey Beat* at 4d (old pence) per word".

Tell me about Mersey Beat.

"It was the first paper in Liverpool to describe the music scene. I launched the first edition on 6 July 1961 and walked around the city centre asking shops to sell it".

Brian Epstein claimed that he had never heard of The Beatles before Raymond Jones came into NEMS in October 1961. What would you say to that statement?

"When I took the first edition to NEMS, I asked to see the manager. Brian Epstein came down from his office and we discussed NEMS selling *Mersey Beat*. He took twelve copies and sold them all. He telephoned me to say with surprise that he had sold out of the first issue. He ordered twelve dozen for the second issue. I delivered them to him and the front cover headline was "Beatles Record in Hamburg". Epstein invited me to the Basnett Bar to talk about *Mersey Beat*. He was interested in the bands and fascinated by the following these bands had in Liverpool. We went to the bar again and then back to our office when Epstein asked if he could be a record reviewer for the paper. From Issue 3, Epstein was the record reviewer. That issue had a Beatles article by Bob Wooler, and beneath it was the advert for NEMS. Epstein, Bob, my wife Virginia and I went to dinner and talked about the music scene in Liverpool.

"That is why Epstein telephoned me and asked me to arrange for him to visit The Cavern. I rang Ray McFall and made the arrangements.

"After playing a lunchtime gig at The Cavern, The Beatles would go into NEMS and enter the booths where you could listen to a record. They picked B-sides to find new songs, but were often thrown out by Epstein. There is no way he didn't know who they were. The Beatles were featured in every issue. Bob Wooler called it the 'Mersey Beatle'".

How did the band decide on the name, The Beatles?

"There have been so many stories, but I was there when it happened. I was in the flat at Gambier Terrace with the group and they had decided they didn't like the name Johnny and the Moondogs and had given up The Quarrymen name by then. Brian Casser had suggested Long John and The Silver Beatles, but none of the group liked it. They idolised Buddy Holly and were singing several his songs in their set. As Holly was backed by The Crickets, they wanted a similar sounding name. Stuart came up with the idea of another insect, a beetle. It was John who then suggested they substituted the 'a' to make it The Silver Beatles. All this nonsense about the film *The Wild One* is wrong. In the film, actor Lee Marvin mentions the name of a motorcycle gang called "The Beetles". However, the film was banned in Britain until 15 February 1968, so it couldn't have been the inspiration".

What about Raymond Jones?

"Raymond Jones was real, but he wasn't the only one asking for the record. Paul McCartney brought two copies of "My Bonnie" to Liverpool; one for Bob Wooler and one for me. Bob played it in every club and told the kids to ask for it at NEMS. I was talking to a guy called Bob Barrack who had spoken to McCartney about the record. Bob went in to NEMS and asked for "My Bonnie" too and ordered it. There were lots of Raymond Jones'".

Why do you think Epstein reinvented history so many times?

"Epstein didn't like to give credit to other people. Bob Wooler was very close to Brian, and Epstein took advice from Bob but rarely was Wooler given any credit. Epstein saw The Beatles as 'his boys' and became upset at anyone who tried to penetrate their inner circle. Epstein was the king of spin. He loved the drama and the theatrical side of the business and was happy to put others down on his way to the top. Epstein told The Beatles to stop taking song requests during a performance. This was a usual habit for all bands, which helped to build a rapport with the crowd. The Beatles were told to stop talking to girls, stop eating, drinking and swearing and, of course, to bow at the end of their performance like the Shadows".

Do you believe this had an effect on the group?

"Definitely. The Beatles had a symbiotic relationship with the crowd: they bounced off each other, which brought out the best in the band. Epstein put them into their suits, which got to John in particular. He saw that Epstein cleaned up these working class boys and put them into suits to have a clean-cut image, whereas the posh university and college boys from the south of England became the tough, hard-living Rolling Stones. John never got over that".

What about the suggestion that Epstein bought 10,000 copies of "Love Me Do" to make it a hit?

"It is ridiculous! Back in 1962, the charts were compiled by different music papers like the *Record Mirror*. To obtain a Top Ten chart, the paper would telephone a random selection of record shops around the country and ask them what their best-selling singles were. They wouldn't ask how many had been sold, just the ten most popular. No record retailer could predict when they would be telephoned, so it makes absolutely no sense for Epstein to invest in so many record purchases. Even if he had been telephoned, he would only tell them the popularity of the record, not the sales".

In the issue of *Mersey Beat* which was printed in August 1962, Harry received the usual written bulletin from Brian Epstein which reported that The Beatles had changed drummers.

Harry's column stated:
"Ringo Starr (former drummer with Rory Storm and the Hurricanes) has joined The Beatles, replacing Pete Best on drums. Ringo has admired The Beatles for years and is delighted with his new engagement. Naturally he is tremendously excited about the future.

The Beatles commented, 'Pete left the group by mutual agreement. There were no arguments or difficulties, and this has been an entirely amicable decision'. On Tuesday September 4th, The Beatles will fly to London to make recordings at EMI Studios. They will be recording numbers that have been specially written for the group, which they have received from their recording manager, George Martin (Parlophone)".

Bill Harry's Mersey Beat announcing The Beatles topping the paper's vote on the best band in Liverpool

The story was a travesty, and many have castigated Harry for printing it. However, he accepted the story on trust. Harry later recalled the incident. "I couldn't figure out what was going on. Epstein had obviously lied to me. He told me it was completely amicable. I thought Pete was absolutely crazy to give it up when they were on the brink".

Within 12 months, Harry interviewed Pete and was the first to print the "truth" about Pete's dismissal and then, years later, Harry co-wrote a book with Pete Best, which gave the true account of the drummer's sacking.

The ground-breaking edition of *Mersey Beat* was number two, because that is the issue that gave the whole front cover over to The Beatles recording in Hamburg and published an Astrid Kirchherr photo for the first time. Brian Epstein placed an order for 144 copies for his NEMS store, and they sold out very quickly. *Mersey Beat* was the only place to really find out about the local bands in detail, plus list where they were playing. It was a unique piece of publishing history that preserves that time in Liverpool, when The Beatles lead the onward march of *Mersey Beat*.

28 OCTOBER 1961
Raymond Jones asks for the record, "My Bonnie", by The Beatles

"Hello, Goodbye"

Brian Epstein's PA, Alistair Taylor, pictured in 2004

Who was Raymond Jones, the fan who first alerted Brian Epstein to The Beatles by asking for a copy of "My Bonnie"? Alistair Taylor said it was him.

Alistair Taylor—Hello Goodbye
In May 2004 I was fortunate enough to spend a couple of hours with Alistair Taylor on a trip from his home in Matlock, Derbyshire to Liverpool. Alistair was known as The Beatles' "Mr. Fix-it" and was a vital cog in the day-to-day operation of NEMS Enterprises—Epstein's shop was called NEMS, which stood for North End Music Stores—the business set up by Brian Epstein to manage The Beatles. Taylor was Epstein's personal assistant and the man to whom John, Paul, George and Ringo turned to if they needed anything.

For the next two hours I enjoyed the company of a most entertaining man. He was great fun, humble and full of stories. He didn't see the need to talk up his part in The Beatles' story, something he had been accused of in the past.

Alistair was born in Runcorn, Cheshire, to the south of Liverpool, on 21 June 1935. After a brief spell in London, where he met his wife, Lesley, he returned north to work for a timber merchant, William Evans in Widnes. The job, he discovered, didn't satisfy him.

So Alistair, how did you come to work for Brian?

"I saw an advert in the local paper for a Sales Assistant in NEMS, 'apply to Brian Epstein'. Naturally, I quickly answered the ad. When I met Brian, we talked about all aspects of music. My love was always for jazz, which was different to Brian who loved classical music. At the end of the interview, which lasted for two hours, Brian said I was over-qualified and he couldn't pay me enough for the position on offer. My heart sank.

"But then he said he wanted to employ me as his personal assistant, for £10 per week. I didn't understand what he wanted, but of course I said yes. It was the beginning of a great relationship with Brian, which had its highs and lows. He sacked me four times, and I resigned a couple of times too.

"Brian was gay. I knew that. He knew that I knew that, and it didn't matter. He knew I wasn't gay, and was happily married. It never interfered in our business relationship. At this point, I want to say something that has been edited out of interviews in the past. I loved Brian. It doesn't have to be complicated by homosexual overtones. It wasn't like that. I loved him. He was awkward, irritating, annoying and frustrating, but I loved him. Full stop.

"Once I had started working there, Brian and I had a little bet on each big record coming out. We would have to say if it was going to be a hit or not. Needless to say, even though he didn't like pop music, he could hear a hit a mile away. I rarely got it right; I can't remember him getting it wrong, ever. The bet was only a G & T (Gin and Tonic) but he was incredible.

"He introduced this remarkable system of record ordering with these little tags so that we knew when we had to re-order. In the end, if Brian put in a large order for a particular record, the other retailers would order them too. Brian was that impressive, and his opinion was often sought".

Who was 'Raymond Jones'?

"I was Raymond Jones. Kids were coming into the shop and asking for this record 'My Bonnie' by The Beatles. We didn't have it and, until somebody put in an actual order, Brian wouldn't do anything. You see, Brian had this claim that if you ordered a record by anyone, anywhere, he would find it. However, no matter how many people asked for it, nobody had ordered it by paying a deposit. Particularly as this was a German import, this was even more important.

"I knew we would sell lots of copies, so I made out the order form and paid the deposit from my own pocket in the name of Raymond Jones, one of our regular customers. Now we had an order, Brian and I set about tracking it down. Of course, it was recorded in Germany and was recorded under the name of Tony Sheridan and The Beat Brothers. Brian ordered the first batch and they sold out in no time at all. So, a few years ago, I announced that I was the real Raymond Jones. And that is it—it was me".

How does this fit? Local radio presenter and writer Spencer Leigh tracked down the real Raymond Jones a few years ago. Bob Wooler even had an address for him at 48, Stonefield Road, Liverpool. Therefore, there was also a local lad called Raymond Jones, who asked Brian Epstein for the record and told him, when asked, who The Beatles were and where they were playing.

But what about Alistair's tale?

Well, we know that Raymond Jones came into the shop and talked to Brian about The Beatles and the record, but maybe did not place the order and paying the deposit required before Brian would track it down. Therefore, Alistair told me that he simply used the real Raymond Jones' details for the order, and paid the deposit himself. Not the normal practice but, as this was a German import, taking a deposit was the standard for NEMS.

Whatever the motive, in this small way Alistair became 'Raymond Jones' but the real Raymond Jones remains an integral part of the story.

The basement record department of NEMS, recreated in The Beatles Story

Of course, the big event was the trip to The Cavern on 9 November 1961. What exactly happened?

"Brian wanted to go and see The Beatles who were so popular. Everyone was talking about them and we had sold so many copies of the record. Brian didn't know where The Cavern was, which of course I did as I had been there when it was a jazz club. He was amazed to realize how close it was.

"We went down into the cellar, and that smell of rotting fruit and vegetables never left The Cavern. It was smelly and horrible, and Brian and I looked out of place in our smart suits. We sat at the back and watched while the place went mad for these scruffy musicians. The noise was terrible. They were loud, awful, unprofessional, scruffy and frankly not that good. But we both couldn't help tapping our feet to the rhythm. They had something.

Don't ask me what it was, because I don't know. If I did I would have been a rich man. I call it ingredient 'X'.

"They played five songs I think, but the one that made us stop and take notice was when they introduced a song of their own called 'Hello Little Girl', which The Fourmost later recorded. It wasn't just that they were prepared to play their own song but that it went down well. Maybe that is what Brian saw in them.

"Anyway, we left and went to the Peacock Restaurant as planned, and that is where Brian dropped the bombshell. He asked me 'Who do you work for? Me or NEMS? What would you say to me managing The Beatles?' I was a little lost for words.

"Brian was a man who was bored easily, and The Beatles came along at the right time. He then made me the offer, which could have made me a wealthy man. He offered me a percentage of The Beatles, there and then. I couldn't contribute anything financially, so I said I couldn't accept his offer. Brian understood but asked me if I would work for him in managing The Beatles. Of course I would. I would have done anything for him. And so that is where it all began. It was the biggest financial mistake of my life, but you can't change things".

How did you get this title of 'Mr. Fix-it'?

"Whatever The Beatles wanted, I fixed it for them. I was Brian's general manager, so I stayed at home while the boys went on tour, because I looked after all the artists for Brian, not just The Beatles. Later on, I sorted out cars, houses, trains and planes and even buying an island. Whenever they went on tour, I made the arrangements. I loved it; it was great fun. I was there when they signed their management contract with Brian, which, of course, Epstein didn't sign. I signed as witness, but Brian wouldn't. I think he wanted a way for The Beatles to get out of it if it didn't work out. He was an honourable man, and was stepping out into a new world. If it did go wrong, he didn't want them tied into a long, complicated contract. That's what he was like.

"They just went along the line and signed, and then I did. I remember Paul saying something like, 'We're going to be stars, but if we don't make it together, I'm going to be a star'. That was Paul for you".

What do you remember about them in Liverpool?

"They were always hanging around the shop. I remember John and Paul coming into NEMS and asking if they could borrow a typist, called Barbara I think. They brought song lyrics in on scraps of paper—once it was on toilet paper—and she typed them up and then threw the scraps in the bin. Imagine what they would be worth now".

So Alistair, with their fame bringing untold riches, and the pick of the girls, surely there must have been scandals and claims?

"The Beatles had managed to get into trouble with local girls, and most of the girls who were pregnant were looked after by Brian. I often had to be the one to hand out the cheques. It is true that many of these girls could have come forward and destroyed the image that The Beatles had tried so hard to portray, but they were willing to settle without undue publicity".

We started to discuss the time when he thought The Beatles had had enough of touring. Most people know that after their last concert in 1966, George famously said that he was no longer a Beatle. But to my amazement, Alistair recalled a much earlier conversation.

"George told me back in 1963 that he was already starting to have second thoughts about fame".

He recalled an incident when The Beatles were flying to London from Liverpool Airport, but George hadn't turned up. The others went to London, leaving Alistair to contact George.

"I rang him at home to find out what was going on. George said, 'I don't want to be a Beatle'. In a panic, I went round to talk to him and George said he didn't like all the pressure and the frenzy of the crowds and the fans. Thankfully, he came to his senses and the matter was never discussed again until they finished touring in 1966".

Brian was determined to get them a record deal, wasn't he?

"Oh yes. I remember seeing him at his desk crying. In the end, he virtually resorted to blackmail. NEMS was the biggest record retailer around, and so he threatened to withdraw his business".

Was NEMS that big? How does that work?

"He could buy his records through a different company, like Decca. It was only anything on HMV (His Masters Voice) that he had to buy from EMI direct, and that wasn't a big concern. The rest of the records he could get elsewhere, so that was a lot of business to them. I believe it was only this that made them do something. Of course, they just fobbed him off on to George Martin who was looking after comedy records, but at least it was something".

It all went 'pear-shaped' at Apple, didn't it?

"I was the face of Apple for the advertising. McCartney asked me to pose as a one-man band in the newspapers to get people to send in their tapes for consideration. Then everyone sent stuff in and it all quickly went mad. Money was being wasted and I could see it. People were leeching off them—it was a disaster.

"The end was no great surprise to me. I was out at a business lunch when I received a phone call from the office. I was told to come straight back. I told them I couldn't as I was in a business meeting. The message was, 'come back now'. I had a feeling what was going on. I made it back to Peter Brown's office. He basically told me that I was out and I had the afternoon to clear my desk. There was Allen Klein's hit list and I was number one on the list—I saw it. I went home and Lesley knew straight away there was something wrong. She even guessed that I'd lost my job. I wanted to get in touch with the lads, not to beg for my job back—I had too much pride for that—but to see if they knew what was happening. I rang them all—one of them I know was in the background when I called—but they wouldn't speak to me. That hurt me. After all I'd done, they couldn't and wouldn't speak to me. I was closest to Paul, spending time at his house more than the others, because he was still living in London. The whole 'Hello, Goodbye' thing happened at Paul's house. I was round there one night and I asked him how he wrote songs. We sat at his piano and he said, 'I'll say one thing, you say the opposite' so we went black, white, yes, no, hello, goodbye. Not long after, the song 'Hello, Goodbye' was written, so I like to think of that as my little contribution".

Alistair was done with The Beatles and, to their shame, he was left to eek out a living washing dishes in a little Bed & Breakfast in Derbyshire. He could have had millions thanks to Brian, but turned his opportunity down. When he was sacked from Apple, they could have looked after him, but they didn't.

Alistair and I had a great journey together and he gave me his phone number to follow up. He gave an interview to Fulcrum TV and then sadly, a few weeks later he died quite suddenly. He had seen so much and been so close to The Beatles' inner circle, and yet had been let down by them. However, being the gentleman that he was, he didn't bear any grudges against them, but rather talked fondly of them.

It was great to meet you Alistair—hello and goodbye.

9 November 1961
Brian Epstein watches The Beatles at The Cavern
"Can't Buy Me Love"

Brian was the eldest son of Harry and Malka (known as 'Queenie') Epstein (pronounced Epsteen, not Epstine, according to his family). Promoter Sid Bernstein (pronounced Bernsteen) recalled laughing with Brian about how their names were partly spelled the same but pronounced differently.

He was born in a private nursing home at 4, Rodney Street in the centre of Liverpool on 19 September 1934, and grew up in the family home at 197, Queens Drive (Childwall). After The Beatles' breakthrough, he moved his parents away from his childhood home and out to a bungalow in Gateacre called 'Treetops', though sadly Brian's father Harry died just a few months before Brian in 1967. 'Queenie' eventually moved into a flat in Crompton's Court near Calderstones Park. Brian also visited his grandparents' home in Anfield, now Epstein's Guest House, where he developed a friendship with Joe Flannery, later to become a Beatles promoter.

Young Brian didn't enjoy school, and didn't settle in any of the many expensive fee-paying schools to which his parents sent him. The schools Brian attended were:

Prestatyn Nursery School, North Wales
Beechenhurst Prep School, Liverpool (Allerton)
Southport College, Lancashire
Croxton Preparatory School, Liverpool
Liverpool College, Liverpool (Allerton)
Wellesley School, Liverpool (Aigburth)
Beaconsfield Jewish School, Sussex
Claysmore School, Somerset
Wrekin College, Shropshire

He was labelled a disruptive pupil at Liverpool College and was expelled for being lazy and lacking concentration. However, his family always suspected it was more likely anti-Semitism.

The Epstein family owned a thriving furniture business, I. Epstein and Sons (Walton). Brian disappointed his parents by revealing that he didn't want to join the family business, but instead wanted to become an actor and later, a dress designer. Brian's only musical accomplishment was a brief period of playing the violin at primary school.

Epstein befriended Brian Bedford, an actor who persuaded him to audition for the Royal Academy for Dramatic Arts. As with most things in his life, it didn't last, and he soon returned to Liverpool where learned the furniture business at Times Furnishing.

He took on the responsibility of dressing the windows and this became an art form in itself. He adopted this role when he became

Brian Epstein, The Beatles' manager

manager of the record department at NEMS (Great Charlotte Street, Liverpool), and later, when Epstein's family opened a new NEMS shop in Whitechapel (Liverpool) and Epstein was installed as manager, his window displays were famous. It was here that he was able to announce that he had the record "My Bonnie", and later that he had all the newest Beatles releases. The rest as they say is history.

At the suggestion of a young Beatles fan, Raymond Jones, Epstein then went to The Cavern to see The Beatles.

Many have questioned over the years if Epstein already knew about the group. Bill Harry claims Epstein knew about them from his *Mersey Beat* paper, which he sold in his shops and contributed to, as it featured The Beatles in every issue. Harry surmised there was no way Epstein could have missed reading articles on The Beatles.

Beatles historian and author Ray O'Brien recently uncovered a fascinating fact. The Max Morris Hall attached to Greenbank Drive Synagogue (Wavertree) hosted performances by most of the big bands in Liverpool. This included The Beatles during the summer of 1961, probably in July or August. This fact is significant because this was the Epstein's synagogue and Harry Epstein was one of the leading fund-raisers there. This was at least two, maybe three, months before his visit to The Cavern.

Epstein met with The Beatles and agreed to a management contract with them, which he didn't sign. He discovered that The Beatles had signed a three-year deal with Polydor when they recorded with Bert Kaempfert in Hamburg, and he called Kaempfert to ask about releasing them from the contract. Polydor decided that it was only interested in Tony Sheridan, the British rock 'n' roll star in Hamburg, and Kaempfert wrote to Epstein releasing The Beatles for absolutely nothing.

Epstein was the guiding light for The Beatles, and the man who kept them together. But, as a homosexual Jew growing up in a Europe that had been ravaged by anti-Semitic uprisings at a time when homosexual acts were still illegal, he was a tortured soul. He kept a private flat at 36, Falkner Street (Liverpool) for his liaisons, outside the glare of his family and the public.

Because of the pressures of managing The Beatles, he grew ever more dependent on various painkillers and drugs. His substance abuse eventually led to his accidental overdose which killed him at the age of 32.

When looking at what led to the break-up of The Beatles, many say it was the death of Brian Epstein. The paradox was that although Epstein's role had diminished when The Beatles stopped touring in 1966, the group needed him to keep everything together. With him gone, the group's day-to-day management was gone.

John and Paul were the main players, but it was never ideal to have a member of the group as leader. John had always had a dominant force to guide him through life. Mimi had brought him up with strong discipline and Epstein had taken over the running of The Beatles. Epstein's death also created the need in John's life for another dominant personality to look after him. Yoko Ono gladly satisfied that need.

Paul had the drive and the motivation, and took on the role of trying to keep them together and focused. He was the impetus behind *Sgt. Pepper's Lonely Hearts Club Band*, *Magical Mystery Tour* and

ABOVE: *The plaque erected at Epstein's Guest House in Anfield, formerly the home of Brian Epstein's grandparents*

Let It Be, but having one band member double as the manager would never have worked, and ultimately it didn't.

That begs the question: What did Brian Epstein do for The Beatles?

Answer: Just about everything.

At the time Epstein entered the picture, Pete Best and his mum Mona were effectively managing the promotion for The Beatles. They were successful in securing many bookings. But it was Epstein who saw their potential and was prepared to back them with his time and money.

Epstein was a great lover of the theatre and frequented Liverpool theatres such as The Playhouse, befriending many of the actors. He spent hours discussing the many nuances of theatrical life with them at a friend's house, situated at 61, Hope Street.

When Epstein became The Beatles' manager he saw the theatrical potential of this dynamic, charismatic foursome who entertained crowds with their on-stage antics, their interaction with the audience and the way they bounced off each other like variety performers. They could sing and tell jokes; they were a modern day Vaudeville act—unlike any other band around at the time.

Epstein wasn't a lover of rock 'n' roll—he was a classical music buff. So why take on this undisciplined, scruffy bunch of loudmouths? I believe he saw them through

theatrical eyes, not rock 'n' roll eyes. He was creating a musical variety show, equally at home in cabaret clubs, theatres and rock 'n' roll venues. However, what Epstein soon discovered was that his boys not only had musical ability, they were original songwriters in their own right. Epstein took a band suited to the clubs of Hamburg and Liverpool and put together an image for the masses.

Epstein became the first manager to properly grasp the role of managing a band—it was more than just plugging in the instruments and playing. He became a theatrical impresario with a new musical sensation. When The Beatles signed their contract with Epstein, they agreed that he would be responsible for their costume, make-up and the songs they played. It was more than just a straightforward management contract.

Epstein made swift changes when he took over:

- He replaced their scruffy clothes with smart suits, like theatrical costumes.

- He reduced their playing time to sets of thirty-five minutes or so—a play in one act—with him providing the set list of songs. Epstein was the director of this musical.

- He renegotiated their fees to £15 from £7—an exorbitant increase. Most Merseybeat groups were delighted because they received increased fees too, which is like a better 'Equity' actor's rate for professional artists.

- He introduced the bowing at the end of songs, which he had pointed out to them when he had taken them to see The Shadows.

- He put a halt to the swearing, eating, drinking and clowning about on stage—they were now serious actors, not jesters. They had to learn their lines and stick to the script—no ad-libbing.

- They made it to the Royal Variety Performance. It's hard to imagine them doing their Hamburg set in front of the Royal Family.

- In the end, he never referred to them as a group or band. He only referred to his 'artists' as 'acts'. A true thespian.

Before they were famous, those who had seen them in Liverpool and Hamburg witnessed the 'real Beatles'. John Lennon once said, "If you haven't seen The Beatles in our black leathers in Liverpool or Hamburg, you haven't seen the real Beatles". After Epstein took over, everything changed.

Under Epstein's watchful eye, The Beatles took on fabricated personas: John was the sharp one; Paul was the cute one; George was the quiet one; and Ringo was the funny one. There were elements of their normal personality in these new creations, but Epstein scripted and directed them initially. When Epstein was asked by Bill Grundy in a 1964 interview about his thoughts on pop music, he responded that he didn't know about it being just good music, but that it was an 'art form'.

By this time, The Beatles would have done whatever it took to become famous. John may have felt donning suits and cleaning up their image was selling out later on, but the contract was quite explicit. Epstein was a hard-nosed business man who knew what it would take to turn The Beatles into world-beaters. The four 'cheeky Scousers', with their renowned sense of humour, were ready to take on the world.

Former publicist Tony Barrow says The Beatles were set up to showcase the song-writing talents of John Lennon and Paul McCartney. George Harrison was an integral

TOP: *Brian Epstein, pictured near his home on Queens Drive, Childwall*
BOTTOM: *Greenbank Drive Synagogue, where the Epsteins worshipped*

part of the music, but not as important as the other two. The drummer was less important, whoever it was.

In the end, Epstein's decision to support the sacking of Pete Best meant that his musical play was complete. Epstein created the greatest show on earth, and how right he was in his belief in them. Ringo charmed America with his droll wit—more humorous than John's sometimes-acerbic sarcasm, Paul's charm or George's Goons-like off the wall observations. It was Ringo who displayed the most natural acting skill in their films—he was seen as the most gifted actor among them.

However, his 'boys' didn't always appreciate him.

In Jann Wenner's book, *Lennon Remembers*, John was quoted as saying, "Brian was a nice guy, but he knew what he was doing. He robbed us. He f***ing took all the money and looked after himself and his family".

In McCartney's biography, *Many Years From Now*, biographer Barry Miles says, "For the most part, Epstein's arrangements with The Beatles were unfair. The Beatles had only agreed to them because they didn't know any better".

In retrospect, Epstein's critics say it was Brian's advisers who exploited his naivety in getting him to agree to deals that did the best for themselves, and not for The Beatles, particularly for the merchandise licensing in America. However, it must be emphatically stated that Epstein was exploring unchartered waters, mixing rock 'n' roll with commerce and that it's easy to be critical years after the fact.

Rex Makin is one man who knew Brian well. The Epstein's neighbour on Queens Drive, Childwall, Makin has been a successful solicitor in Liverpool for many years, and Brian often asked him for advice, both legal and personal. "Brian never moved without me", he claimed in an interview in the *Liverpool Echo*. "I advised him on everything. I knew him better than anyone. He used to call me on a daily basis when he went to lunch. At Paul McCartney's 21st birthday party, Lennon beat up Cavern DJ Bob Wooler and broke his nose. Wooler wanted to sue Lennon, but, because of my relationship with Brian, I settled the matter between them in a way which would today be held improper, for £200 odd plus costs, and that was the end of that".

Makin was also a personal friend of the family and when Brian's father died in June 1967, he and Brian sat in his back garden and talked. "Sadly", Makin says, "just two months later, I was making Brian's funeral arrangements".

In February 2008, it was suggested that a statue to Epstein be erected in Liverpool City Centre. Makin, however, was opposed to the idea. "Brian was an introspective person and, unfortunately, he was the victim of clingers-on, who remain to this day. He was a conflicted soul and would have laughed at the idea of a statue".

Sid Bernstein
I met and spoke to Sid Bernstein, the American promoter who staged the Shea Stadium concerts in 1965 and 1966. He came to Liverpool in August 2004 to unveil a plaque honouring his friend, Brian Epstein. Sid, at the age of 86, recalled the days of The Beatles with great affection.

I asked Sid how it all started.

"I have a love affair with England, which was formed during World War II when I was a G.I. stationed at bases like Grantham. I was soon then to leave the peace and tranquillity of England for the battlefields of France and Germany.

"After the war, I stayed in touch with England by taking the *Manchester Guardian* and *The People* newspapers. This way I kept up to date with what was happening on this side of the 'pond'. I noticed one day a single column of about twenty lines about a four-piece band creating waves in Liverpool called 'The Beatles'. I liked the sound of them and decided to enquire further.

"I found the phone number of Brian Epstein—I still remember it today: Childwall 6158. Brian's mum answered the phone politely and began to ask me questions about who I was. I soon heard Brian's footsteps and him picking up the receiver. There then followed a little amusing interchange as I explained who I was. I was Bernstein (pronounced Bernsteen) and Brian was Epstein (pronounced Epstine) and so that took a moment to get right, and certainly brought a nice touch of humour to the proceedings. I remember Brian's voice. It was like a classically trained actor, so beautifully English and warm".

Sid went on to explain that he had read about The Beatles and wanted to bring them to the United States. Brian quickly said, "Why would you want to commit financial suicide?" No one else had been interested from the U.S. and Brian couldn't believe his ears.

"Don't worry", I replied, "I have the finance in place for it—I want to bring them to Carnegie Hall". Sid had two things going against him: he didn't have the money and Carnegie Hall didn't host pop concerts.

"Brian and I eventually struck a deal over the phone and agreed everything verbally— we never had a signed contract", Bernstein said.

The Carnegie Hall concert on 12 February 1964 was a triumph for Bernstein. The 2,900 tickets for each of their two performances were sold out within a day.

The Shea Stadium concert on 15 August 1965 will go down as one of the greatest, and most significant, concerts in music history. This was the start of stadium concerts which are commonplace today. Shea Stadium, home to the New York Mets baseball team, held 55,600 screaming fans, a new world record. With gate receipts of $304,000, it was also the highest grossing pop concert for its time.

Sid unveiled a new plaque, dedicated to Brian, at Epstein's Guest House, the Epstein family home where Brian's dad Harry was born. It was also where the family furniture business was run, and where Brian used to play with his neighbour, a boy called Joe Flannery who became his lifelong friend and fellow promoter.

The previous night, Sid was joined on stage at The Grosvenor Ballroom, Wallasey, by Joe Flannery, Allan Williams and Sam Leach—a legendary line-up. They were four influential men from the early history of The Beatles.

Bill Covington
Bill Covington also knew Brian Epstein well. Covington was a member of the band The Rustiks, who were signed to NEMS by Brian. I asked him about his group, what Brian was like as a manager and touring with The Beatles.

ABOVE: *American promoter, Sid Bernstein,*
who booked The Beatles at the Shea Stadium
TOP RIGHT: *Promoters Sam Leach, Sid Bernstein,*
Joe Flannery and Beatles manager Allan Williams
BELOW: *The Rustiks, whom Brian Epstein managed*

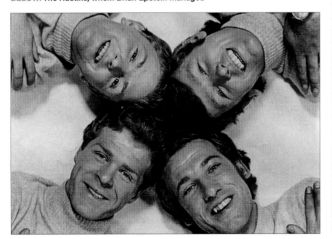

"The Rustiks reached the final of Westward TV's 'Beat Competition' in July 1964. We won the competition and were offered a recording contract with Decca Records. Out of the blue a management offer was tendered from Brian Epstein, who was one of the judges. The group had major exposure with appearances on The Beatles' tour, which started at Bradford on 9 October 1964.

"In March 1965 we spent ten days at the Festival of Valencia in Spain. In June we returned to Spain playing U.S. air bases, and appeared with The Beatles in Madrid on 2 July 1965".

Bill talked about his memories of Brian.

"I found Brian to be a generous man in the sense that he supplied The Rustiks with funds to buy clothes. Brian had a defined image of how he wanted his bands to look. Brian's idea of 'pop' bands was that they had to look presentable to the public. Therefore, he made sure his acts were in suits. So he was quite prepared to spend to achieve his objective. No other management that I've been involved with has spent money freely and unconditionally. So my memory of him is of a generous man.

"I would say that he was generous with his spirit, too. When he signed The Rustiks to NEMS he did so in a spirit of largesse. I can't think of another reason why he did sign us to NEMS. The Rustiks were not a band who were likely to have a successful recording career. The fact was made clear to Epstein on numerous occasions by members of his staff. True to his word, Epstein honoured the terms of our contract and did everything he could for us. I have no complaints about him at all".

Bill Parr
Bill Parr is another Liverpudlian who knew Epstein well. He remembers Epstein and The Beatles with great warmth. Bill worked for Rushworths music shop in Liverpool, not far from NEMS.

Bill remembers when Brian Epstein visited the instrument workshops to have a cup of tea with him.

"He would often call in to see what wood had been received so that he could order a new guitar. He would look at the various pieces of wood like oak or ash, and then ask for a guitar to be made out of that particular piece. In the workshop we would do a rubbing of the set-up of a guitar, order the heads and then assemble the guitar: this often took up to a week to make. Epstein would then choose his wood and say 'Hey Billy, can you make a guitar out of that piece please'. We would then go off and make it in the workshop.

"Brian was generous to all the staff there, and would often give us a £1 note and tell us to go and get some cakes. It was the little things like that which made him stand out.

"Sometimes before they had to disappear to wherever they were playing that day, The Beatles would assemble in the café below Rushworths. The Beatles would inevitably go on the hunt around the place. If I saw them, I would ask them 'what are you scrounging for?' We'd chat for a while, so I promised them I'd teach them how to read wood—what type it was, whether it was any good. They'd all borrow books from the music shop; well it is better than having to buy them! I promised to educate them and once said to Paul "Let's start with you, you're young". Paul took exception to that and told me proudly that he'd left school. Paul was known by us all there as 'our baby' because of his youthful looks.

"Often in the café, I would sit down and talk to The Beatles; they were all good friends and very sociable. They had a good sense of humour and liked the banter in the morning. One of my games was to arm-wrestle with them. I'd start with Ringo and work my way through them all, teasing them that they weren't as good as the others.

"One morning, I received the call to say I was needed the next day for a job. I had to take a piano to The Cavern and set it up on the stage. The four Beatles took me there and I gave them the instructions.

"As you may know, the entrance to The Cavern was narrow and there were a lot of steps. There was only one way in. I had to take the piano apart—it was a Brinsmead Upright Piano—and lower the pieces by rope to the bottom of the steps. I then had to reassemble it, and set it up on the stage. I then told Ringo to play it. 'I don't play the piano, I'm drums,' he protested. 'Well go and learn it then!' I said.

"One interesting little fact is that when we were sitting in the café, naturally there would be several 'lad's' jokes, the ruder the better when men are together. However, if there were any ladies present, one of The Beatles didn't like that type of humour, and would cough when the jokes turned blue. Can you guess who it was? Astonishingly, it was John Lennon. Who would have believed that? It seems that maybe not all of Mimi's discipline was wasted.

"As they were constantly in Rushworths they would always take a look at the new instruments coming in to the shop and have first pick if they wanted it. However, there was a problem when somebody left a match near the sheet music, and set fire to it, which could have been disastrous. The finger was pointed at The Beatles, though it

English composer, Lionel Bart, with Brian Epstein at The Cavern in 1963

"Brian was into drugs and becoming more and more dependent on them. I could see how this changed his character, with him being more depressed. Many have suggested that The Beatles didn't need him any more, but Lennon summed it up when he said, 'Well we've f***ing had it now'. All four Beatles were quite clear on this: if Brian couldn't be their manager then nobody else could".

How did Alistair recall that night?

"I remember coming home from San Francisco, walking through the door and saying hello to my wife Lesley, when the phone went. Epstein's secretary rang and said she couldn't get an answer from Brian. I had to apologise to Lesley and head off there. Lesley wasn't impressed, but I had a feeling something was wrong. We went in to the flat, and I just remember Brian lying there and I immediately knew he was dead.

"I looked around, and presumed it wasn't suicide, because firstly there was no note, but more importantly, I could see his pill bottles next to his bed, half full with the lids on. There were some letters on the bed and his favourite chocolate biscuits on a plate.

"He did not commit suicide in my opinion".

Taylor's statement was confirmed by the coroner who stated that it was an "incautious self-overdose". The amount of drugs in his body was consistent with a build up over the previous weeks, and this would have had the side effect of making the user more and more forgetful. The official cause of death was 'Carbrital poisoning'. '*Time, place and circumstances*: 3.00 p.m., Sunday 27 August 1967 at 24, Chapel Street, Westminster. Found dead in bed. *Coroner's conclusion:* Incautious self-overdosage. Accidental death'.

Brian Epstein's body was brought back to Liverpool, and his funeral was held in his local synagogue at Greenbank Drive in Wavertree. Brian Epstein was buried in the Jewish Cemetery (Aintree). His contribution to the group's success has been diminished over time, but to those in the know, it is immeasurable.

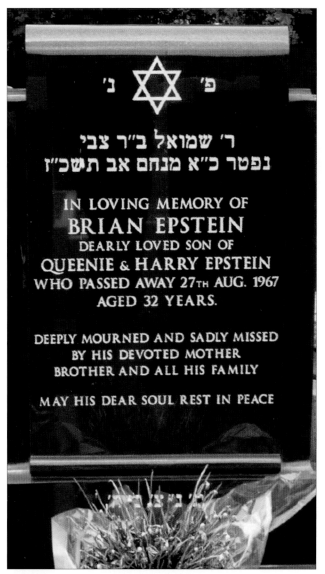

ABOVE: *Brian Epstein's grave in the Jewish Cemetery, Aintree, Liverpool*
RIGHT: *Here the weary are at rest—the Jewish Cemetery gates*

was never admitted or denied, and so The Beatles and the other groups were banned from the shop".

Brian Epstein's death
On 27 August 1967, Brian Epstein was found dead in his London flat. Assistant Alistair Taylor discovered his body. Alistair remembered that awful day.

"Brian had called me on several occasions threatening to commit suicide, and when I went round to his flat, he would be sitting there quite calmly having a drink and wondering what the fuss was about.

10 November 1961
The Beatles appear at Sam Leach's first "Operation Big Beat"
"Ask Me Why"

'Operation Big Beat' was a spectacular November 1961 event that was staged in the Tower Ballroom, New Brighton (Wirral), one of many such events in the early sixties. The Beatles were the main attraction at a venue which held over 4,000 people, their biggest ever gig, until the band later started playing stadium shows.

Sam Leach, The Beatles' friend and promoter, put together a night of rock 'n' roll on a scale that had never been seen before in and around Liverpool. Between 7.30 p.m. and approximately 1.00 a.m., five of Liverpool's top groups took to the stage in turn, including Rory Storm and the Hurricanes with a bearded Ringo Starr on drums.

At a Jacaranda event in December 2003, hosted by the British Beatles Fan Club, I had the pleasure of talking to Leach, who had recently launched his book *The Rocking City* and told me of some of the great times he spent with The Beatles.

You are forever linked with those incredible "Operation Big Beat" events at the Tower Ballroom in New Brighton. What were they like?

"I would book all the top artists and feature them back-to-back in some of the best Merseybeat shows ever seen. Unfortunately, a fire in 1969 destroyed this once-great landmark. The Beatles made one dramatic appearance on 10 November 1961.

"I'd put in a massive investment to promote this evening, and then fog struck. I was worried that not many people would turn up, and The Beatles told me they would play for nothing so that I wouldn't lose out—that's what they were like. The Beatles opened and then had to disappear over to Knotty Ash Village Hall, and were due back at the Tower at midnight. No one expected them back.

"To my surprise and delight, the crowds flocked in—a record 4,124 people. The Beatles made it back eventually, Neil Aspinall driving carefully to get them there. They were electric. There were screaming girls, fainting and going hysterical over their performance. It was the first time this had happened on this scale".

Another great venue not known to many fans, but located close to The Cavern, was the Iron Door. Previously a traditional jazz club, Sam remembers The Beatles playing there many times. Although it was also a converted warehouse, it was newly painted and smelled fresh, unlike The Cavern. It had been renamed the Liverpool Jazz Society, but would forever be referred to as the Iron Door. Leach's memory is still sharp concerning the club.

TOP: *Beatles promoter Sam Leach*
ABOVE: *'Operation Big Beat' Poster*

"When I took over holding my band nights, it became one of the most famous clubs in Liverpool, even though it was quite close to The Cavern. Regular cloakroom girls Pat Davies and her friend Ruth decided one busy night to ask me if their friend could help out. They were rushed off their feet, so I agreed. Her name was Priscilla White, known better these days as Cilla Black.

"On one infamous night, The Beatles were worried about their equipment, and the damp conditions there. There was a real risk of five fried Beatles. So, John, Paul, George, Stuart and Pete played on rubber mats to avoid being electrocuted. In the end, I believe it was the Iron Door events that ended The Cavern's jazz days, and they reluctantly gave in to rock 'n' roll. This latest big event at the Iron Door had led Ray McFall, together with Bob Wooler's persistence, to re-think the future. Ten days later, The Cavern announced the debut of The Beatles".

When did you begin promotions, working with Brian Epstein?

The Tower Ballroom, New Brighton, home of Sam Leach's 'Operation Big Beat'

"I met with John Lennon and Paul McCartney at the Kardomah Café after a phone call from Paul McCartney, who asked me to meet him and John urgently. John said 'look, we know we have an unwritten handshake with you, but we've been approached by this fella Brian Epstein who has real money. Have a look at him and see what you think'.

"I accompanied John and Paul to NEMS, and then John and Paul left Epstein and me alone to talk. I proposed a joint venture, but Epstein turned me down. From then on, Brian Epstein set about separating The Beatles from me.

"On 1 February 1962, Epstein advertised the first gig under his management as 'The Grand Opening of The Beatle Club', arranged by me. Set above the Thistle Café in West Kirby on the Wirral, panic had set in when Epstein found out that John Lennon had laryngitis, and was ready to cancel the show, but I insisted it must go on. On my recommendation, Epstein engaged Rory Storm to substitute. Epstein's first concert as The Beatles' manager was Paul, George, Pete and Rory. The fee was £18, of which Epstein received only 10 per cent, which just about covered his petrol and expenses.

"Then, at the Rialto on 6 September 1962, Epstein was worried about the threat of violence at this inner-city venue. I promised them bodyguards, but Epstein wasn't happy. He asked The Beatles to pull out, but John and Paul sided with me against Epstein. Brian felt humiliated and he was determined to break The Beatles' loyalty to me.

"The next day at the Tower, Epstein decided to put me under financial pressure by demanding all the outstanding monies from the previous day's Rialto concert. I told him I wouldn't have it until after the show. Epstein took the tickets out from NEMS and told me The Beatles would not be playing unless he received the outstanding £19.

"Paul McCartney begged Epstein to let them play. The Beatles travelled to the Tower with the situation still unresolved. There was a small crowd—the weather was bad and it was not long after Ringo had joined them. I gave Epstein the £19, hoping that would resolve things, but Epstein then demanded the fee of £35 for that night before they would go on.

"The DJ announced that they would not be appearing. Paul, John, Epstein and I were locked in argument in the office. Paul and John were pleading with Epstein. I didn't have all the money. Epstein warned Paul and John: 'You went against my wishes appearing at the Rialto last night. Do it again, and it's all over for us'.

"I told them to abide by their manager's wishes and left the room. The Beatles didn't appear that night. In 1964 I sent Brian Epstein a cheque for the outstanding money, which he acknowledged".

What other memories do you have of them?

"There was a great one at the Cassanova Club in Dale Street, where they appeared at an afternoon session one Sunday—the launch of the club. The Beatles were playing regularly at The Cavern and Ray McFall, The Cavern's owner, told The Beatles they couldn't play at the Cassanova. I had promoted the concert but I was in a dilemma. Suddenly, The Beatles turned up.

"Apparently, someone had let off stink bombs in The Cavern and they had to shut it down for the afternoon. So they turned up and played for me. The Beatles were threatened with being banned from The Cavern. What would have happened then? The Beatles never officially appeared again at the Cassanova, but billed as Rory Storm and the Wild Ones, John, Paul and George would come along and play— whoever was free at the time got up on stage".

December 1961
Tony Barrow and The Beatles
"The Word"

Liverpool-born Tony Barrow was The Beatles' Press Officer between 1962 and 1968, and worked for Brian Epstein at NEMS Enterprises.

Tony's full-time job was as an album sleeve writer for Decca Records. He also moonlighted for the *Liverpool Daily Post* and the *Liverpool Echo* under the *nom de plume* 'Disker', reviewing the latest releases for his '*Off The Record*' column.

While perusing old copies of the *Liverpool Daily Post*, I stumbled across one review from a momentous day in Beatles history: 6 July 1957, the day John met Paul. What did 'Disker' (Tony Barrow) write about that day?

"The whispers that Elvis Presley is on the way out have grown into yells and screams from some. 'All Shook Up' is still spinning Mr. Elvis a tidy income but I have an idea the magic has worked for the last time. Who can replace him? I'd nominate Capitol's Tommy Sands with his smooth natural personality".

So Barrow didn't always get it right. He made up for it with his incredible way with words and people.

Epstein asked Disker to mention The Beatles in one of his columns, but since they did not have a record for review, this would not be possible. However, Epstein was surprised to learn that Disker and Tony were the same person. Here was the introduction he was looking for. He took a poor quality acetate to Tony, and asked him to persuade his associates at Decca to grant The Beatles an audition. Tony pointed out that Epstein was a formidable record retailer in the north-west of England, and that he was well-known across the country. Decca agreed but the audition did not go well.

Later, when he was looking for a PR man, Epstein remembered Tony. He had initially approached future Rolling Stones manager Andrew Loog Oldham, who turned him down. At first, Tony also rejected the proposal, but when Epstein offered him twice the pay that he was earning at Decca, he accepted the job. His task was to look after some of NEMS' other clients like Cilla Black and Billy J. Kramer, as Epstein's press officer for The Beatles was Derek Taylor. However, Barrow gradually became more involved with The Beatles and accompanied them on many trips. At the request of Paul McCartney, he taped The Beatles' final concert at Candlestick Park on 29 August 1966.

It was Tony who arranged many of the press conferences and media interviews, and coined the phrase 'the Fab Four' while writing the sleeve notes for The Beatles' album covers. Tony also came up with the idea of the famous Christmas records for the fans, which he scripted, though it's apparent the boys did improvise.

He had a great view of the lives of The Beatles. His 2005 book, *John, Paul, George, Ringo and Me*, was a fairly straightforward autobiography of the man who helped craft their image. I spoke briefly with Tony Barrow during his book tour.

"I didn't want to do a tell-all, gossip and secrets type of book which would all be based on hearsay or rumour, and inconsequential to the story. I wanted just to tell my story as I saw it, being around the biggest pop sensation ever", Tony explained. "I couldn't believe that no one had used that title before with all the Beatles' names in it, so I thought, why not? This is my story, told through my eyes, and it just happened to be that it was The Beatles I was with. It is almost like writing a diary of what I saw. I hope readers will like it. It doesn't make any sensational claims, just a good story of a great time in my life".

It was appropriate, then, that Tony was asked to help announce a very special coup for The Beatles Story visitor attraction in Albert Dock, Liverpool. On 13 April 2005 they announced that they had acquired some unique pieces of The Beatles memorabilia. Tony delighted in retelling his stories, but seemed to do so out of respect and not for self-gain. He explained the exhibits, and the organ in particular.

"At the heart of the exhibition was the Vox organ, which had been played by John at Abbey Road and was taken over for the famous 1965 Shea Stadium concert. When The Beatles were booked to play there, they had to review the way they performed their concerts. Instead of being up close and personal with their fans, they were in the middle of a massive stadium, a long way from the crowd. Each action and facial expression had to be exaggerated so that the fans would see what they were doing.

"And so, when they came to perform 'I'm Down' for the first time at a concert like this, John decided to use this organ. If you have seen the film of the Shea gig, you will remember John going, as he would say "all Jerry Lee Lewis", running his elbow up and down the keyboard, to the obvious delight of the crowd. In fact, George was next to John and laughing so much that he could hardly play his guitar—not that anyone would notice by then.

"I remember Brian Epstein standing as usual at the side of the stage, bathing in the reflected glory of 'his boys', while still trying to look nonchalant. By the end of the concert there were tears of joy on Brian's face".

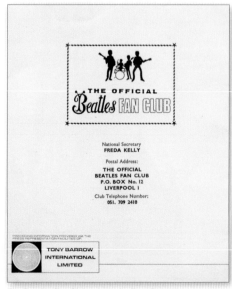

The Beatles Fan Club release by Tony Barrow

1 JANUARY 1962
The Decca audition
"A Hard Day's Night"

The Beatles' January 1962 Decca audition is a watershed moment in music history. Legend has it that Brian Poole and the Tremeloes had been in the studio either the previous day or the same day as The Beatles, and it was up to Decca's Recording Manager Dick Rowe to make the final decision between the two bands. He unwisely chose Brian Poole and The Tremeloes.

There have been many words written about this event, and Rowe has been vilified in history for his decision. A & R (Artistes & Repertoire) man Mike Smith also received his fair share of criticism for getting their hopes up and sending them away happy. The Beatles admitted coming away from the session in a confident mood, which is why they were shocked when they were later turned down by the label.

Mike Smith was happy to discuss his part in the story. He recalled travelling to Liverpool to see The Beatles at The Cavern and was impressed with the group. He recommended further inspection in the studio.

Mersey Beat reported Smith's trip to see the foursome:

"Commenting upon the outfit's recent recording test, Decca disc producer Mike Smith tells me that he thinks The Beatles are great. He has a continuous tape of their audition performance which runs for over 30 minutes and he is convinced his label will be able to put The Beatles to good use".

However, Smith since claimed that when The Beatles played for Decca officials, they weren't very good. It was New Year's Day 1962 and their equipment was in a terrible state and their performance was not terribly impressive. He also disliked their song selection—or rather the songs Brian Epstein had chosen for them. Smith felt their set list didn't show the true scope of their talent. Having listened to the recordings that survived, Smith is correct in his assessment that they were not great that day.

I turned to Brian Poole to see if he could enlighten me about the Decca audition. Poole has admitted that he had befriended Mike Smith some time before and his group had been into Decca months earlier, not the day before. His group had already recorded for Decca and was working on its first single and album by the time The Beatles arrived. There was no competition over the two bands and there was no decision for Decca to make between two bands, as Decca has claimed. Decca officials wondered if they could afford to take a chance on another "guitar band", particularly one that failed to bowl over executives. This supports the theory that Decca gave The Beatles an audition to pacify Brian Epstein, since his NEMS record shops were influential in the trade. The Beatles did have the last laugh—in more ways than one.

Mike Smith remembers seeing The Beatles in London after they became famous. In true Scouse fashion, they stood on the pavement and gave him a two-fingered salute. Decades later, he smiled at their cheek. He couldn't blame them now, could he?

Tony Barrow, the man from Decca who helped arrange the audition, playing John Lennon's Vox organ

10 April 1962
Stuart Sutcliffe's death
"In My Life"

Toward the end of 1961, Stuart Sutcliffe collapsed at the Art College in Hamburg and was sent home to Liverpool. His fiancée, Astrid Kirchherr, said he had been suffering a series of headaches and surmised that he had been working too hard.

Stuart returned to Hamburg the next day but in February 1962 he collapsed again. Stu was brought back to Astrid's and taken to his room. This time he stayed there, writing thirty-page letters to John, working on drawings and paintings, or just walking round and round his room. He suffered from violent headaches and temper tantrums, which made it difficult for Astrid and her mother to look after him.

There are stories of Stu being involved in a fight in a Liverpool or Hamburg alley where he was kicked in the head, which ultimately lead to his death. The one fight that is a matter of record occurred at Lathom Hall in Seaforth, Liverpool during 1961, though the exact date is unknown.

Pete Best remembered it well. The Beatles had played and were in the bar after the gig. "Stuart stepped outside and was jumped by a local gang", Pete said. "This girl ran in and told us what was happening and John and I ran out to help. Stuart was getting a kicking and so we just dived in. We rescued Stu but he was badly beaten and his face was covered in blood. John broke a finger I think, too".

When Stu returned home, his mother Millie was shocked at her son's appearance. He refused to see a doctor and went straight to bed. Millie felt that there was a connection between this attack and his death. Stuart had been to see a doctor in Germany and had x-rays taken to try to establish the result of his headaches. No fault could be seen, and when Sutcliffe visited Liverpool, he and his mother visited Sefton General Hospital with those x-rays, and again no obvious injuries could be detected.

One other commonly quoted theory is that Lennon had a fight with Stuart in Hamburg, in which he kicked Stuart in the head and in turn this led to Sutcliffe's death.

Could John Lennon really have killed his best friend?

Bill Harry recalls speaking to Millie about her son, and she told Bill that Stuart had fallen down the stairs at Astrid's house where he was staying, following more headaches and blackouts.

The official cause of death was "cerebral paralysis because of blood seeping into the right ventricle of his brain".

Who, or what, really caused Stuart Sutcliffe's death?

The medical diagnosis

A fan of The Beatles, and a doctor, Steve Dutton has researched the possible causes of death with some interesting conclusions.

The possible causes of cerebral haemorrhage are: Stroke, brain tumour, trauma (a blow to the head), aneurysm, and AVM, a malformation in the connection between an artery and a vein.

Stroke
This is virtually unheard of in people Stuart's age as it is the result of high blood pressure.

A brain tumour
A tumour may cause bleeding; however, the presence of a tumour large enough to cause bleeding would have been obvious on autopsy.

Trauma
A blow to the head can cause three possible types of bleeds:

1. Epidural bleed. A ruptured artery rapidly pumps blood into the skull and the brain is compressed by the growing blood clot. The patient becomes unconscious within hours after the injury and dies within about twenty-four hours if it is not treated. There would be no headaches so Lennon could not have been responsible.

2. Subdural bleed. A ruptured vein oozes blood into the skull. The patient deteriorates slowly over about two weeks, (occasionally several weeks) with unsteady gait progressing to confusion, then lethargy and coma. It would show up on an autopsy, and he would have been comatose long before his eventual death. If Lennon had been responsible, Stuart's death would have been at least four months before, which is way out of the time frame for this type of injury.

3. Intracranial bleed. A severe blow to the head can cause bleeding deep into the brain, frequently with rupture into the ventricles. Death can be rapid but the patient may last up to about three days and in which the patient is near comatose or comatose. This fits the case only if the fall down the stairs occurred just before he died. Sutcliffe did have a fall shortly before his death, though this on its own was not enough to kill him. Again, John was not present in the necessary time frame to have caused the injury.

Aneurysms are weak spots in arteries. They are present from birth and gradually enlarge. They most frequently rupture in patients over thirty. Although there may be some warning headaches, most often there is a single, explosive headache. Half of aneurysm patients die immediately. The location of most aneurysms makes bleeding into the ventricle very possible. An aneurysm is certainly a strong possibility in Stuart's case.

AVM, also present from birth, is a malformation in the connection between an artery and a vein. The veins in the area have arterial blood pumped into them. Because veins are not made to handle the high pressure of arterial blood, they become enlarged and eventually bleed. They frequently have repeated small bleeds causing severe episodic headaches before a large bleed occurs and seizures ("fits") are common. The large bleed can be fatal. AVM ruptures are most common in teens and young adults. Bleeding into just one ventricle is less likely with an AVM than an aneurysm, but the history of headaches, age, and rapid death make AVM a very strong possibility.

Summary:

The causes of death that best fit the scenario are therefore aneurysm and AVM, with both of these being congenital and unrelated to any blow to the head. More importantly, John Lennon was not with Stu in the four months prior to his death. No head trauma of the type suggested causes cerebral bleeding and death that long after injury. Therefore, John could not have been responsible for Stuart Sutcliffe's death.

Stuart had fallen down the stairs in Astrid's Hamburg home, after which he complained of severe headaches. It was this fall that most probably contributed to his untimely death.

Millie and Astrid talked about Stuart after his death. Millie had a premonition something was amiss when Stuart was ill. "At half-past four I was in my bedroom at home in Liverpool", recalled Millie. "I felt as if a great strong cold wind came through that house, lifted me up and laid me across the bed. For fifteen or so minutes, not a muscle in my body was capable of movement. That was the time, I discovered later, when Stuart was dying".

Astrid commented after the post-mortem, "Stuart's brain was expanding—getting too big for the space it floated in. It's a very rare medical condition, but it can happen. Even if Stuart had lived, he would have been blind and probably paralysed. He wouldn't have been able to paint. He would have preferred to die".

On 10 April 1962, as Paul, John and Pete boarded a plane from Manchester Airport bound for Hamburg, Astrid was working in her photo studio in Hamburg when she received a phone call from her mother. Stuart was having another of his spells. Astrid rushed home and she and her mother bundled Stuart into an ambulance to take him to the hospital. On the way there, Stuart died in Astrid's arms.

The news reached Millie from Astrid in two telegrams, which were delivered out of sequence. The first said he had died; the second that he was seriously ill. Stuart's father was away at sea and not reachable. Millie had to break the news to her two daughters. She then booked the first flight she could, which, by chance, was the same one Brian Epstein and George Harrison took to Hamburg. Epstein gave her a lift to Manchester, and the two men sat with her on the plane. At the Hamburg airport, Astrid was waiting with John, Paul and Pete.

Astrid was plunged into black despair by Stuart's death and for a while seemed to give up on life. She later said, "It was John who saved me. He convinced me, after Stu was gone, that I couldn't behave as if I were a widow. He pretended to be heartless, but I knew what he said came from the heart. 'Make up your mind,' he told me. 'You either live or you die. You can't be in the middle'."

Stuart Sutcliffe, buried in the grave with his father, Charles, in Huyton, Liverpool

6 JUNE 1962
The Beatles at EMI
"Please Please Me"

After the disappointment of the Decca audition of 1 January 1962, Epstein had managed to secure a meeting with EMI officials at London's Abbey Road Studios in June. It has often been referred to as an audition, but this was a proper recording date too.

George Martin met with Brian Epstein on 9 May and decided to offer The Beatles a recording contract subject to seeing them in person. Martin arranged for the contract to be drafted, and sent to Epstein on 24 May, post-dated for 4 June. Epstein returned the paperwork to Martin on 5 June, the day before The Beatles walked through the door of Abbey Road Studios. Because the contract had been prepared, The Beatles were ready to record a debut single that day, but the session also doubled as an audition for Martin to confirm whether he was prepared to sign off on the contract.

Often seen as the straw that broke the camel's back for Pete Best's career with The Beatles, it has been said that Martin told Epstein that Pete's drumming wasn't good enough and that he was bringing in a session drummer.

While researching the *Best of The Beatles* DVD, the interviewers spoke to key members of the EMI sound crew who were involved that fateful day, most notably Ron Richards, Norman Smith and Ken Townsend. Richards was left in charge of producing the recording as Martin did not usually oversee these sessions and was in his office for most of the time. It was revealed that Martin only dropped in when they were performing "Love Me Do".

The first thing that engineers Smith and Townsend noticed was the awful state of their equipment. They couldn't use it, particularly as Paul's bass amplifier was making a "farting noise" because it was so poor. They were forced to improvise and raided their boxes of spare leads to come up with something better.

In the Mojo book *Ten Years That Shook The World*, author and Beatles historian Mark Lewisohn looked into the Pete Best affair. He quoted Ron Richards as saying to Martin, "He's (Best) useless, we have to change this drummer. Poor old Pete, but he wasn't very good".

Richards said decades later that he had "a thing about drummers" and was very particular about drumming on records which is very different to drumming live—it takes a certain style of rhythm and is hard to record, even with modern technology.

As Richards and Martin listened to the recording, Richards said that he wanted to bring in a seasoned session drummer. That turned out to be Andy White, a friend and drummer with whom

Abbey Road Studios in London

he had worked many times. EMI only had a small budget and limited studio time, so Richards' request was granted.

Martin's short term aim was to bring in a session drummer to produce a satisfactory recording and he did not consider it necessary to change the physical line-up by dismissing Pete. It was Richards who put Pete through his paces, and admitted that no other regular "live" drummers could have done what he asked—not even Ringo. When Townsend was interviewed, he commented that he didn't even see the need for a session drummer at all.

Martin said that there was nothing wrong with Pete's drumming as far as he was concerned, but this was not conveyed clearly enough to Epstein, who had little understanding of studio protocols. Consequently, Martin has felt partly responsible for Best's dismissal over the years, though he was only passing on the comments of his producer and engineers, who have admitted that in hindsight, they were a bit harsh on Pete.

The session was not brilliant, but the record deal was agreed upon and a recording date set for September. John, Paul, George and Pete had secured the contract that would make three of them rich beyond their wildest dreams. For Pete, the nightmare was about to unfold.

16 AUGUST 1962
Pete Best is dismissed
"I'm Down"

Many theories abound regarding the controversial sacking of Pete Best as The Beatles were on the threshold of stardom. Pete was never told the reason why by anyone in the group and will probably never get a straight answer in his lifetime.

Some of the most commonly quoted reasons are his refusal to get a Beatle haircut or that he was a poor drummer. It's also been said that he was anti-social and a nonconformist. John, Paul and George all knew Pete from The Casbah: Pete was not unknown.

Did He Fit In?
If it was a problem, who would this most affect? John Winston Lennon, yet Pete was closer to John than to any of the others. If there was such a clash or problem with his background or personality, it never openly surfaced.

He Wasn't From Liverpool
The only two of the six Beatles who weren't Scousers were Stuart—who was from Edinburgh in Scotland, with Scottish parents—and Pete who was born in India with a father from Liverpool, but his mother grew up in India. Did it make a difference? Maybe what he didn't know was that unless you had that ingrained working class "scouse" mentality, you would never survive in The Beatles.

In March 1966, John Lennon gave an interview in which he claimed that The Beatles were "more popular than Jesus". By the time the US press and radio stations had whipped up a furore, Lennon had received death threats and their US tour was in doubt. The reaction from fans forced the band to close ranks and brought them closer together. Ringo, as a Scouser, could understand their mentality and knew what it took to break into this close-knit group. Once in, the Fab Four were impenetrable. Even so, he said in *The Beatles Anthology* that it took years to feel part of the group. He also said, "I had to join them as people, as well as a drummer".

Mean, Moody, Magnificent
There was a suggestion that Pete was moody. Bob Wooler described Pete as "mean, moody and magnificent" and many have taken this the wrong way. Wooler was a genius of alliteration, and so intimated that Pete reminded him of a film star, with those "bedroom eyes" and film-star good looks gave him the excuse to use it. Many, however, have taken this the wrong way, and assumed it to mean that he was moody and miserable.

Jealous Guys?
Did Pete's popularity make the other Beatles jealous? This feeling also wasn't helped when Bob Wooler introduced The Beatles at The Cavern with: "It's time for John, Paul, George and... Pete", at which point the screams reached an unbelievable crescendo. Ray Ennis of the Swinging Blue Jeans recalled on one occasion when Pete was singing "Matchbox" in The Cavern, that John, Paul and George were asked to sit down on the edge of the stage by the female fans so that they could see Pete.

For their gig at Litherland Town Hall on 7 August 1961, the newspaper advertisement proclaimed "Hear Pete Best sing tonight". When *Mersey Beat* announced the recording contract had been secured, the congratulatory ad was accompanied by a photo of Pete on his own, not of the four Beatles.

Paul McCartney, it has often been suggested, was the most jealous. During the *Teenagers' Turn* showcase in Manchester in March 1962, Lennon, McCartney and Harrison walked on stage to applause, but when Best walked on, the girls screamed. Best was surrounded at the stage door afterwards by attentive girls, while the other members were ignored after signing a few autographs. Paul's father, Jim McCartney, was present at the time and admonished Best by saying: "Why did you have to attract all the attention? Why didn't you call the other lads back? I think that was very selfish of you". Did this increase Paul's desire to see Pete removed from the group?

That their female admirers loved Pete. However, when you are dealing with young men, egos are involved and so many believe, as do I, that this would have been a factor.

The Beatles enjoyed moderate success from August 1960 to August 1962. They refined their act and repertoire in Hamburg and Liverpool before Epstein "cleaned" them up and secured the record deal in June 1962 that would launch them to stardom. This was all gained with Pete's help, but he wouldn't be there with them when they broke through. Instead, Ringo Starr was drafted in at the last minute to join their wild roller-coaster ride to fame.

Pete remembered that fateful day in August 1962 when he received the life-changing news. "Epstein saw me the night before and said that he wanted to see me in the morning, which was not unusual. However, when I arrived there Epstein was agitated and I knew something was wrong. Finally he came out with it: 'I don't know how to tell you this, Pete, but the boys want you out and Ringo is joining them on Saturday'. Epstein by this time was almost in tears". Pete left Epstein's office and went home to tell Mo. He just told her, "They kicked me out of The Beatles", and broke down.

Pete Best, before he was dismissed from The Beatles

Chronology

Let us look at the chronology of events that led up to Pete's dismissal in the summer of 1962.

1 January 1962 - The Beatles audition for Decca. They are turned down, but John, Paul and George do not tell Pete straight away.
18 May 1962 - George Martin issues a contract for The Beatles, which he sends to Brian Epstein, which he signs and returns to EMI.
4 June 1962 - Contract is effective from this date for 12 months.
6 June 1962 - The Beatles' first meeting and recording session at EMI with George Martin. It is after this session that Martin tells Brian that he will use a session drummer for the record.
July 1962 - George Martin watches The Beatles at The Cavern.
July 1962 - Following this appearance, George Martin confirms the recording contract to Brian Epstein, and announces that the first recording session will take place on 4 September, and that The Beatles should work on "Love Me Do" and "How Do You Do It".
16 August 1962 - Pete Best is dismissed.
18 August 1962 - Ringo Starr joins The Beatles.
22 August 1962 - Granada television film The Beatles at The Cavern.
23 August 1962 - John Lennon marries Cynthia Powell.
4 September 1962 - Second recording session at Abbey Road, this time with John, Paul, George and Ringo.
11 September 1962 - Third recording session at Abbey Road, with session drummer Andy White brought in to drum for the debut record, leaving Ringo to play the maracas.
5 October 1962 - "Love Me Do" is released as The Beatles' first record, with Ringo on the drums.

The Contract

The contract stipulated that there would be six records/ titles per annum, no flat fees, and they would receive 1d (1 penny) per record. This royalty would be paid to Brian Epstein on behalf of The Beatles. There were also options to increase the royalty in years two and three.

In sacking Pete, was there a breach of contract? The contract signed in February 1962 between The Beatles and Brian Epstein meant that within the first twelve months of the contract, either party could walk away without giving notice. If either party decided, after February 1963, that they wanted to part company, then they would have to give at least three months notice in writing. If they were to get rid of Pete, it would have to be done by Brian as manager, and before February 1963. And then, to add to this, they had suddenly had the confirmation from Granada TV that they were going to be filmed at The Cavern for a program at a later date. Decisions had to be made, and fast. Should he stay, or should he go? When was the decision taken? It would be foolish to appear on TV with one line-up, and then release the debut single with a different drummer? After all, record sleeves in those days always had a photo of the group on the cover. It is therefore reasonable to suggest that the TV appearance hastened Pete's exit, which by now was inevitable.

In 1965, Pete successfully sued Ringo for comments in a Playboy interview, and Brian Epstein for breach of contract. Although the settlement was "less than £50,000", it was a significant moral victory for Best.

Off The Record

Best was replaced, but Ringo Starr didn't pass the audition either, and session drummer Andy White was brought in to drum on three songs. It doesn't mean that Pete or Ringo were bad drummers, but underscores that Pete's dismissal wasn't down to drumming ability alone. Ringo had the same problem. They were 'live' drummers used to playing in big halls and concert venues. Drumming for a record is a different skill altogether, which Ringo was given the opportunity to develop with The Beatles.

Baffled In The Studio

If the EMI recordings from June are the only evidence on which to judge Pete's drumming, it is possible to understand the decision to replace him. However, listen to "My Bonnie": his drumming is steady, much brighter and livelier than the sessions at Decca or EMI. Does the way it was recorded make a difference? This is where it can get technical, so I enlisted the help of Don Dorsey, a recording engineer who has worked in Abbey Road.

He discussed with me the differences between drumming in a live band and in a recording studio.
"A recording studio environment is quite different to a live environment", Dorsey explained. "In a live hall all band members are relatively close together and all their sound output mixes in the environment—the drummer hears everything. In a recording studio it would be customary for the drummer to be separated from the rest of the band with a large wall-like sound baffle.

"The purpose of baffles is to keep sounds from one player intruding too much into the microphones of the others. As a result, to hear other band members well, headphones must be used and the sound would be nothing like a live appearance. From a producer's viewpoint though, everything must go quickly, easily and smoothly. Working with an unknown drummer would probably cause any producer who knew an experienced drummer to choose the latter just so the project could be completed with ease. To a producer, the term 'session drummer' means 'I know he can and will do the job because he's done it before'.

After reading Dorsey's technical insight it is no surprise that EMI, with a limited budget and studio time available, opted for a session drummer. Ringo was a mate who had sat in with The Beatles when Pete wasn't available on a couple of occasions and was not a regular occurrence as some have made out.

The Best Drummer?

I spoke to Mike Rice, who was a drummer with Liverpool band The Senators in the sixties. I asked him for an impartial view on Pete and Ringo.
"They were both good drummers, and personally I preferred Pete to Ringo, but there wasn't much between them. He does what I believe drummers should do and that is keeping a good rhythm, a strong beat, without too much fancy work. He was dynamic with the sound he was punching out. People tried to analyse it. It was the bass drum that stood out—the atom beat—but there was so much more to it than that. He could use his snare and put a variety in the beat, not just the straight 4/4 atom beat".

Rice shot down the notion that Pete was sacked because he wasn't a good enough drummer.
"I'd say it was wrong. I watched drummers all the time. You listened for the sound and knew which drums and cymbals he was hitting without watching, and he was drumming right. If you get it wrong it is very noticeable.

"Ringo, in my opinion, was the safe option and would not dominate the sound like Pete did. Maybe that was the problem. Ringo had such a great attitude and was a good drummer. He had the least ego and did a good job, so I'm not knocking him. He was—and still is—a great drummer".

Drummer Required

It wasn't just Ringo who was approached to replace Pete as some have claimed. According to Spencer Leigh's book, *Drummed Out*, John met former Quarrymen banjo player Rod Davis in March 1962. Davis told him that he had made a record and played guitar, banjo, fiddle and other string instruments. John said, "You don't play drums, do you? We need a drummer to head back to Hamburg". Davis admitted it was his second bad career move! Dakota's drummer Tony Mansfield recalled that Epstein also approached the band's manager, Rick Dixon, to ask about his availability.

Then there's the matter of musician Johnny "Hutch" Hutchinson. He was regarded as the best drummer in Liverpool and sat in for Pete before Ringo arrived, and surely would have been the favourite. Bob Wooler told Epstein that Hutchinson would suit The Beatles perfectly. Epstein asked Hutchinson, "What do you think, John?" Hutchinson responded without hesitation. "I wouldn't join The Beatles for a gold clock. There's only one group as far as I'm concerned and that's The Big Three. The Beatles couldn't make a better sound than that and anyway, Pete was a very good friend of mine and I couldn't do the dirty on him like that, but why don't you get Ringo? Ringo's a bum—Ringo will join anybody for a few bob". Hutchinson sat in with The Beatles between Pete's departure and Ringo joining. Bob Wooler noted that there was considerable friction on stage between Hutchinson and Lennon. "The Beatles didn't want a drummer who would be a force to be reckoned with", observed Wooler, "hence, Johnny Hutch didn't stand a chance".

George Martin

Regardless of who was considered better, the only fact that mattered was what George Martin said after the June 1962 session. He has given slightly different versions of what he said, but the core facts remain the same. Martin recalled: "When I saw them—The Beatles—I thought the three front-men worked well, but the guy at the back, Pete, was the best looking, but he didn't say much or have the charisma of the others. More importantly, his drumming was ok, but it wasn't top-notch in my opinion, so I mentioned it to Brian Epstein. I said, 'I don't care what you do with them as a group, but from purely a sound point of view, I would like to get someone else in to play drums. Is that ok? They took it as the final word: the catalyst to bring about change and poor Pete got the boot. I've always felt a bit guilty about that, but I guess he survived."

In his book, *All You Need Is Ears,* Martin gave a second version of what he said to Brian. "At the end of the test I took Brian to one side and said, 'I don't know what you're going to do with the group as such, but this drumming isn't good enough for what I want. It isn't regular enough. It doesn't give the right kind of sound. If we do make a record, I'd much prefer to have my own drummer—which won't make any difference to you, because no one will know who's on the record anyway." From George Martin's point of view, it is clear that he never, at any stage, suggested that Pete be dismissed from The Beatles. It is what Brian, John, Paul and George did with Martin's comments that led to Pete's dismissal.

Interestingly, Paul McCartney commented in the *Anthology* that "George Martin told us": this is a different scenario. It was always stated that George Martin spoke to Brian only, but Paul has clearly stated in different sources that George Martin spoke to him, and probably John and George too. A clear division was there for even Martin to observe.

George Martin was not in on most of the June session and was only brought in later on by his producer. He had delegated that responsibility to engineers Norman Smith and Ken Townsend, and to producer Ron Richards, who oversaw the session. It was Richards who put Pete through his paces, and admitted no other regular 'live' drummers could have done what he asked—not even Ringo. "I just got a bit, oh God, where do we go from here", said a despairing Richards. George Martin was only agreeing with, and passing on, the comments of his producer and engineers, who have admitted in hindsight that they were a bit harsh on Pete. Norman Smith said, "I personally didn't see a reason for a session drummer to be brought in".

Paul later recalled that when George Martin told them about changing the drummer, he thought, 'No. We can't!' It was one of those terrible things you go through as kids. Can we betray him? No. But our career was on the line. Maybe they were going to cancel our contract." The decision was taken, and Pete was out, but did they misunderstand George Martin's comments, or did his comments suit their purpose?

The Session Drummer

Richards had made his decision, so when it came to making the record, Pete Best wasn't acceptable, and George Martin agreed that they should bring in a session drummer for the task of providing the rhythm on The Beatles' debut record. Richards told Martin that he was going to bring in one of the best session drummers he had ever worked with: Andy White. "I did a lot of work for Ron Richards, not EMI," said White, "and so he was instrumental in me being there that day."

However, there is a problem here with timing. George Martin made it clear that he told Epstein in June that he was going to provide a session drummer for the recording. The first recording session at Abbey Road on 4 September involved John, Paul, George and Ringo, and they recorded versions of "Love Me Do" and the Mitch Murray song, "How Do You Do It", which George Martin had asked them to work on for their first single. In the end, The Beatles convinced Martin that they should only release their own songs, and so "How Do You Do It" was given to Gerry and The Pacemakers who had a number one hit with it.

But, if George Martin was bringing in a session drummer to make the record, where was this other drummer on 4 September? Andy White's version, recorded on 11 September, was issued on the album *Please Please Me*.

In George Martin's book, he makes no mention of this day at all in relation to the session drummer. Why? "On 11 September 1962, we finally got together to make their first record". But that isn't what happened. They turned up to a recording session on 4 September to make a record. The next day, Martin and Ron Richards listened repeatedly to the acetate and determined from the playback that it lacked drive: there was a problem now with Ringo's drumming. Paul has since observed that "Ringo at that point was not that steady on time", and Norman Smith decided that Ringo "didn't have quite enough push". Andy White was brought in for a third attempt at recording the debut single.

What did White recall about the 11 September session? "I didn't know about a previous drummer to Ringo or who I was playing for, and it was only later that I heard that there had been a change of drummer. Ringo never spoke to me: I think he was shocked seeing somebody else setting up the drums when he came in." George Martin remembered it well too. "The boys meantime had brought along a guy and they said 'we're going to get Ringo to play with us' and I said 'we just spent good money and booked the best drummer in London. I'm not having your bloke in; I'll find out about him later. Poor Ringo was mortified and I felt sorry for him, so I gave him the maracas."

Martin also said on the *Anthology* DVD, "When Ringo came to the session for the first time, nobody told me he was coming. I'd already booked Andy White and told Brian Epstein this". Ringo was devastated when he turned up to see that he had been replaced. Even being handed the maracas and tambourine couldn't pacify him. It doesn't add up: the dates and stories don't tally.

My Theory

I am often asked for my opinion on Pete Best's dismissal, so this is my theory.

Many authors just create their theories from hindsight. They start at Ringo and begin to make comparisons between him and Pete Best. Who was the better drummer? Who was the better looking? Who had the better personality? Who fitted in best? However, I would like to start at a point before Ringo appears on the scene. When Pete signed the recording contract as a member of The Beatles, he was entitled to his equal cut of the profits. Yet, if George Martin was going to use a session drummer for the records, why should John, Paul and George give their drummer a quarter share of the proceeds when he wouldn't even be playing? The money from the record sales would therefore be better cut three ways instead of four. That way, they could hire a session drummer on a fixed weekly rate instead of sharing a chunk of the profits, which weren't expected to be great at this stage. Their royalty rate at the time was only one penny per record.

When Ringo joined the group, he signed for £25 per week on a probationary basis, not a quarter–share, full member of The Beatles. Peter Brown, who had worked closely with Brian Epstein since their days in NEMS in Liverpool was quoted as saying, "The terms were that Ringo would be paid £25 per week for a probationary period, and if things worked out he would be made a member". At that stage, the other three Beatles were taking £50 per week, plus they were due a share of the proceeds from their records and performances. George Martin had made it clear that he would be providing the drummer, and had stated to Brian that he wanted to bring in a drummer purely from a sound point of view: purely for recording.

He was surprised when Ringo walks in, not knowing who he was and what he was doing there. He hadn't asked for Pete to be sacked, and turning up with another drummer wasn't the solution: a seasoned professional session drummer was. Ringo obviously expected to play, but at that time, to John, Paul and George, he was the replacement drummer on probation on £25 per week. They did the maths: this was the perfect solution, and it wasn't the first time either.

Consider what happened to Nigel Walley, The Quarrymen tea-chest bass player who became their first manager. It was Nigel, a childhood friend of John's, who booked their first proper gig at the local golf club and then got them into The Cavern for the first time. He also made other bookings. However, once The Quarrymen had built up a following, it was Paul who suggested that Nigel's managerial fee be cut off because he didn't contribute: Nigel left the group. Likewise, Ken Brown was eased out of The Quarrymen at The Casbah over fifteen shillings (75 pence), because Ken didn't play and so John, Paul and George demanded Ken's share, to split it three ways instead of four. Allan Williams was the recipient of similar treatment. Williams

procured bookings, drove the group personally to Hamburg and set them up. On The Beatles' second visit to Hamburg, when they moved to another club, they dropped Williams and did not pay him his usual commission because they arranged the booking themselves. In all three situations, it was a financial decision, with the non-contributing person eased out of the picture.

Only on 20 June 1963—nearly a year after he joined them—when Beatles Ltd. was set up did Ringo Starr become an equal member of the band. Even then he was on a lesser share of The Beatles performances from concerts. Ringo eventually became a fully-fledged Beatle and his performances as a drummer and a personality ultimately made him a very popular member. However, he spent nearly twelve months as a session drummer with The Beatles trying to earn his place in the band permanently.

In my theory, Ringo doesn't feature in the plan yet, because this was all about getting rid of Pete from the band, as the other members didn't feel that Pete fitted in, and that he shouldn't take a share the profits, because he wasn't going to appear on the records. Once that decision was made, thoughts then turned to a replacement, who would be happy to join them on a fixed rate. The incentive for any replacement drummer was the record deal. Enter Ringo, a drummer they knew well, who happily signed up to the deal on offer. So my theory is that the final, and clinching decision as to why The Beatles got rid of Pete, was because they wanted to split the profits from the records three ways instead of four, with the non-contributing person eased out. Pete was dismissed, like Ken Brown, Nigel Walley and Allan Williams, over money, because George Martin had told Brian, John, Paul and George that Best wasn't going to drum on the records.

And In The End

The Beatles had played together for two years, with Pete as drummer. It was only when George Martin told Brian that Pete wasn't going to be playing on the records that John, Paul and George acted, swiftly. It could be surmised that they weren't sure how long fame would last, and they were determined to grab every penny while they could. History shows they had no problem sticking it to friends and associates with little or no remorse. If they were going to enjoy maybe six months of fame and fortune, they could split the profits three ways instead of four, then pay Ringo a flat rate. If they became successful Ringo could join them permanently. If fame eluded them, then John, Paul and George could at least split their meager earnings three ways, instead of four.

Whatever the main reason was, clearly several factors were taken into account and that between them, John, Paul, George and Brian decided Pete had to go. When there were suggestions from George Martin to bring in a session drummer, they didn't think twice about dropping Pete. As Allan Williams commented, "All groups are users. They are ruthless". Alistair Taylor once said that Pete was simply not a Beatle. John was even quoted as saying the same: "Pete Best was a great drummer but Ringo was a Beatle". Pete was a great drummer, says John, and thereby adds to the fact that Best was not sacked because of his lack of ability as a drummer. However, it does show that there was something missing between Pete and the others in the group. Paul stated in an interview that "we had Pete Best who was a really good drummer, but there was just something; he wasn't quite like the rest of us. We kind of had a sense of humour in common, and he was nearly in with it all, and it's a fine line between what is nearly in and what is exactly in." Paul clearly puts the theory that Pete wasn't a good enough drummer to bed, once and for all: there was something else.

We will probably never know exactly what happened, but as author Spencer Leigh concludes, it was most likely a combination of many elements. Pete was a Beatle for two years and played an important role in the formation of the band until August 1962. He was a vital cog of the band that took Hamburg and Liverpool by storm and secured a recording contract. What brought it to an end will probably never be revealed, but his contribution nonetheless cannot be ignored.

23 AUGUST 1962
Cynthia Powell marries John Lennon
"All My Loving"

Cynthia and John Lennon pictured in 1963

Cynthia Lennon (nee Powell) was John Lennon's first and long-suffering wife. They met at the Liverpool College of Art, while in 'lettering' class, taught by one of the few teachers that would accept John. The two were so different, yet very attracted to each other. John thought Cynthia 'posh' because she grew up in Hoylake on the Wirral. In truth, Woolton, where John grew up, was more middle-class than Hoylake. John was confident, loud and rude. Cynthia was shy, quiet and polite. They were a classic example of how opposites attract.

As they came to know each other, the pair discovered they had some similarities. John had lost his mum when he was aged seventeen; Cynthia lost her dad at the same age. Both Mimi and Cynthia's mum took in lodgers after their spouses died so that their respective children could attend college.

Another characteristic they shared was poor eyesight. Like John, Cynthia was virtually blind without her glasses. They loved the cinema but their vanity prevented them from wearing their glasses as they watched.

When they met in class, John consistently borrowed stationery from her. Lennon was a class clown and Cynthia knew he was a bad influence. Yet she couldn't help feeling attracted to him. When John commented that another girl looked like French actress Brigitte Bardot, Cynthia went home and bought a blonde hair dye kit. John immediately took notice. When he asked her to dance one evening, she replied, "I'm engaged". Ever the wisecracker, Lennon replied, "I didn't say I wanted to marry you".

After the dance they had a drink at Ye Cracke on Rice Street and then retired to Stuart's Gambier Terrace flat where they made love for the first time.

Their relationship flourished and the two often took the ferry to New Brighton and the nearby sand dunes. John grew intensely possessive and was jealous of the attention she received from the opposite sex, so much so that once, after she danced with Stuart, John took her to one side and slapped her across the face, knocking her head against the pipes. He walked away, leaving her in a daze. Cynthia decided to end their relationship. They didn't see each other for three months but the two missed each other. John apologised for his actions and it never happened again.

Cynthia moved to a flat in Garmoyle Road, Wavertree, which she shared with Paul McCartney's girlfriend Dot Rhone. Unknown to Cynthia's mum or John's Aunt Mimi, John spent the night at the flat on numerous occasions. One evening in the summer of 1962, Cynthia confronted John with the news that she was pregnant. "Right, we'll have to get married then", said Lennon gallantly.

At short notice, a wedding was arranged at Mount Pleasant Registry Office on 23 August 1962. Paul McCartney, George Harrison and Brian Epstein attended, as well as Cynthia's brother, Tony, and his wife. Brian, as best man, picked up Cynthia in his car and took her to the registry office. Mimi didn't attend the wedding but gave John the £10 to buy the ring from a jeweller in Whitechapel. Their son, Julian, was born on 8 April 1963.

Cynthia believes that she was the inspiration for some of John's songs. On their first Christmas together, John inscribed a card with the words inside: 'I love you, yes, yes, yes'. Sound familiar? The lyrics were later changed to "yeah, yeah, yeah" in the worldwide smash, "She Loves You".

The Lennon's marriage ended abruptly in 1968 when Cynthia returned home from holiday to find John with Yoko Ono and wearing Cynthia's dressing gown. In 1970, Cynthia married Italian hotelier Roberto Bassanini, whom she had started dating after the split from John, but they were divorced in 1973. During Lennon's split from Yoko in 1973–74, May Pang, Lennon's lover, tried to reconcile John with Julian. John had been an absent father for most of Julian's life and Pang attempted to renew the father-son relationship. Cynthia recalled, "I met May Pang the first time when I went to see John after he had split up with Yoko. She was a very young girl and she was so kind and so lovely to Julian. I've never forgotten that". The two have maintained their decades-long friendship.

ABOVE: *Cynthia Lennon signs her book, John, in Liverpool during its launch in 2006*
OPPOSITE: *Ringo practicing with The Beatles at The Cavern in February, 1963*

Cynthia married John Twist, an engineer from Lancashire, in 1976. She wrote her first book, cleverly titled *A Twist of Lennon*, which was published in 1978.

After John was murdered in 1980, she was discouraged from attending any official events and Julian only received a small token inheritance from his father's will. Cynthia was devastated by this action, which she blamed on Yoko.

Cynthia Lennon currently lives in Majorca, Spain and still makes appearances at Beatles festivals. She released her book *John* in 2006.

Cynthia and Julian attended the 2006 Cirque du Soleil premiere of *Love* in Las Vegas, making her first public appearance with Yoko since 1989. They were joined by Olivia and Dhani Harrison, together with Sir Paul McCartney. "It's a coming together of all the families, as we hadn't seen each other in so many years", said Julian.

Tony Booth's paintings of The Beatles
"I've Just Seen A Face"

Just days after Ringo joined The Beatles in August 1962, Tony Booth asked Brian Epstein if he could create a painting of the new Fab Four. Booth, a local commercial artist, had worked for Epstein before. He also promoted a Beatles' gig at the Apollo Roller Rink on the Wirral as well as designing Cavern membership cards and posters.

When Booth saw the first black and white photo of the Fab Four, he asked for a copy. Epstein gave it to him, though only after asking for half-a-crown. "After all, business is business", said Epstein.

Booth took a cue from Andy Warhol and decided to paint the picture in the pop-art style made famous by the white–haired artist. Epstein was so impressed by Booth's work that he brought the painting to The Cavern. Epstein arranged for the "boys" to sign it in their "best handwriting".

The original painting lay forgotten in Booth's studio for almost four decades, where he had been using the reverse as a makeshift cutting board. When rediscovered, it was valued at £100,000, and is now safely locked away in his bank vault.

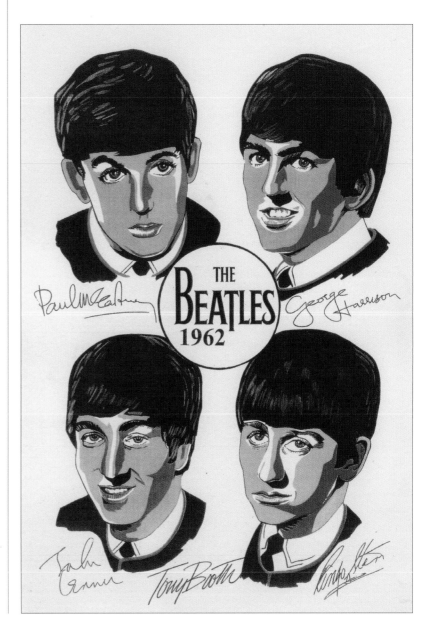

ABOVE: *Artist, Tony Booth* RIGHT: *Tony's 1962 painting of The Beatles*

4 SEPTEMBER 1962
The Beatles record at EMI Studios
"Love Me Do"

Pete Best had been dismissed and was replaced by Ringo Starr. So how did session drummer Andy White end up keeping time on "Love Me Do" instead of the newest Beatle?

The Beatles had rehearsed and made some test recordings on 4 September with EMI producer Ron Richards at the helm. The next day, Richards and George Martin listened to the acetates and couldn't make up their minds on why the music wasn't gelling. All fingers pointed to the drummer.

Like Pete Best before him, Ringo had no real experience in the recording studio, and was about to suffer the same fate as Best and be replaced by a session drummer. Engineer Norman Smith said Ringo "didn't have quite enough push", but that it was a skill he could acquire. "We had a record to make and I needed someone who could deliver exactly what the song required on every take", Smith recalled.

On 11 September 1962, Ringo entered the studio expecting to record and was greeted by a young Scot named Andy White. Pete and Roag Best later met up with Andy in America and Roag interviewed him for the documentary, *Best of The Beatles*. Andy knew of The Beatles, as his wife was from Liverpool, and was one of the famous "Vernon's Girls", an English musical ensemble of female vocalists, formed at Vernons' football pools company in Liverpool during the 1950s. Interestingly, Andy worked with Ron Richards on several occasions, and recorded with The Beatles at the beginning of September at Abbey Road.

Andy was asked which drummer he had been brought in to replace. White told Roag that he wasn't aware of a change of drummer or any of the history, which wasn't his concern, as he was brought in to drum on three tracks with The Beatles. He was there to replace the guy who drummed on the 4 September session.

White spent most of the day rehearsing with The Beatles and learning the songs. It was a long session because there was no written music, and they recorded ten takes of "P.S. I Love You", eighteen of "Love Me Do" and an unspecified number of "Please Please Me".

Ringo never spoke to White and had been surprised to see another drummer there. He was relegated to playing the maracas and tambourine in the background.

In the end, Ringo's recording of "Love Me Do" from the first session on 4 September was issued on the single while Andy White's "P.S. I Love You" appeared on the flip side. However, Andy's version of "Love Me Do" appeared on the album *Please Please Me*. Afterwards, Ringo commented, "I was shattered, I thought, they're doing a Pete

Best on me. How phony the record business was—getting other musicians to make your records for you". Ringo openly held a grudge against George Martin for years.

Andy White also confirmed that he was sworn to secrecy about his role on the three tracks, which is why it was kept quiet for so long. George Martin probably went back to using Ringo's original version of "Love Me Do", because he realised that he could in fact provide a steady beat for the record and his style broke through.

Eventually Ringo was given the proper studio time and became an integral part of The Beatles' recording career. He has become one of the most respected rock drummers in the world. Like a lot of movie stars, he had that little something extra, which no one can quite define in words. In hindsight, The Beatles without Ringo Starr in the equation is hard to imagine.

Brian Epstein talking to EMI Record Producer George Martin, in Abbey Road Studios

27 OCTOBER 1962
Monty Lister records The Beatles for radio
"I Want to Tell You"

The Beatles recorded a curious radio interview on 27 October 1962 for the patients of the Cleaver and Clatterbridge Hospitals, located on the Wirral, across the Mersey from Liverpool. The group was quizzed by radio host Monty Lister and two of his friends, Malcolm Threadgill and Peter Smethurst, for his regular show, 'Sunday Spin'. The interview took place at 8.45 p.m., prior to going on stage at Hulme Hall, Port Sunlight, and was broadcast on the hospital radio station the next day.

I met Monty Lister in 2004, just before he hung up his headphones at BBC Radio Merseyside. He still remembers their encounter fondly, especially as he had the cheek to undertake the interview without first clearing it with Epstein and how unhappy the manager was afterwards. For Lister, it was a nice story about a local band that everyone was talking about, so it would be ideal for his hospital radio show.

The following is a brief extract of that interview. It's not exactly earth-shattering, cutting-edge journalism, but a nice piece of history.

MONTY LISTER: *Well, it's a very great pleasure for us this evening to say hello to an up-and-coming Merseyside group, The Beatles. And I know their names, and I'm going to try and put faces to them. Now, you're John Lennon, aren't you?*
JOHN: Yes, that's right.
MONTY LISTER: *What do you do in the group, John?*
JOHN: I play harmonica, rhythm guitar, and vocal.
MONTY LISTER: *Then there's Paul McCartney. And what do you do?*
PAUL: Play bass guitar and uh... sing? I think. You know, that's what they say.
MONTY LISTER: *Then there's George Harrison. How do you do. What's your job?*
GEORGE: Uh, lead guitar and sort of singing.
MONTY LISTER: *By playing lead guitar, does that mean that you're sort of leader of the group, or are you...*
GEORGE: No, no, just—well, you see, the other guitar's the rhythm. Ching, ching, ching, you see.
PAUL: It's solo guitar, you see. John is in fact the leader of the group.
MONTY LISTER: *And over in the background here, and also in the background of the group, but making a lot of noise is Ringo Starr.*
RINGO: Hello
MONTY LISTER: *You're new to the group, aren't you, Ringo?*
RINGO: Yes, um, nine weeks now.
MONTY LISTER: *Were you in on the act when the recording was made of "Love Me Do"?*
RINGO: Yes, I'm on the record.
MONTY LISTER: *You're on that disc.*
RINGO: I am. It's down on record, you know. I'm the drummer.
MONTY LISTER: *Well, Paul, you tell us. How did you get in on the act in Germany?*

PAUL: Well, it was all through an old agent. We first went there for, uh... a fella who used to manage us, a Mr. Allan Williams of The Jacaranda Club in Liverpool. And he found the engagement, so we sort of went there, and then went under our own...
JOHN: Steam.
PAUL: Steam... Yes, you know the airplanes.
MALCOLM THREADGILL: *I understand you've made other recordings before on a German label.*
PAUL: Yeah.
MALCOLM THREADGILL: *What ones were they?*
PAUL: Well, we did make, first of all, we made a recording with a fella called Tony Sheridan. We were working in a club called the Top Ten Club in Hamburg. And we made a recording with him called "My Bonnie", which got to number five in the German hit parade, but...
JOHN: Achtung.
PAUL: It never, it didn't do a thing over here.
MALCOLM THREADGILL: *Who does the composing between you?*
PAUL: Well, it's John and I. We write, you know, sort of the songs between us.
JOHN: It's equal shares.
PAUL: Yeah, equal shares and royalties and things, so that, you know, we just both write most of the stuff.
MONTY LISTER: *We're recording this at Hulme Hall, Port Sunlight. Did any of you come over this side before you became famous, as it were? Do you know this district?*
JOHN: I've got relations here. Rock Ferry.
MONTY LISTER: *Have you?*
JOHN: Yes. Oh, all sides of the water, you know.
PAUL: Yeah, I've got a relation in, uh, Claughton Village.
MONTY LISTER: *Yes.*
PAUL: Upton Road.
RINGO: I've got a friend in Birkenhead.
MONTY LISTER: *I wish I had.*
GEORGE: I know a man in Chester.
MONTY LISTER: *Now, that's a very dangerous thing to say. There's a mental home there, mate.*

And that was it, a little interview for local hospital radio, but perhaps a foretaste for those chaotic and hilarious interviews on their U.S. tour.

ABOVE: *Hulme Hall, Port Sunlight, where Ringo made his debut with The Beatles*
OPPOSITE: *Monty Lister, holding the microphone, interviews The Beatles at Hulme Hall, 27 October 1962*

19 February 1963
Michael Ward photographs The Beatles in Liverpool
"Here, There and Everywhere"

On 19 February 1963, The Beatles became big news when they were told that their single, "Please Please Me" was No. 1 in the U.K. charts.

Photographer Michael Ward had been dispatched from London to cover the story of the latest pop sensations. Ward had decided he didn't want to take the easy option and go for studio prints. He didn't know much about the group, but on that day, his photographs captured The Beatles as people and as part of their hometown. They walked the streets of Liverpool freely—something that they would shortly not be able to do.

Ward photographed them at various locations around Liverpool, including the Pier Head, the docks, NEMS music store and the Queen Victoria Monument. He shot them talking to fans, drinking mugs of tea and walking through the streets of Liverpool's city centre.

He finished the day by photographing The Beatles rehearsing in The Cavern before capturing them on stage in one of their last ever appearances at the Mathew Street club.

Ward's images captured a group on the threshold of untold wealth and fame, before they became the most famous foursome on the planet.

ABOVE: *The Beatles on the Victoria Monument, Derby Square, Liverpool*
LEFT: *Paul and John on stage in The Cavern*

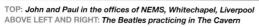

TOP: *John and Paul in the offices of NEMS, Whitechapel, Liverpool*
ABOVE LEFT AND RIGHT: *The Beatles practicing in The Cavern*

18 JUNE 1963

Paul's 21st birthday party, John Lennon beats up Bob Wooler

"Birthday"

When ex-Cavern DJ Bob Wooler died in 2002, there were many Beatles fans who asked "Bob who?" But summing Bob Wooler up as an ex-DJ is like saying The Beatles were just a band. The full impact of his importance to the Merseybeat scene in '60s Liverpool has rarely been appreciated by those outside the area. Wooler, by his own admission, was more of a fan of Frank Sinatra's music than he was of The Beatles, but he was a visionary and a man who saw the potential and talent in people.

As a promoter and DJ at The Cavern, he introduced and worked with many of the legends of '60s music, from the Merseybeat bands and British groups like The Who to the giants of American soul music.

Since The Cavern did not sell alcohol, the only way to get people through the door was to book the biggest bands around. Each band had its own following and Bob was a master at attracting marquee names and the best musicians. His reputation within Liverpool meant that he was considered the "guru of Merseybeat". When promoters wanted to bring their bands to Liverpool, Bob was the man who made it happen.

Radio host Spencer Leigh is renowned for his knowledge of The Beatles and Merseybeat, with his twice–weekly radio show on BBC Radio Merseyside. He developed a fascinating relationship with Bob Wooler while writing his biography, *The Best of Fellas*. I interviewed Leigh at Radio Merseyside and asked him about the book.

Do you think that Bob's role in the growth of Beatlemania was properly recognised?

"He was always wary about others overstating their part—he was not a boaster, but was never a fan of others making things up. He was modest and always wanted to put the record straight on several things".

What stories did Bob have about The Beatles?

"In the book, Bob tells of the time when The Beatles received their new suits and The Cavern had just been painted, and they dirtied them. The book is at its best when Bob is talking about Brian Epstein and the other managers and promoters and their in-fighting. Epstein was a visionary and could see how he could make money from them. Bob stayed local and was happy here. Epstein offered him a job in London, but Bob said he was 'a big fish in a little pond, and didn't want to be a little fish in a big pond'. Bob and Epstein were good friends, and Bob was looked up to as a 'father' figure and gave advice to many local bands. He also talks about John's Aunt Mimi and reveals that she did not oppose John's music career as some people have made out. Bob said that, 'John was always on time at The Cavern often because Mimi would make sure he was prompt, as it was an important appointment'. McCartney, of course, would engineer a late appearance if he wanted to appear further down the bill".

What did Bob make of The Beatles?

"Bob was very impressed with The Beatles, and was 'flabbergasted' at their Litherland Town Hall appearance after their return from Hamburg. It was then that Bob started promoting The Beatles around the clubs, and then of course made The Cavern his home".

Did Bob have any regrets?

"He regretted the fact that he was quite shy away from the microphone and didn't further his own career—he worked in Bingo—his 'calling' as he would say. Bob was probably lined up for Radio 1 when it was launched—he could have walked into a job—though it was alleged he turned up drunk: Bob insists he didn't turn up. He would have loved that.

"Bob was a frustrated songwriter, and there are several of his songs in between the chapters in the book. The Dakotas, who performed at Bob's tribute concert, had released a single 'I'll Keep You Satisfied', which had Bob's song 'I Know' on the B-side. George Martin put music to his lyrics, but Bob wouldn't pursue his career as a songwriter. He loved the idea of his song lyrics being published in the book, though of course he didn't live to see this happen".

What about the sacking of Pete Best?

"Bob felt so sorry for him and the way he was treated. He always said that if the only drumming George Martin heard was on that recording for 'Love Me Do', then you could understand, because he did go to pieces that day. Bob referred to my book *Drummed Out* and agreed with the *Murder On The Orient Express* theory that there was no single reason for it—just everybody had a reason why they didn't want him, and they used George Martin's reason on the day to finally sack him. Bob was particularly appalled at the way it happened, and wanted to write an article in *Mersey Beat* about it, and had many an argument with Brian Epstein over it".

What did Bob say about the infamous fight between him and John Lennon, in which he referred to his vacation in Spain with Brian Epstein?

"He didn't want to comment on the fight involving himself and John Lennon, which ended with Bob receiving a black eye, broken ribs, cuts and bruises, all dealt by Lennon at Paul's 21st birthday party in Dinas Lane, Huyton. 'That is between John,

Brian and me—it's private' was all he would comment. Despite knowing that his work would probably never be published without the sensationalism the modern tabloids demanded, Bob didn't want to succumb to the temptation.

"The fight with John Lennon, of course, had to be in the book. He argued that the people buying the book 'would understand that I don't want to talk about it' but I argued that you couldn't have this book without mentioning it. There are enough comments that could be put together, and the opinion that he said something along the lines of 'How was the honeymoon?' and Lennon hit him.

"John was very drunk and had to be dragged off the helpless Wooler. As The Beatles were becoming a household name, the scandal could have ruined them. Although they never fully revealed what had taken place, Brian Epstein arranged an "out-of-court" settlement of £200 with Bob, and his agreement not to discuss the incident, and John sent a telegram to Bob as an apology.

"As The Beatles exploded onto the world, The Cavern was overrun with fans. Where they would previously have all-night sessions running from Friday night through to Saturday, and all-day sessions during the month, they were now having to let fans in for three hours, throw them all out, and then let a new crowd in".

By early 1964, the work was too much for one man to handle. Bob needed help. At a charity football match featuring a Merseybeat XI, Bob was hired for commentary. At half time, Billy Butler, a member of The Tuxedos, was substituted. Bob turned to Billy and said, 'Can you commentate on the second half because I know nothing about football and, judging by your performance, neither do you'. That second-half commentary turned out to be Billy Butler's audition.

Bob asked him to come down to audition one evening as a DJ at The Cavern. He passed the test and became the man Bob Wooler relied on to play the music each night. Bob would introduce the main acts, which, of course, included The Beatles on countless occasions. He would then concentrate on the promotion of the best local, national and international bands around".

I met Billy Butler, who is a presenter on BBC Radio Merseyside and has been involved in local radio in Liverpool for many years. I asked about his memories of Bob.

"Bob was a genius with words. He could write adverts for the paper like no other, and make the words jump out at you", commented Billy. He says he learnt everything about promoting from Bob. "He was the master of the written word, but also a stickler for accuracy".

"Wooler argued with his good friend Allan Williams to the point of frustration about inaccuracies that surrounded The Beatles in particular. It got to the point where Bob renamed Mathew Street as 'Myth-ew Street'. His standard line was if one journalist started a rumour and committed it to print, another would copy it and the whispers would grow into folklore".

The former Beatles' manager Allan Williams, unveiling the plaque to Bob Wooler, with former Cavern DJ Billy Butler

He once asked a journalist if he would rather hear it from 'the horse's mouth, or the other end' pointing in Allan Williams' direction. Wooler had a great sense of humour, and his close friends like Allan Williams and Billy had a great affection for him.

"Bob put the Mersey into Merseybeat; in fact, the Merseybeat was his heartbeat", said Billy.

"The *Mersey Beat* paper became a must-buy for music fans, thanks to Wooler's regular column, which enabled them to follow their favourite band. Bob was never tempted to move away to the bright lights of London. Liverpool was his home, his world, and he would never leave. His legacy to Beatles' fans is that he gave the Fab Four a platform to show their talents and form a bedrock of local support that would launch them on to the world's stage. He knew so much about The Beatles but, when compiling his biography, he refused to comment on any scandals or incidents".

And finally Billy, how would you sum up Bob Wooler?

"He was a lovely man, decent, honest and modest. He was a very private man and never talked about his personal life. He probably never appreciated the enormous influence he had on The Beatles and the other Merseybeat bands. He would never claim credit for something he did not do, but neither did he take credit for what he did achieve".

If you were one of those who asked 'Bob who?' you will have a better idea of a great man who achieved so much and yet never sought nor received the credit he truly deserved. Allan Williams and Billy Butler unveiled a permanent memorial to this great man at The Cavern in 2005.

How should history remember Bob Wooler? The Beatles and the Merseybeat bands without The Cavern is unthinkable. The Cavern without Bob Wooler is also unthinkable. That shall be his legacy to us.

9 OCTOBER 1963
The Mersey Sound
"From Me to You"

As Beatlemania tilted into full swing in 1963, the BBC sensed something special was happening. They wanted to capture The Beatles' magic on celluloid.

The Beatles were in Liverpool for four days in August 1963 to film the new documentary, originally to be called 'The Beatles', and later 'The Mersey Sound'. On 27 August at The Little Theatre in Southport, they performed "Twist and Shout" and "She Loves You" without an audience, because the screaming would have been distracting. Director Don Haworth then incorporated the audience, which had been shot the previous night at the Odeon in Southport, into the film.

The thirty-minute documentary was shown on BBC television in London and the North on 9 October 1963, John's 23rd birthday, and then on 13 November, it was broadcast to the entire country.

The rights to show an extract of "She Loves You" from 'The Mersey Sound' were sold by the New York office of the BBC to 'The Jack Paar Show' on the NBC network. When Brian Epstein found out about NBC's plans, he angrily contacted the BBC, because, three months earlier, he had sold the exclusive rights to 'The Ed Sullivan Show' on the rival CBS network. There followed a frantic exchange of letters, and telephone calls. The BBC in London attempted to rescind the agreement but was unable to do so. The performance was aired on U.S. television and created an excitement about this new English pop phenomenon that would pave the way for their forthcoming tour.

ABOVE: *The Beatles in November 1963* OPPOSITE: *Bob Wooler (in bow-tie) watches over The Beatles at the Press Conference in Liverpool's Speke Airport on 10 July 1964*

7 DECEMBER 1963
The Beatles answer a call for help!
"Help!"

Beatlemania was in high gear in late 1963.

The Beatles returned to Liverpool on 7 December 1963 for a concert at the Liverpool Empire and to record an episode of 'Juke Box Jury' for TV. Using the same audience from The Beatles Northern Area Fan Club performance, the group was filmed between 2.30 p.m. and 3.15 p.m. for broadcasting that evening. About thirty minutes later they taped a concert segment for 'It's The Beatles', followed by an interview for 'Top of the Pops'. They then made a mad dash up London Road to the Odeon Cinema for two more performances that evening.

It was just another crazy day in the life of The Beatles as their fame spread across the United Kingdom. However, for Michael Turner, a six-year-old boy, it was a most memorable day. Michael's sister Flora remembers it well.

"Michael was nearly seven. He loved all The Beatles, but most of all, he loved George Harrison", Flora said. "So, as the boys were coming to Liverpool to do 'Juke Box Jury' at the Empire, we decided to get him a ticket for his birthday".

Flora and her friends stood in line all night waiting for tickets. They purchased four tickets each, including one for Michael. Unfortunately, a few days before the concert, Michael came down with the measles, which put an end to his Beatles dream. "He was heartbroken", Flora recalled.

Flora knew where Louise and Harry Harrison lived and hit on a novel idea—send them a telegram explaining Michael's predicament. The day of the concert Flora was in her room getting ready for the big show, when there was a knock on the door. Moments later Flora's mother told her that Mrs. Harrison was asking for her.

"So, off I went—rollers in my hair and all". Flora said, "At the door was a woman, wearing a greyish coat and holding something in her hand. 'We received your telegram,' she said 'and George wanted you to have this!' I invited her in, but they were on their way to the theatre. 'The boys are in the car', she added".

"The boys are in the car? They certainly were. Smiling and waving at me—in my rollers. You can imagine how I felt. I waved back and thanked George's mum. She was a nice lady".

Louise delivered an autographed photo from all four Beatles, dedicated to Michael. They all wished him well.

That selfless act made lifetime fans out of both Michael and Flora. "It cheered a sick little boy when he felt disappointed—and no matter what is written about them, I will never forget what George's mum, George and the other Beatles did", Flora said.

The Beatles at the Liverpool Empire Theatre

9 FEBRUARY 1964
The Ed Sullivan Show
"I Wanna Hold Your Hand"

On 3 January 1964, the extract of "She Loves You" from 'The Mersey Sound' was shown on American television as part of 'The Jack Paar Show'. At the end of the program, Paar sarcastically remarked "It's nice to know that England has finally risen to our cultural level".

Even though Epstein had tried to stop the transmission, the brief appearance served only to whet the appetite of American fans. On tour in Paris, France on 16 January 1964, The Beatles returned to their hotel and were told that "I Wanna Hold Your Hand" had jumped from No. 43 to No. 1 on the U.S. charts. It sold an amazing 250,000 copies in three days. A week later sales had topped one million. A meteor was about to hit the States.

The timing was perfect. On 7 February 1964, an American Airlines Boeing 707 touched down at the newly-named JFK Airport to be met by 3,000 screaming fans.

In front of 728 hormonally-challenged teenagers on 9 February, The Beatles performed live on 'The Ed Sullivan Show'. Approximately 73 million people tuned in, setting a new world record for a television show. The Beatles had arrived as foreigners but were instant hometown heroes. They invaded and conquered America with alarming ease, and the rest of the world followed.

By the time The Beatles left the U.S. on 21 February 1964, the country was Beatle crazy. Memorabilia like wigs, figures, buttons, towels, talcum powder and games were available. For British bands, for The Beatles and Epstein, conquering America meant conquering the world. It was Eldorado and the pot at the end of the rainbow, all rock and rolled into one. The dream had become a reality. Beatlemania had become a worldwide phenomenon and the group's faces were splattered on magazines and newspapers around the globe. But, it was more than a passing fad. The Beatles transcended mere pop music and left an indelible mark on popular culture that will never be seen again.

The Beatles' next step was to preserve their fame on celluloid and they filmed a full-length motion picture, *A Hard Day's Night*. Directed by Richard Lester, it was scripted by Liverpool writer Alun Owen. Although shot in only a few weeks in March 1964, it remains one of the best films of its genre.

Brian Epstein was naturally keen to get the film into the cinemas as quickly as possible, and the northern premiere could only take place in one city—Liverpool. It was the perfect excuse to "get back to where they once belonged".

The Beatles in February 1964 with Ed Sullivan as they prepared to take America by storm

10 JULY 1964
The Beatles come home to Liverpool
"All You Need Is Love"

The Beatles conquered America and the rest of the world in 1964, but one city remained absent from their ever expanding list of conquests: their hometown of Liverpool. The previous year they had been the undisputed kings of Liverpool, but they had left the safety of their hometown and had hardly set foot in the city since they last played The Cavern in August 1963.

For John, Paul, George and Ringo, this was a different proposition. These were the friends and family they had left behind; the fan club which had followed them through thick and thin and forced to share their heroes with the rest of the world. Would they welcome them back as hometown heroes or with ambivalence?

The July 1964 civic reception almost didn't happen. The Lord Mayor had approached Brian Epstein earlier in the year, and his response of 6 February was not encouraging.

Thank you very much for your charming letter of the 4th instant. As you probably know the boys and I set forth for the United States tomorrow morning. On their return the boys have an intense filming schedule, which will take them up to the end of April. They will then be resting for most of the month of May. So therefore while I look forward very much to accepting your kind invitation, for which the boys and I are most appreciative, I think the actual date may have to be left in abeyance for the present.

With many thanks and best wishes.

Yours respectfully,
Brian Epstein

At that stage, the proposed civic reception seemed in doubt. Epstein's master stroke was to combine the northern premiere of *A Hard Day's Night* with a trip to the Town Hall.

ABOVE: *The Beatles on the balcony of Liverpool Town Hall with the Lord Mayor Alderman Louis Caplan and his wife at the civic reception held in their honour on 10 July 1964*
OPPOSITE: *Fans welcome The Beatles home to Liverpool's Speke Airport*

ABOVE: *Paul and George, posing with one of the stewardesses, before they descended from the plane to meet their fans*
OPPOSITE: *The Beatles arrive at Speke Airport, Liverpool, on 10 July 1964*

The date was set for the homecoming: 10 July 1964, soon after The Beatles' triumphant tour of Australia.

On the flight home their thoughts were occupied with this visit to Liverpool. One of the travelling journalists who had accompanied the group down under was from the *Liverpool Daily Post and Echo,* named, ironically, George Harrison—no relation whatsoever. Harrison's observation was astute: "Probably for the first time in their show-biz lives our world-famed troubadours are nervous. They aren't sure how their fellow citizens will react to this home-coming triumph. The four boys are thrilled to their fringes at the honour Liverpool is bestowing upon them. But in the back of their mind is a niggling doubt".

Harrison spoke to each of The Beatles about how they were feeling as they came closer to their return to Liverpool. Even though all the preparations had been made, Paul McCartney didn't know if it would click with Liverpool people.

"I can't somehow see all the kids I used to go to school with from Mather Avenue and their parents, turning out to watch young Paul McCartney drive by in a big car, along the road where we used to play together. I don't think I'd bother to go and cheer for somebody else", McCartney said honestly, "and I've got a feeling that they won't do it for us either.

"And who is going to stand outside the Town Hall just to see us arrive? Only a couple of years back hardly anybody in Liverpool had heard of us. Now this! I'm keeping my fingers crossed and hoping that everything comes off all right, but I have butterflies in my tummy over it".

Harrison (the reporter) observed that the manner of The Beatles was one of humility and that "there still isn't a big head among the four of them. They just can't believe they are important".

John Lennon, never normally short of words, could hardly explain how he felt about the forthcoming event. "The only time I've ever been at the Town Hall was when they sent me from art school to draw it. Going back like this, in state, or whatever they call It, Is a bit scary". Ringo, however, was more forthcoming. "It's a funny feeling. Makes you feel small and yet ten feet tall. I mean, all those other places in Australia and New Zealand where we went to civic receptions, they were only parties of people we didn't know, like. But this is different", Ringo enthused. "It's Liverpool. Think of being in that parade from Speke to the Town Hall with some of our old mates probably looking at us and saying; 'I knew that lot when they were poor'. And that wasn't so long ago either, was it?" he said with a smile.

Even the "quiet" Beatle had an opinion. George spoke to his namesake with his own perspective. "It's great that our own home town should do this for us", he said seriously, "but deep down I have the feeling that there are a lot of Liverpool folk who deserve this honour far more than we do. After all", he continued modestly, "what have we done? Sang some songs around the place and made money. It doesn't seem much compared with some things that have been done by many Liverpool men and women who've never been honoured".

The Beatles landed at Liverpool's Speke Airport when the British Eagle Britannia aircraft taxied in shortly after 5.20 p.m. The reception at the airport eased their minds when crowds of screaming fans watched them descend from the aircraft.

The press conference in the airport lounge was an untidy exercise. Reporters could hardly ask their questions and certainly could not hear most of the answers because of the noise from the shrieking fans outside.

They left the airport and drove off at a speed of 10 mph, which soon slowed to a crawl. Several times the motorcade was brought to a halt before arriving at the Town Hall. Main roads in the city centre had already been closed off. Liverpool Chief Constable Joseph Smith said that "more than 100,000 people had greeted The Beatles between the Airport and the Town Hall". It was by far the biggest event he could remember. Later estimates had the number closer to 200,000, and yet very few authors have ever mentioned this glorious homecoming. It may not have been numerically the biggest reception The Beatles ever experienced, but it was the most important to them.

Nearly 400 teenage girls fainted and forty-seven people were treated in various city hospitals. At one stage, St. George's Hall, where the ballroom was normally reserved for grand dances, became a temporary emergency casualty centre. The entire Liverpool police force was on hand to provide crowd control outside the Town Hall, the focus of the celebrations. Teenagers were bowled over like ninepins in the crush as The Beatles drove to the site for a civic reception. Afterwards they would make their way the short distance across the city to the Odeon Cinema for the northern premiere of *A Hard Day's Night*.

As the numbers grew, local police locked arms to stop the intense swaying. Luckily an army of approximately 200 St. John's Ambulance and Red Cross volunteers were on duty to deal with the hysteria.

The Beatles having a laugh with the Liverpool City Police Band inside Liverpool Town Hall

The volunteers fought their way into the crowd to resuscitate people who had fainted in the excitement and screaming girls were treated with sponges of cold water thrust in their faces. A St. John's spokesman said to a local reporter, "We have never experienced a night like this before. It made even the biggest football match seem soft in comparison". The local hospitals worked overtime with the casualties. One hospital official said, "It's just like the blitz all over again". This time it was a Beatles blitz on its hometown, which surrendered with a display of affection unparalleled anywhere in the group's lifetime.

On their short walk into the Town Hall, The Beatles were greeted by the Liverpool City Police Band. Paul helped himself to a trumpet, John grabbed a horn and Ringo whipped the conductor's baton from the hands of a laughing Chief Inspector George Marriott. Their prowess with wind instruments did not compare with their ability on the guitars and drums. The police band went on to play a selection of hits by The Beatles.

George Harrison's mum Louise said to the *Liverpool Daily Post*, "This is the greatest night of my life. I knew Liverpool people would not let the boys down. I knew they would turn out to welcome them back home. You can take it from me that George and John, Paul and Ringo too are thrilled at this great day. They were nervous, you know, but Liverpool has shown that they still love them".

John Lennon was equally thrilled by the reception. "Man, this welcome is fantastic", he said. "It's the greatest we've ever had. It beats our reception at Adelaide—our previous best—by miles. The boys are flabbergasted. This is the proudest moment of our lives. There's only one word for it, staggering. We have been all keyed up for days wondering what reception we would get. In fact, we were rather nervous about it all. We never expected many people would turn out. We thought there would only be a few people standing on the odd street corners. Just to think nobody would have turned their head to give me a second look a few years ago when I was at the College of Art in Hope Street. Mind you, those were great days just as the present are. And it's great to see my old pals who were at the college or in beat groups in the city at the time".

John was interrupted by Ringo. "These are lovely salmon butties (sandwiches) Mr. Lord Mayor. Fab. Can I have another?" He then commented about their homecoming. "We are completely overwhelmed by this reception. Everyone seems to have turned out to see us. There's no doubt about it, the people in our hometown are our greatest fans. We are grateful to them for giving us such a reception".

John added, "What has delighted us more than anything is that everybody from the top nobs to the humblest Scouser have been so nice and friendly".

One notable absentee from the balcony was Brian Epstein, who was responsible for taking the Fab Four out of Liverpool. "I lost the way when I became separated from the boys and their families. So I just stayed downstairs with the rest of the guests. I couldn't find the way to the staircase to the gallery", Epstein told the paper. Epstein's action that day was indicative of his generous character in staying out of the spotlight.

The four musicians were presented with an oblong cake decorated with a map of the world that read: "The City of Liverpool Honours The Beatles". The Fab Four donated the cake to Alder Hey Children's Hospital in West Derby, where Paul's mother Mary had started her nursing career.

Liverpool's favourite sons had returned in triumph to where it all began. Having conquered the world, re-conquering their hometown made them nervous. When they saw 200,000 fans turn out to applaud and congratulate them, it took their breath away.

The *Liverpool Daily Post's* headline said it all, "They love us, yeah, yeah, yeah".

ABOVE : *View from the Town Hall balcony in 2007* BELOW: *The Town Hall balcony from Castle Street*

11 July 1964
Leaving Liverpool
"Ticket To Ride"

ABOVE: *Paul and John wave goodbye as the Fab Four leave the Town Hall reception* OPPOSITE: *Castle Street from the Town Hall balcony as the fans wait to see The Beatles appear*

After their triumphant civic reception at Liverpool Town Hall, The Beatles were driven to the Odeon cinema for the northern premiere of their debut movie, *A Hard Day's Night*. Fans had queued for hours in the rain for a glimpse of their heroes, which was in vain as the group was whisked through the rear entrance into the cinema.

At 1.30 a.m. the following morning, The Beatles boarded a plane at Liverpool's Speke Airport and headed for London, a ninety-minute flight. A few hours later they appeared live on the ITV's 'Thank Your Lucky Stars' program.

The Beatles all set down roots in and around "Swingin' London" in the summer of 1963. For the fans in Liverpool, there were mixed feelings that went along with their departure.

Liverpudlians were glad for the band and their success, but were a bit selfish, too. They didn't want to share The Beatles with the rest of the United Kingdom, let alone the world.

If 1964 was the year that they conquered the world, then 1965 was when they cemented their place in music history, culminating in the record-breaking Shea Stadium concert. The home of the New York Mets baseball team barely contained the 55,600 screaming fans who watched The Beatles arrive and perform on a small stage in the middle of the field. To The Beatles and promoter Sid Bernstein, it was a major triumph. It was not that long ago that they had been inches away from their adoring fans in The Casbah and The Cavern in Liverpool or Hamburg, where they learned how to work a crowd.

They did make one final appearance in Liverpool at the Empire on 5 December 1965. This really was "Hello, Goodbye". However, playing live was soon to become a thing of the past. Exactly seven years to the day since the re-formed Quarrymen opened The Casbah, The Beatles' final live gig was held at Candlestick Park in San Francisco on 29 August 1966.

The band wanted to push new frontiers in the recording studio. On 30 January 1967, Subafilms, headed by Liverpool-born Tony Bramwell, began shooting the promotion for their new single,

the double-A-sided "Strawberry Fields Forever" and "Penny Lane". They were filmed in 35mm colour for U.S. television, though the finished films only appeared in the United Kingdom in black and white.

Sadly, even though the songs were about Liverpool, they were mainly filmed on the National Trust property in Knole Park (about twenty miles from London) and Angel Lane in East London. Filming was completed during the following week and clips of both of these short films appeared around the globe.

The Beatles managed to stay together for three more years but each member was pulled in a different direction as he grew older. On 10 April 1970, the dream was officially over. If the fans thought that was the end of their association with Liverpool, it wasn't.

Ringo's first solo album was released in March 1970. *Sentimental Journey* was produced by George Martin and the album cover featured The Empress, his local pub, which is at the top of Admiral Grove where he grew up. An album of old standards, they were the songs he remembered from childhood. Ringo, like John, left England for America in the 1970s, and after the passing of his mother Elsie in 1987, he hardly returned to Liverpool. He has, however, supported his childhood area by donating money to St. Silas School for an adventure playground, and to his old school Dingle Vale Secondary Modern—renamed "Shorefields" in the 1970s—where the "Starr Fields" were opened in 2007 for the children in The Dingle and the local community. Ringo also paid homage to his hometown with the January 2008 launch of his new album, *Liverpool 8*. The reference is to the postal district of The Dingle.

OPPOSITE: *Ringo appeared on a specially arranged stage in a blue metallic box above the columns at the front of St. George's Hall, Liverpool in January 2008*
ABOVE: *Paul McCartney performing at Anfield on 1 June 2008 during Liverpool's European Capital of Culture year*
BOTTOM: *Financially supported by George Harrison, the renovated Victorian Palm House in Sefton Park*

"Liverpool I left you, but I never let you down", sang Ringo at the opening ceremony of Liverpool's European Capital of Culture celebrations on 11 January 2008. Over 50,000 people congregated in front of St. George's Hall to witness a forty-five-minute show. Ringo sang his new song to rapturous cheers and applause. One of Liverpool's favourite sons was home again. The year 2008 was truly a sentimental journey for Ringo.

George's triple-album *All Things Must Pass* was released on 27 November 1970. The massive work demonstrated the pent-up frustration that he must have felt when his songs had been overlooked for so many years. He also had the honour of being the first solo Beatle to make it to No. 1 on the charts with "My Sweet Lord". George's music reflected his strong religious convictions that had been awakened in the sixties and his journey took him away from Liverpool.

George's Liverpool connections gradually meant that his trips back home became fewer and fewer. His love for gardening was reflected in his desire to help restore the Victorian Palm House that had been left to rot at the heart of Sefton Park. George backed the campaign and became a trustee. Sadly he was unable to make the trip to Liverpool for the reopening because of his deteriorating health. Though he didn't give much thought to his hometown after he left, his hometown never forgot him.

Liverpool mourned the quiet Beatle's death on 29 November 2001 by gathering on the plateau of St. George's Hall. A tree was planted in St. John's Gardens to celebrate his life, and a tribute concert was staged in Liverpool on 24 February 2002. The audience applauded as Paul McCartney, paid tribute to George before he sang "Yesterday" *a cappella*, changing the words appropriately to "Why *he* had to go, I don't know, *he* wouldn't say". It was a tasteful nod to his "little Beatle brother".

John's ties with his Liverpool-based family were strained for many years and contact was limited because of his ongoing deportation case in America, which took him several years to fight and win. On 5 October 1975 the U.S. Court of Appeal overturned the order to deport John and he was granted residency status. The authorities announced, "Lennon's four-year battle to remain in our country is testimony to his faith in this American dream".

Lennon later made amends and renewed his ties with his half-sisters Julia and Jackie, talking fondly of his childhood in Liverpool in letters and telephone calls. He asked for photos and other possessions that reminded him of his childhood to be sent to him, including his Quarry Bank School tie. He was so fond of the tie that he wore it at his son, Sean's fourth and his thirty-ninth joint birthday party on 9 October 1979.

In June 1964, Lennon was interviewed on radio about his hometown. He had been annoyed at the media's description of Liverpool. "We see in papers all over the world—isn't it wonderful they (The Beatles) rose from the slums", he said. "Lots of people imagine that Liverpool is one big slum which it isn't". None of the group came from a slum area, Lennon said. His description of Liverpool was "black, you know, like all the northern cities are". This was because of the colour of the buildings blackened from soot. He defended Liverpool loyally. "The people and the goings on in Liverpool are almost as interesting as the things in London—it just so happens London's a bit bigger".

During that interview, Lennon was asked about the popularity of The Beatles and how long it would last. "Obviously", Lennon thought, "we are not going to stand on the stage singing "Twist and Shout" when we're thirty with long hair".

Life was just starting over for John in 1980 with the release of *Double Fantasy*, his first album in five years. Lennon, now aged 40, was ready to share with the world his message of the joys of domesticity when he was murdered by a deranged fan on 8 December 1980. In Liverpool, fans gathered at St. George's plateau for a candle-lit vigil to mourn the passing of a genius. A tree was planted at a ceremony in St. John's Gardens, Liverpool, on 9 October 2000, and children from Lennon's primary school, Dovedale, sang "Imagine" as a tribute.

In 2007, Ringo Starr gave his support to Starr Fields in The Dingle

Images of John Lennon were projected on the Liverpool waterfront buildings as a tribute to him in 2005, 25 years after he was killed

Strangely enough, this wasn't the end of Lennon's association with Liverpool. Through his widow Yoko Ono, Lennon has been remembered in many ways. Yoko has supported several projects in Liverpool, including a generous donation of £30,000 to Dovedale School, purchasing Mendips, financially contributing to Strawberry Field and the renaming of the city's municipal airport to Liverpool John Lennon Airport.

In 2007, Yoko launched the "Imagine Appeal" at Alder Hey Children's Hospital and supported Liverpool's bid for "European Capital of Culture" for 2008.

Out of all The Beatles, it was Paul McCartney who flew the highest flag for Liverpool and over time has become the city's greatest ambassador. Paul cherished his Liverpool roots and has been the one who has maintained his links with his home town throughout his life. He has supported many local charities, both publicly and privately. After the April 1998 death of his wife Linda from breast cancer, Paul helped establish the Linda McCartney Centre at the Royal Liverpool Hospital to help women with cancer.

McCartney remembered Liverpool in his solo song writing with songs like "Let 'Em In" mentioning his brother Mike and Auntie Jin. As he progressed into classical music, he produced the *Liverpool Oratorio* in October 1991. Lyrically, it follows his life in Liverpool from birth, through school and growing up with the sentiment remaining that "Not for ourselves but for the whole world were we born, and we were born in Liverpool", inspired by the Liverpool Institute school motto.

One of McCartney's more public expressions of support for his home town was his intervention after his school, the Liverpool Institute, closed its doors in 1985. Plans had been discussed to demolish the building and so Paul stepped in. He formed a committee to establish the Liverpool Institute for Performing Arts (LIPA). Paul didn't just sign a cheque and do the obligatory round of publicity, he completely devoted himself to LIPA, mobilising local support for the initiative. It took £20 million to get the LIPA project off the ground, which was opened on 7 June 1996 by Her Majesty, Queen Elizabeth. A regular visitor to the institution, McCartney teaches students, attends graduation and has given his time and support whenever it has been needed to help LIPA and its students.

Macca has played many memorable gigs in Liverpool. In the first of his two King's Dock triumphs—in 1990—he paid tribute to John Lennon when he sang a medley of "Help", "Strawberry Fields Forever" and "Give Peace a Chance". The second concert was in 2003, and in 2008 he returned for a Capital of Culture celebration concert at the home of Liverpool Football Club.

The Beatles left Liverpool in 1963 and moved on to London and the rest of the world. Did they leave, or just relocate? As is commonly stated by Liverpudlians everywhere, "You can take the boy out of Liverpool, but you can't take Liverpool out of the boy".

Thousands of fans from all over the world still flock to Liverpool to visit the city that produced the greatest band in the history of popular music. Brian Epstein was once asked by an interviewer if it was important that The Beatles came from Liverpool.

"Oh yes", Epstein replied. "It is essential".

Epstein was later to lament; "But alas, and I regret this most profoundly, we also outgrew our beloved, lovely, Liverpool".

TOP: *Paul presenting a LIPA Pin to a 2005 graduating music student with LIPA's principal, Mark Featherstone-Witty in the background*
BOTTOM: *The new LIPA building with the Art College on the right of the complex*

The Beatles pose on the flight deck of the plane

Liddypool

The Songs

Liddypool 🎵 The Songs
"Only A Northern Song"

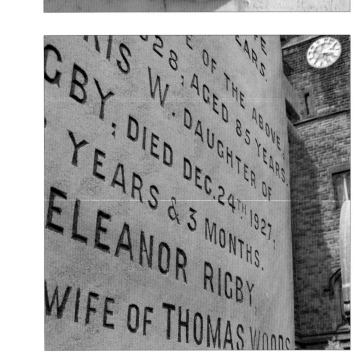

TOP LEFT: *Allerton Fire Station plaque*
TOP CENTRE: *Vintage double-decker bus, like the one that
Paul and George met on, as they travelled to the Liverpool Institute*
TOP RIGHT: *The cast iron shore, Dingle, mentioned in "Glass Onion"*
ABOVE: *The grave of Eleanor Rigby in St. Peter's cemetery*

The following is a list of The Beatles' songs with relevance to Liverpool. You can cross-reference the song with the appropriate area, which is in brackets, where appropriate.

"A Day In The Life"

The BBC banned "A Day In The Life" because of the line, "I'd love to turn you on" which they took to be a reference to drugs. However, Paul McCartney's contribution to this song was about his morning bus ride to school on the number 86 bus, and not about drugs. He famously sang in the middle section, "woke up, got out of bed, dragged a comb across my head" and sings "made the bus in seconds flat". He then "went upstairs, and had a smoke, somebody spoke and I went into a dream". Paul said, "It was just me remembering what it was like to run up the road to catch a bus to school, having a smoke and going into class. It was a reflection of my school days. I would have a Woodbine (cigarette) and somebody would speak and I would go into a dream". Upstairs was the only place you could smoke on the old double-decker buses. The route took him along Mather Avenue, passing the fire station mentioned in "Penny Lane", through the Penny Lane roundabout and on into town, to the Liverpool Institute.

"Cayenne"

One of Paul's first songs, an instrumental piece composed using his first guitar, was penned even before he met John Lennon. He made a tape recording of it in 1960, and although never officially recorded by The Beatles, an early demo appeared on *The Beatles Anthology*.

"Do You Want to Know a Secret?" (see Liverpool - 36, Falkner Street)

Although sung by George Harrison, it was written by John Lennon while living in Epstein's flat in Falkner Street. It appears to be written for Cynthia Powell, John's first wife.

"Eleanor Rigby" (see Woolton - St. Peter's Church)

"Eleanor Rigby, died in the church and was buried along with her name, nobody came", Paul wrote. But now they do—at St. Peter's Church in Woolton to see her grave.

"Getting Better"

A true collaboration between Paul and John, this was a real mixture of their feelings at the time. John wrote of his education at Dovedale School and Quarry Bank. "I used to get mad at my school, the teachers who taught me weren't cool, holding me down, turning me round, filling me up with your rules". John didn't look back on his schooling with affection, but his frustration was aimed more at the teachers than school itself. He was angry that his artistic talents weren't developed or recognised.

"Glass Onion"

In the song "Glass Onion", John mentions standing on the cast iron shore. This is a part of The Dingle Shore, also nicknamed "The Cassie". It was reclaimed in the 1980s as part of the International Garden Festival site which had a Beatles garden complete with a Yellow Submarine.

Haymans Green

This album, released by the Pete Best Band in 2008 takes its title from the address of The Casbah Coffee Club, which resided in the basement of the Best's family home at 8, Haymans Green. This autobiographical album charts his life from growing up in Liverpool through his time with The Beatles in Liverpool and Hamburg and beyond.

"Hello Little Girl"

This was the first of John's songs that The Quarrymen performed from about 1958 onwards. He maintained that the inspiration was the Cole Porter song "It's De-Lovely". The Beatles never released it as a record, though they did perform the song at the Decca audition. It was a hit for Liverpool group The Fourmost, in September 1963. It was also the song that made Brian Epstein sit up and listen at The Cavern. The song was later released on *The Beatles' Anthology 1*.

"I Am the Walrus"

This was a typical Lennon "nonsense" song, which had various influences. One of these was supposedly a letter received by John from a pupil at Quarry Bank School, stating that he was going to study songs by The Beatles in class. John therefore made it

TOP LEFT: *Brian Epstein's flat at 36, Falkner Street where John and Cynthia lived after they married*
TOP RIGHT: *Gerry Marsden, Bill Harry and three members from The Fourmost, pictured in 2007*
ABOVE: *Penny Lane tram terminal in 1926*

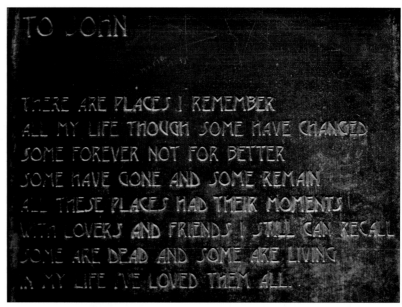

as unintelligible as possible, challenging the teachers to understand him.

Another influence was the playground chant he would have picked up from the skipping girls at Dovedale School:

> Yellow matter custard, green snot pie,
> All mixed together with a dead dog's eye,
> Slap it on a butty, ten foot thick,
> Then wash it all down with a cup of cold sick.

The Walrus came from Lewis Carroll's poem "The Walrus and the Carpenter". In 2006, a schoolbook of John's reached over £126,000 at auction. The book, completed by John when he was twelve-years old, included an illustrated page of "The Walrus and the Carpenter", showing his knowledge and appreciation for a poem that he would return to in this song.

In 1970, John gave an interview to journalist Sam Beckett in which he said "I am the eggman" was a term referring to Jerry Furber, a Liverpudlian who delivered eggs to Mendips when John was a boy. Calling at his house on a regular basis would be a milkman (his Uncle George), a bin man, a rag-and-bone man, a fruit man and an "egg man". Every Saturday, Jerry would come round and Mimi and would give him 5d for a dozen eggs. John remembers one day while Jerry

was in the house, he looked inside the van, "there were just so many eggs. There would be a tap on the door and he would shout 'Egg man'. I'd never seen anything like it", he declared, "I wanted his job". He said he had never mentioned Jerry before because he was a private man and Lennon didn't want to inflict the media on him.

"I Saw Her Standing There"

This early rocker was a collaboration between Paul and John. Paul had most of it worked out driving home to Forthlin Road in 1962. His first two lines were originally "She was just seventeen, never been a beauty queen" but it didn't sound right to McCartney. Lennon suggested a real 'Scousism' with the line, "She was just seventeen, you know what I mean?" "You know what I mean" is often tagged on to the end of a sentence in Liverpool as a rhetorical question. They quickly scribbled the song down in an exercise book Paul had brought home from school as a Lennon-McCartney original.

"In My Life" (see Allerton and Wavertree)

John wrote a nostalgic song about his childhood, mentioning places he remembered. These lyrics only came to light years later. Each place mentioned has an explanation in this book. The places John wrote about in these original lyrics were:

> Penny Lane is one I'm missing
> Up Church Road to the clock tower
> In the circle of the Abbey
> I have seen some happy hours
> Past the tram sheds with no trams
> On the 5 bus into town
> Past the Dutch and St. Columbus
> To the dockers umbrella that they pulled down
> In the parks I've spent some good times
> Calderstones was good for

John couldn't get the song to work and replaced most of the lyrics. However, the reference to "Penny Lane" sparked an idea in Paul's head and inspired him to begin writing about the Penny Lane of their childhood (see Allerton & Mossley Hill).

The following places were mentioned in John's original draft of the song.

"In My Life"—Penny Lane
This line, though not used in the final song, inspired Paul to write about his childhood memories of Penny Lane.

"In My Life"—Up Church Road
Running up from the Penny Lane roundabout is Church Road. Bluecoat School is also on Church Road, and at the top is the Abbey Cinema and Picton Clock. This was George's route to and from Dovedale School.

"In My Life"—Picton Clock (see Wavertree)
The "clock" referred to by John is Picton Clock. It was a popular meeting place near George's home and the Abbey Cinema.

"In My Life"—The Abbey (see Wavertree)
The "Abbey" was the old Abbey Cinema that stands on the roundabout at the top of Church Road, where it meets Wavertree High Street.

"In My Life"—The tram sheds (see Wavertree)
The tram sheds were on Smithdown Road, about 200 yards from Penny Lane.

"In My Life"—The Dutch (see Wavertree)
John mentioned "the Dutch". This was the Dutch Café, which was an all-night café at 316, Smithdown Road.

"In My Life"—St. Columbus (see Wavertree)
John's original lyrics referred to "St. Columbus". St. Columba's (not Columbus) was a church at the junction of Smithdown Road and Greenbank Drive.

"In My Life"—The docker's umbrella
This was John's reference to the overhead electric railway that ran from Seaforth Docks in the north to The Dingle in the south. It was known as the "docker's umbrella" because dockworkers used it as a shelter from the rain.

"In My Life"—Calderstones (see Allerton)
Calderstones Park was one of the favourite places for John Lennon's gang to meet, where they would watch the girls go by.

"In My Life"—There are places I'll remember
Next to the entrance of The Cavern in Mathew Street is a plaque on the wall, which is often missed, with the words of the final draft of the song that was recorded. Make sure to look for it next to the door.

"In Spite Of All The Danger" (see Kensington)
Credited to McCartney and Harrison, this is the first original song recorded by The Quarrymen at the studio in Kensington in July 1958.

"I'll Get You"
This was the B-side to "She Loves You" and, although mainly written by John, was one of the few songs composed with Paul at Mendips.

"I've Just Seen A Face"
Paul played this song for his family in Liverpool—then known as "Auntie Jin's Theme". Auntie Jin was the sister of Paul's father, Jim McCartney.

"Let 'Em In"
This song makes mention of two special members of the McCartney family. It appeared on the 1976 album *Wings at the Speed of Sound*. The song mentions 'Brother Michael' and his favourite 'Auntie Jin,' who lived in Dinas Lane, Huyton.

"Let It Be"
Paul's anthem "Let It Be" flashes up images of the Virgin Mary, and of his own mother Mary, who he had lost at fourteen to cancer while living at Forthlin Road. He described it as one of his 'semi-religious' songs.

Mary often said in her soft voice 'let it be' to calm a situation. He wrote this as a reference to the pressure he was under with The Beatles, especially after a dream he had when his mother came to him to give him strength. He had used this imagery in "Lady Madonna", a tribute to his mother, and all mothers. When the virgin Mary was visited by the angel to be told that she would become the mother of Jesus, she said, "Let it be to me as you have said". "Let It Be" is the translation of the Hebrew word 'Amen' said at the end of prayers.

"Like Dreamers Do"
Written back in the late 1950s by Paul, The Quarrymen performed "Like Dreamers Do". It was also incorporated into The Beatles Cavern set. The song was performed at the Decca audition on 1 January 1962.

In John's original lyrics for "In My Life" he mentions the docker's umbrella.
This was a reference to the Liverpool Overhead Railway, pictured here in the 1930s,
in front of the Cunard Building and the Liver Building

Liverpool Oratorio

Paul McCartney's 1991 classical album, *Liverpool Oratorio*, received critical acclaim on its release. It has been performed at Liverpool's Anglican Cathedral, and features a semi-autobiographical journey through Paul's entire life in Liverpool.

Liverpool 8 (see Dingle)

Although Ringo had mentioned Liverpool in songs like the modestly titled "I'm The Greatest" and "Snookeroo", it was when he launched his new CD, *Liverpool 8* in 2008, that he decided to dedicate an album to the town of his birth. Its title track was an autobiographical look at his life. He picks up on those places and people that were important to him in the following lyrics.

"I was a sailor first, I sailed the sea". His first job was working on the ferry from Liverpool to North Wales and back. Not quite sailing the sea.

"Then I got a job, in a factory". His apprenticeship was served in Henry Hunt & Sons Ltd. in The Dingle, making equipment for schools.

"Played Butlin's Camp, with my friend Rory". He gave up his apprenticeship at Hunt's to play professionally with Rory Storm and the Hurricanes at Butlin's Holiday Camp.

"Liverpool I left you, said goodbye to Madryn Street". Madryn was the street where he was born.

"Said goodbye to Admiral Grove". Admiral Grove was the street where he lived from the age of five.

He also mentions Hamburg where he went with "George and Paul, and my friend John". His chorus makes the claim that, "Liverpool I left you, but I never let you down". Those words came back to haunt him when he made a derisory comment aimed at his home town on television, which made him very unpopular in Liverpool. "I never let you down"?

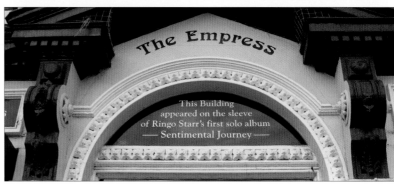

TOP: *The Dingle looking over Madryn Street and Kinmel Street to The Empress pub on the left, and the towers of the Liver Building on the horizon*
ABOVE *The Empress celebrates being made famous by Ringo*

"Maggie Mae" (see Liverpool—Lime Street)

A short rendition, and spelled differently, of the old Liverpool folk song "Maggie May" appeared on the *Let it Be* album in 1969. It was a standard song for skiffle groups, including The Quarrymen. The story is of an infamous Liverpool prostitute who plied her trade at Lime Street station. It was a perfect folk song that transferred nicely to the new skiffle scene. Such was the affection for the song that Paul McCartney 'just chucked it in for Liverpool' at his Kings Dock concert in June 2003.

Menlove Avenue (see Woolton—Mendips)

Menlove Avenue is the posthumous album of John Lennon songs named after the road on which Mendips is found.

"Michelle"

This song grew out of the 'art parties' that were thrown by John's art tutor Austin Mitchell. The parties were very Parisian and John recalled how Paul sat there, strumming a guitar and pretending to be French. After much cajoling by John, he wrote this song. McCartney then approached Ivan Vaughan's wife Jan, who was a French language teacher, and she helped him with the French lines that make this song stand out.

ABOVE: *Paul would walk through the Dam Woods, to Hale Village, above, and onto Hale Beach*
RIGHT: *Gambier Terrace, Hope Street, Liverpool, where John shared a flat with Stuart*

"Mother"

John's song from his first solo album, *Plastic Ono Band,* is both moving and painful. The album was influenced by his primal scream therapy in 1970. The song's central theme goes back to the event that probably defined his life. At the age of five, he was forced to choose between his mother and his father after Alf had taken John to Blackpool. He stood by his father, but as his broken-hearted mother turned and walked away, he shouted "Mummy don't go". Then as he grabbed her hand, he turned around to his father and shouted "Daddy come home". All he wanted was for his mum and dad to live together again as a family. It never happened. John returned to Liverpool with Julia who took him back to Mimi's house. This song, for me, defines John more than any other of his works.

"Mother Nature's Son" (see Speke—Dam Woods and Hale)

Influenced by his nature trips through the Dam Woods in Speke and Hale Village, to the Lighthouse, Paul's love for nature was brought to the fore while in India. He finished the song at his father's house in Baskervyle Road, Heswall.

"Norwegian Wood" (see Liverpool—Gambier Terrace)

Pete Shotton felt that "Norwegian Wood" was John's reference to both his unfaithfulness to Cynthia and his recollections of those days in Percy Street when they had burned the furniture—made of Norwegian wood—in the fireplace, and asked guests to sleep in the bath, which John had done on more than one occasion. Rod Murray remembered, "We burned the furniture because we didn't have any money to buy coal".

"Penny Lane" (see Penny Lane Walk)

This street is the most famous in all of Liverpool thanks to Paul, who waxed nostalgic about his hometown in "Penny Lane", where his childhood memories are found "there beneath the blue suburban skies".

"Please Please Me"

John wrote "Please Please Me" in his front bedroom at Mendips. John loved the homophonic 'Please' and 'Pleas' in Bing Crosby's 1932 song, entitled "Please". He listened intently as his mum Julia sang this song to him when he was little. "Oh please, lend your little ears to my pleas". John, like Julia, loved to play with words. *Please Please Me* eventually became the title of The Beatles' debut album.

"Polythene Pam"

John originally stated that the central figure was a 'mythical Liverpool scrubber'. It later turned out that it was a story about two people he had met. Pat Hodgett was a Cavern regular known for her habit of eating polythene, and was called 'Polythene Pat'. However, the person dressing up in polythene was a girl introduced to John by beat poet Royston Ellis, while on tour in the Channel Islands in 1963.

The Beatles perform at The Cavern in February 1963

"Put it There"
Released by Paul in 1989, the moving song is about his father Jim. Paul recalled his father saying to him, "Son, put it there if it weighs a ton". It was Jim's way of saying that he would carry his son's burden.

Sentimental Journey (see Liverpool 8: The Dingle — Empress)
Ringo's first solo album features The Empress pub on the front cover. The pub is on the corner of Admiral Grove where he grew up.

"She Loves You"
Many songs were written at Forthlin Road, including the finishing touches to "She Loves You". Paul and John spent hours filling schoolbooks with songs: twenty of them eventually became tracks for The Beatles.

"Strawberry Fields Forever" (see Woolton Walk)
One of Lennon's most memorable songs, it was written in 1966 while filming *How I Won the War*. Lennon reflected on his childhood in the grounds where "nothing is real, and nothing to get hung about".

"No one I think is in my tree" relates to the elm tree that used to stand at the bottom of his garden at Mendips. According to Mimi, John spent hours in his tree, reading, writing or drawing — it was his special place. (It was cut down years ago as it became diseased).

However, John also later compared it to his childhood. No one was 'in his tree' — they weren't on his intellectual level. He often stated that he was a genius and his teachers should have realised it.

"Nothing to get hung about". For many fans this means, 'having no hang-ups, worries'. This phrase actually comes from a saying that John used on Mimi when he was in trouble, which was often. Mimi would tell him off, but you can imagine the young Lennon shrugging his shoulders and answering back, "Yes, whatever, but it's nothing to get hung about Mimi". In Britain, the ultimate penalty in law was to be hanged. Therefore, whatever John did wrong, it wasn't serious enough to get hung.

When it came to recording the song, there were two versions that John liked and wanted piecing together, though he didn't fully grasp that they were recorded at different tempos. George Martin slowed down the second part so that they matched. It was a work of genius.

John's song is pure fantasy and nostalgia, and some interesting memories are captured here. Not all of these have translated as easily as others, or are as well known. This is possibly one of the most enduring examples of The Beatles, and John, at their best. It is a masterpiece that stands the test of time, yet still captures a moment of individual song writing that typifies the era it was created for. Maybe nobody was in John's tree.

"That Was Me"
From Paul McCartney's 2007 album, *Memory Almost Full*, "That Was Me" is a nostalgic trip back to his childhood growing up in Liverpool. In the lyrics, he mentions: "scout camp" where he went with his brother, after Paul and John had first met at St. Peter's Church on 6 July 1957: "blanket in the blue bells" was Bluebell Woods near his home in Speke: the "Royal Iris, on the river", the ferry where The Beatles played on the River Mersey: "sweating cobwebs *(a Liverpool phrase, from 'sweating cobs' or perspiring greatly):* "in the cellar, on TV", a reference to their performance on TV with Ringo's first appearance at The Cavern in August 1962: "a cappella at the altar", his choir singing days at St. Barnabas' Church, Penny Lane.

"The Other Side of Liverpool"
From Ringo's 2010 album, *Y Not*, "The Other Side of Liverpool" was another nostalgic song following on from his *Liverpool 8* album. In this song, he shows a darker side to growing up in The Dingle.

"The other side of Liverpool is cold and damp".

For most of working class Liverpool in the 1940s, they could only dream of central heating, warm baths and indoor toilets. The cold and damp toilet was in the little brick outhouse at the bottom of the yard. Ringo said:

"The Dingle was one of the roughest areas in Liverpool, and Toxteth still has quite a reputation. It was really rough. Liverpool was dark and dreary, but it was great fun to be a kid."

"Only way outta there, drums, guitar, and amp The other side of Liverpool, where I came from My mother was a barmaid".

"Mum didn't do too much for a while", recalled Ringo. She was in a bit of pain after my dad left, and she ended up doing any down-home job she could get to feed and clothe me. She did everything: she was a barmaid, she scrubbed steps, worked in a food shop".

"At the age of three my father was gone." As is well known, Richard Starkey Senior walked out on Elsie and young Richard. Their family home at 9, Madryn Street became too expensive, and so they moved to Admiral Grove.

"Working Class Hero"
"A working class hero is something to be", sang John in one of his most famous solo songs. Working class? John was brought up in the Penny Lane area, better than a working class area like The Dingle. He spent his childhood in his Aunt Mimi's house at Mendips in middle-class Woolton.

The rest of the song is a brief history of his childhood, through bitter eyes. Lennon sings about being hurt at home and hit at school, something that happened regularly at both the Dovedale and Quarry Bank Schools.

"Yellow Submarine"
"In the town where I was born, lived a man who sailed to sea". Paul had the inspiration for writing a children's song one night. It was released on the B-side of "Eleanor Rigby" in August 1966. A model of the Yellow Submarine was made for the International Garden Festival in the 1980s, and currently resides outside Liverpool John Lennon Airport.

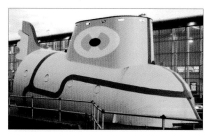

The Yellow Submarine, which is displayed outside Liverpool John Lennon Airport

Paul and John rehearse at The Cavern in February 1963

Liddypool
The Venues

Liddypool The Venues
"There Are Places I'll Remember"

There was more to the Liverpool club scene than just The Cavern. Everybody around the world knows about the famous club but there were venues all over Merseyside that showcased the music of the new 'Mersey Sound'. The Beatles played many great venues, but some unusual ones as well.

Kay Shepard used to follow the bands to the various clubs, especially to see her boyfriend (and now her husband) Wally Shepard who was with Earl Preston and the TTs.

What was the music scene like in Liverpool?

"My first experience with the Merseybeat scene was in 1960 at the tender age of 14. There was a small hut in Westvale, Kirkby, by where I used to live. It only held about forty people and I remember that it was the first time I saw Earl Preston and the TTs. I was hooked. The music was fantastic and, of course, Wally was in the band. He was only 17 so, when they finished at 10.30 p.m., my dad would be outside waiting for me to walk me home, God love him.

"I then progressed to the Aintree Institute. I absolutely loved that place. Every Thursday, Friday and Saturday, The Beatles were on; also Earl Preston and the TTs were on most weekends. Earl was such a good-looking guy and all the girls would be screaming for him. Walking up those stone steps, feeling the bass guitar thumping in your chest was so exciting. There was one time when they held a band competition between The Beatles and Earl Preston and the TTs. The winner of the competition went on the response of the audience and believe it or not, the TTs won. I remember George Harrison saying to Wally, 'Don't forget your friends on the way up'.

"We were coming out of the Merseyside Civil Service Club in Lower Castle Street one Sunday night to get the bus home. I can remember there was a gang of us walking towards the Pier Head to the bus stop and Paul McCartney, John Lennon and George Harrison were walking behind us calling to us. We were all acting cool, not answering them. There used to be a hut at the Pier Head that sold pies and drinks and when we reached there, we were sitting on a bench and Paul McCartney said to me, 'What time is your bus?' I told him 11.00 p.m. he said, 'Can't you get a later one?'

"The last one left at midnight. I said I could do, so I told my friends not to make a noise going past our house, as mum would wake and know that I wasn't with them. There at the Pier Head I had a bit of a kiss and cuddle with Paul and made it home around 12.30 a.m. As soon as I put my key in the door, it was opened by my mum, who gave me a good hiding. With every smack, she spoke, 'I will Paul McCartney you'.

"One of my friends had knocked and told my mum where I was. Oh, the good old days".

The Night Boppers were a band that hailed from Atherton in Lancashire and appeared on the same bill as The Beatles. Dave 'Tempest' Peacock was the lead singer of the Night Boppers and he told me about his brief appearance alongside The Beatles.

Why were you appearing in Liverpool?

"We'd never heard of The Beatles or anyone else. We did two gigs in one night— Formby Hall in Atherton and one in Bury. As I was singing, I saw 'two suits' with trilbies. Who are they? I thought, they're not local. They came to our dressing room afterwards and they assumed as I was the singer, that I was the leader, but I wasn't. It was Dennis Taylor, our saxophone player. They were Liverpool guys who were both agents. It turned out to be Jim McIver and Dougie Martin of Ivamar Promotions. Because the Liverpool bands were going to Hamburg, they were searching for new bands to replace them. We got about sixteen gigs around Liverpool, and that's how it started".

Did you know the other bands?

"No, not really, because after we'd played we had to travel back home to Atherton so we never socialised with them. The Night Boppers played on the same bill as The Beatles on two occasions. On 11 March 1961, we appeared as the second billed act going on before them for, 'The Beatles Farewell Show' as they were soon returning to Hamburg. This was the last gig Stuart played here with them".

Paul McCartney signed Dave Peacock's picture of the Night Boppers

Were you doing the same songs?

"We'd never heard the Merseybeat stuff. We played covers of American songs but they threw some songs in that we hadn't come across. They were playing different sets to us. The Beatles were right in front of us by the stage, and they were looking up at us. Bob Wooler said they were looking worried, but we were different, not competing. You wouldn't have recognized the songs they were doing the way they were playing them.

"They then went up on the balcony and watched us from there. We had a saxophone player and we left everything back stage. Prior to us going on someone had been in the dressing room and one of the locks had been broken on his saxophone case, and I'm not saying who it was, but The Beatles had been seen in the vicinity.

"To be honest, I was a bit scared, even though I was a wrestler. I was scared of starting anything in Liverpool. I thought, 'We are from a little town and we're going to get killed'. I swear to you I toned down the act and tried not to look at the girls as there were lots of teddy boys and I didn't want to upset them; I was just glad to get away. When The Beatles went on stage after us, I thought we'd better watch them and show that we appreciated them. I was standing close to John Lennon and watched him. I looked at the others and I thought he was impressive. John was chewing away—I'd never seen anyone chewing and singing. He had this long nose and was looking down it with this gunslingers stance. He looked right at me. I gave him the thumbs up and he gave me a smile back. I wished I'd have stayed and had a photo but you didn't know back then. I'd never seen anyone like him, except Elvis. As I came off-stage the first person I looked at was Pete Best and I thought, 'He's better looking than me'. I'd never seen such a handsome fella. A very nice man and we still exchange Christmas cards.

"Years later, I sent a letter to Paul McCartney and he took it home to Sussex and sent it back with a nice note, 'To Dave and the Night Boppers, have a great reunion, here's to the old days', which was nice. He didn't have to do that; he could have thrown it in the bin.

"I also obtained a copy of promoter Dave Forshaw's diary showing, 'Night Boppers' and 'Beatles Rock Combo' showing Pete Best's name, as he did The Beatles' bookings".

The search for the venues played by The Quarrymen as they progressed through to The Beatles has perhaps been one of the favourite parts of my research for this book. Since starting this book in 2001, some of these venues have been demolished to make way for new houses or apartments, and very few are in their original state. Despite this, there is an excitement in the eyes of the remaining residents when they reminisce, for their memories are often as fresh as if it were yesterday.

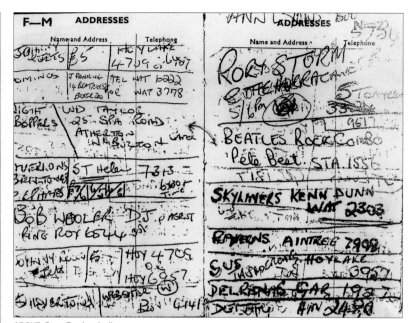

ABOVE: *Dave Forshaw's diary showing The Beatles Rock Combo and next to it, Pete Best's telephone number, as he was handling the bookings for The Beatles with Mona*

BELOW: *The Night Boppers on the bill with The Beatles*

THE BEST JIVE DANCES IN THE AREA ARE AT

AINTREE INSTITUTE
(By the Black Bull)

EVERY SATURDAY

compered by Mr. "Big Beat" BOB WOOLE

THIS WEEK —
THE BEATLES FAREWELL SHOW
Fantastic Night Boppers, Ray and the Del Renas with Joan, Cliff Roberts Rockers, Ravens.

7-30 — 11 p.m.   Admission 4/-

WEDNESDAYS	**FRIDAYS**
7-45 to 11-0 p.m.	7-45 to 11-0 p.m.
Admission 2/6	Admission 3/-
Dominoes	**Ravens**
Del Renas	**Johnny Sandon's Searchers**

"Get Back"

Here you will find an alphabetical listing of the venues where The Black Jacks and The Quarrymen, right through to The Beatles, played. Cross-reference it with the area of Merseyside in the Liddypool—The Guide section (in brackets) for more information.

Aintree Institute

Aintree Institute, Walton Vale (Aintree)
The Beatles made their debut at the Aintree Institute on 7 January 1961, and played there approximately thirty times in that year.

Air Training Corps Club, Birkdale (Southport)
The Beatles played once here on 9 March 1961.

Albany Cinema

Albany Cinema, North Way, Maghull (Aintree)
The Beatles made their only appearance here on 15 October 1961 with Ken Dodd as the headlining act. It has been demolished.

Alexandra Hall, (Crosby)
In the heart of Crosby, The Beatles appeared here once on 19 January 1961. It has been demolished.

Alexandra Hall

Allerton Synagogue, (Allerton)
Allerton Synagogue played host to The Beatles, probably in December 1961. The synagogue was demolished in 2006 and rebuilt in 2008.

Apollo Roller Rink, Moreton (Wirral)
The Beatles made a single appearance here on 26 March 1962.

Allerton Synagogue

The Balfour Institute, Smithdown Road (Wavertree)
The Balfour Institute, now demolished, was on the corner of Smithdown Road and Garrick Street in Wavertree. The Quarrymen played there, though the date is unknown.

Barnston Women's Institute, Barnston (Wirral)
The Beatles played here three times for the Heswall Jazz Club, the first of these on 24 March 1962.

The Apollo Dance Club

Blair Hall, (Walton)
The Beatles played here in Walton (north Liverpool) five times in 1961. Their first appearance was on 5 February 1961. The building was demolished.

Blair Hall former site, Walton

The Blue Angel (Liverpool)
The Wyvern Club was opened by Allan Williams and was where The Silver Beatles auditioned for Larry Parnes. Pete Best was given an audition here by The Beatles before they invited him to join the group, now renamed The Beatles, to head for Hamburg. After Williams returned from Hamburg, he renamed the club, Blue Angel.

Blue Angel

British Legion Club, Dam Wood Road (Speke)
George played his first gig at this club as The Rebels with his brother Pete and friend Arthur Kelly.

Busmen's Social Club, Picton Road (Wavertree)
The Quarrymen appeared here early in 1959 as well as the Social Club in Finch Lane.

British Legion Club, Speke

Cabaret Club, Duke Street (Liverpool)
Brian Epstein arranged this show at the Cabaret Club, 28, Duke Street, on 25 July 1962.

Cambridge Hall, Lord Street (Southport)
The Beatles played here once on 26 July 1962.

The Cassanova Club, London Road

The Casbah Coffee Club, Haymans Green (West Derby)
The re-formed Quarrymen opened the Casbah on 29 August 1959, and The Beatles played here more than forty times. The Beatles were the last band to play there when it closed on 24 June 1962.

Barnston Women's Institute, where The Beatles played in March 1962

Cassanova Club, Dale St

The Cavern Club stage

Childwall Golf Club

David Lewis Theatre

Embassy Club

The Empire Theatre, Lime St

Cassanova Club, Dale Street (Liverpool)
The Beatles played at its opening on 10 January 1960. The club later moved to London Road.

Cassanova Club, London Road (Liverpool)
The new Cassanova Club was opened at 39, London Road. The Beatles made their first of six appearances here on 11 February 1961.

Cavern Club (Liverpool)
The Beatles' lunchtime debut was here on Thursday 9 February 1961. They went on to make nearly 300 more appearances at this historic club.

Childwall Golf Club, (Childwall)
Nigel Walley arranged a gig for The Quarrymen in the summer of 1957 when the group was trying to get established.

David Lewis Theatre (Liverpool)
The Liverpool-based Beatles Fan Club hired this hall, in the shadow of the Anglican Cathedral, on 17 October 1961. The building has been demolished.

The Embassy Club, Wallasey (Wirral)
The Silver Beatles appeared here once in July 1960.

Empire Theatre, (Liverpool)
The Quarrymen's first recorded engagement was here on 9 June 1957 at a Carroll Levis audition. The Beatles appeared here on 28 October 1962 and their last ever Liverpool appearance was here on 5 December 1965.

Floral Hall, The Promenade (Southport)
The Beatles played here four times, the first of these on 20 February 1962.

Florence Institute, Mill Street (Dingle)
Ringo played the Florence Institute with the Eddie Clayton Skiffle Group as the resident band.

Garston Swimming Baths (Garston)
The Quarrymen made several appearances at the Garston Swimming Baths, though specific dates are not known.

Florence Institute

Garston Swimming Baths

The Grafton Rooms

The Grosvenor Ballroom

Garston Stevedores & Dockers Club (Garston)
Playing in June 1958, this was one of the few Quarrymen gigs that featured John Duff Lowe. The building has since been demolished, and a new building erected on the site.

Gaumont Cinema, Allerton Road (Allerton)
The Quarrymen made a couple of unrecorded appearances at the Gaumont Cinema, now demolished.

Glen Park Club, Lord Street (Southport)
The Beatles only appeared at the Glen Park Club once, on 5 November 1961.

The Grafton Rooms, (West Derby)
The Beatles appeared at this Liverpool ballroom, The Grafton Rooms, four times in 1962–63.

Greenbank Drive Synagogue, (Wavertree)
The Beatles appeared at Greenbank Drive Synagogue in the Max Morris Hall during the summer of 1961.

The Grosvenor Ballroom, Wallasey (Wirral)
The Silver Beetles first appeared at The Grosvenor Ballroom on 4 June 1960. The line-up included John, Paul, George, Stuart and drummer Tommy Moore. The Beatles appeared here regularly for Allan Williams.

Haig Hall (Wirral)
The Quarrymen appeared at Haig Hall in November 1957. It has since been demolished.

Greenbank Drive Synagogue, where The Beatles appeared in 1961

Holyoake Hall

Hulme Hall stage door

Irby Village Hall

The snug in The Jacaranda

Percy Phillips' Studio

The Kingsway Club

Knotty Ash Village Hall

Hambleton Hall, Page Moss (Huyton)

The Beatles appeared at Hambleton Hall fifteen times, the first of these on 25 January 1961.

Heswall Jazz Club
(see Barnston Women's Institute)

Holyoake Hall (Allerton)

Holyoake Hall is opposite the tram sheds on Smithdown Road, a few hundred yards from Penny Lane. The Quarrymen played here in skiffle competitions in 1958. The Beatles appeared twice at this venue in July 1961.

Hulme Hall, Port Sunlight (Wirral)

Hulme Hall was the site of Ringo's first appearance with The Beatles on 18 August 1962.

The Institute, Neston (Wirral)

The Silver Beatles appeared at The Institute six times in 1960, the first of these on 2 June.

Irby Village Hall, Irby (Wirral)

Found on Thingwall Road in Irby, on the Wirral, The Beatles made one appearance here on 7 September 1962.

Iron Door (Liverpool)

The Iron Door was opened on 9 April 1960. The Silver Beetles played here on 15 May 1960. The club became the Liverpool Jazz Society, and The Beatles debuted here on 6 March 1961 at an all-night affair. They played at the club five times. In 1962, the club changed its name again to the Storyville Jazz Club, and The Beatles made two further appearances here. By the end of 1962, it had returned to its original name of the Iron Door.

The Jacaranda, Slater Street (Liverpool)

The Silver Beetles played here on 30 May 1960. It was Allan Williams' club, and he became their manager.

38, Kensington (Kensington)

This was the recording studio where The Quarrymen made their first recording.

Kingsway Club, The Promenade (Southport)

The Beatles played the Kingsway Club eight times, the first of these on 22 January 1962.

Knotty Ash Village Hall (West Derby)

Mona Best booked The Beatles for many appearances at the Knotty Ash Village Hall. Their first appearance was on 15 September 1961 as a Casbah promotion.

Labour Club

Lathom Hall stage area

Lee Park Golf Club

Lewis's Department Store

Labour Club, Devonshire Road (Southport)

The Beatles appeared here once on 9 March 1961. A Labour Club is the local headquarters of the national Labour Party, which was traditionally frequented by working class men to enjoy a pint of beer with their friends.

Lathom Hall, (Seaforth)

The Beatles played Lathom Hall ten times, but their first appearance was as The Silver Beats on 14 May 1960.

Lee Park Golf Club, (Netherley)

Lee Park Golf Club was the site of The Quarrymen's audition for Alan Sytner in July 1957, owner of The Cavern.

Lewis's Department Store, Renshaw Street (Liverpool)

The Beatles appeared at a Young Ideas Dance on the top floor '527 Club' on 28 November 1962.

Litherland Town Hall, Hatton Hill, (Litherland)

Litherland Town Hall is the birth site of Beatlemania on 27 December 1960. It was a popular venue for The Beatles in north Liverpool. It is now a Health Centre.

Liverpool College of Art, Mount Street (Liverpool)

Billed as The College Band, John, Paul, George and Stuart appeared here in late 1959 at the Saturday evening student dances.

Liverpool Corporation Passenger Transport Employees Social & Athletic Club, Finch Lane

The Quarrymen played at this club in 1959, a gig organized by George Harrison's father.

Hambleton Hall

Liverpool Jazz Society (See Iron Door)

The Locarno Ballroom, (West Derby)
The Quarrymen performed here in skiffle contests in the late 1950s, and The Beatles made their first appearance at The Locarno Ballroom on Valentine's Day, 14 February 1963.

The Locarno Ballroom

Lowlands, Haymans Green (West Derby)
The Quarrymen auditioned at Lowlands in June 1958, but never appeared again. The club was in Haymans Green just down the road from The Casbah. It was here that George Harrison played with the Les Stewart Quartet.

Macdonna Hall/Thistle Café - West Kirby (Wirral)
Brian Epstein advertised this 1 February 1962 event as 'The Grand Opening of The Beatle Club' since this was their first gig under his management.

The Majestic Ballroom, Birkenhead (Wirral)
The Beatles made sixteen appearances at the Majestic Ballroom, their first on 28 June 1962.

Lowlands, in Haymans Green

The Mandolin Club, (Toxteth)
The Beatles sometimes rehearsed at The Mandolin Club before heading off to The Cavern for a lunchtime session. They would also return here in the afternoon for further practice.

The Mardi Gras Club, Mount Pleasant (Liverpool)
Contrary to previous records, Ringo didn't make his debut at the Mardi Gras. Brian Linford, manager of the club from 1960-1969 confirms that they didn't embrace beat music until 1964.

Macdonna Hall, above the Thistle Café, West Kirby

Melody Inn, Wallasey (Wirral)
The Beatles appeared at the Melody Inn once in 1961. It burned down in 1969.

Merseyside Civil Service Club, Lower Castle Street (Liverpool)
This downstairs club was host to The Beatles on four occasions in November 1961.

Merseyside Civil Service Club

Moreton Co–operative Hall, Moreton (Wirral)
The Beatles appeared in this Co-operative Hall in Moreton.

The Morgue, Broadgreen (West Derby)
Situated in an old house in Oak Vale Drive, Rory Storm's short-lived club opened on 13 March 1958, with Al Caldwell's Texans. The Quarrymen also played here before it was soon closed on 22 April. The building has been demolished.

NEMS, Whitechapel, in 1963

The New Cabaret Artistes Club was situated to the left of the buildings above

New Clubmoor Hall

The Odd Spot Club

The Beatles at the Majestic Ballroom on 28 June 1962

Mossway Hall (Croxteth)
The Beatles' only appearance at Mossway Hall occurred on St. Patrick's Day, 17 March 1961.

NEMS, Whitechapel (Liverpool)
The Beatles made a guest appearance at the NEMS store in Whitechapel in early 1963 following the release of their debut album, *Please Please Me.*

New Brighton Pier, (Wirral)
Pete Best remembers The Beatles playing at the New Brighton Pier in 1960 and 1961. It was demolished in 1978.

The New Cabaret Artistes Club, Upper Parliament Street (Toxteth)
Allan Williams booked The Silver Beetles at his and Lord Woodbine's illegal 'strip' club at 174a, Upper Parliament Street early in 1960. It has been demolished.

New Clubmoor Hall, Back Broadway (Walton)
It's been noted by various sources that Paul McCartney made his debut with The Quarrymen here on 18 October 1957, but it is most likely that this was the first time he appeared with them at a paid gig.

New Colony Club, (Toxteth)
This club at 80, Berkley Street was run by the famous Lord Woodbine. The Beatles made a few unrecorded appearances here in1960.

The Odd Spot Club, (Liverpool)
The Beatles made two appearances at The Odd Spot Club, Bold Street, their first on 29 March 1962.

Odeon Cinema, London Road (Liverpool)
The Beatles gave two performances at the Odeon Cinema on 7 December 1963.

Odeon Cinema, (Southport)
The Beatles appeared at the Southport Odeon Cinema from 26 August to 31 August 1963.

Pavilion Theatre, (Aintree)
The Silver Beetles appeared here during 1960, though the date has not been recorded.

Pavilion Theatre, Lodge Lane (Dingle)
John's first group, The Black Jacks, played here. The Quarrymen also appeared here in skiffle competitions though, as The Beatles, they made just the one appearance on 2 April 1962.

Prescot Cables Social Club

Peel Hall, Peel Street (Dingle)
Ringo's first group, The Eddie Clayton Skiffle Group, appeared here several times.

Plaza Ballroom (St. Helens)
The Beatles appeared at the Plaza Ballroom five times, the first on 25 June 1962.

Prescot Cables Social Club
The Quarrymen appeared here several times in 1959.

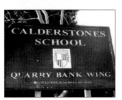

The Quarry Bank sign at Calderstones School

Quarry Bank School (Allerton)
Now called calderstones School, The Quarrymen played their alma mater in October 1956 at one of their own school dances.

Queens Hotel, The Promenade (Southport)
The Beatles made just the one appearance at the Queens Hotel on 6 December 1962 in the Club Django, on the ground floor.

Rialto Ballroom (Dingle)
The Beatles played here on Thursday 6 September 1962. The original club burned down in the Toxteth Riots in 1981, to be replaced by a new Rialto.

Rosebery Street (Toxteth)
The street party was held on 22 June 1957 with The Quarrymen playing on the back of a lorry.

Royal Iris (Liverpool)
The Beatles made their first appearance on this ferry on 25 August 1961 with jazz clarinetist Acker Bilk.

Queens Hotel

Starline Club, (Toxteth)
The Beatles often practiced at the Starline Club and made a handful of unrecorded appearances here in 1961.

St. Aloysius Church (Huyton)
The Quarrymen made various appearances at St. Aloysius Church, the first time in September 1957.

St. Aloysius Church

St. Barnabas' Church Hall, Penny Lane (Allerton)
The Quarrymen appeared at St. Barnabas' in 1957 and at the Vespa Scooter Club annual dance on Penny Lane in the summer of 1958.

St. Edward's College (West Derby)
The Beatles made a Sunday evening appearance at a college dance on 8 October 1961.

St. John's Church

St. Barnabas' Church Hall

St. John's Church Hall, (Tue Brook)
This church hall hosted eleven shows by The Beatles, the first on 17 February 1961. It was often booked by Mona Best.

St. John's Hall, (Bootle)
The Beatles made five appearances at St. John's Hall, the first one on 6 January 1961.

St. Luke's Hall, (Crosby)
The Quarrymen appeared once at St. Luke's Youth Club in November 1957.

Storyville Jazz Club (See Iron Door)

Former site of the Storyville Jazz Club in Temple Street

St. Paul's Presbyterian Hall, Birkenhead (Wirral)
The Beatles made two appearances at St. Paul's, the first on 10 February 1962.

St. Peter's Church, (Woolton)
Saturday, 6 July 1957 was the day that John Lennon met Paul McCartney here. The Quarrymen appeared first in the field in the afternoon, and then in the church hall in the evening. They made several unpaid appearances in the church hall, including Paul's first shows.

St. Luke's Hall

Stanley Abattoir Social Club, Old Swan
The Quarrymen appeared at the Stanley Abattoir Social Club in 1957.

Technical College, Birkenhead (Wirral)
The Beatles made three appearances at the Technical College in February 1962. The building has since been demolished.

Ticket to see The Beatles at St. Paul's

The Royal Iris

St. Peter's Church Hall

Stanley Abattoir Social Club

Technical College, Birkenhead

25, Upton Green

Wavertree Town Hall

Tower Ballroom, New Brighton (Wirral)
The Beatles appeared here twenty-seven times in total. It has been demolished.

Town Hall, Newton-le-Willows (St. Helens)
The Beatles made one appearance here on 30 November 1962, in an evening's entertainment billed as "The Big Beat Show 2".

25, Upton Green, (Speke)
George Harrison's house was the venue for The Quarrymen to play for George's brother Harry's wedding reception on 20 December 1958. By this time, The Quarrymen were just John, Paul and George.

Victoria Hall, Bebington (Wirral)
The Beatles made one appearance at Victoria Hall on 4 August 1962.

Wavertree Town Hall (Wavertree)
The Quarrymen appeared at Wavertree Town Hall several times during 1957 and 1958, though most have not been recorded.

Wilson Hall, (Garston)
Wilson Hall was the place for Paul McCartney's debut appearance with The Quarrymen apart from some unrecorded Saturday appearances at St. Peter's Church Hall. The suggested date that George Harrison was invited to come and watch The Quarrymen here is 6 February 1958, and he played "Raunchy" as his audition for the group. The Quarrymen played at this location several times.

Winter Gardens (Garston)
The Quarrymen appeared at Winter Gardens in June 1957.

Woolton Village Club (Woolton)
The Quarrymen played the Woolton Village Club on Saturday, 24 January 1959.

Wyvern Club, Slater Street (Liverpool)
The Silver Beetles auditioned at Allan Williams' Wyvern Club for Larry Parnes on 10 May 1960, after which Parnes arranged for them to back Johnny Gentle for his Scottish tour. Pete Best played an audition here on 12 August 1960 to join the group, now known as The Beatles— they had dropped The 'Silver'—for their trip to Hamburg. The Wyvern was reopened by Williams as the Blue Angel.

YMCA Birkenhead (Wirral)
The Beatles appeared at this YMCA (Young Men's Christian Association) once in September 1962. The building has been demolished.

YMCA, Hoylake (Wirral)
The Beatles appeared here on 24 February 1962. This was the group's only appearance here, and they were so bad that they were booed off the stage. The building has since been demolished.

Zodiac Coffee Club, Duke Street (Liverpool)
Not an official venue for them, The Beatles played an impromptu jam session at the Zodiac Coffee Club with other local bands, which included The Big Three, Gerry and The Pacemakers and Rory Storm and The Hurricanes, featuring Ringo Starr on drums.

The stage at the YMCA Birkenhead, before the building was demolished

Victoria Hall, Bebington, Wirral

Liddypool
The Guide

Liddypool ⟨⟩ The Guide
Guide to The Beatles' Liverpool

This guide has been created as a result of my exhaustive research for this book, and it is arranged to help you discover The Beatles' Liverpool. There are walking tours in Liverpool City Centre, Allerton & Mossley Hill (including Penny Lane), Wavertree, Liverpool 8: The Dingle, Toxteth and Aigburth, plus Woolton (including Strawberry Field). There are also maps and information about the rest of Liverpool's suburbs, Southport and the Wirral. These would need a professional guided tour or a car to explore further.

Once you have found the area you are interested in touring, there is a brief introduction. Also included is an index of the places mentioned and what relevance they have to The Beatles.

Each map contains references which can be found in that chapter: for example, A16 on the Allerton Map is cross-referenced with the Allerton & Mossley Hill (including Penny Lane) chapter, and the index at the beginning of the chapter tells you that the map reference is Penny Lane. Each chapter lists locations in alphabetical order, so simply look up P = Penny Lane and find the information you require.

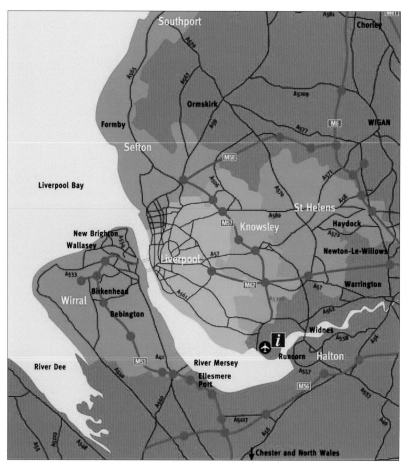

ABOVE: *The North-West of England, with Liverpool on the banks of the River Mersey*
OPPOSITE: *The Penny Lane roundabout in 2008*

Please bear in mind that many of these locations are private houses. Treat these places with the utmost respect and take into account that the occupiers deserve their privacy. They won't take kindly to cameras being pointed through their front windows or tourists knocking on their door.

Taking an official Liverpool Beatles Tour is recommended as many of these places are often out of the way and hard to find. Liverpool (and Merseyside) is a deceptively large place. Locations featured here stretch from Southport in the very north of the county to Speke and Hale at the very south of Liverpool, and across the River Mersey to the Wirral. Take the suggested routes or make up your very own 'magical mystery tour'.

Liddypool Walking Tours

There are several walking tours that have been created to enable you to explore The Beatles' Liverpool.

Much of Liverpool's city centre has been pedestrianised and there are three tours to help you find Mathew Street and The Cavern, the Town Hall, Liverpool Institute and Liverpool Art College and much, much more.

If you want to explore Penny Lane, there are three routes that help you discover more than just a road and a song, but a childhood area that John, Paul and George knew so well.

To find Strawberry Field and where John and Paul first met, you need to follow the Woolton Walk, discovering a village that was home to John Lennon in Mendips, and where The Quarrymen found out that 'nothing is real'.

Finally, uncover Ringo's Dingle birthplace and childhood along a route that takes you in to the heart of Toxteth and Ringo's working class upbringing amid a close community of family and friends.

There are many long and winding roads that lead you in the footsteps of The Beatles. For each walking tour there is a map, including references, plus some suggestions of a route to take to see the best of everything.

Liverpool City Centre Walking Tours

These tours have been selected so that you can see the most important locations, but please feel free to follow the map and create your own magical mystery tour.

The numbers in the directions below refer to the map references on page 233.

Tour 1 – The Cavern Quarter Tour

Make your way to number 8: The Cavern on Mathew Street. This walking tour is about half a mile (0.8 km) and can be completed in 30 minutes.

8   From **The Cavern Club,** walk down **Mathew Street** towards Stanley Street.

9   Cross over Stanley Street where you will see the **Eleanor Rigby Statue.**

14 Go down Stanley Street towards Whitechapel. On the right is where **Hessy's Music Centre** used to be.

19 At the bottom corner is where the **Kardomah Coffee Bar** was.

40 Turn left on Whitechapel and cross over to see the location of the former **Rushworths shop.**

27 Walk back along Whitechapel to the former site of **NEMS**, next to Thorntons.

47 Walk up Button Street where you will find **The White Star pub.** Turn left and walk up Harrington Street to North John Street.

49 Turn right, and on your right is the **Hard Days Night Hotel and shop.**

6   Continue along North John Street, and on your left is **46 Watson Prickard.** At the end of the road, turn left along Dale Street. On your left is where the **Cassanova Club** was situated.

44 Continue along Dale Street to **Liverpool Town Hall** on your right.

17 Turn around and walk back along Dale Street to Temple Street and turn right to find the former site of the **Iron Door.**

Tour 2 – The Walker Tour

*Make your way to 45: the **Walker Art Gallery** at the top of William Brown Street. This walking tour is about 1.5 miles (2.4 km) and will take about 1 hour.*

45 Walk down William Brown Street.

43 Enter **St. John's Gardens** which is behind **41 St. George's Hall.**

10 Exit the gardens at William Brown Street and cross over Lime Street to the **Empire Theatre.**

29 Walk to the left of the Empire and into London Road on the right, where you will find the **Odeon Cinema.**

34 Turn right down Hotham Street and through **Lime Street Station** and cross over to Bolton Street. On the right you will see the **Punch & Judy Café.**

20 Walk to the end of Bolton Street and turn right down Copperas Hill. In front is **Lewis's Department Store.**

1   On your left is the **Adelphi Hotel.**

26 Walk across the front of the Adelphi and up Mount Pleasant. On your right is **64, Mount Pleasant.**

37 Turn right down Rodney Street where, on the right, you will find number **4, Rodney Street.**

Tour 3 – The Metropolitan Tour

*Make your way to **30: Oxford Street Maternity Hospital** on Cambridge Street. This walking tour is close to 3 miles (4.8 km) and takes about 2 hours.*

30 Exit Cambridge Street onto Oxford Street, and turn left onto Hope Street.

33 Locate the **Philharmonic Dining Rooms** on your right.

32 Cross over Hardman Street and continue on Hope Street. On your left is the **Philharmonic Hall.**

48 Walk along Hope Street. Cross over, and on your right is Rice Street. Walk down Rice Street, and on your right is **Ye Cracke.**

22 Return to Hope Street and turn right. In front of you is **Liverpool College of Art** at the top of Mount Street.

23 Next to the **Art College** on Mount Street is the former **Liverpool Institute.**

21 Walk down Mount Street and turn left onto Pilgrim Street. **LIPA** is on your left. Turn left up Duke Street.

12 Turn right on to Hope Street and on the left is **Gambier Terrace.**

16 Walk along Hope Street and turn left to find **22, Huskisson Street** on your right.

31 Turn left and locate **9, Percy Street.**

4   At the end of Percy Street turn right and find **12, Canning Street.**

5   Carry on along the street to locate **83, Canning Street** on your left.

11 Retrace your steps down Canning Street and turn right on to Catherine Street and left to find **36, Falkner Street.**

39 Return to Catherine Street and turn left. At the end is the location of the former **Royal Liverpool Children's Hospital.**

3   Turn left down Myrtle Street which runs into Hardman Street and Leece Street to the bottom, then left onto Berry Street. Turn right down Seel Street to the **Blue Angel.**

18 Walk down Seel Street and turn right into Slater Street for **The Jacaranda.**

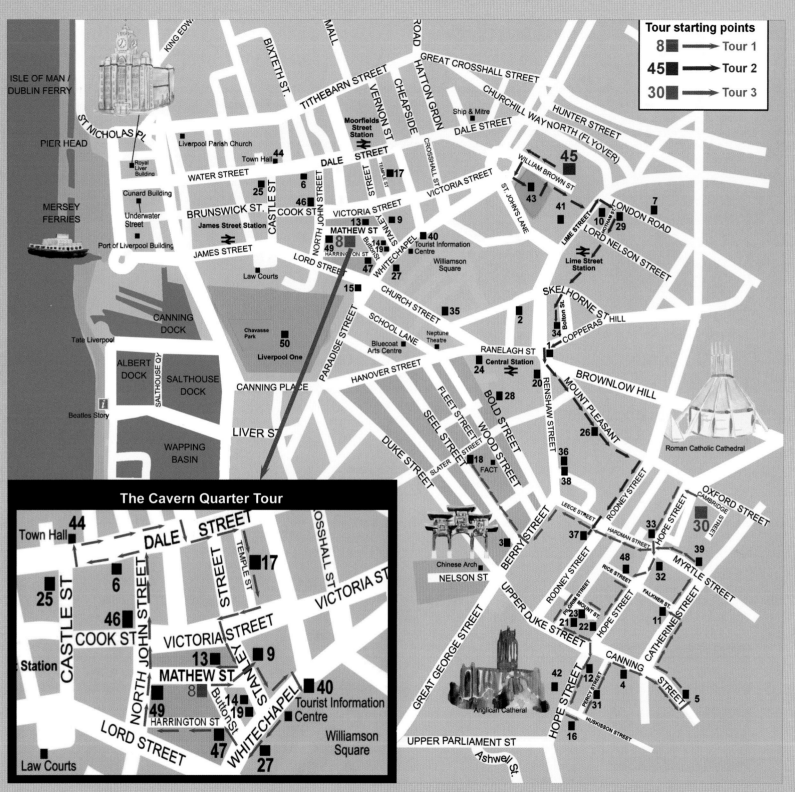

The Cavern Quarter Tour

Liverpool City Centre Map

Liverpool City Centre

"There's A Place"

A. Hannay & Co.

Jim McCartney, Paul's father, started work at A. Hannay & Co. in 1916 at the age of fourteen. It was at 14, Chapel Street near to the waterfront and was a cotton broker's office. It has since been demolished.

Adelphi Hotel

Adelphi Hotel - 1

The Adelphi was once the grandest hotel in Liverpool. It is the venue for the annual Beatles convention at the end of August. The hotel is connected to The Beatles in several ways. Alf Lennon and Julia Stanley (John's parents) met on the steps outside the Adelphi before walking up Mount Pleasant to get married on 3 December 1938. Alf also worked here as a bellboy.

John Dykins, Julia Lennon's partner, worked here as a wine waiter and it was also where Brian Epstein met and started a two-year courtship with actress Sonia Seligson.

Ringo remembers seeing his hero, Johnny Ray, having coffee and waving to fans in the Adelphi. The moment struck a chord with Ringo, who decided that being famous suited him well.

"Free as a Bird" is a song written and recorded as a demo in 1977 by John Lennon, to which Paul, George and Ringo added extra lyrics, performing alongside John's vocal recording.

In the "Free As A Bird" video, the film-makers used the Adelphi Hotel for the art deco parlour scene, and featured several references to Beatles songs

American Consul

Fascinated by all things American, Ringo visited the American Consul in Liverpool to consider emigrating to the United States. He was required to secure work in a selected factory to qualify. The forms arrived from the U.S., but he found them too hard to understand. Soon after he gave up the idea.

The Beatles Story, Albert Dock

Anglican Cathedral

John Duff Lowe, occasional pianist with The Quarrymen, failed his audition for the Liverpool Cathedral Choir along with his friend Paul McCartney. He later retook it and passed but Paul didn't bother. The Royal Liverpool Philharmonic Orchestra performed Paul's Liverpool Oratorio here on 27 June 1991 and a performance of his classical work, *Ecce Cor Meum*, in 2008.

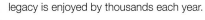
Liverpool Anglican Cathedral

The Basement

A regular haunt of Epstein's was The Basement club in Mount Pleasant. It has since been demolished.

The Beatles Story

The Beatles Story, an award-winning visitor attraction, is situated at the Albert Dock (see map on page 233, red number 11) and is a 'must-see' for Beatles fans. The Beatles Story was the vision and dream of Mike and Bernie Byrne, and their legacy is enjoyed by thousands each year.

The Beehive pub, Paradise Street

Beehive pub, Paradise Street

Brian Epstein frequently went for an after-work drink here.

The Big House

This Mount Pleasant pub is where Alf and Julia Lennon celebrated after they exchanged wedding vows, and were treated to a meal and drinks by his brother Sydney.

Blackler's Store, Great Charlotte Street - 2

George served a brief apprenticeship as an electrician at Blackler's Store. Blackler's was eventually replaced by the J D Wetherspoon pub.

Blue Angel - 3

Blue Angel, Allan Williams' club

Formerly known as the Wyvern Club, this was Allan Williams' establishment at the top of Seel Street. It was frequented by The Beatles and many of the Merseybeat bands. The Blue Angel was where Ringo met Maureen Cox. They started dating regularly and she eventually became his first wife on 11 February 1965.

Brian Epstein met with Allan Williams at the Blue Angel to discuss signing a contract with The Beatles.

Brownlow Hill Registry Office

George Harrison's parents, Harold and Louise, were married at Brownlow Hill Registry Office on 20 May 1930.

Cabaret Club, Duke Street

Trying to expose The Beatles to a wider audience, Brian Epstein arranged this show at the Cabaret Club at 28, Duke Street. The 25 July 1962 gig was a disaster—they were the wrong band for the wrong audience. This was the first time they wore their new dark-blue mohair stage suits. The club has since been demolished

12, Canning Street, Stuart's flat

12, Canning Street - 4

Stuart Sutcliffe rented a small flat on the top floor at 12, Canning Street for his second year at Liverpool Art College in 1957.

83, Canning Street - 5

Stuart Sutcliffe's first flat was at 83, Canning Street, not far from the art college. He shared the flat with friend Rod Murray.

Cassanova Club, 22, Dale Street - 6

Named after Liverpool band Cass and the Cassanovas, this club was initially in The Temple, Dale Street. The Beatles appeared here at an afternoon session on the day of the club's launch. The Beatles had a regular following at The Cavern and owner Ray McFall considered them his exclusive band. McFall told The Beatles they couldn't play at his club and the

83, Canning Street, Stuart's flat

Cassanova, as well. Sam Leach had promoted the concert at the Cassanova so he had a bit of a problem. Fortunately, The Beatles turned up because someone had let off stink bombs in The Cavern and it was forced to close for the afternoon. Unfortunate for McFall, but fortunate for The Beatles and Leach. They fulfilled their promise to Leach but never officially appeared at the Cassanova again.

Cassanova Club, London Road - 7

The new Cassanova Club opened above Sampson & Barlow's Restaurant at 39, London Road. The Beatles' first appearance was on 11 February 1961.

The Cotton Exchange, on the right

Cavern Club (See Mathew Street) - 8

Cotton Exchange

Jim McCartney moved to the Liverpool Cotton Exchange from Hannay's. He was eventually promoted to the role of salesman.

The David Lewis Theatre

The Beatles Fan Club hired this hall on 17 October 1961. The Beatles had no PA equipment and were forced to improvise. The crowd, which included Paul McCartney's father, watched as his son and Pete Best each belted out a few tunes. Paul crooned ballads while Pete sang robust versions of "Matchbox" and "Peppermint Twist", and a song made famous by Elvis Presley—"A Rose Grows Wild in the Country". When Pete forgot the words, he leapt around the stage and shook hands with the fans. The David Lewis Theatre has been demolished.

The Eagle Hotel, Paradise Street

The Eagle Hotel

This building was an American Consulate among other uses, and eventually became a pub. The Eagle was on Paradise Street. This establishment was run by Paul's uncle Bill (his mum's younger brother) and Auntie Dill.

It was also the place where Alf Lennon drank a few pints of 'Dutch courage' before getting married, hoping to find one of his mates who could act as witness. No one suitable appeared, so he phoned his brother Stanley.

Eleanor Rigby Statue - 9

Erected on Stanley Street, Tommy Steele sculpted this bronze statue of Eleanor Rigby and donated it to Liverpool for half a sixpence. It is dedicated to 'all the lonely people'.

Tommy Steele with the statue of Eleanor Rigby that he sculpted

Empire Theatre - 10

Liverpool's biggest theatre is the Empire, which recently underwent a multi-million pound refurbishment. It was the venue for the big acts of the day.

Paul saw skiffle king Lonnie Donegan here when he was fourteen and queued for his autograph— George found out where Donegan was staying and obtained his autograph as well. Brian Epstein took

Liverpool's Empire Theatre, Lime St

The Beatles to see The Shadows at the Empire for the express purpose of showing them how smartly dressed they were and how they bowed at the end of their act.

The Quarrymen's first recorded engagement was here on 9 June 1957 at a Carroll Levis audition. They didn't qualify. Two years later in October 1959, John, Paul and George entered as Johnny and the Moondogs and came in third. That same competition saw Rory Storm and the Hurricanes, featuring their new drummer Richard Starkey, placed second behind Kingsize Taylor and The Dominoes.

The Beatles appeared here several times over the years, the first on Sunday 28 October 1962. They were on the bill with Little Richard and Craig Douglas, for whom they also acted as backing band. The Beatles' last ever Liverpool concert took place here on 5 December 1965.

European Peace Monument - 50

To mark what would have been the 70th birthday of John Lennon, a new Peace Monument was unveiled by Cynthia and Julian Lennon at Chavasse Park, on 9 October 2010.

The European Peace Monument for John Lennon in Chavasse Park

Everyman Theatre, Hope Street

The Everyman Theatre, previously Hope Hall, has been a thriving hot spot for local talent for years. It was also host to poetry readings, which were attended by John, Paul, and George.

Falkner Street

John Lennon liked eating lunch at the chip shop on Falkner Street. His usual order was chips and potato scallops, which are slices of potato in batter. He rarely paid because of his ability to scrounge money from friends and strangers.

36, Falkner Street - 11

This was a ground floor flat rented by Brian Epstein in the early '60s—primarily for his secret homosexual liaisons away from his family.

After John Lennon and Cynthia Powell married, Epstein invited

36, Falkner Street, Brian Epstein's flat

the newly-weds to live here. The flat extended the full length of the ground floor, and had a small walled garden. Their bedroom, however, was at the front of the house, overlooking Falkner Street. It was here in Epstein's flat where John wrote, "Do You Want to Know a Secret?"

Gambier Terrace, Hope Street - 12

Gambier Terrace with its Georgian facade is in the shadow of the Anglican Cathedral. Stuart and John shared Flat 3, Hillary Mansions, with Rod Murray. When *Backbeat* was filmed, they used Gambier Terrace as one of the locations. The Beatles also rehearsed in the flat many times.

The Grapes
(See Mathew Street) - 13

The Hard Days Night Hotel, North John Street - 49

The Hard Days Night Hotel

Standing on the corner of Mathew Street and North John Street, this multi-million pound development opened for business in January 2008. Every room has a unique piece of Beatles art and it is a must for fans. Local sculptor Dave Webster has created four statues of The Beatles with the title, "Together Again". The statues are thirty feet above the street and represent the reunion of the solo Beatles, together again for one last performance in Liverpool. The hotel also incorporates the UK's first Beatles Superstore, licensed by Apple.

Hessy's Music Centre - 14

The Beatles and most other Merseybeat bands bought (mainly on credit) their musical gear at Hessy's. Hessy's also gave free lessons with a guitar purchase. John's Aunt Mimi bought him his first decent guitar at Hessy's for £17. Armed with £46 he had borrowed from his grandfather, Ringo purchased a new drum kit in 1958. Hessy's delivered it to his Admiral Grove address. It was also from Hessy's that Stuart bought his bass guitar with the proceeds from his art competition. One of Brian Epstein's first acts as manager was to clear The Beatles' debts of almost £200 at Hessy's.

Hessy's in Stanley Street

Hope Street Registry Office

Brian Epstein sent John to the Hope Street Registry Office to obtain a marriage license.

The former site of Horne Brothers, Lord Street

They set the wedding date for 23 August 1963, the day after Cynthia Powell's mother returned from Canada.

Horne Brothers - 15

After fitting them with new suits, Brian Epstein sent The Beatles to the barber-shop in the basement at Horne Brothers to smarten them up. Epstein had been a regular customer there for years. It is now a McDonald's.

22, Huskisson Street

22, Huskisson Street - 16

The Stanleys, John Lennon's maternal family, were brought up in this 19th Century Georgian house. A wealthy relative left some money to the family and had purchased several properties in Liverpool, including this one.

Plaque at the site of the Iron Door

Iron Door - 17

The Iron Door was opened on 9 April 1960 by Geoff Hogarth and Harry Ormesher. The Silver Beetles made one appearance at the Iron Door. It then changed its name to the Liverpool Jazz Society in March 1961 and, although jazz bands still appeared regularly, they began promoting beat music. When promoter Sam Leach held his band nights here, it became one of the most famous clubs in Liverpool. The Beatles made five appearances here in 1961. In 1962, the name had briefly changed once more, this time to the Storyville Jazz Club, and The Beatles made two appearances in March 1962. By the end of the year, it was the Iron Door once more.

The Jacaranda, Slater Street - 18

This was a coffee club which was opened in 1958 at 23, Slater Street, Liverpool. The club was run by Allan Williams. John, Paul, George and Stuart hung around the 'Jac' or 'Rock and Dole' as they called it—looking for a free cup of coffee or toast, and badgered

The Jacaranda, Slater Street

Williams to find them work. They stood in for the Royal Caribbean Steel Band when they were on the road, and played in the basement.

Williams recalled the day George Harrison came upstairs to borrow brushes and mops. Williams mistakenly thought they were cleaning up. When he went to investigate, he found a group of young ladies on the floor, holding the broom handles, which had microphones attached to them. The boys didn't have the money to purchase microphone stands.

In an effort to keep them occupied, Williams gave them work painting the toilets. Stuart was commissioned to paint a mural in the basement, which he did with his flatmate and fellow art student Rod Murray, but sadly these were destroyed years later after dampness caused the plaster to fall off, with only a fragment surviving. However, if you go down into the basement, it's been recreated and what you can see is very close to the original.

Before heading off for Butlin's Holiday Camp—where Rory Storm and The Hurricanes were booked for the summer season—Ringo visited The Jacaranda one day with fellow band mates Rory Storm and Johnny Guitar. There he saw three scruffy lads playing with their guitars. It was John and Paul trying to teach Stuart to play bass guitar. It was the first time Ringo laid eyes on the group.

The Silver Beetles played here on 30 May 1960.

Jacey's Cinema

George often skipped school from the Liverpool Institute to take in a movie with friends at Jacey's Cinema in Clayton Square. The original Clayton Square buildings were demolished years ago, and replaced by the Clayton Square shopping complex.

The former site of Joe's Café at 139, Duke Street

Joe's Café, Duke Street

Joe's Café at 139, Duke Street was owned by Joe Davy (later to own The Cavern for a short period). This café was popular with many bands like The Beatles because it catered to the late-night crowd. It was here that Brian Epstein had asked The Beatles to meet him to discuss their future after they were turned down by Decca Records.

Kardomah Coffee Bar, Whitechapel - 19

John and Paul escorted the Beatlettes (local female fans) to this local coffee bar and bought them a cup of tea or coffee. Promoter Sam Leach met with Lennon and McCartney at the Kardomah after a frantic phone call from Paul. The two told Leach that they had been approached by Brian Epstein to manage them and wanted his opinion.

The former site of the Kardomah Coffee Bar

Lewis's Department Store - 20

Lewis's Department Store's sculpture known as 'Dickie Lewis'

Dickie Lewis is the famous naked male statue on the front of Lewis's Department Store in Renshaw Street. The statue is named 'Liverpool Resurgent'—a maritime theme for the bow of a ship, though where the naked man comes in is anyone's guess. The statue was sculpted by Jacob Epstein and became a favourite meeting place for locals.

"In my Liverpool Home", a local folk song, includes the line "meet under a statue exceedingly bare". No one referred to the statue by its given name, so it is affectionately known as 'Dickie Lewis'.

John often met Cynthia Powell at the landmark statue. She was frequently propositioned when John was late because the statue was a stone's throw from Lime Street—a popular standing place for ladies of the night.

Paul and John routinely visited Lewis's on Saturday mornings to go through the record department's selection for the week, saving pocket money and buying records when they could. Peter Brown who later became Brian Epstein's personal assistant, had previously run the Lewis' record department. Paul also worked here for a short time as a second man on one of their delivery vans

The Beatles made an appearance on the top floor at the Lewis' staff "Young Idea Dance" on 28 November 1962 in the 527 Club.

Lime Street Station

Lime Street Station

Lime Street Station is the main railway station in Liverpool, the gateway to the world for The Beatles and Brian Epstein. It was the direct rail connection for London: Decca, Abbey Road Studios and, by the end of 1963, their homes as well. It wasn't long before catching the train was impossible because of the fans, and flights from Liverpool's Speke airport became the norm for the group.

Linda McCartney Centre

Linda McCartney Centre

Paul's first wife Linda McCartney tragically died of cancer on 17 April 1998. The Linda McCartney Centre for research and treatment of cancer was opened at the Royal Liverpool Hospital on 24 November 2000.

Liverpool College of Art - 22

Located in Hope Street, the Liverpool College of Art (also known as the Art College) was originally part of the Mechanics Institute. Stuart Sutcliffe left Prescot Grammar School in 1956 with five 'O' levels. His admittance to the Art College at sixteen was regarded as a great achievement. He attained his Ministry of Education National Diploma in design and painting on 1 August 1960.

Stuart was a member of the Student Union which booked acts for the college entertainment. Since the Liverpool Institute was next door, Paul and George often joined John and Stu in the canteen for lunch. Stu arranged for them to rehearse at the Art College and booked them for many Saturday night dances. In return, the college bought PA equipment, which the group liberally borrowed for their gigs.

Liverpool College of Art

John enrolled at the Art College in the autumn of 1957, turning up in tight jeans and a long black jacket. He put his normal trousers over the top to fool Mimi, and then took them off at the bus stop. He met Cynthia Powell here in lettering class.

John produced a pantomime at the Art College in December 1959, where he appeared as an ugly sister in their version of *Cinderella*. Stuart lent his talents to the skit as the Snow Fairy.

The Art College is now part of John Moores University. Moores was the art aficionado who bought Stuart's painting at the Walker Art Gallery, which enabled him to buy his guitar and join The Beatles.

In front of the building is a fabulous piece of art called 'A Case History'. It is your mission, should you choose to accept it, to find the cases with the names of Paul McCartney, John and Yoko, Stuart Sutcliffe and George Harrison. (There is a map on the side of the college to help you out if you can't find them).

Liverpool Institute - 23

The Liverpool Institute was a grammar school in Mount Street and adjacent to the Art College. It opened on 15 September 1837 (it had previously been the Mechanics Institute). In 1890, one-half of the facility became the Art College. The building is now the Liverpool Institute of Performing Arts (LIPA), which was set up by Paul McCartney.

Liverpool Institute, Mount Street, which Paul and George attended

The motto of the school was 'Non nobis solum sed toti mundo nati', which translated from the Latin means, 'Not for ourselves alone but for the whole world were we born'. How appropriate for a band who would leave Liverpool and conquer the world.

Paul and George attended here as did Ivan Vaughan, Len Garry, Tony Bramwell and Neil Aspinall. Paul was taught by John's uncle, Alfred 'Cissy' Smith. Paul was an able student and his foray into the acting world saw him take on the part of an Assessor in *Saint Joan* by George Bernard Shaw. He also won a music prize here in 1959.

Paul befriended Quarryman Len Garry, who was also at the Institute. Len remembers morning assembly and practicing their 'counterpoint harmonies' during hymns, especially when singing "Onward Christian Soldiers". Paul also remembered that he and Mike were caned regularly at school by the 'sadistic' Head Master, affectionately known as 'The Baz'—standing for bastard. On his last day of school, Paul performed "Long Tall Sally" and "Tutti Frutti" on the desks as his parting shot.

George Harrison had passed his eleven-plus exam at Dovedale School and progressed to the Institute. He was delighted to have won his place there, but he soon regretted it. A constant rebel against conformity, George rarely wore his uniform correctly and let his hair grow long. He was terrorized, as were many lads, by teacher Frank Boot, who 'slippered' the boys when they stepped out of line. On his last day, George gave his gym shoe to Boot as he said that he had used it on him more than he had used it himself.

George's grades weren't up to par. He spent his days sagging-off school (playing truant) and retreated to the confines of the cinema. He kept this secret from his parents but they eventually discovered the truth when George didn't qualify for his preliminary exams. He left school without any qualifications.

Liverpool Institute for Performing Arts (LIPA) - 21
One of Paul McCartney's long-time ambitions was fulfilled when his old school, The Liverpool Institute, was transformed and reopened as the Liverpool Institute for Performing Arts (LIPA) in 1996.

This philanthropic effort was one of Paul McCartney's biggest civic victories. He still takes a personal interest in the school, and comes back to award the degrees on graduation day. Paul has invested a lot of energy and his personal fortune into this project, countering local allegations that The Beatles haven't contributed to Liverpool.

Liverpool Stadium
Still a popular venue for bands in the 1970s, the Best family owned Liverpool Stadium in St. Paul's Square in the City Centre. Pete's dad, John, and grandfather, Johnny Best, Sr., promoted many successful boxing matches at this venue.

Although it never resounded to the rock 'n' roll of The Beatles, the stadium was a great venue. It was here that Allan Williams co-promoted an Eddie Cochran and Gene Vincent concert with Larry Parnes. However, shortly before the Liverpool event, the two rockers were travelling through Wiltshire, England, when their taxi was involved in a fatal crash that took Cochran's life. Vincent, though injured, agreed to perform at the Liverpool show. Without Cochran, Williams bolstered the concert by placing Gerry and The Pacemakers, Rory Storm and the Hurricanes (with Ringo on the drums) and Derry and the Seniors on the bill. The Silver Beatles watched from the stands.

Liverpool University
The Silver Beetles backed famous beat poet Royston Ellis at Liverpool University in 1960.

The Lyceum, Bold Street

The Lyceum, Bold Street - 24
Formerly Reece's Lyceum Café, The Beatles met here for coffee and composed a few songs on napkins.

Manchester Street, Roman Catholic Bookshop
According to art student Richard Tate, the light-fingered John Lennon enjoyed stealing literature from this Roman Catholic Bookshop near the Mersey Tunnel entrance. The shop was demolished long ago.

Mathew Street - 8
Mathew Street has become Beatles Street for all of its bustling Fab Four activity.

The Cavern Club
The Cavern was situated at 10 Mathew Street, and was opened by Alan Sytner as a jazz club in 1957. The Beatles made their debut here on 9 February 1961, and played nearly 300 times at the club. The original Cavern was demolished in 1973 and the new building here is Cavern Walks shopping arcade. Beneath Cavern Walks is a reproduction of the original Cavern Club.

In 2004, it was discovered that nearly fifty per cent of the original Cavern Club site had survived when a photo owned by Bob Wooler came to light, which showed that the entrance is now the fire exit for the current Cavern Club.

The Cavern Wall of Fame

A brick wall featuring the names of every band and performer who appeared at The Cavern Club. It is on the wall outside The Cavern pub (on the other side of Mathew Street to The Cavern Club).

The Cavern Wall of Fame

Statue of John Lennon

This statue of John is a good likeness, and it stands by the Cavern Wall of Fame. In August 2002, close family and friends of uncle Charlie Lennon scattered some of his ashes at the feet of John's statue. What was left of Charlie's ashes were scattered on the River Mersey.

The Guinness Book of Hit Singles Wall of Fame

Here is a wall of bronze discs for every No. 1 record by a Liverpool band or performer, which currently totals more than fifty. That's more than any other city in the world, including all The Beatles chart toppers. It is not-so-tastefully painted in pink now; perhaps taking a cue from the Scaffold's 1967 hit "Lily the Pink".

Arthur Dooley's 'Four Lads Who Shook The World'

This sometimes controversial sculpture is by Liverpool sculptor Arthur Dooley, who has depicted The Beatles as cherubs, held in the arms of a lady Madonna. One of the four cherubs, Paul, disappeared, and someone once suggested he had taken 'Wings' and flown.

Arthur Dooley's sculpture in Mathew St., 'Four Lads Who Shook The World'

Cavern Walks

A shopping arcade dedicated to The Beatles was constructed above the site of the original Cavern.

There is a sculpture of The Beatles inside, though don't get too excited as the artist didn't go for an exact likenesses. It is said the only thing the figures have in common with The Beatles is the fact that they all have heads.

The statues of The Beatles in Cavern Walks

Above the doorway outside is the design of doves and roses by

Cavern Walks doorway moulding

Cynthia Lennon, in memory of John. The dove is a sign of peace and the rose was his favourite flower.

Up the stairs is the From Me To You shop, the only Apple-licensed store in Liverpool qualified to sell official merchandise.

The Grapes

Just down from The Cavern on Mathew Street, The Grapes was a popular watering hole for The Beatles and Brian Epstein. It was also here that Pete Best and Neil Aspinall drowned their sorrows after Pete was sacked from The Beatles. Being the only original pub in Mathew Street, the Grapes still has a photo in the back room that was taken of the four—John, Paul, George and Pete—in the snug there. It was established in the late 17th Century in what was then Pluckingtons Alley. The stables have gone but some of the Victorian wallpaper and original wooden beams are still there.

The Grapes pub, Mathew Street

The Beatles Shop

The Beatles Shop is at the bottom of Mathew Street. Above the entrance there is another Beatles sculpture, by David Hughes. The Beatles Shop boasts the world's largest collection of memorabilia from records to books and other collectibles.

Merchant Navy Building

On the corner of the Strand near the Pier Head, John and Nigel Walley decided to join the Merchant Navy in July 1957. However, the forms needed to be approved by a parent or guardian. When Mimi heard about it, she immediately put a stop to the half-baked idea. She didn't want another Alf Lennon in the family. The building has since been demolished.

Mersey Ferries

Although "Ferry Cross the Mersey" was Gerry Marsden's big hit, it very well could have been written for The Beatles. A ride on Liverpool's famous ferry service—that has been going since the 12th Century—is a must, if only to look back at the World

Heritage Site waterfront. Follow in John Lennon's footsteps for he spent many an hour on the ferries, going across from Pier Head to Seacombe (on the Wirral). He then walked three miles to New Brighton, often with college friends Helena Anderson and Ann Sherwood.

Ringo was a barman on the St. Tudno ferry, which ran between Liverpool and Menai, in North Wales. The job didn't last long. Early in his tenure Ringo showed up drunk and insulted the boss. Paul often took ferry rides to clear his head. He'd bring with him a book of poetry, a play or a novel, and spent time alone reading.

Merseyside Civil Service Club - 25
This downstairs club was host to The Beatles on four occasions in November 1961.

Mount Pleasant Registry Office where John and Cynthia were married

64, Mount Pleasant - 26
This once grand Georgian terrace, the second oldest domestic building in Liverpool, contained the Registry Office where John and Cynthia Lennon were married on 23 August 1962. Paul McCartney, George Harrison and Brian Epstein attended as well as Cynthia's brother Tony and his wife, Margery. The persistent noise of a pneumatic drill disrupted the ceremony and provided comedic fodder for those in attendance.

Cynthia recalled the event in her book, *A Twist of Lennon*. "None of us heard a word of the service; we couldn't even hear ourselves think".

When the registrar asked for the groom to step forward, George Harrison stepped up as a cheap laugh. "The registrar saw nothing funny in either the drilling or George's joke", she recalled, "so we all struggled to keep our faces straight".

NEMS, Whitechapel

NEMS - 27
The main office of NEMS (North End Music Stores) was in Whitechapel, opposite Button Street, near the bottom of Mathew Street. Located at 12-14 Whitechapel, next to Thorntons, this shop was opened in 1959 by actor and singer Anthony Newley.

The record department of NEMS was in the basement. The Beatles would toil there for hours listening to the latest records. Epstein's offices were on the first floor, which is where he held his meetings with The Beatles. When Epstein later set up

NEMS Enterprises to manage The Beatles' affairs, he took up the entire top floor. DJ Bob Wooler referred to Epstein as the 'NEMporer' at the 'NEMporium'.

The Beatles made a guest appearance at the NEMS store to sign copies of their 1963 single "Please Please Me". They also gave a brief acoustic performance.

Neptune Theatre, Hanover Street
According to Beatles historian and writer Ron Jones, this theatre was dedicated to Brian Epstein in August 1997 on the 30th anniversary of his death. It is still a community theatre, owned and run by Liverpool City Council. In 2010, the council announced that after it has been refurbished, the theatre would be renamed "The Epstein Theatre" in Brian's honour.

The Northern Hospital (left) in 1968

Northern Hospital, Leeds Street
The Northern Hospital was on the corner of Leeds Street, opposite the old St. Paul's Eye Hospital (on the corner of Old Hall Street). It was in the Northern Hospital that Mary McCartney was taken when she was diagnosed with breast cancer. She was dead within a month of the diagnosis. Her dying regret was that she would have liked to have seen her two boys grow up. She would have been very proud of both of her sons. The hospital has since been demolished.

The Odd Spot Club - 28
The Beatles made two appearances here in 1962. The club at 89, Bold Street, was where John 'Bobby' Dykins—Julia Lennon's partner—worked as a waiter. Bold Street was also home to Peter Kaye, who took the first official promotional photos of The Beatles with Ringo Starr.

Odeon Cinema - 29
The Beatles played here on 7 December 1963 for two performances. The afternoon was a special performance for the 2,500 members who made up The Beatles Northern Area Fan Club.

Oxford Street Maternity Hospital, where John Lennon was born

Part of the evening performance was filmed and shown on BBC TV the same evening along with 'Juke Box Jury', which had been filmed earlier at the Empire. The programme was watched by an estimated twenty-three million people. This cinema also premiered their debut motion picture *A Hard Day's Night* in the north of England. The Odeon was the location for the films *Backbeat* and Paul McCartney's *Give My Regards to Broad Street*. John often ditched Art College to take in a movie at the Odeon Cinema with girlfriend Thelma Pickles, who most likely paid for his ticket. The cinema closed in 2009

Oxford Street Maternity Hospital - 30
John Winston Lennon was born here on 9 October 1940 in a room on the second floor. The blond-haired child weighed seven-and-a-half pounds. The notice of his birth in the *Liverpool Echo* read: "LENNON—October 9, in hospital to JULIA (nee Stanley), wife of ALFRED LENNON, Merchant Navy (at sea), a son—9, Newcastle Road".

A new plaque has been placed on the hospital wall commemorating this event, which is entitled "This is not here" (after one of Yoko Ono's New York exhibitions).

Mimi told biographer Hunter Davies about John being born in the middle of a heavy bombing raid. There had been a raid the night before—on the 8th—but the next one wasn't until the 10th, with not many more over the next couple of weeks.

This large building has been converted into apartments, called 'Lennon Studios'.

9, Percy Street - 31

Stuart Sutcliffe moved into a flat at 9, Percy Street, with his friend Rod Murray. It was just around the corner from the Liverpool College of Art, where Stu practiced Elvis Presley songs on a guitar purchased by his father. Stuart's sister Pauline remembers her brother reminisced when he and John Lennon tape-recorded themselves doing impressions of "The Goons". John played the Peter Sellers part while Stuart was Harry Secombe. They also taped Gene Vincent and Elvis songs on the recorder.

9, Percy Street, where Stuart Sutcliffe lived

The Quarrymen occasionally rehearsed at Stuart's flat, with Rod Murray joining in on the washboard. They were evicted in 1959 when their landlady, Mrs. Plant, entered the flat and found various rules had been broken. She especially didn't like it when she discovered one of her chairs was being used for firewood.

Philharmonic Hall, Hope Street - 32

Buddy Holly and the Crickets appeared at the Philharmonic Hall on 20 March 1958. John and Paul made it a point to see their idol. It was Buddy Holly who made it cool to wear glasses, which gave John the confidence to wear his in public.

The Philharmonic Hall, where Buddy Holly played on 20 March 1958

Epstein also frequented the Philharmonic Hall and indulged his love of classical music by reserving the finest seats to listen to the world-famous orchestra.

On 10 May 1963, George Harrison helped judge a 'beat group' competition with Dick Rowe—the Decca man who famously turned The Beatles down. It was here that George told him that if he didn't want to make the same mistake twice, he should sign the Rolling Stones. Rowe immediately headed south for London to sign them.

It was also here in 1999 that Paul's third orchestral work, *Working Classical,* was premiered. Paul and members of his family were in attendance.

Philharmonic Dining Rooms, Hope Street - 33

Known locally as 'The Phil', this popular pub sports Victorian marble gents' toilets that are a worldwide tourist attraction. Don't believe me? Go in and see for yourself, but, ladies, make sure they are empty first!

Philharmonic Dining Rooms

The Beatles often drank here as an alternative to Ye Cracke. John once said that the price of fame was not being able to go to 'The Phil' for a drink.

The Punch & Judy Café - 34

Opposite Lime Street Station, this café was where Paul and John waited for Epstein on return trips from London to enquire if he had landed them a record deal. They spent many a day in there waiting in vain.

Reece's Café - 35

After John and Cynthia Lennon's wedding on 23 August 1962, the party ran down Mount Pleasant in the pouring rain to Reece's Café in Clayton Square for a wedding breakfast, courtesy of Brian Epstein. Because Reece's Café wasn't a licensed premises, the toast was made with water.

The Punch & Judy Café

Reece's Café

81a, Renshaw Street - 36

It was in this small office that Bill Harry and his girlfriend (and later his wife) Virginia started the first Liverpool music paper, the *Mersey Beat*. The publication which launched its first edition on 6 July 1961, was essential for anyone interested in the local music scene. John Lennon and Brian Epstein were regular contributors and the paper religiously followed The Beatles' progress.

81a, Renshaw Street, the Mersey Beat offices

4, Rodney Street - 37

The Harley Street of Liverpool is the office of several private doctors. It was here in a private nursing home that Brian Samuel Epstein was born on 19 September 1934.

The Roscoe Arms - 38

'The Roscoe' was beneath the *Mersey Beat* offices in Renshaw Street and became the place for the bands, managers and promoters to seal their deals over a quiet drink.

Royal Iris

The famous Mersey Ferry hosted the first of its many rock 'n' roll cruises featuring Merseybeat bands on 25 August 1961. The Beatles made four appearances on the cruises that started at The Pier Head and cruised the River Mersey for the next four hours.

4, Rodney Street

Royal Liverpool Children's Hospital, Myrtle Street - 39

Royal Liverpool Children's Hospital, Myrtle Street

Just before his seventh birthday, Richard Starkey was rushed here by ambulance in 1947 with stomach pains. It was soon discovered that he had developed peritonitis after his appendix burst. The hospital was located close to the fruit shop in Myrtle Street where Elsie Starkey, Ringo's mum, worked for a short time.

Rushworths Music House, Whitechapel, before it closed in 2002

Rushworths Music House, Whitechapel - 40

Situated on the corner of Whitechapel and Richmond Street, Rushworths was once the biggest musical instrument suppliers in Liverpool, the store supplied guitars to many Merseybeat bands including The Beatles. They managed to import John and George's special Gibson guitars from America. Chairman James Rushworth presented John and George with the guitars before they set off on tour. Rushworths was the place that Jim McCartney had bought a young Paul McCartney his first trumpet and where Paul exchanged his trumpet for his Zenith guitar.

St. George's Hall - 41

This neoclassical building dominates this section of Liverpool. Designed by Harvey Lonsdale Elmes, it was built to hold Liverpool's musical events in a grand ballroom that had an ornate mosaic floor.

In a bid to recreate the Chelsea Ball, Allan Williams rented St. George's Hall for a party. He arranged for Stuart and John to create a few floats for the ball with some help from Paul and George. They created a magnificent guitar-shaped float, which was customarily destroyed at the end of the evening.

In 1980 on the plateau in front of St. George's Hall, an estimated 25,000 people congregated after the death of John Lennon. Fans also gathered here after the announcement that George had died in 2001.

St. James' Cemetery - 42

Paul and John skipped school from the Institute and Art College and crossed the road into St. James' Cemetery. There they sunbathed and smoked 'loosies' (loose cigarettes) which they purchased at the tuck shop. Paul referred to this location in his *Liverpool Oratorio* many years later in the lines where he wrote, "Cross the road and over the cemetery fence, down the hill to where the gravestones lie inviting in the sun".

St. John's Gardens, where a tree was planted in memory of John Lennon

St. John's Gardens - 43

A tree was planted here on 9 October 2000 to commemorate John Lennon's 60th birthday. Julia Baird, John's half-sister, planted the oak tree. Pupils from Dovedale School sang "Imagine" during the ceremony.

On 3 December 2001, an oak tree was planted to commemorate the life of George Harrison.

St. John's Gardens. This tree was planted after George Harrison died in 2001

Storyville Jazz Club - 17 (see Iron Door)

The Storyville Jazz Club was on Temple Street, just off Dale Street in Liverpool. On 9 April 1960 it was opened as the Iron Door, and was then renamed the Liverpool Jazz Society. For a brief time in 1962, it was known as the Storyville Jazz Club, and The Beatles made two appearances here.

Town Hall, Liverpool - 44

The City of Liverpool held a civic reception for The Beatles at the Town Hall on 10 July 1964. There they looked over the balcony to view the streets filled with adoring fans. In the downstairs foyer is a brass plaque bearing the names of John, Paul, George and Ringo, acknowledging their award of the Freedom of the City.

Walker Art Gallery - 45

Stuart Sutcliffe's work entitled 'Summer Painting' was selected for the John Moores Liverpool Exhibition in 1959. It was the only student piece accepted. Moores, a Littlewoods Pools millionaire, bought Stu's painting for £65. It was with this money that Stuart made a down payment on an electric bass guitar and joined his friend John Lennon's group. This painting was in fact one portion. The other half never made it down from Stuart's Percy Street flat and rotted outside the back door for months.

Two years after his death, the gallery held an exhibition of Stuart's work. In 1984, local Beatles historians Ron Jones and Mike Evans arranged a similar show called 'The Art of The Beatles', which was opened by Cynthia Lennon.

Watson Prickard, North John Street - 46

As one of the main stockists of school uniforms, Paul and Mike McCartney visited Watson Prickard Department Store at the start of each school year. It is only fifty yards from the top of Mathew Street. This was also Brian Epstein's tailor for many years.

The White Star pub - 47

The Beatles sometimes visited this pub after appearing at The Cavern. The White Star was named after the famous shipping line, for whom both George's father, Harry, and John's father, Alf, worked as stewards.

The Wyvern Club (see the Blue Angel) - 3

The Wyvern Club was later renamed the Blue Angel after the Roy Orbison hit. John, Paul, Stuart and George auditioned here as The Silver Beatles for Larry Parnes to back Liverpool's Billy Fury. Ringo also auditioned with Rory Storm and the Hurricanes.

Ye Cracke - 48

This pub is on Rice Street near the Liverpool Art College. John and Cynthia often met here for drinks, and John and Stu also met with friends Bill Harry and Rod Murray to discuss art and were known as 'The Dissenters'. A plaque has now been erected to commemorate the meetings.

Zodiac Coffee Club, Duke Street

This coffee house was a popular venue for local bands, including The Beatles. The club also played host to an impromptu jam session which included The Beatles, The Big Three, Rory Storm and the Hurricanes and Gerry and The Pacemakers. It has since been demolished.

Ye Cracke, Rice Street

ABOVE: *The Walker Art Gallery, William Brown Street, where Stuart Sutcliffe's painting was exhibited*
OPPOSITE: *The rear of Liverpool's Town Hall, where The Beatles were entertained at a civic reception on 10 July 1964*

The Penny Lane Walking Tours

Walk 1 - The Penny Lane Walk

This walk is approximately half a mile (0.8km) and will take about 30 minutes, allowing for photographs.

Refer to the insert map on page 247 for this walk. It starts at the famous Penny Lane roundabout - **(A16)**, which is actually called Smithdown Place, by Sgt. Pepper's Bistro—the Shelter in the middle of the roundabout. You will discover many places here, beneath the blue suburban skies.

Find the barber-shop, now Tony Slavin. To its left is the Penny Lane Surgery, which was Martin's Bank. On the opposite corner is a pharmacy and next to it is the white building, the former Barclays bank. The Lloyds TSB bank is on the other side of the roundabout. Cross over at the lights in front of the shelter to see where the 'pretty nurse' stood, selling her poppies. Cross over again and you will be by the Lloyds TSB bank. Next to it is the Barnardo's shop, the former Albert Marrion photo studio and opposite is St. Barnabas' Church - **(A19)**. Then walk down Penny Lane to find the Penny Lane chip shop - **(A17)**: and opposite is St. Barnabas' Church Hall, now called Dovedale Towers - **(A18)**. Then walk over the bridge to the end of Penny Lane where, on your left, through the fence, you can see Liverpool College - **(A12)**.

Turn around and walk back up Penny Lane to the roundabout. There are two more Penny Lane walks for you.

Walk 2 - The Penny Lane Walk 2

The second walk is nearly 5 miles (8km) and you should allow up to 3 hours to complete it at a leisurely pace.

Starting at the Penny Lane roundabout - **(A16)**, this walking tour takes you down Smithdown Road into Wavertree and back to Allerton and Penny Lane. Facing St. Barnabas' Church - **(A19)**, and Penny Lane, cross over towards the white building—the former Barclays Bank— onto Smithdown Road. Cross over at the lights and walk to your right along Smithdown Road. Follow the blue arrows to discover:

On your left is Holyoake Hall - **(A11)**, and further along is a Bathroom and Plumbing shop, which was the Dutch Café - **(WA16)**. Continue along the road, and cross over at the lights towards Wavertree 'Mystery' - **(WA22)**. Walk under the bridge and turn right into Garmoyle Road. On your right you will find 93, Garmoyle Road - **(WA11)**. Turn left down Lidderdale Road to find the former site of Lidderdale School - **(WA18)** on your left, which is now apartments. Opposite the end of Lidderdale Road is the tower of St. Columba's Church - **(WA14)**. Cross over at the traffic lights and walk down Greenbank Drive. On your left is Greenbank Drive Synagogue - **(WA13)**.

Follow Greenbank Drive to the end and turn left on Mossley Hill Drive, and then turn left up Greenbank Lane. At the top, turn right onto North Mossley Hill Road, and then left up Penny Lane. Walk over the bridge and then turn right onto Dovedale Road, where on your left you will find Dovedale School - **(A8)**. Follow the arrows back to Penny Lane - **(A16)**.

Walk 3 - The Penny Lane Walk 3

This walking tour is almost 5 miles (8km) and will take approximately 3 hours.

It starts from the Penny Lane roundabout - **(A16)**, and goes up Church Road - **(A7)**, into Wavertree and Childwall.

Walk up Church Road - **(A7)**, where on your left is the shopping area which was the Penny Lane tram sheds - **(WA17)**. Cross over Church Road to find 9, Newcastle Road - **(A14)**. Return to Church Road and turn right. Cross over the road again towards Bluecoat School – **(WA10)**. Continue up Church Road and on your left is Holy Trinity Church - **(WA4)**.

Continue up to the roundabout where you will see The Abbey Cinema - **(WA7)**, which is now a supermarket, and Picton Clock - **(WA6)** in the centre of the roundabout. Turn left down the High Street and cross over to the white building, which is Wavertree Town Hall - **(WA5)**.

Turn right and then right again, into Chestnut Grove. At the end of the road, to your right, is Arnold Grove. Find 12, Arnold Grove - **(WA1)**, on your right. Return to the end of the road and then turn right, and right again, into Albert Grove. Here is 9, Albert Grove - **(WA2)**. Walk back down Chestnut Grove to discover the church of Our Lady of Good Help - **(WA3)**. Retrace your steps to - **(WA6)** and then follow Childwall Road. Turn right onto Lance Lane. Turn left onto Woolton Road and on your left is Mosspits School - **(WA8)**. Turn left onto Queens Drive and follow the green arrows. Next to the pedestrian crossing, on your left, is the former site of the Graham Spencer Studio - **(C2)**, which is now a double-glazing showroom. Spencer took the photograph of Epstein's artists from across the road in the car park of the Fiveways Pub (see page 293). Cross over to the Fiveways Pub, then walk back up Queens Drive to find 197, Queens Drive - **(C4)**.

Head back up Queens Drive to the roundabout and turn right onto Allerton Road. On your right is the former site of Woolworths - **(A25)**.

The walk finishes at the Penny Lane roundabout - **(A16)**.

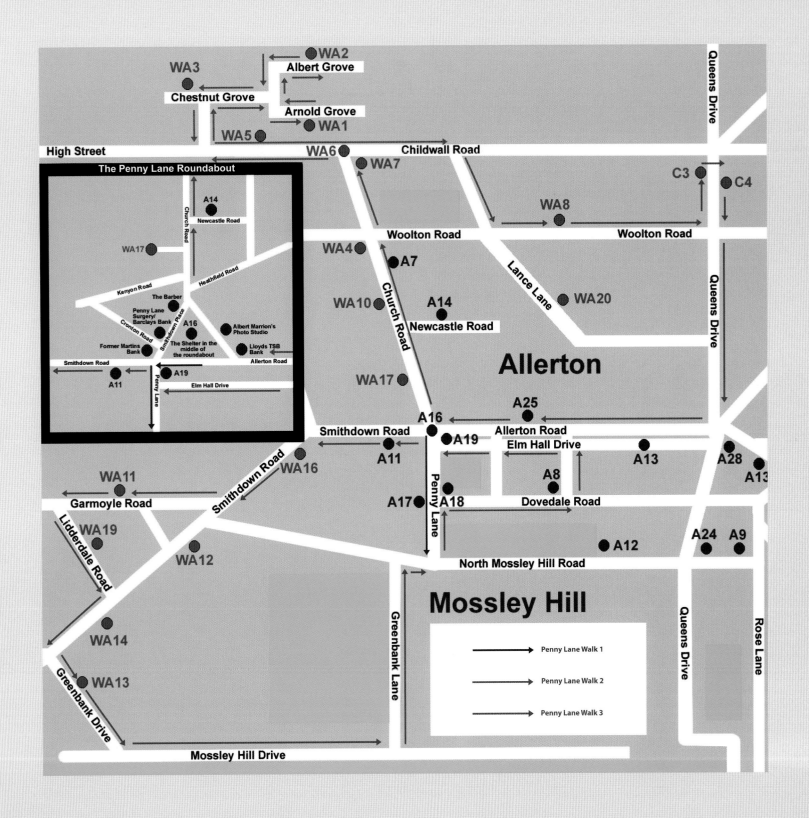

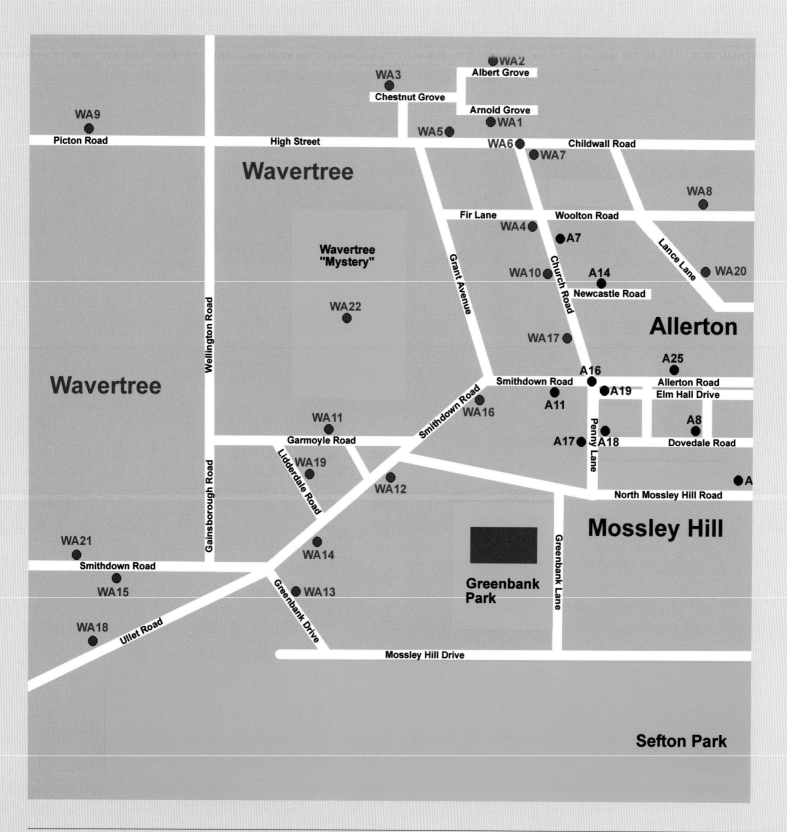

WA2
Albert Grove
WA3
Chestnut Grove
Arnold Grove
WA9
WA1
Picton Road
WA5
High Street
WA6
Childwall Road
WA7

Wavertree

WA8

Fir Lane
Woolton Road
WA4
A7

Wavertree
"Mystery"
WA10
Church Road
A14
WA20
Newcastle Road

Grant Avenue

WA22

Wellington Road

Wavertree

WA17

Allerton

A25

A16
Smithdown Road
Allerton Road
WA16
Elm Hall Drive
A19
A11
A8
WA11
Garmoyle Road

Smithdown Road

WA19
Lidderdale Road
A17
A18
Dovedale Road
Penny Lane
WA12

Gainsborough Road

North Mossley Hill Road
A

Mossley Hill

Greenbank Lane

WA21
WA14
Greenbank
Park
Smithdown Road
WA15
WA13
Greenbank Drive
WA18
Ullet Road

Mossley Hill Drive

Sefton Park

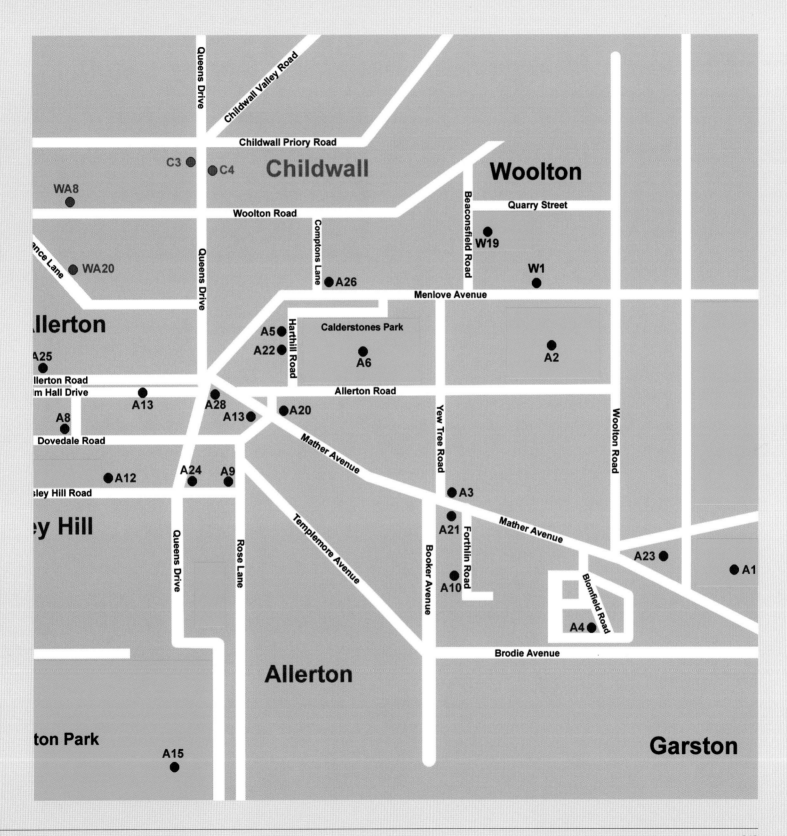

Allerton & Mossley Hill (including Penny Lane)

"Here beneath the blue suburban skies"

Allerton has many claims to fame, besides the obvious Beatles connections. The oldest man-made structure in Liverpool was a prehistoric burial mound, uncovered when the construction of Menlove Avenue was started. This mound near Calderstones Park was excavated in the 18th Century, and yielded a few burial urns. The walls and the roof of this burial mound were the 'Calder Stones' which are now in one of the Park glasshouses.

CITY OF LIVERPOOL MOSSLEY HILL

The following places are found within this chapter:

- Allerton Cemetery - **A1**
- Allerton Golf Course - **A2**
- Allerton Synagogue - **A3**
- Beechenhurst Prep School - **A26**
- 1, Blomfield Road - **A4**
- Calder High School - **A5**
- Calderstones Park - **A6**
- Church Road - **A7**
- 69, Dovedale Road
- Dovedale School - **A8**
- Elmswood Nursing Home - **A9**
- 20, Forthlin Road - **A10**
- Gaumont Cinema - **A28**
- Holyoake Hall - **A11**
- Liverpool College - **A12**

- Mather Avenue
- NEMS, 44, Allerton Road - **A13**
- 9, Newcastle Road - **A14**
- Palm House, Sefton Park - **A15**
- Penny Lane - **A16**
  - Penny Lane roundabout
  - St. Barnabas' Church - **A19**
  - Albert Marrion's Photo Studio
  - Penny Lane - the song
  - The Barber
  - The Banker
  - The Shelter
  - The Pretty Nurse
  - The Fireman and the Fire Station - **A20**

- Grove Mount, Penny Lane
- Dovedale Towers/ St. Barnabas' Church Hall - **A18**
- Penny Lane chip shop • Strange and Strange - **A17**
- Police Training School, Mather Avenue - **A21**
- Quarry Bank School - **A22**
- Springwood Primary School - **A23**
- St. Anthony of Padua Catholic Church - **A24**
- Vernon Johnson School of Dance - **A27**
- Woolworths, Allerton Road - **A25**

Allerton Cemetery - A1

John's mother, Julia Lennon, was buried here at 10 a.m. on Monday 21 July 1958 in the Church of England section 38, grave no. 805. It is a private grave and not clearly marked. A new headstone was erected in 2010.

The simple stone in the centre marks Julia Lennon's grave

Allerton Golf Course - A2

John often sat in the brick shelter on the golf course with his girlfriend Thelma Pickles while waiting for Mimi to leave the house. Once the coast was clear, they would sneak into Mendips.

It's often been wrongly reported that Pete Shotton found Paul McCartney at the golf course, and told him he could join The Quarrymen. However, Shotton has refuted that version and recalled the meeting took place on Vale Road.

Paul remembers how he and John played a few rounds of golf here. The golf course was a convenient short cut between John and Paul's houses—a trail they often took.

Allerton Golf Course

Paul recalls walking from John's house across the golf course in the dark nights, singing with his guitar strapped over his back. He said he wrote the basic chords and lyrics of a couple of songs on those walks home, such as "Love of the Loved" and "World Without Love".

Allerton Synagogue - A3

Situated on the corner of Mather Avenue and Yew Tree Road, Allerton Synagogue, built in the 1950s, played host to The Beatles in December 1961. The gig was most likely arranged through Epstein's contacts. The building, replaced in 2005, was barely 500 yards from Paul's home at Forthlin Road.

The new Allerton Synagogue

Beechenhurst Prep School - A26

Beechenhurst Prep School was the kindergarten attended by Brian Epstein on Menlove Avenue. He didn't enjoy his time there and all he could remember was hammering bits of wood through holes. Beechenhurst School closed in 2009, and is now Carleton House.

Beechenhurst Prep School

1, Blomfield Road - A4

Julia Baird is John's half-sister, the daughter of John Dykins and Julia Lennon. Julia had separated from Alf Lennon and had set up home with her new partner, John Dykins. When baby Julia was two, the family moved to 1, Blomfield Road on the Springwood Estate. John visited there frequently. When he and Mimi had a row, he stayed with Julia for the weekend. John and Julia reunited in his teenage years and spent a lot of time re-establishing their relationship.

Julia Lennon's home at 1, Blomfield Road

Calder High School - A5

Next to Quarry Bank boy's school, Calder High School was where John Lennon often trespassed on to the girl's school grounds.

Calderstones Park - A6

Calderstones Park is a big public park, very close to John's home on Menlove Avenue. The park is next to Quarry Bank and a good place to 'sag-off' (play truant) from school, according to John. Quarry Bank School has now been renamed Calderstones School.

The Linda McCartney Play Area in Calderstones Park

Affectionately termed 'Colly Park' by Lennon, John and Paul spent many a lazy afternoon there. They usually met on a grassy slope they called 'the bank', near the Mansion House, the original home of the Brocklebank family. It was here they assembled with their bikes and watched the world (mostly girls) go by. Later converted in part to a café, the group spent a lot of their pocket money on drink and food there.

In the middle of the park is a large lake where boats were available for rent. One day, Len Garry ordered a boat, while the others hid. Len got in on his own, and then the other four—John, Pete, Ivan and Nigel—appeared from behind the boathouse and jumped in the boat before the owner could do anything. John's Long John Silver pirate impressions were a hit, providing the on-board entertainment. Their shenanigans eventually ended up with them being banned from the boating lake.

Near the park entrance was a bowling green. One day the unruly lads thought they'd have a bit of fun at the expense of the regulars. They nominated Pete Shotton as spokesman, who told the attendant he was sixteen and old enough to play, but John started larking about, and Pete apologised for him saying he was from a 'special school'—a local term for children with social or learning difficulties. They carried on playing, crashing their bowls into those of the older members of the bowling club.

At the corner of Harthill Road and opposite Quarry Bank School was the grand entrance to Calderstones Park with the statues of the Four Seasons. This was John's meeting place where he hurled insults and told amusing stories before heading to school. He cycled through the park every day on his way to and from home.

Paul planted a special tree in memory of Linda in the park in 1999. There is also a special playground there that he opened in her name.

TOP: *The front room of Paul McCartney's home at 20, Forthlin Road, where Paul and John composed many songs*
BOTTOM: *View along Penny Lane from St. Barnabas' Church, with the Wirral peninsula and North Wales on the horizon*

Church Road - A7

Running up from the Penny Lane roundabout is Church Road, the main route to school for George Harrison, that would lead him to Penny Lane and Dovedale School. (See Songs—"In My Life")

69, Dovedale Road

The home of John Lennon's school friend, Mike Hill, was where John had his rock 'n' roll epiphany. John and Mike, together with their friends, would regularly listen to rock 'n' roll records together here, but it was Little Richard's "Long Tall Sally" that struck a chord with the young Lennon. "This boy at school, Mike Hill, had been to Holland and said he had a record by someone who was better than Elvis", recalled Lennon. "When I heard it, it was so great I couldn't speak".

Dovedale School from St. Barnabas' Church

Dovedale School - A8

The author has been associated with Dovedale School for the last few years, as his daughters Philippa, Lauren and Ashleigh attended there. At the time of writing, he is Chair of Governors at the junior school and have helped with the Parent and Teacher Associations in both schools.

The renovated playground at Dovedale School

The school is split into infants school from ages four to seven and the junior school from ages eight to eleven. Both John Lennon and George Harrison attended the infant and junior schools. George and John were in different years and it is unlikely they met. Peter Harrison, George's older brother was in John's class from the age of eight until eleven. John's friend Ivan Vaughan only attended the junior school.

John was enrolled here on 6 May 1946 with his address noted as 251, Menlove Avenue. Mimi took John to and from school on the bus.

Dovedale School entrance

Aged eleven, John started to work on a series of comic books with the title *Sport, Speed and Illustrated*. He added a postscript 'Edited and illustrated by JW Lennon'. It contained pictures of film stars and football players, which he pasted in among cartoons, poems and short stories he composed. He was also contributing editor to the *Daily Howl*, a school paper which exhibited his poems and pictures.

A fellow pupil was Liverpool comedian Jimmy Tarbuck, who once commented about John, "He later became a pacifist, but he did not mind a playground fight". On the passing of his eleven-plus exam in 1951, his uncle, George Smith, bought John an emerald-green Raleigh Lenton bicycle.

On 6 May, 1946, John Winston Lennon was enrolled at Dovedale School

George Harrison was enrolled at Dovedale School on 19 April 1948

George was enrolled in Dovedale School in April 1948. There are some revealing quotes about George at Dovedale. School friend Ashley Thom remembers an incident with their teacher Mr. Lyons, who caned George. When Harold Harrison found out, he angrily marched to the school and punched the teacher, with a warning not to touch his son again.

George said he was sad to leave Dovedale. He was reasonably athletic, enjoying football and cricket.

Elmswood Nursing Home, owned by the Salvation Army, where Julia Lennon gave birth to a daughter, Victoria Elizabeth, on 19 June 1945

Elmswood Nursing Home - A9

Commissioner Catherine Bramwell-Booth opened Elmswood, located on North Mossley Hill Road, as a Salvation Army Nursing Home on 25 January 1940. Julia Lennon became pregnant after an affair with a soldier, known as Taffy Williams, and gave birth here to a girl, Victoria Elizabeth Lennon, on 19 June 1945. Victoria was put up for adoption, arranged by Mimi, to a Norwegian sea captain and his Liverpool-born wife. They lived in Liverpool for a short time before moving to Norway. John never met Victoria despite searching for her for years. She had been renamed Ingrid Pederson, and was tracked down by a journalist a few years after John had been murdered.

20, Forthlin Road - A10

In 1955, the McCartney family made their move from a vast council estate in Speke to the more suburban Forthlin Road—now a National Trust house and open to visitors. Mary McCartney's work as a district nurse took her around Allerton, Woolton and the local schools.

The McCartney's home at 20, Forthlin Road

They moved in for a weekly rent of 39 shillings and 10 pence (about £2). Their joy soon turned to sorrow when on 31 October 1956, Mary died of breast cancer. With Jim left to bring up his boys—a job he accomplished with success—Paul and Mike both lost themselves in their creative hobbies. For Paul, music was his escape.

The house had many updated features for its day, particularly the inside toilet, which was considered a luxury when compared to a freezing cold outhouse. One recent visitor, Donna Cook, commented that, "Paul's room was so small he'd have to go outside to change his mind".

Forthlin Road proved to be the inspirational 'studio' for many early Lennon and McCartney collaborations. Jim actively encouraged his boys' musical hobbies and was more than happy for them to practise there.

The family's fortunes had changed after The Beatles struck it big, and in 1964 Paul moved his dad to Heswall, on the Wirral, to the new home, 'Rembrandt'.

Gaumont Cinema - A28
One of the smaller venues The Quarrymen ever played was at the Gaumont Cinema in Allerton, though no dates of their appearances are available. The building has been demolished.

Yoko Ono visits Dovedale School

If there is one person who has been almost universally targeted by the fans for the break-up of The Beatles, it is Yoko Ono. The world's press, especially the British media, have great joy in focusing on everything Yoko does or says that could be seen in a poor light. Hardly ever does the good news get through.

Yoko Ono has unselfishly given so much to Liverpool, particularly since John Lennon's death. She has been generous with her time, money and the use of Lennon's image to help children and improve the city. Her generosity will make a big difference to the lives of the local children for years to come.

A decision was made by a group of concerned parents and teachers to set up a charity called the 'Friends Of Dovedale Infant School' (FODIS) to raise the funds required for a new playground. A committee consisting of a dozen volunteers, including the author, was ably led by recently-retired head teacher Wen Williams, whose hard work over the years has recently been recognized. We had plans drawn up and realised we needed about £27,000 to achieve our goal.

One look at the school's history showed several famous people had passed through its halls, including BBC newsreader Peter Sissons, horror writer Clive Barker, comedian Jimmy Tarbuck, singer and songwriter John Power, and of course, John Lennon, George Harrison and Ivan Vaughan. We wrote to them and their families to see who was in a charitable mood. Much to our surprise and delight, we were contacted by Ono's lawyers offering to help. Lennon's widow asked for a budget, which was sent, and it was hoped that her interest would get our appeal off to a great start. Her representatives sent a cheque for £30,000—covering our total costs and then some.

Since Yoko's generous donation, the school has transformed the playground, installing 'pencil-shaped' fences and all manner of equipment for the children to enhance their playtime.

Yoko has visited the school twice, meeting the teachers and children. On the second visit, she was so pleased with the playground renovation that she wanted to further honour John by donating an additional undisclosed amount. This has helped with the funding of additional building work at the school.

Yoko Ono with Dovedale Head Teacher Wen Williams, in July 2001

Holyoake Hall, Smithdown Road

A view from St. Barnabas' Church overlooking Holyoake Hall to the Liverpool skyline

Holyoake Hall - A11

Holyoake Hall is opposite the tram sheds on Smithdown Road and about 200 yards from Penny Lane. The Quarrymen played here regularly in 1958, as did The Beatles on the 15th and 22nd of July 1961.

Liverpool College - A12

Brian Epstein attended many schools, including Liverpool College, a private school at the bottom of Penny Lane and North Mossley Hill Road. Epstein was later expelled for 'rude behaviour towards a teacher'. He had been caught doodling girls on the blackboard amongst other offences. Epstein felt that anti-Semitism was a contributory factor. The family was not pleased when the school insisted that Epstein attend on Saturday mornings when he would usually go to the synagogue with his father to observe the Sabbath.

Mather Avenue

Paul and Mike were sent to a house on Mather Avenue, at the top of Forthlin Road, for piano lessons. The two weren't keen on practicing, and didn't follow through with their lessons.

NEMS, 44, Allerton Road - A13

Now a solicitor's office, this was a handy record shop for John and his friends to visit, listen to records and scribble down song lyrics before being thrown out. They frequented the shop at lunchtime, often sneaking out of school.

9, Newcastle Road - A15

After his birth at Oxford Street Maternity Hospital, John was brought back to Newcastle Road and lived here for the majority of his first five years. Julia's father worked for the Liverpool Salvage Company and was often away from home. When Alf Lennon returned from sea, this was where he and Julia set up home. They briefly shared the house with Julia's parents, who initially blessed their marriage.

Newcastle Road is just a couple of hundred yards from the Penny Lane roundabout within the area referred to locally as 'Penny Lane'.

Palm House, Sefton Park - A15

This Victorian glass greenhouse fell into disrepair in the 1970s, and a board of trustees set about restoring it to its former glory. George Harrison joined the board and made a significant contribution to the fund. It reopened in 2001 and George had hoped to perform there, but ill health prevented him from doing so.

Penny Lane - A16

It is best to refer to the map on page 247 to help understand the geography of Penny Lane, and the reference points.

Penny Lane was named after James Penny, an 18th Century slave trader who had supported the political leaders of the city by arguing against the abolition of slavery. Six other powerful slave traders were so honoured. In 2006, the Liverpool City Council considered a proposal to rename these streets after abolitionists such as William Wilberforce. However, when the Council realised that Penny Lane was one of the most significant tourists attractions in the city would be affected, it decided to leave the name unchanged.

However, the song, "Penny Lane" is not really about the road of that name—it is mainly about the roundabout at the top of Penny Lane called 'Smithdown Place'. But that would not have worked lyrically as 'Smithdown Place is in my ears and in my eyes'.

The roundabout is at the centre of what then became known as the 'Penny Lane' area. All three—the road, the roundabout and the area— are significant in the story of The Beatles and the song, "Penny Lane".

Seen from the top of St. Barnabas' Church, this roundabout is like the hub of the wheel where the suburbs of Wavertree, Mossley Hill and Allerton converge and it became a popular meeting point.

The Penny Lane street sign

LEFT: *Penny Lane roundabout from St. Barnabas' Church* RIGHT: *Penny Lane roundabout in 1957*

Much has changed over the last century, when it was mainly surrounded by fields, including Allerton Road Farm, going away from the roundabout.

Penny Lane was also the terminus for the trams from the city centre. The local City Council hadn't even extended the trams beyond Penny Lane by 1926, though this followed shortly after when the line was extended up to Woolton along Menlove Avenue. St. Barnabas' Church, on the corner of Penny Lane, hadn't been built yet—the original church building occupied the site where Holyoake Hall is now.

Before discussing the song "Penny Lane", there are three places left which need to be mentioned. Paul McCartney suggested other locations he had considered including Winters, the fashion store, Liverpool Victoria Insurance and the Penny Lane Cake Shop on Church Road. There was indeed a fashion store next to Barclays Bank, called Winters. There was also a Withers on Penny Lane, and at the corner of the road was the Co-operative Insurance, not Liverpool Victoria Insurance, but we can forgive him for his memory. The Penny Lane Cake Shop was a child's delight, selling popular day-old cakes for only 1d (one old penny).

Penny Lane roundabout - A16

The best way to experience Penny Lane is to stand in the middle of the roundabout. Penny Lane is more than just a place where there were a few shops.

"Penny Lane" is about John, Paul and George's childhood—literally in their ears and in their eyes. The area was the centre of The Beatles' lives from a very young age.

● John lived his first few years in Newcastle Road, just off the roundabout. This is where he was pushed in his pram and later walked around with his mum when she was shopping there.

● Aunt Mimi enrolled John into Dovedale School, and he jumped off the bus with her at the Penny Lane roundabout, and waited here for the return trip to Mendips.

● The bus that John rode to the Liverpool Art College passed through Penny Lane roundabout everyday.

● 12, Arnold Grove, George's home, was at the top of Church Road, which leads off Penny Lane roundabout.

● George walked down Church Road, across the roundabout and down Penny Lane on his way to and from Dovedale School.

● The Harrisons moved to Speke from Arnold Grove, so George caught the bus to Penny Lane on weekdays, to attend Dovedale School.

● When Paul and George attended Liverpool Institute from the age of eleven, they passed through Penny Lane roundabout everyday on their journeys to and from school.

● The Quarrymen frequently travelled to and from their gigs by bus, and they often took refuge in the Penny Lane shelter in the middle of the roundabout where they waited to change buses.

● Paul was in the choir at St. Barnabas' Church on the roundabout.

● In April 1963, Cynthia was shopping in Penny Lane when her labour pains started. She was rushed to Sefton General Hospital where she gave birth to Julian.

● Julia worked in a tearoom on Penny Lane where she met a soldier called Taffy Williams, with whom she had an affair and later became pregnant, giving birth to a girl.

● The first time Cavern DJ Bob Wooler met The Beatles was at the bus stop at Penny Lane.

A former fellow Dovedale School pupil Jimmy Tarbuck was known as 'The Terror of Woolton'. One day at Penny Lane, John wasn't wearing his glasses, and was forced to squint. Tarbuck perceived Lennon as being aggressive and challenged him to a fight. Tarbuck was strangling John with his Quarry Bank School scarf until his friend Pete Shotton intervened and explained about John's poor eyesight. Tarbuck relented and let go of him.

St. Barnabas' Church

St. Barnabas' Church - A19

Opposite the shelter is St. Barnabas' Church, which opened in February 1914. The "Penny Lane" video of the single included shots of Penny Lane, including an aerial shot of the roundabout from the top of the church tower.

It was at St. Barnabas' that Paul remembered singing in the choir. Brian Johnson, who joined the St. Barnabas' Church choir back in 1953, and is still a member, believes that Paul sang occasionally with the choir, but there are no records to prove that he was a long-term member.

Paul returned to the church on 29 May 1982, when he was best man at his brother Mike's wedding.

Albert Marrion's Photo Studio - A16

Albert Marrion's Photo Studio

Albert Marrion was the first photographer to take formal photographs of the Fab Four, and his photos often appeared in *Mersey Beat*. He had a studio on the Penny Lane roundabout next to the Lloyds TSB Bank, though it is now a Barnardo's charity shop. Paul often stood in front of the shop looking at the photos in the window.

'Penny Lane' — the song

The song has immortalized this small suburban area of Liverpool, making Penny Lane one of the most famous streets in the world.

Paul described the song as part fact and part nostalgia. "It was childhood reminiscences: there is a bus stop called 'Penny Lane'. There was a barber-shop called 'Bioletti's' with head shots of the haircuts you can have in the window and I just took it all and dressed it up a little bit. It was all based on real things; there was a bank on the corner so I imagined the banker and the little children laughing at him. The fire station was a little bit of poetic licence; there's a fire station about half a mile down the road, not actually in Penny Lane. So the banker and the barber-shop and the fire station were all real locations".

Tony Slavin's barber-shop, formerly Bioletti's

The Barber - A16
"Penny Lane there is a barber showing photographs"

Right on the corner of the roundabout by Church Road is a hairdresser's shop called Tony Slavin. The original barber-shop was called 'Bioletti's', but it is no more. This is the barber-shop where Paul, George and John received haircuts.

It is found at the north-west corner of the roundabout.

The former Barclays Bank and Bioletti's barber-shop at Penny Lane

The Banker - A16
"On the corner is a banker with a motor car"

Back in the 1950s, Liverpool resident Keith Newman remembers that there were three banks on this roundabout. What is now Penny Lane Surgery is a former Barclays Bank. Opposite was a Martins Bank, so that when Barclays purchased Martins Bank, the two banks were amalgamated. On the other corner was, and still is, a Trustees Saving Bank, now a Lloyds TSB, and it is the only one of the three that remains a bank. Therefore the phrase could have been inspired by any of these three banks, all on different corners of the roundabout. Staff within the Barclays Bank spoke for years about a manager who was the famous 'banker' in the song, and is the most likely candidate.

A deserted Penny Lane roundabout in 1957
"On the corner is a banker with a motor car"

The shelter - A16
"Behind the shelter in the middle of the roundabout"

The "shelter in the middle of the roundabout" is a bus shelter; a waiting room of sorts. It was the terminus and the place to change buses because of its proximity to the bus depot. The shelter became Sgt. Pepper's Bistro many years ago, though it has been closed since 2004.

The Lloyds TSB bank on the corner of the Penny Lane roundabout

The white building on the left is the former Barclays Bank, which was one of the banks on the Penny Lane roundabout. The other building was Winters, the fashion store

The Fire Station, near Penny Lane

The Pretty Nurse - A16
"The pretty nurse is selling poppies from a tray"

It was behind the shelter in the middle of the roundabout where the 'pretty nurse' stood. The nurse was not a drug-induced fictitious creation of Paul McCartney as some have claimed. She was Beth Davidson, a childhood friend of John Lennon's, who later married Pete Shotton, Lennon's best friend. To raise money for Remembrance Day, Beth and her friends sold poppies every 11 November from a cinema-style tray.

She was first identified in the magazine of the British Beatles Fan Club when Stan Williams, a friend of the author, told his story. Stan attended Dovedale School with John Lennon, and he remembered standing by the shelter at Penny Lane talking to Beth in October 1954 when John and his friend Pete Shotton

approached her and stopped to talk. That is the memory that John captured and retold for the song. Paul has admitted that John helped him with the last verse, but that he did not realise that the 'pretty nurse' did in fact exist. John placed his best friend's wife into a Beatles' song without anyone noticing.

Beth Davidson and Margaret Jones

Stan Williams, top left with Ivan Vaughan top right and Beth Davidson, second from the left, front row

Is there more evidence? The last line is, "And though she feels as if she's in a play, she is anyway". This lyric has always seemed a bit surreal, but can be explained.

As a child, Beth and her friends performed plays in the backyard of her friend Annetta Scott's house in Borrowdale Road. Annetta had persuaded her father to build them a stage, an impressive structure with backdrop curtains and lights and seating for over a dozen people. Stan and his friends had to audition for parts and then help print out tickets on a 'John Bull' printing kit. They charged everyone 1d (one penny) to come and watch their performances. When she was older, Beth performed in school plays and at her church and youth clubs.

Beth lived as if she 'was in a play'—well, now 'she is anyway' sang Paul.

With Stan's help, I placed this story into the Liverpool Echo in 2004 and received two phone calls shortly after the article ran. The first was from Margaret Porter (nee Jones) and the other from Diane Page (nee Shaw). They both remembered Beth and could corroborate Stan's story.

Margaret, who had lived next door to Annetta, was a friend of Beth's from childhood to her untimely death from cancer in 1977. They had acted in the plays together, attended the same school and she was a bridesmaid when Beth married Pete Shotton. She had known John before Beth did and even dated Len Garry from The Quarrymen. Margaret, Beth, John and Pete and the gang often attended the Saturday night dances at St. Barnabas' Church Hall on Penny Lane.

The Fireman - A20

Lastly, we have the 'fireman'. The fireman himself could be in Penny Lane, but as Paul has admitted, he used poetic license. The fire station is along Allerton Road at the start of Mather Avenue, where they keep their clean machine.

Allerton Road fireman and his clean machine

The Penny Lane chip shop, where John, Paul and George bought their chips

Liverpool College on Penny Lane, where Brian Epstein had been a pupil

Paul passed the fire station every day on his way to and from school, and he picked the fireman because his father had been a volunteer fire-watcher during World War II. This was a fact that Paul was proud of and mentioned when he sang "Freedom" for New York firefighters after 9/11.

Grove Mount, Penny Lane
Moving down Penny Lane, Grove Mount can be seen on the left. In the video for "Free as a Bird", a fairground helter-skelter was hired and set up on the Grove Mount playing fields. This was an obvious reference to "Helter Skelter". This was the original site of Dovedale School.

Dovedale Towers/ St. Barnabas' Church Hall - A18
St. Barnabas' Church Hall was a popular dance hall where John and his friends would meet. Now called Dovedale Towers, the dance hall was affectionately known locally as 'Barnys'.

Quarrymen drummer Colin Hanton remembers it well. "Barny's was a great place, and if you didn't have a tie on you didn't get in. There was a dress code—very different from today. You had to get past the doormen—I think the police ran it—and if you couldn't dance, you just stood against the wall. There was no alcohol served, just cold drinks. We usually went to the pub beforehand. John's mum Julia came to see us here at the Vespa Scooter Club Dance—she was the only one at the side of the stage clapping. We were pretty rubbish but we enjoyed it".

Penny Lane chip shop - A17
Across the road from Dovedale Towers is the Penny Lane chip shop. It was here that John and his friends would get their 'four of fish and finger pies'. Paul and John admitted that there was a sexual connotation to 'fish and finger pie' in the song. It was an old colloquial saying: a bit of smut for the lads.

Strange and Strange - A17
Next to the chip shop was a business called 'Strange and Strange'. The lyric "very strange" could have possibly referred to this office.

From the top of the bridge, there's a great view up and down Penny Lane. At the very top, St. Barnabas' Church can be seen on the roundabout.
If you travel to Liverpool on the train from London, you will pass right under the bridge of Penny Lane.

Just past the shops on your right you'll see where a section of the "Free as a Bird" promotional video was filmed. The alley scene, where children can be seen running was staged here—(references to "Little Child", "Lady Madonna", "Piggies", "I Am the Walrus").

St. Barnabas' Church Hall, now Dovedale Towers

Police Training School, Mather Avenue - A21
When he was sixteen in 1957, Pete Shotton enrolled at the Police Training School, just around the corner from Forthlin Road. He stayed there for two years and during his 'passing out parade' (when the trainees qualified), Paul, George and John stood on the roof of Paul's Forthlin Road outhouse, which overlooked the parade ground, and marched up and down with mops and buckets. Unsurprisingly, Pete found it hard to keep a straight face during their mock parade.

The Police Training School

Quarry Bank School - A22
The school, on Harthill Road Allerton, was opened in 1922. It was constructed from stone from the local quarry from which it takes its name. It was here where John Lennon attended school from the age of eleven. He rode his bicycle to school with Pete Shotton every weekday along Menlove Avenue and around the edge of Calderstones Park. In 1985, Quarry Bank School was renamed Calderstones School.

On entering Quarry Bank School, boys were divided into 'houses' named after the area of Liverpool in which they lived. John, Pete Shotton, Eric Griffiths and Rod Davis were all placed in Woolton.

Quarry Bank School, where The Quarrymen were formed

John held a few good memories of Quarry Bank as he asked Mimi for his school tie, which he took with him everywhere, even while in New York. He wore the tie for his thirty-ninth and Sean's fourth joint birthday party on 9 October 1979, and slept with a picture of Quarry Bank School above his bed.

The motto of the school was 'Ex Hoc Metallo Virtutem'—'From this rough metal we forge virtue'.

Ron Bentham, a fellow Quarry Bank pupil formed the Quarry Bank Jazz Combo in 1956. John was rejected when he wanted to join the group. They deemed he wasn't good enough to play with them—and they were probably right.

There are many great stories about John's time here.

● Pete Shotton found a stash of dinner vouchers in the bins at school. He could hardly contain himself. After telling John, they took them all back to John's bedroom to count. By the time Mimi checked in on them, they had counted 1,500. The boys quickly hid them under John's bed and made a tidy sum selling them at half face value over the next few weeks, bringing in about £5 a week, which was quite a windfall in those days.

● Lennon and Shotton were often in school detention, but worse was to come. After being late too many times, Head Master Mr. Pobjoy sent them home on suspension. What would Pete tell his mum? What would John tell Mimi? They decided they dare not turn up, and visited Julia instead. She found their predicament hilarious. For the next few days John met Pete and left for school at the normal time. The two then cycled to Julia's house where they served out their suspension.

● Another of Lennon's japes was having fun with Mr. McDermott, their Religious Instruction teacher. Lennon spent an evening cutting strips out of cereal boxes and making dog collars. As the teacher started to waffle, every pupil put on his dog collar. After a few minutes, he looked up and suddenly realised what they had done. He took it all in and then burst out laughing. He liked it so much he made them keep the collars on.

● Another time John and Pete were called before Deputy Head Mr. Gallaway. While looking up their names in the punishment book, John came up behind him and tickled the remaining strands of his hair. Gallaway swiped away what he thought to be an imaginary fly, much to Lennon and Shotton's amusement. This carried on for a few minutes before John and Pete burst out laughing uncontrollably; to the extent that John peed himself. The puddle that formed below him was spotted by the teacher, who asked Lennon what it was. Quick as a flash, he responded, "I think the roof is leaking, sir".

● One of their most hard-faced stunts was a dare from John Lennon. Len Garry and Bill Turner, who had a day off from their school, the Liverpool Institute, turned up at lunchtime and pretended to enrol themselves into Quarry Bank School. They joined John Lennon's art class and Lennon introduced

the two new pupils to the teacher. Garry and Turner took out their Institute scarves and put them on and nobody noticed. Pete Shotton, who was in another classroom, couldn't resist taking a look, making the excuse of saying Lennon had taken his pen. Lennon broke into a straight-faced tirade against Shotton for interrupting his work. In fact, so good was he that Pete Shotton was given a detention.

● An interesting story comes from William Pobjoy, who was Lennon's Head Master at Quarry Bank in John's last year. He described his student as 'a boy of great talent'. When asked by Pobjoy to list his interests in priority order, John's first choice was salmon fishing. Apparently, when he stayed with his aunt in Scotland, they would go salmon fishing. He even told Yoko about his love for Scottish salmon. "There was nothing like it" he declared.

Springwood Primary School - A23
Rod Davis attended Springwood Primary School, in Allerton, near Garston. He was an excellent pupil and even skipped a year. Colin Hanton also attended Springwood for a year, but returned to Bootle after his mum died, when he was only nine years old. The old school was demolished and replaced with a new building in 2005.

Springwood Primary School

St. Anthony of Padua Catholic Church - A24
George often made a three-mile trek to St. Anthony of Padua Catholic Church in Mossley Hill to attend Cubs (young Boy Scouts). His mother attended church on Christmas and Easter and major festivals. George took his first Holy Communion there at the age of eleven.

St. Barnabas' Church and St. Barnabas' Church Hall—see Penny Lane - A19

Vernon Johnson School of Dance - A27
Desperate to learn how to dance, John Lennon and Pete Shotton joined the Vernon Johnson School of Dance off Allerton Road. They didn't stay for too long and Lennon never learned to dance.

Woolworths, Allerton Road - A25
John's mum, Julia worked in Woolworths and this was one of John's favourite places to shoplift sweets with school friend Pete Shotton. The shop closed in 2009.

St. Anthony of Padua Catholic Church, where George was a Boy Scout

Wavertree

"Here Comes The Sun"

Wavertree has existed as a community for about 2,000 years. The name possibly means a 'settlement near a spring on the wasteland' as there was a monk's well nearby. A small cemetery was unearthed on Olive Mount in 1867, containing prehistoric burial urns which are now displayed in the World Museum, Liverpool. The area was mainly farmland with its own mill and quarry. To discover Wavertree, follow the Penny Lane Wavertree Walks 2 and 3 on page 247.

- Abbey Cinema - **WA7**
- 9, Albert Grove - **WA2**
- 12, Arnold Grove - **WA1**
- The Balfour Institute - **WA21**
- Bluecoat School - **WA10**
- Busmen's Social Club - **WA9**
- Capaldi's - **WA12**
- 93, Garmoyle Road - **WA11**
- Greenbank Drive Synagogue - **WA13**
- Holy Trinity Church - **WA4**
- 77, Lance Lane - **WA20**
- Lidderdale School - **WA19**
- Massey & Coggins
- Mosspits Primary School - **WA8**
- Our Lady of Good Help - **WA3**
- Picton Clock - **WA6**
- Sefton General Hospital - **WA15**
- St. Columba's - **WA14**
- The Dutch - **WA16**
- The Tram Sheds - **WA17**
- 53, Ullet Road - **WA18**
- Wavertree "Mystery" - **WA22**
- Wavertree Town Hall - **WA5**
- 26, Wellington Road - **WA23**

Abbey Cinema - WA7

The Abbey Cinema that became Lennons Supermarket

The 'Abbey' referred to in the original lyrics of "In My Life", was the old Abbey Cinema on the roundabout at the top of Church Road and Wavertree High Street.

The Abbey became a favourite meeting place for 'the gang'. consisting of John Lennon, Pete Shotton, Ivan Vaughan, Nigel Walley, Len Garry and Bill Turner. John, in particular, spent many hours here watching Westerns at Saturday morning matinees, sitting in the balcony, flicking objects down on to the girls below and generally making a nuisance of himself. The boys spied on young ladies and sat next to them when they worked up the nerve. They didn't always watch the film.

The Abbey Cinema eventually became a supermarket, ironically owned by a chain of stores called 'Lennons'.

George Harrison's home, 12, Arnold Grove

9, Albert Grove - WA2

This residence, owned by George Harrison's maternal grandparents John and Louise French, is the next road over from George Harrison's Arnold Grove home. George visited John and Louise many times when his parents were at work.

12, Arnold Grove - WA1

George Harrison was born on 25 February 1943 at the family home,

The row of Victorian terraced houses in Arnold Grove, including George's house at number 12, fourth door from the right

12, Arnold Grove, Wavertree. Arnold Grove is a small cul-de-sac off the High Street near the Picton Clock and Abbey Cinema.

The Harrisons moved into this residence after their 1930 wedding. It is a two-up, two-down terraced property, with a yard and alley to the rear. As with most of the housing of this type, there was no indoor bathroom or toilet. Instead, they used an outhouse in the backyard. George was bathed in the kitchen sink as a baby and then progressed to a tin tub, brought in from the yard and placed in front of the fire.

The Balfour Institute - WA21

The Balfour Institute was part of the Mabel Fletcher College and was on the corner of Smithdown Road and Garrick Street in Wavertree. Pete Shotton's girlfriend, Beth Davidson, arranged for The Quarrymen to play at one of their dances. It was an appearance not recorded anywhere else before. The building has been demolished.

Bluecoat School - WA10

Alf Lennon and his sister Edith were sent to the Bluecoat Orphanage on Church Road because they lost their father, Jack, to liver disease when Alf

Bluecoat School

was seven. The orphanage is now Bluecoat Grammar School (and only a couple of hundred yards from Newcastle Road, John's first home). Nigel Walley, one time Quarrymen member, also attended Bluecoat School.

Busmen's Social Club

Busmen's Social Club - WA9
George Harrison's father, Harold, arranged various gigs for The Quarrymen, since he was the Busmen's social committee secretary. The Quarrymen appeared here at the Picton Road club early in 1959 as well as the Finch Lane Social Club, which has been demolished.

The former site of Capaldi's ice cream parlour

Capaldi's - WA12
Capaldi's was an ice cream parlour on the corner of Smithdown Road and Nicander Road. It was one of the few places in the area that had a jukebox. John Lennon and his friends frequently stood outside and listened to the new rock 'n' roll from America, featuring stars such as Elvis Presley, Buddy Holly, Chuck Berry and Little Richard.

93, Garmoyle Road, Cynthia Powell's flat

93, Garmoyle Road - WA11
It was while John Lennon was living at Gambier Terrace with Stuart that he met Cynthia Powell. Cynthia was living at 93, Garmoyle Road in Wavertree, and John virtually moved in here. It was also at this location where Julian was conceived. When confronted with the news, John said to Cynthia, "There's only one thing for it Cyn, we will have to get married".

Greenbank Drive Synagogue - WA13
This was the synagogue the Epstein family regularly attended. Brian Epstein's funeral was held here on 27 August 1967, and his body was carried from here to the Jewish Cemetery in Long Lane, Aintree. The Max Morris Hall was attached to Greenbank

Greenbank Drive Synagogue, where the Epstein family regularly attended, and where The Beatles played

Drive Synagogue and hosted performances by most of the big bands in Liverpool, including The Beatles during the summer of 1961, before Epstein became their manager.

The synagogue closed in January 2008 after the congregation dwindled to forty worshippers. It has been saved from demolition by being upgraded by English Heritage to a Grade 2 listed building status. Built in 1937, it is considered one of the finest art deco buildings of its time.

Holy Trinity Church - WA4
George's grandparents, Henry Harrison and Jane Thompson, were married here on 17 August 1902. George walked past the church every day on his way to and from Dovedale School, while he lived in Arnold Grove.

77, Lance Lane - WA20
Len Garry lived in Lance Lane and The Quarrymen rehearsed there several times.

Holy Trinity Church

77, Lance Lane, home of Len Garry

Lidderdale School, where Ivan Vaughan attended

Lidderdale School - WA19
This was Ivan Vaughan's first primary school, located on Lidderdale Road. He later transferred to Dovedale School, where he travelled each day with John Lennon. Lidderdale School has since been demolished.

The former site of Massey & Coggins

Massey & Coggins
Situated in Bridge Road in Wavertree, Paul landed a job winding coils at Massey & Coggins. The job didn't last long and Paul decided music was a better option. The business is no longer in existence.

Mosspits Primary School - WA8
Mosspits Primary School on Woolton Road in Wavertree was John's first school. He enrolled here on 12 November 1945 while still living in Newcastle Road. His mother, Julia, took a job nearby so that she could take and pick up John from school.

When Mimi took John to live with her, she initially accompanied John to school on the bus. He bullied a young girl named Polly Hipshaw and was removed from Mosspits School by Mimi, who then enrolled him in Dovedale School.

Our Lady of Good Help - WA3
Our Lady of Good Help was the church where George was christened. It was a short walk to the church from Arnold Grove. The name on the christening papers is listed as 'Georgius Harrison'.

Picton Clock - WA6
Picton Clock was built by the famous local historian James Picton in memory of his late wife, Sarah. Picton Road is named after James as well as Picton Library next to the Liverpool World Museum. This clock was referred to in the original lyrics of "In My Life".

Sefton General Hospital - WA15
Sefton General Hospital on Smithdown Road was the main hospital for the south end of the city. The site has now been replaced by an ASDA Supermarket (part of the Wal-Mart group), with new homes built on the rest of the property.

During its heyday, many Beatle-related events took place at the hospital:

● Rod Davis of The Quarrymen was born here on 7 November 1941.

● Sefton General Hospital was where Julia Lennon was taken after she was hit by an off-duty policeman on Menlove Avenue on 15 July 1958. She was pronounced dead on arrival.

● Len Garry was rushed here by ambulance, unconscious, in 1958. He was in Sefton General Hospital for seven months with tubercular meningitis, and his career with The Quarrymen was over.

Picton Clock, from John's original lyrics of "In My Life"

● George Smith, Mimi's husband and John Lennon's uncle, was rushed to Sefton General from Mendips. He died here on 5 June 1955 from a brain haemorrhage.

● Stuart Sutcliffe visited Sefton General Hospital after returning from Hamburg in 1961. He saw a neurosurgeon who didn't detect anything wrong with him, after examining the x-rays. Not long after his visit, Stuart died.

● Cynthia Lennon gave birth to Julian on Monday 8 April 1963 at 7:45 a.m. John exclaimed on seeing Julian, "Who's going to be a famous little rocker like his dad, then?" They arranged a private room for Cynthia, but it was surrounded by glass windows. Many faces appeared at the glass, looking at the new Liverpool celebrity, John Lennon. It was Cynthia's first taste of what it would be like living in the public eye.

● Julia Lennon's partner, John 'Bobby' Dykins, also died here in 1966 after a road accident on Penny Lane.

The main hospital building has been demolished.

St. Columba's - WA14
St. Columba's was a church at the junction of Smithdown Road and Croxteth Road. It is now sheltered housing, retaining the church tower. St. Columba's had a youth club, which was attended by Pete Shotton's girlfriend Beth. Beth's friend, Stan

Sefton General Hospital

St. Columba's Church

The Dutch Café, Smithdown Road

The last tram shed, Smithdown Road

The Sutcliffes lived at 53, Ullet Road

Williams, remembers Pete Shotton and Lennon coming into the club one evening and starting an argument with the youth leaders. When they were told to leave, Beth led a walkout to support her boyfriend, never to return.

The Dutch - WA16

This was the Dutch Café in the song, "In My Life". The Dutch was located at 316, Smithdown Road and was an all-night café, frequented by taxi drivers. It also became a haunt for The Beatles where they could grab a bacon buttie after a gig. Pete Shotton later became the owner of the café after dropping out of the police force. It has the original windmill decoration, recenty restored, on the building.

The Tram Sheds - WA17

The last tram shed—mentioned in John's original draft of "In My Life"—that remains, is on Smithdown Road, a few hundred yards from Penny Lane. It would have been passed by John when taking the bus into town, as Liverpool discarded trams to replace them with buses. The bus terminal and depot were behind the Penny Lane roundabout, off Prince Alfred Road.

53, Ullet Road - WA18

The Sutcliffe family moved to Ullet Road on the edge of Sefton Park. It was here where Stuart returned having been beaten up after the gig at Lathom Hall. His face was smothered in blood with extensive bruising on his forehead. His mum remembers Stuart coming home and practically collapsing in his bed. When she went to wake him in the morning, the pillow was covered in blood. Stuart refused to see a doctor. It was only on his return from Hamburg after he had been suffering with headaches that he was convinced to see a doctor.

It was also here where Astrid made her first visit to Liverpool. She stayed with the Sutcliffe family, but Astrid and Stuart were not allowed to sleep together. Soon after they stayed with Allan Williams and his wife.

Wavertree 'Mystery' - WA22

Wavertree 'Mystery' park, known locally simply as the 'Mystery', was donated to Liverpool by an anonymous benefactor, hence the mystery. The donor was later revealed to be Philip Holt of the famous Holt shipping line but the name has stuck.

John, Ivan and George regularly walked across the park to take a dip at

John Lennon's swimming certificate from Picton Swimming Baths

Picton Swimming Pool while at Dovedale School. It was at the swimming pool that John achieved his twenty-five yard swimming certificate, one of the few mementos he kept from Dovedale.

Wavertree Town Hall - WA5

Standing on the High Street near George Harrison's home at Arnold Grove, The Quarrymen appeared here several times during 1957 and 1958, though no record was kept of the dates. They also made several other unrecorded appearances. It was also here where George's birth was registered. There is still the motto above the door, which reads 'Sub umbra floresco'. Translated it means, 'I flourish in the shade'. The motto is quite appropriate for George Harrison, the Beatle who flourished in the shade of John Lennon and Paul McCartney to become a great songwriter in his own right. This former Town Hall is now a pub with function rooms for hire.

26, Wellington Road - WA23

Harold Hargreaves Harrison, George's father, was born here on 28 May 1909. The house has been demolished.

Wavertree Town Hall, where George Harrison's birth was registered

The Woolton Walk

The Woolton Walk is approximately 5 miles (8 km) and will take about 3 hours to complete.

The walk starts at Mendips, 251, Menlove Avenue - **(W1)**, home of John Lennon. Walk on Menlove Avenue and turn into Vale Road. You pass the former site of the Vale Road Den - **(W3)**. On the opposite side of the road is the wall that marked the boundary of Strawberry Field. As you walk round the corner of Vale Road, you will find the homes of Ivan Vaughan - **(W6)**, Nigel Walley **(W5)** and Pete Shotton - **(W4)**, plus "The Tip" - **(W7)**.

At the corner of Vale Road and Linkstor Road is where Pete Shotton asked Paul McCartney to join The Quarrymen. Continue down Vale Road to the end, and then turn left on to Allerton Road, Woolton. On your left is the dairy cottage - **(W9)**. Behind the cottages, and next on your left is Tesco, which is the former site of the dairy farm - **(W8)**. Opposite the dairy cottage is the former site of Liverpool Convalescent Home - **(W10)**. Follow Allerton Road to the left into Woolton Village, and on your right at the junction is Woolton Baths - **(W11)**.

Turn left down Quarry Street. Up to your right, at the corner of Mount Street and St. Mary's Place is the former site of St. Mary's Catholic Primary School - **(W30)**. Carry on along Quarry Street and you will pass Woolton Quarry - **(W12)**, on your right. Carry on along Quarry Street and you will pass Quarry Street Newsagents - **(W13)** (now a hairdresser's shop). Turn right up Linkstor Road to the end and turn right on to Church Road. St. Peter's Church - **(W14)**, is on your right, with the grave of Eleanor Rigby. Opposite is St. Peter's Church Hall - **(W15)**. Keep walking down Church Road and turn left into Allerton Road. On your right is Woolton Village Club - **(W21)**. Continue to the end of the road. Opposite is the former site of Jo's Milk Bar - **(W17)**. Turn left along Woolton Street and then left again into Mason Street where you will see Woolton Cinema - **(W16)**, on your right.

Follow Mason Street back to Church Road and turn right, going up the hill, past St. Peter's Church. On your right is Reynolds Park - **(W18)**, which is a good place for a stop, if you need one.

Follow the road to the end, then turn left into Beaconsfield Road where you come across the famous gates of Strawberry Field - **(W19)**. Follow Beaconsfield Road to the bottom, and cross over into Yew Tree Road, with Calderstones Park—**(A6)** from the Allerton Map—on your right.

Follow Yew Tree Road into Booker Avenue to the junction with Mather Avenue, and on the corner is the site of Allerton Synagogue - **(A3)**. Turn left along Mather Avenue and cross over, past the Police Training School - **(A23)**, and right into Forthlin Road, looking for 20, Forthlin Road - **(A10)**.

This is the end of this tour. You can return to Mather Avenue, where there is a bus stop, or you could turn left along Mather Avenue where, after a 20 minute walk, you will find yourself at the Penny Lane roundabout (see page 246).

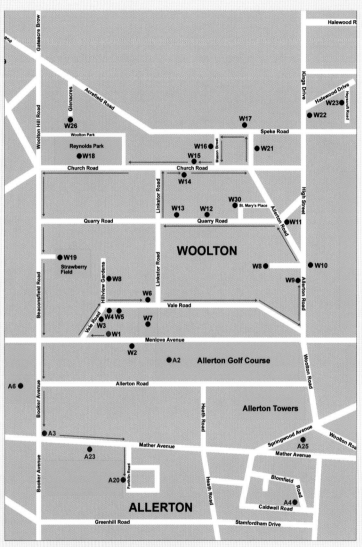

OPPOSITE: *The original mansion that became the Salvation Army's Strawberry Field Children's Home*

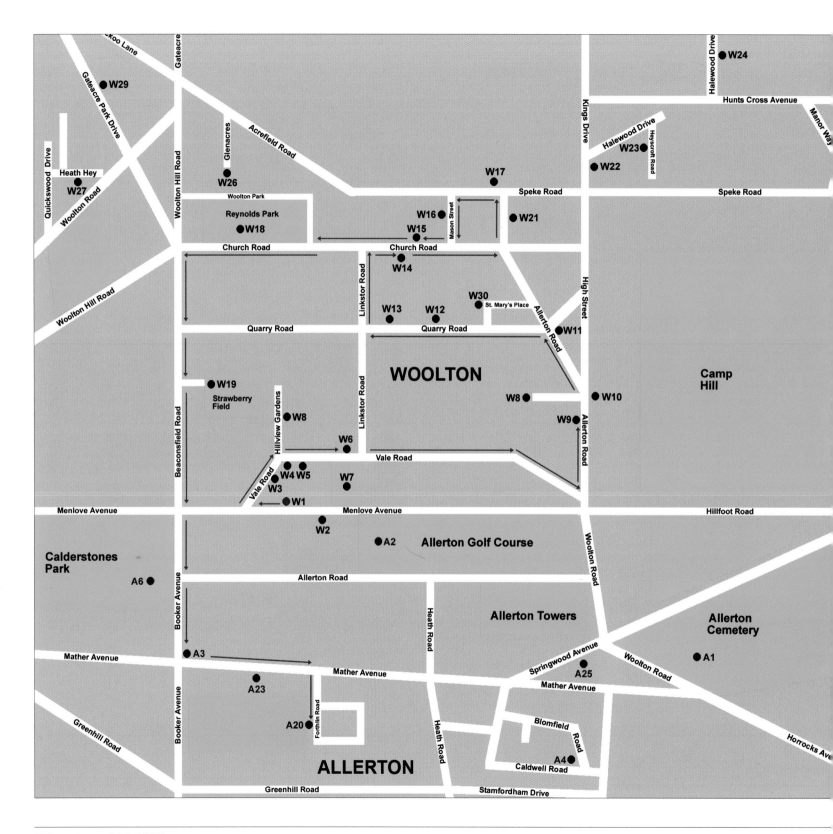

GARSTON

The gravestone in St. Peter's Church cemetery, displaying the name of Eleanor Rigby

gwood Avenue

Woolton (including Strawberry Field)

"Let me take you down"

The name "Woolton" is possibly an old Anglo-Saxon or, more likely, a Norse name meaning "Wulf's enclosure".

Many small quarries sprang up locally, but the biggest was Woolton Quarry, which was opened by James Rose, known to locals as the "King of Woolton". He regenerated the area, building houses for the rich and the poor. His quarry went on to provide the stone for Liverpool's Anglican Cathedral.

In the early 19th Century there was a large influx of Irish people fleeing the great famine and by 1851 nearly twenty-five per cent of Woolton's population was Irish. That was expressed in a plethora of pubs, which

numbered approximately forty by the end of the century. A massive house-building project resulted in the construction of many semi-detached homes; one of which was Mendips, soon to become the home of John Lennon.

Woolton Village is within the confines of Woolton and is a designated conservation area, which gives protection to the original feel of the village, and restricts development. As you drive through Woolton, you can almost imagine yourself anywhere in England—it has that "English Village" feel. This is where John Lennon grew up—not the dirty, grimy picture you might have in your head of Liverpool. On closer inspection you'll see that Woolton has hardly changed in fifty years. Woolton officially became a part of the City of Liverpool in 1913.

- 3rd Allerton Scout Group
- Allerton Towers - **W28**
- Ashe's Grocers
- Dairy Cottage - **W9**
- Dairy Farm - **W8**
- Fosters Field - **W20**
- 137, Gateacre Park Drive - **W29**
- 96, Halewood Drive - **W24**
- Heath Hey - **W27**

- 4, Heyscroft Road - **W23**
- Jo's Milk Bar - **W17**
- 129, Kings Drive - **W22**
- Liverpool Convalescent Home - **W10**
- 174, Macketts Lane - **W25**
- Mendips - **W1**
- Menlove Avenue
- 298, Menlove Avenue - **W2**
- Quarry Street Newsagents - **W13**

- Reynolds Park - **W18**
- St. Mary's Catholic Primary School - **W30**
- St. Peter's Church - **W14**
- St. Peter's Church Hall - **W15**
- St. Peter's - The Graveyard - **W15**
- Strawberry Field - **W19**
- "Strawberry Fields Forever"
- 'The Tip' - **W7**
- 'Treetops', Glenrose Road - **W26**

- Vale Road 'Den' - **W3**
- 83, Vale Road - **W6**
- Vale Road, 'Vega'- **W4**
- Vale Road, 'Leosdene'- **W5**
- Woolton Baths - **W11**
- Woolton Cinema - **W16**
- Woolton Quarry - **W12**
- Woolton Village Club - **W21**

Woolton Village from St. Peter's Church

3rd Allerton Scout Group
This was the Woolton-based Boy Scout group that John attended for a short time in his youth.

Allerton Towers

Allerton Towers - W28
One of the local parks in Woolton, Allerton Towers is where John and The Quarrymen hung out to admire the opposite sex.

Ashe's Grocers
Ashe's was a grocer's shop in the heart of Woolton Village which became the key provider of tea-chests for the budding skiffle group movement in the late '50s. The Quarrymen could buy tea-chests here for 2 shillings and sixpence (12.5 pence), and transform them into a tea-chest bass. This is an instrument peculiar to skiffle and not often understood.

The dairy cottage, Allerton Road

Dairy Cottage - W9
This small house at 120a, Allerton Road, was attached to the dairy farm owned by George Smith, Mimi's husband, and is on Allerton Road in Woolton.

At Mimi's invitation, Julia Lennon lived here for a short time with John while Alfred was away on his voyages. Harriet, Mimi's sister, also lived here with her husband, Norman, and became guardians to Julia and Jackie, John's half-sisters. John later bought Harriet a larger home in Gateacre Park Drive.

The site of George Smith's dairy farm

Dairy Farm - W8
The dairy farm was owned by Mimi's husband, George Smith and his family. George made daily trips on his horse-drawn cart around the village, delivering the milk straight from the churn. Occasionally, John delivered milk with his Uncle George and looked after the horse, including cleaning the stables.

When George Smith's father died, the dairy farm was sold to the Bear Brand manufacturers, who advertised on the back of the programme for the summer fete at St. Peter's. (George Smith was later employed as a night watchman on the site of the estate that bought his farm from him and took over the land).

Fosters Field - W20
Foster's Field was a deserted piece of land, which had a murky pond full of frogs. One day, John Lennon and Pete Shotton built a raft to float across the pond. Halfway across, their raft capsized and they were soaked. Having been warned to keep away from the pond, they couldn't go home wet. They therefore lit a fire to dry their clothes first.

137, Gateacre Park Drive which John Lennon bought for his two half-sisters, Julia and Jackie Dykins

The site was developed for houses and became a mud bath. However, people soon moved into the completed houses, including a policeman and his shapely, buxom wife. It was from a vantage point on the slopes from which Pete and John could spy her sunbathing topless—something she would do with regularity. They spent an inordinate amount of time one summer admiring her figure.

137, Gateacre Park Drive - W29
John bought a four-bedroom house in Gateacre Park Drive, which was intended for his two half-sisters, Julia and Jackie. John's Aunt Harriet and Uncle Norman had assumed the responsibility for the girls after their mother Julia had been killed. After both John and Harriet died, it was discovered that the home was still in John's name, through Apple. Julia Baird has told how Yoko Ono planned to evict them, but, following a protest, she allowed Norman to stay. This house became an important place to Julia and Jackie because they claim it was John's gift for them.

9G, Halewood Drive

The house was handed over to the Salvation Army on 2 November 1993 as a gift from Yoko and it is currently used as a home for retired officers.

96, Halewood Drive - W24
This is the childhood home of Eric Griffiths, founder member and guitarist with The Quarrymen. The group often rehearsed here.

Heath Hey - W27
When Beatlemania became too much for Elsie and Harry Graves, Ringo moved his mother and stepfather to a bungalow in Woolton.

The house in Heath Hey that Ringo bought for his mother and stepfather

4, Heyscroft Road, where Colin Hanton lived

4, Heyscroft Road - W23

This home in Woolton Village was where Quarrymen drummer Colin Hanton lived. On the opposite side of Woolton from John, The Quarrymen practiced here on Saturday afternoons.

Jo's Milk Bar - W17

One of the most popular meeting places for The Quarrymen was at Jo's Milk Bar in Woolton Village. Its central location made it an ideal rendezvous for the young musicians. Jo was the attractive barmaid who ran the place and was popular with The Quarrymen gang because she fussed over them. On one occasion, with encouragement from Jo, John played his guitar and sang, eliciting applause from patrons. In payment, Jo made them milk shakes.

129, Kings Drive, Rod Davis' home

129, Kings Drive - W22

Quarrymen banjo player Rod Davis lived at this Woolton residence where The Quarrymen sometimes rehearsed in the garden.

Liverpool Convalescent Home - W10

Sited opposite the dairy farm, this is where Mimi started her nursing career in 1927. While here, she struck up a relationship with the milkman George Smith, who later became her husband.

174, Macketts Lane - W25

The Harrison family moved to 174, Macketts Lane in Hunts Cross (on the edge of Woolton) in 1962. Fans camped outside the house and fan mail was delivered in sacks. The Harrisons were extremely nice to these uninvited visitors, but eventually, they placed a screen on the front window to give them some privacy.

174, Macketts Lane, where The Harrison family moved from Upton Green in Speke

George moved the family in 1965 to Appleton, near Warrington, Cheshire, to a bungalow set in three acres—a far cry from Arnold Grove. A few industrious fans still found the house and received the usual courtesy and welcome from George's parents, for which they are fondly remembered.

Mendips - W1

The home at 251, Menlove Avenue, was named Mendips after a range of hills in the South of England. Set within a still picturesque and attractive suburb, the naming of the house was a typical middle-class affectation that Mimi was quick to adopt.

How Mendips was acquired has been a mystery for years but has finally been cleared up by John's half-sister Julia Baird. George and Mimi Smith rented a house behind Mendips, known as 'Vega'—the house where Ivan Vaughan later grew up. They witnessed

John's bedroom in Mendips

John's small bedroom in Mendips, where he would write his stories and poems, and listen to the radio

the previous tenants preparing to leave and stored their furniture at the bottom of the garden by the fence that separated the two homes. The day the tenants vacated Mendips, Mimi and George lifted their furniture over the fence and moved in. With long-term possession being important under the laws in England, this forced the owner to sell the property to them. Essentially they were squatters. The house had three bedrooms, a bathroom and inside toilet.

John's bedroom, above the front porch, was small and his bed sat under the window. His room was invariably untidy and Mimi eventually was banned from entering. His walls boasted posters of Elvis Presley and Brigitte Bardot, and he had his books and radio. Uncle George had installed a speaker by taking an extension lead up the stairs from the radio in the morning room downstairs. This private retreat was where John spent hours reading and thinking. He wrote poetry and most nights sang himself to sleep. Sally his dog, curled up at the foot of his bed to sleep and kept his feet warm. One of John's jobs was cutting the lawn at Mendips for pocket money,

Yoko at Mendips in 2008

On 3 April 2008, I met Yoko Ono at Mendips, in my capacity as Chair of Governors at Dovedale School. With the head teachers and deputy head teachers, we brought with us a few of the children from the infant and junior schools to meet Yoko, at her invitation.

As the children sat quietly, waiting for their special guest to arrive, I was able to explain some of the history of Mendips, and in particular several of the paintings and photographs on the wall. One of these was a picture of a football match that John had painted in 1952 when he was in his last year at Dovedale School. It showed the players from Arsenal Football Club, dressed in red scoring a goal, and famously appeared on the cover of Lennon's 1974 album, *Walls And Bridges*.

When Yoko Ono arrived, wearing a Quarry Bank School tie, she unexpectedly brought with her two film crews who crowded the small room. She was introduced to the younger children by infant school head teacher Jane Noble, and she took the time to shake each child by the hand and exchange a few words. The school had prepared a photograph album showing all the changes that had been made to the school with Yoko's donation. Nik Smith, head teacher in the junior school, then introduced the older children and myself. I had prepared a copy of a photograph of John at Dovedale School in 1951 and had written down a few of the stories from John's school friends that appear in this book. "As you know", Yoko said to the children, "John was very fond of Dovedale School and of Liverpool too. I want to thank you very much for these gifts, which I didn't expect".

"Now, I have something to show you", Yoko said. "Come with me and I'll show you John's bedroom". Yoko disappeared up the stairs like the Pied Piper of Hamelin. She took time to show the children the bedroom where John spent his formative years and explained to them how important it was.

"John's bedroom was only small, but that doesn't matter", she said. "What is important is what is in your mind. That is why John was so special, because his imagination was his future. Any of you", she commented, looking directly at the children, "can be famous no matter where you come from or how little your room is. Maybe in twenty years time I will see you and come to visit you because you will be famous".

CLOCKWISE: *Yoko poses with the group from Dovedale School. The pupils examine the memorabilia, in the back room at Mendips, and Yoko talks about John. Some of the children look at the paintings John did in his last year at Dovedale School, which appeared on the cover of his* Walls and Bridges *album*

pushing the heavy mower up and down the grass. Mimi insisted he finish this chore before he went out with his friends.

When Paul rehearsed with John, they were usually found in the enclosed porch by the front door. Mimi didn't like the noise of the guitars, and the room offered respite for her and great acoustics for John and Paul.

The morning-room—between the entrance hall and the kitchen—was John's favourite hangout when he had friends. As with most homes in Liverpool, the front room was out of bounds to all but the most important of visitors because it was the showroom and not for general use. Paul remembers walking in there for the first time and thinking how posh they were, particularly with all the books on the shelves, almost all of which John had read.

When they were growing up, John and his friends inevitably found trouble and mischief. One of Pete Shotton's recollections is of them building a rope swing on a tree at the edge of Menlove Avenue. Their idea of fun was to swing out in front of the buses and play 'chicken' (to see who could pull out at the last possible moment without being splattered on a bus.)

Mendips was sold in October 1965 for £6,000, after John had bought Mimi a house in Poole, Dorset in August of that year. Mendips was later bought by Yoko Ono and given to the National Trust.

Mendips and Songs
John wrote "Please Please Me" in Mimi's front bedroom at Mendips. Pete Shotton remembers when Lennon rushed him into the morning-room where he had his record player and played the first acetate of "Please Please Me". John was thrilled beyond belief that the music coming out of the record player was his own.

"I'll Get You", the B-side to "She Loves You" was one of the few songs written by John and Paul at Mendips.

Menlove Avenue
Menlove Avenue was the road where Julia Lennon was knocked down by an off-duty policeman on 15 July 1958. The driver had not passed his driving test, had no insurance, and was speeding.

Menlove Avenue from Mendips

The street hasn't changed much since John lived there apart from the central reservation in the middle of the road which is where the tram tracks had originally run. At either side of the track was a privet hedge.

Menlove Avenue was also the name of a 1986 posthumous album of John Lennon songs that echoes back to the road where he grew up. They were essentially outtakes from the recording sessions for the *Walls and Bridges* and *Rock 'N' Roll* albums.

298, Menlove Avenue

298, Menlove Avenue - W2
Across the road from Mendips was the home of Bill Smith, a member of The Quarrymen for a brief time. Smith, it was deemed, was not dependable and was duly replaced.

Quarry Street Newsagents - W13
This little hairdresser's shop holds one of the smallest, yet significant pieces in The Beatles' jigsaw. Pete Shotton's mother was the owner and one day she overheard a customer and Harry Gibbons, the caretaker of the church hall at St. Peter's, talking about the summer fete. Mrs. Shotton immediately thought of The Quarrymen and asked Gibbons if they could play at the event since they attended Sunday School and Youth Club at St. Peter's. Gibbons arranged an audition with organiser Harry Foster, and so the first steps were taken towards that momentous appearance at the fete on 6 July 1957 that would change musical history.

The site of Quarry Street Newsagents which is now a hairdresser's shop

If that conversation had not taken place, The Quarrymen most likely would have never played. The trickle down effect would have been that John Lennon probably would have never met Paul McCartney. No meeting, no Beatles.

Reynolds Park - W18
Reynolds Park, just off Church Road in Woolton, was a favourite alternative to Calderstones Park for Lennon's gang. It is a little gem of a park hidden away in Woolton and well worth a visit. It was in this park where Len Garry and John Lennon spotted two girls standing next to a tunnel. One of these girls was Barbara Baker, who became Len's girlfriend for a while. Later, she dated John Lennon.

Reynolds Park, where John met girlfriend Barbara Baker

St. Mary's Catholic Primary School - W30
Colin Hanton, drummer with The Quarrymen, attended St. Mary's Catholic Primary school in Woolton.

St. Peter's Church - W14
St. Peter's Church is famous as the site where John Lennon met Paul McCartney. However, there is other history here as well. Lennon attended Sunday School from the age of eight. Most of the original Quarrymen attended St. Peter's—Rod Davis, Pete Shotton, Ivan Vaughan and Nigel Walley. Eric Griffiths married in the church in 1963. John sang in the church choir with friends Pete Shotton, Nigel Walley and Dave Ashton. They only did it for the half a crown payment. John spent most of the time inventing words and his own 'harmonies' to the hymns.

They attended rehearsal one evening during the week, two services on Sundays, and then for funerals and weddings, for which they were paid extra. John and Pete had the distinction of being thrown out of the choir for continually being disruptive and giggling.

Following his own free will, according to his Aunt Mimi, John was confirmed at the age of fifteen into the Church of England at St. Peter's. His confirmation was for materialistic reasons Lennon later said, who thought he'd better do something in case he 'didn't make it'. Lennon was also a member, for a short time, of a Boy Scout group that met here.

St. Peter's Church Hall - W15

The earliest public performances by The Quarrymen were at St. Peter's Church Youth Club, where they would perform for free—most of them were members of that club. Paul McCartney's first performances with The Quarrymen were in St. Peter's Church Hall.

Eleanor Rigby's gravestone

St. Peter's - The Graveyard - W15

John Lennon's uncle is buried in St. Peter's graveyard. When John Lennon saw the gravestone, he discovered that his Uncle George Smith's middle name was 'Toogood' and that his ancestors were the Toogoods from Woolton. He was so proud that he showed the grave to all his friends. It was too good to be true. If John had showed Paul this gravestone, surely he would have seen the Eleanor Rigby gravestone too? Which brings us to the subject of the famous song, "Eleanor Rigby".

In St. Peter's graveyard there is a gravestone with the name 'Eleanor Rigby'. Paul says he made the name and the character up, and the song is fictitious. He wrote the lyrics and story, and then worked on giving the characters names. 'Daisy Hawkins' was the original title of the lead character but the name didn't seem to ring true with Paul.

The inspiration for "Eleanor Rigby" first came from a building in

Rigby's Buildings in Dale Street—an inspiration for the song "Eleanor Rigby"?

Bristol, when he was visiting there with Jane Asher. Opposite The Theatre Royal in King Street was 'Rigby and Evans Ltd'., a wine merchant. Steve Turner, in his book, *A Hard Day's Write*, also points out that 'Rigby & Evans Ltd'. was owned by Frank Rigby from Liverpool, who owned a company in Dale Street in Liverpool City Centre in the 19th Century.

Tribute to Tom McKenzie in Cavern Walks

To go to The Cavern, Paul would have leapt off the bus at the top of Mathew Street, and close by, at the end of North John Street, is 'Rigby's Building', Thomas Rigby's pub, one of the oldest in Liverpool. Surely Paul would have seen it hundreds of times. One wonders if the Bristol building subconsciously reminded him of the one in Liverpool, which reminded him of the gravestone.

The name Eleanor came from Eleanor Bron (pictured below), the actress in *Help!* Paul put Eleanor and Rigby together and thought it sounded right. He didn't know why, it just was.

Many years later, after the song became famous, it was discovered that there was a grave in St. Peter's graveyard with the name of Eleanor Rigby on its headstone. Had Paul seen the grave and not remembered? Was this coincidence? Paul later admitted to author Barry Miles that he must have seen the gravestone in his youth because The Quarrymen played at the Youth Club quite often. Therefore, it must have been hidden in his subconscious, unlocked years later by a series of completely unconnected events. Eleanor Rigby, buried in St. Peter's graveyard, lived in Pit Place, just off Quarry Street in Woolton. In 1990, McCartney donated an accounts register from Liverpool's City Hospital to charity - revealing that an E. Rigby worked there. The document has been signed by her, suggesting her to be a scullery maid.

Not far from Eleanor Rigby's grave is a headstone with the name of McKenzie—the last name of the priest in the song. Tom McKenzie worked for two years as a compere, PA transporter and host at many Beatles gigs around Liverpool. The musicians referred

Actress Eleanor Bron, after whom Paul named the fictional lady in the song, Eleanor Rigby

to him as 'Father' McKenzie and there is a plaque dedicated to his memory in Cavern Walks. Father McKenzie once reported that during a conversation with The Beatles, he had told them how, during the war, he would darn his socks in order to keep awake whilst on air raid watch and that this was reflected in the lyrics in "Eleanor Rigby"—"Father McKenzie, look at him working, darning his socks in the night when there's nobody there. What does he care?"

Children in Strawberry Field, pictured in the 1950s

McCartney had originally named the priest 'Father McCartney'. He had second thoughts and assumed everyone would think he was writing about his dad. Pete Shotton remembers a night when they were searching for names, and claims that he suggested 'Father McKenzie' after scouring the phone book.

Strawberry Field - W19

Strawberry Field (not Fields) was a Salvation Army children's home in Beaconsfield Road off Menlove Avenue. Much has been written about this place made famous in the song.

The earliest reference to Strawberry Field dates to 1870. Originally it was a field where strawberries were grown. A wealthy ship-owner, George Warren, purchased the land and built the house. Later, Alexander C. Mitchell, another shipping magnate, owned the property until his death in 1927, and his widow sold the estate to the Salvation Army in 1934.

The charity was able to purchase the mansion and convert it to a home for approximately forty homeless girls from the poorest slums of Liverpool, most of whom were orphans, using a legacy from Mary Fowler, a Liverpool woman. On 7 July 1936, the house and grounds were opened by Commissioner Bates in the presence of General Evangeline Booth, who was the fourth General of the Salvation Army, and daughter of William Booth, the founder. It was the fourth home of its kind opened in England by the Salvation Army. In the mid-1950s, boys under five years of age were taken into the Strawberry Field home, and even later, older boys were admitted.

Thinking about Strawberry Field, Lennon later recalled, "I used to go to garden parties as a kid with my friends Nigel and Pete. We would go there and hang out and find empty lemonade bottles and get a penny back on them. We always had fun at Strawberry Field". Lennon commented that he felt he had something in common with the children there; his dad had left him and his mum had given him away, so he too was without his parents.

The Vale Road entrance to Strawberry Field had a high wall, which to John was the real Strawberry Field—not the famous red gates on Beaconsfield Road. Once they scaled the wall, John and his friends played for hours in the grounds. Much to Mimi's displeasure, John played with the children from the home. Mimi didn't want her little boy playing 'with the commoners'. John enjoyed gathering conkers from the large trees on the grounds. For those unfamiliar with this custom, conkers are the produce of the horse chestnut tree. Every autumn the boys engaged in one of the oddest contests whereby they'd thread a piece of string through the conker, and proceeded to bash each other's suspended conker to bits. Having the best remaining conker was an honour. The only time John and his friends visited the big house at Strawberry Field was when they attended the annual summer fete mentioned earlier. They later admitted to stealing items from the stalls.

Bill Parr remembers that the unmarried mothers who lived in the small cottage in the grounds sent signals to boys. If the coast was clear to come over the wall, the girls hung out a piece of washing on the line. If it was blue, it was the signal to stay away. If not, they were made welcome. They were known locally by the lads as the 'naughty girls'.

The early 1970s saw the demolition of the original house and the erection of the Salvation Army's first purpose-built home for children. Major Ida Cawthorne was at Strawberry Field in 1973 and she recalled "We had large amount of ground so we sold some of the land in order to fund the building of a modern house for the children. The site of the old house was turned into a play area with slides and swings. The adults were a bit sorry to see the house go, but the children were thrilled with the new building". With the release of The Beatles' "Strawberry Fields Forever", and the relationship between the home and John Lennon was revealed, nothing would be quite the same again. In 1979, The Beatles connection was renewed when new accommodation for staff and older boys and girls was named Lennon Court following a donation from John. The following year Lennon was murdered.

The house where John wrote "Strawberry Fields Forever" in Almeria, Spain

The flag of the Salvation Army in Strawberry Field

The empty playground after Strawberry Field closed

John had promised his son, Sean, that one day he would take him to Strawberry Field, but his death meant he was unable to do so. However, John's widow, Yoko Ono, did not let his promise go unfulfilled. In 1984, almost fifty years after General Evangeline Booth's motorcade stopped off at Strawberry Field for its opening, a three-car cavalcade brought Yoko and Sean to John's childhood haunt.

The pair made two visits that day. During the first visit, the children were not present as they were at school, though hordes of reporters and camera crews were. At the end of the visit, Yoko asked the officer-in-charge, Captain David Botting, if she and Sean might return privately that evening. This time there was no press, but the children were home from school. Yoko signed autographs for them and looked at their homework and drawings, while Sean played games with the children. Before leaving, Yoko told the kids, "John loved this place. He was just an ordinary Liverpool lad".

The author is a member of a rock 'n' roll children's charity called "Merseycats", formed by the Merseybeat musicians from the sixties to raise money for local children's charities. The charity has been supporting Strawberry Field for many years, including paying for the construction of a new playground, which was opened in 2000 to mark what would have been John's 60th birthday.

Sadly, in January 2005, the Salvation Army announced the closure of Strawberry Field, an action that was initially condemned. However, the nature of modern childcare has changed dramatically and there were only three children in residence with some twenty-five coming in on weekends for respite care. Social Services and the Salvation Army acknowledged that the place for children should be within a loving family, and so they placed all the children within foster families. Discussions are ongoing at present as to the long-term future use of the site, a process that Beatles fans want to be involved in. On 31 May 2005, Strawberry Field closed its doors as a children's home for good. The Salvation Army still owns the site and runs it as a prayer retreat and meeting place, called 'The Boiler Room'.

"Strawberry Fields Forever"

The song was written in Spain by John Lennon while filming *How I Won the War*. A Spanish journalist, Adolfo Iglesias, tracked down the house in Almeria where John stayed. It is a big house on a hill, surrounded by trees and bushes, just like Strawberry Field back home in Liverpool. Lennon was bored and probably homesick,

The wall in Vale Road which John Lennon jumped to reach the grounds of Strawberry Field

and longed for those carefree days of his youth. Once John and his friends had climbed the wall on Vale Road and jumped down into the wild gardens of Strawberry Field they had entered an imaginary playground. Once you were over the wall, nothing was real: it was whatever you wanted it to be. In John's mind, Strawberry Field would always be forever.

'The Tip' - W7

'The Tip' was a piece of land that ran between Vale Road and Menlove Avenue, and a short cut between John's and Pete Shotton's homes. Before the war this was a big lake, which was mistaken by the Luftwaffe as the docks, and was subjected to heavy bombing. The council decided to fill it in with the rubble from bombed houses and it became known as 'The Tip'.

'Treetops', Glenrose Road - W26

'Treetops' was the house where Harry and 'Queenie' Epstein moved in the sixties. After Brian Epstein's death, The Beatles returned from a trip to Bangor to visit his mother 'Queenie' at home to offer their condolences. 'Queenie' asked them not to come to

Salvation Army Captain David Botting with Sean Ono Lennon and his mother Yoko at Strawberry Field in 1984

'Treetops', in Gateacre, The Epstein's home

the funeral because she felt their presence would draw a large crowd and wouldn't be appropriate. They respected her wishes and mourned in silence.

Vale Road 'Den' - W3

On the first bend of Vale Road was an old disused garage. John and his friends used this garage as a den. It was here that John and Pete Shotton decided to become 'blood-brothers'. John sawed away at this wrist with a knife. However, the knife was blunt and didn't draw blood. The two boys improvised and swore allegiance to each other without the blood.

83, Vale Road, Pete Shotton's home.

83, Vale Road - W6

Pete Shotton was brought up at 83, Vale Road, a house his parents rented located behind Mendips. Situated in the garden was a small air raid shelter, where Shotton remembers the very first Quarrymen rehearsals taking place, which included many Lonnie Donegan songs.

Vale Road, 'Vega' - W4

Immediately behind John's house, Mendips, was Ivan Vaughan's house 'Vega'—their gardens connected at the back. Ivan rigged string between a tree in his garden and one in John's. Like many kids in those days, they passed messages to each other through tin can phones.

Vale Road, 'Leosdene' - W5

Nigel Walley lived near Ivan at 'Leosdene' on Vale Road. Nigel was Pete Shotton's first friend from the age of about three.

Woolton Baths - W11

Woolton Baths (swimming pool) was often frequented by Lennon and friends Pete Shotton, Ivan Vaughan and Nigel Walley. Paul visited here with his brother Mike. There was a great toy shop opposite the baths where John shoplifted. His method was almost foolproof—he created a distraction for the elderly lady behind the counter and when she looked in the opposite direction, slipped a toy into his pocket.

Woolton Cinema - W16

Situated in Mason Street in Woolton Village, this cinema became the regular haunt of Lennon and his cohorts. Woolton Cinema, or 'The Picture House' as it was originally known, is a one-screen cinema just yards around the corner from St. Peter's Church. The cinema opened on Boxing Day 1927 and survived World War II and the multiplex invasion of the '80s and '90s. The cinema was an important part of growing up in the 1950s, when not many people owned a television set. The young John Lennon and

Woolton Cinema, formerly the Woolton Picture House, in Mason Street, where John and his friends used to visit regularly

The Quarrymen were regular visitors, naming it the 'Bug House', and feasting on Westerns and Jerry Lewis comedies on Saturday mornings.

With the author's help, The Quarrymen and Mike McCartney became involved in the battle to save the cinema from closure in 2007. Three local businessmen purchased the Woolton Picture House with the full intention of running it as a cinema and keeping The Beatles connection. On hearing of the success of the appeal, Paul McCartney sent a message: "Mike told me the news, well done all involved. My very best wishes".

Woolton Quarry, after which The Quarrymen were named. The quarry has been disused for years and houses have been built right next to the rock face

ABOVE: *The Beatles photographed in 1963*

Woolton Quarry - W12

At the heart of Woolton just behind where John, Ivan, Nigel and Pete lived was Woolton Quarry, which was part of the reason for the choice of name for their new skiffle group—The Quarrymen. There was a public footpath through the quarry from Church Road, which Colin, Rod and Eric used to cross from the other side of the village when going to John or Pete's house for rehearsals. The quarry was active until about 1950.

On the top of the quarry is St. Peter's Church, and the field where The Quarrymen played. They were watched by a teenaged Paul McCartney, who toyed with the idea of joining them.

Woolton Village Club - W21

The Quarrymen played here on Saturday, 24 January 1959. This was the last known booking for them and the group effectively disbanded after this gig. Woolton was the birth and death of The Quarrymen.

The Dingle Walk

The Dingle Walk is about 6 miles (9.7 km) long and you will need to leave yourself 4 hours to complete it.

Start at Liverpool Anglican Cathedral on the corner of Hope Street. Walk up the hill of Upper Parliament Street and turn right at the lights. On the corner is the Rialto - **(D12)**.

Cross over Princes Road and follow it on the left and into Princes Avenue. Walk along and on your left will be Rosebery Street - **(D13)**, though it has mostly disappeared now.

Turn right down Upper Warwick Street and on the corner with Windsor Street on your right is the former site of Henry Hunt & Son Ltd. - **(D7)**. On the opposite corner is the former site of the Starline Club - **(D15)**.

Walk up the road to your left, Windsor Street. On your right is the former site of 57, Copperfield Street - **(D2)**. Turn left on to High Park Street. On your right is St. Silas School - **(D14)**.

Carry on down and stop at The Empress pub - **(D4)**. Turn left and on your right is 10, Admiral Grove - **(D1)**.

Turn back to High Park Street and cross over the road to Madryn Street to your left. Walk down and on your left is 9, Madryn Street - **(D8)**, and find house numbers 10, 21 and 59.

Turn right at the bottom of Madryn Street and follow South Street to the very end. Turn left down Devonshire Road West and then right down Belvidere Road. Take the first right along Peel Street to the very end. On the left corner is the former site of Peel Hall - **(D10)**.

Turn left down Park Road. On the bottom right corner is the Gaumont Cinema - **(D6)**. Follow the road round to the left and then cross over at the corner of Aigburth Road. On your right is the former site of Dingle Vale Secondary Modern School - **(D3)**. Turn around and retrace your steps. Carry straight on at the lights past the Gaumont on your right.

Turn left from Dingle Lane on to Dingle Vale where you will find Starr Fields - **(DA3)**. Turn around and walk along Mill Street until you find the Florence Institute - **(D5)**.

Finish the walk by heading back to the Anglican Cathedral.

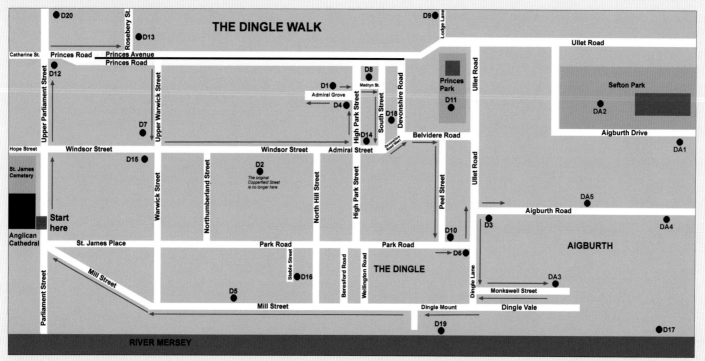

Liverpool 8: The Dingle, Toxteth and Aigburth

"Sentimental Journey"

The Dingle was originally part of Toxteth Park, but as with some parts of Liverpool, areas within designated suburbs take on a personality of their own. The Dingle is an area within the suburb of Toxteth with its own distinct idiosyncrasies, like many areas of Liverpool. People from The Dingle see themselves as different from those in Granby, or Princes Park, even though they too are in Toxteth. The Dingle was named after a stream that ran through this area along what is now Park Road and into the River Mersey at Dingle Vale.

Toxteth's history stretches back many centuries. A stone-age axe head was found in Toxteth Park and the area is mentioned in the famous 12th Century Domesday Book as 'Stochestede'. The word implied that it was an area for livestock.

In 1207, King John established Liverpul as a port; a gateway to Ireland. Toxteth Park became a royal hunting park reserved exclusively for the use of the royal family. The park stretched from St. James' Church (in the shadow of the Anglican Cathedral) right through to Aigburth and across to Mossley Hill, and the area stayed this way for close to 400 years.

The park was sold at the beginning of the 17th Century and families began living in The Dingle near to the river. The Puritans built the Ancient Chapel which was opened in 1618, which still stands at the bottom of Park Road.

Richard Mather set up as pastor there and was quite radical. Following persecution, he left for America in 1635.

The Dingle is a traditional working class area of terraced housing that was settled primarily by Welsh labourers who came to Liverpool to work in the docks in the late 19th Century. This helps to explain why many of the streets have Welsh names, for example, Madryn Street. The Dingle was a real community when Richard Starkey was born there in 1940 and residents could walk freely in and out of each other's houses. Sadly, it has changed quite a bit since the 1980s when the city renovated the area by demolishing many streets of houses and relocating the residents, which in turn broke up the communities. It never recovered. Now they are planning to do it all again and will knock down Ringo's birthplace on Madryn Street, along with all the 'Welsh' streets in the community.

People in the United Kingdom usually associate Toxteth with the inner-city riots that swept through the country in the summer of 1981 and brought the area national notoriety. There were running battles with the police, with hundreds of thousands of pounds worth of damage. Many buildings burnt to the ground, including the Rialto Ballroom, one of Liverpool's great dance venues. The local church in The Dingle, St. Philemon's, housed many of the police drafted in from around the country. The Dingle, like the rest of Liverpool, is on the rise again.

The Dingle and Toxteth

- 10, Admiral Grove - **D1**
- 11, Admiral Grove - **D1**
- 3, Admiral Grove - **D1**
- Cast Iron Shore - **D17**
- 57, Copperfield Street - **D2**
- 36, Devonshire Road - **D18**
- Dingle Vale Secondary Modern School - **D3**
- 43, Elswick Street - **D19**
- Empress pub, High Park Street - **D4**
- 49, Fern Grove
- Florence Institute, Mill Street - **D5**
- Gaumont Cinema - **D6**
- 8, Head Street
- Henry Hunt & Son Ltd. - **D7**
- 9, Madryn Street - **D8**
- 10, Madryn Street - **D8**
- 21, Madryn Street - **D8**
- 59, Madryn Street - **D8**
- The Mandolin Club

- The New Cabaret Artistes Club - **D20**
- New Colony Club
- Pavilion Theatre, Lodge Lane - **D9**
- Peel Hall - **D10**
- Princes Park - **D11**
- R.A.O.B., Devonshire Road - **D18**
- Rialto Ballroom - **D12**
- Rosebery Street - **D13**
- St. Silas Church - **D14**
- St. Silas School - **D14**
- Starline Club, Windsor Street - **D15**
- Steble Street Baths - **D16**

Aigburth

- 37, Aigburth Drive - **DA1**
- Sefton Park - **DA2**
- Starr Fields - **DA3**
- Stella Lovell School of Dance
- St. Charles Catholic Church - **DA4**
- Wellesley School, 11, Aigburth Road - **DA5**

The Marina in Toxteth

3, Admiral Grove - D1

The home of Mrs. Kay Conroy, a good friend of Elsie Starkey who baby-sat Ritchie many times.

Fans in 10, Admiral Grove: Gordon Bates, Margaret Grose (current occupier), Pattie Bates, Annamarie Siligrini, Felicia Meglino and Julian Bates

10, Admiral Grove - D1

Elsie Starkey moved her and her son to 10, Admiral Grove in 1944, when Ritchie was nearly five, and they lived there until Beatlemania overtook their lives in 1963. Ritchie was only three when his parents divorced, and Elsie could not afford the rent on the Madryn Street home, so she exchanged houses with her mother. It was a simple two-up, two-down terraced house. There was no bathroom, or inside toilet. Bathing was a tedious process that involved bringing in the old tin bath from the backyard, placing it in front of the fire and filling it with boiling water. The toilet was in an outhouse at the bottom of the backyard.

Margaret (right) showing Nola her famous home at 10, Admiral Grove

Ritchie practiced with The Eddie Clayton Skiffle Group in the living room at Admiral Grove. While they were practicing one day, Annie Maguire, his mum's best friend, said "See you on the Palladium, son. See your name in lights". Little did she know that would come true.

10, Admiral Grove, where Ringo lived from the age of five

At the corner of Admiral Grove on High Park Street, was a newsagent shop and general store, which was the official 'office' for the Eddie Clayton Skiffle Group. The Starkeys, like most families in the neighbourhood, didn't have a telephone and it was here that the group made their bookings. It was in this same shop on High Park Street that Ritchie marked up the newspapers for delivery, to earn extra pocket money.

In 1962, when George Harrison was keen to recruit Ringo into the band, he sought him in Admiral Grove. Although Ringo was away, working at Butlin's Holiday Camp, Elsie arranged to contact him. Ringo's 21st birthday party was held at Admiral Grove on 7 July 1961. Many entertainers like Cilla Black and Gerry and The Pacemakers came and somehow, they managed to squeeze up to eighty people into his house.

The visitor's book at 10, Admiral Grove, with a message from Ringo's son and daughter, Zak and Lee Starkey

Once The Beatles had become famous, Ringo's parents were inundated with fan mail, and occasionally fans would turn up at the house and steal parts of the door or scribble on the walls. Elsie and Harry were nothing but gracious in return, even when some of the fans were downright cheeky and asked to sit in Ringo's chair or lay down on his bed. Eventually, Ringo bought Elsie and Harry, his step-father, a house in Woolton, which was much more private.

The Admiral Grove house is now the home of Margaret Grose, who has been dubbed the 'First Lady of Liverpool' by fans. Margaret used to live in number 12 and was a friend of Elsie's and so she knew Ringo when he was a teenager. She has become a friend to Beatles' fans from all over the world and she shows the inside of the home where Ringo grew up (by special arrangement). As a result, with pen pals all over the world, she has become a cultural ambassador for Liverpool and is able to convey the true nature of a Liverpudlian—generous and welcoming. She has not seen Ringo since he left Liverpool, although she was visited by Ringo's children, Zak and Lee, in July 2006.

11, Admiral Grove - D1

This house adjacent to number 10 belonged to Eddie Miles, Ringo's good friend with whom he formed the Eddie Clayton Skiffle Group.

Cast Iron Shore - D17

Mentioned in the song, "Glass Onion", this part of the shoreline on the River Mersey was as close to a beach as The Dingle-dwellers could get.

57, Copperfield Street - D2

Alfred Lennon was born at 57, Copperfield Street in Toxteth in 1912. The Victorian terraced houses in the area have since been replaced by new housing. Many of the streets were named after Charles Dickens' characters. As well as Copperfield Street, there were Micawber and Nickleby Streets. Some that remain nearby are Dorrit, Dombey, Pickwick and Dickens Street. Charlie Lennon, Alf's brother, remembered answering the door here one night to be confronted by John Dykins, Julia Lennon's lover, who had come looking for Alfred to demand a divorce for Julia. Charlie told him to leave, as Alfred would never grant her request.

36, Devonshire Road - D18

The Royal Antedeluvian Order of Buffaloes (R.A.O.B.)—Dingle Lodge 4303—a working-men's club similar to the Freemasons held its meetings in an extension at the back of the building at this address. The club room opened onto the bottom of Madryn Street (where Ringo was born). Charlie Lennon, John's Uncle, was a member for sixty years, and was very proud of his association with the 'Buffs'. The neighbours could always tell when it was closing time at the club when the members rolled home after a night of drinking. The club has since closed.

Dingle Vale Secondary Modern School - D3

Ringo attended Dingle Vale Secondary Modern School (now called 'Shorefields Comprehensive') in 1951 at the age of eleven, though he contracted tuberculosis and missed his last two years of school. While recuperating at a children's hospital on the Wirral he became interested in playing the drums and never looked back. One school report read, "He is a quiet thoughtful type, although working rather slowly.

The former site of Dingle Vale Secondary Modern, Ringo's school

He is trying to do his best". He excelled at drama, did fairly well in art but was a poor music student. Having missed a good chunk of school, Ringo returned at age 15 to retrieve his papers only to be told that they couldn't find his records.

With Ringo's financial support, the school created 'Starr Fields' with a community centre and playing fields for the local children.

43, Elswick Street - D19

This was the home of Ian James, a school friend of Paul McCartney. It was Ian's guitar that Paul first played before he purchased his own. They attended the Liverpool Institute together, and Ian helped Paul to learn various chords and songs. The 'Rex' guitar was kept by Ian James and auctioned in July 2006 with a provenance from Paul. It read, "The above guitar, belonging to my old school pal Ian James, was the first guitar I ever held. It was also the guitar on which I learnt my first chords in his house at 43, Elswich (sic) Street, Liverpool 8".

Paul later showed John Lennon some of these chords—those that he had learned from Ian—when they first met at St. Peter's Church on 6 July 1957.

The Empress, High Park Street - D4

At the corner of Admiral Grove and High Park Street sits The Empress pub. This landmark was featured on the front of Ringo's

The alley between Kinmel Street (on the left) and Madryn Street (on the right) leading up to The Empress pub, top left

album *Sentimental Journey*. Ringo recalled the days as a child when his mum listened to classics such as "Bye, Bye, Blackbird" and Doris Day's "Sentimental Journey", hence the name for his debut solo album.

If you look closely at the photograph on the album's front cover, you can spot Ringo in the doorway and his mum Elsie and stepfather Harry in the window downstairs.

The Empress pub, on the corner of Admiral Grove and High Park Street

The cover of Ringo's debut album, Sentimental Journey, where you can see Ringo in the doorway, and his mum, Elsie, and stepfather, Harry, in the bottom window. Admiral Grove is to the right

49, Fern Grove

Tommy Moore, the short-lived drummer with The Silver Beetles, lived on Fern Grove, just off Lodge Lane.

Florence Institute, Mill Street - D5

In the heart of The Dingle is the Florence Institute. Ringo played there in his youth at the Boys Club in the 'Florey' (as locals refer to it) with the Eddie Clayton Skiffle Group.

Gaumont Cinema - D6

At the bottom of Park Road in The Dingle sat the Gaumont Cinema, a favourite haunt of Ritchie's and his mate Roy Trafford. It was here that Ritchie developed his love for all things American, particularly Western films.

8, Head Street

One of the homes in Liverpool owned by the Stanley Family, this was the house where Julia Stanley, John's mum, was born. All the homes in Head Street were demolished in the 1970s.

Henry Hunt & Son Ltd. - D7

Registered at 21a, Maud Street just off North Hill Street in The Dingle was Henry Hunt & Son Ltd., manufacturers of gymnastic

Ringo's birthplace: 9, Madryn Street

apparatus and Ritchie Starkey's place of employment. It was a five-minute walk from his home at Admiral Grove. The building has since been demolished.

The main buildings were on Windsor Street, taking up the addresses at numbers 85, 87, 89, 91 and 93. It was a good apprenticeship and the place where Ringo and his next-door neighbour Eddie Miles formed the Eddie Clayton Skiffle Group. When Ringo decided to turn professional with Rory Storm, his family and girlfriend told him not to turn his back on a good career, but he didn't listen to the advice, and never returned to the factory.

These buildings were demolished years ago.

9, Madryn Street - D8

Richard Starkey was born on 7 July 1940 in the front bedroom of 9, Madryn Street. He was delivered by forceps, weighing in at 10 lbs.

This working class house was typical of thousands of similar homes built in Victorian Liverpool at the end of the 19th Century. The houses were larger than Admiral Grove where Ringo grew up, but still had no bathroom or toilet inside. Occupants used the outhouse at the bottom of the concrete yard behind the house.

After his parents split up, little Richard's grandparents, who lived at 59, Madryn Street, spent a lot of time babysitting the toddler. He was soon nicknamed 'Ritchie' to distinguish him from his father, after whom he was named.

10, Madryn Street - D8

Across the road at number 10 was the home of Ringo's childhood friend, Marie Maguire. Her mum Annie was Elsie Starkey's best friend. The Maguire family moved into this house in June 1943.

21, Madryn Street - D8

Home of Nancy Starkey, Ringo's paternal aunt, while he was growing up in Madryn Street and Admiral Grove.

59, Madryn Street - D8

Home of John and Annie Starkey, Ringo's paternal grandparents, and where Ringo's father moved to when he left the family home of 9, Madryn Street.

The Mandolin Club

The Beatles spent many hours at The Mandolin Club before and after lunchtime Cavern sessions. It was here that Paul McCartney rather tactlessly showed Pete Best how he wanted him to play the drums. The club was a converted cinema in Smithdown Lane. This has since been demolished.

The New Cabaret Artistes Club - D20

Allan Williams booked The Silver Beetles at his and Lord Woodbine's strip club at 174a, Upper Parliament Street. It was an old cotton merchant's house, with big white pillars and black railings. Williams had auditioned a well-proportioned stripper named Janice from Manchester, who demanded live music, unlike the other strippers who performed to a record player. Williams agreed because he knew she would be good for business, and so he convinced the lads to play there, even though they were against the idea. They backed Janice on a stage that was seven feet square, and in return they received 50p a man per night for a week. As they were drummer-less, Paul played drums that week. Janice fancied young George—though she was warned off. The punters often complained about The Silver Beetles because they couldn't concentrate on Janice. The building has since been demolished.

New Colony Club

Situated at 80, Berkley Street, this was run by the famous Lord Woodbine (Harold Phillips). The Beatles made a couple of appearances here in 1960. They liked the club and often hung out when they had nothing to do. It has since been demolished.

It was at one of Lord Woodbine's clubs that Pete Best's brother Rory had a memorable encounter. "The Beatles were playing there and I knocked on the door. Many of these clubs were in Toxteth and were mainly for the local African and Caribbean population. A little flap in the door opened and out popped a big black face. 'Are you colour prejudiced?' came the voice. I said 'No', expecting to be let in. But he just said, 'Well we are' and slammed it shut on me. I then had to explain that I was with The Beatles and they let me in".

The Pavilion Theatre, Lodge Lane

Pavilion Theatre, Lodge Lane - D9

The 'Pivvy' has seen many famous music hall and variety acts in its time, and even a young Julia Lennon appeared there in a dance troupe. Before becoming The Quarrymen, the group was briefly called The Black Jacks, and they appeared in a skiffle contest in late 1956. The judges ensured that they didn't even finish their rendition of "Maggie May" and so after this failure they changed their name. They made a couple of appearances at the Pavilion as The Quarrymen in skiffle contests during 1957. The Beatles played at the Pavilion Theatre on the evening of 2 April 1962 when they appeared with the Royal Waterford Showband from Ireland.

Peel Hall - D10

The Eddie Clayton Skiffle Group with Ringo on the drums made its debut at Peel Hall as did another Dingle lad, Gerry Marsden, with

Ticket for The Beatles appearance at the Pavilion Theatre, Lodge Lane

The rebuilt Rialto, bottom left, with the dome, at the end of Berkley Street

his skiffle group. Gerry later formed Gerry and The Pacemakers, and was also managed by Brian Epstein. He achieved a feat greater than The Beatles, when his first three records went to No. 1 in the charts.

Gerry is still a legend among Liverpool Football Club fans, who sing his hit, "You'll Never Walk Alone", before each football match.

Peel Hall, on the corner of Peel Street and Park Road, was the local Orange Lodge (Protestant Order) Hall where Ringo was a member of the accordion band. He remembers playing a tin drum during one Orange Day parade when the 'lodge' marched around the area, something they still do to this day.

Princes Park - D11

At the heart of Toxteth is Princes Park, created from King John's hunting ground. This was a destination point for Ritchie and his mates when they 'sagged-off' school.

'Prinny' Park was an ideal place to play. There was a long track down the outside, which was perfect for a hand built go-kart, as was the great 'roly-poly' hill at the bottom near Ullet Road.

Rialto Ballroom - D12

On the corner of Berkley Street and Upper Parliament Street, The Quarrymen played in a couple of skiffle contests at this popular ballroom and dance hall. On 6 September 1962, during a Sam Leach promotion, Epstein was worried about the threat of violence at this inner-city venue. Leach promised them bodyguards, but Epstein wasn't satisfied, and he asked them to pull out, but John and Paul sided with Leach. Epstein felt humiliated, and he decided he had to break The Beatles' loyalty to Leach and eventually squeezed him out financially. The original Rialto was burned down in the Toxteth riots of 1981.

The Quarrymen performing in Rosebery Street on 22 June 1957:
Colin, Len, Eric, Rod, John and Pete

Rosebery Street - D13

Rosebery Street was the site of one of the first proper gigs for The Quarrymen where they played from the back of a lorry at a street party on Saturday 22 June 1957. The gig was arranged through Colin Hanton's friend Charles Roberts. Julia Baird remembers them calling themselves Johnny and the Rainbows because they sported different coloured shirts. It was also here that John's poor eyesight meant he was staring hard to see who was standing in front of him. This glare was misunderstood for aggression. Word went round that the lads in the crowd were going to 'get Lennon'. As soon as they had finished playing, the boys dived into their friend's house and called the police, who escorted them to safety.

St. Silas Church - D14

St. Silas Church, situated on the corner of Admiral Street and High Park Street, was built in 1864. As a boy, Alf Lennon and his sister and brothers were christened here and then sent to Sunday School.

Ringo's parents were married at the church in 1936 and Ritchie was christened here in July 1940 and attended Sunday School from the age of four. He was also a member of the church choir. The church suffered bomb damage during October 1940—when Ritchie was three months old—and was closed until December 1942.

St. Silas Church, where Ringo was christened in 1940

It was finally closed in 1952 and demolished in 1954. Years later Ringo made a generous donation to the church of 'St. Philemon with St. Silas'—after the two parishes were combined—towards a minibus for the older members. St. Silas was the church affiliated with Peel Hall Orange Lodge, and was where they would hold their services.

St. Silas School - D14

Ringo's primary school was St. Silas School on High Park Street—just 200 yards from the top of Admiral Grove. Ringo was five when he started here in 1945, though his schooling was disrupted by illness. St. Silas was erected in 1870. It was a red Victorian building, one of the National Schools, erected by the Church of England to teach children reading, writing, arithmetic and religion.

St. Silas School, before it was demolished in the 1970s

A fellow classmate of his was Ronnie Wycherley, who later achieved fame as Billy Fury. He had many hit records and it was for the chance to back Billy Fury that The Silver Beatles auditioned at the Wyvern Club. Their playing didn't impress Larry Parnes enough, and so they ended up backing Johnny Gentle instead.

Having missed a whole school year through illness, Ritchie fell behind. He was considered almost illiterate and was taught with the children in the year below. This wasn't enough and his mum asked her neighbour's daughter, Marie Maguire, to come in a couple of times a week to help with his reading and writing.

Starline Club, Windsor Street - D15

The Starline Club was a former cinema that stood behind the pub on the corner of Windsor Street with Warwick Street. It was a popular rehearsal hall for The Beatles back in 1961, but it has since been demolished.

Steble Street Baths – D16

Opened in 1874, Steble Street Baths was one of Liverpool's many public bath-houses that helped stem the number of deaths from cholera and other diseases associated with a lack of cleanliness. There was also a wash-house for boiling and cleaning clothes. Most homes in The Dingle had running water and an outside toilet, but no bath. The usual routine was for the families to visit a public bath-house. Vera Dowbiggin was a Bathroom Attendant at Steble Street, and she remembers how the patrons would pay 6d for a bath, plus a piece of soap and hire of a Liverpool Corporation towel, having paid a deposit. For this they would get a hot bath in one of several private bathrooms.

Ringo pictured in 1963 in the NEMS offices in Liverpool

Steble Street Baths

Sefton Park where Julia Stanley met Alf Lennon

Aigburth

Aigburth is named after the Anglo-Saxon for "place of the oaks". It is estimated that the Anglo-Saxons were here around 1,500 years ago, and that there was possibly a village near the River Osklesbrook that runs through what is now Sefton Park.

Much of the area of Aigburth and Garston was owned originally by the monks of Whalley Abbey, who gave local tenants the right to farm the land. The monks also had a farm here. There is still a Monksferry Road, marking the place where the ferries of the 12th Century monks would come ashore. Follow the map on page 282 for directions.

37, Aigburth Drive, where the Sutcliffe family lived

37, Aigburth Drive - DA1
Stuart Sutcliffe's family lived in Ullet Road, on the other side of Sefton Park, before moving to Aigburth Drive. The home is near the gates of Sefton Park by the lake and is now called the Blenheim Lakeside Hotel.

Sefton Park - DA2
When you walk through Princes Park, you'll immediately cross into Sefton Park. In 1928, fifteen-year-old Alf Lennon met a fourteen-year-old Julia Stanley in Sefton Park. Alf amused her and a romance ensued. They spent many hours walking here.

There was a big bandstand in the middle of the park, and Paul was taken there by his dad to watch the brass bands.

Starr Fields - DA3
Visited by Ringo in January 2008, Starr Fields has been created for the community and his former school, Dingle Vale Secondary Modern, which was renamed Shorefields. There are all-weather sports pitches and a new community hall.

Stella Lovell School of Dance
Roy Trafford dragged his mate Ritchie along to this dance school at 14a, Linnet Lane, just off Lark Lane. (In an interview, Trafford recalled the name as Skellen's, not Stella's). The school advertised in the local press for its "Rock and Roll Classes" which must have attracted the boys. Ritchie was a surprisingly accomplished dancer, a skill he shared with his parents who took their dancing seriously. The building has gone, and has been replaced by flats.

St. Charles Catholic Church - DA4
It was at St. Charles Church on Aigburth Road that Paul's maternal grandparents, Owen Mohin and Mary Teresa Danher, were married. Owen came to Liverpool from Ireland, via Glasgow.

Wellesley School, 11, Aigburth Road - DA5
When Brian Epstein was expelled from Liverpool College, he was moved on to Wellesley School, in Aigburth. It was a private fee-paying school in a grand old Georgian house and the Head Mistress was Miss E. M. Beresford. It was 200 yards from Dingle Vale Secondary Modern, where Ringo attended. These were the two extremes of education then, yet neither Epstein nor Ringo achieved any school qualifications.

The former site of Wellesley School, Aigburth Road, where Brian Epstein attended

South Liverpool and Suburbs

Belle Vale, Netherley and Childwall: Huyton and Croxteth:
West Derby: Kensington: Garston: Speke

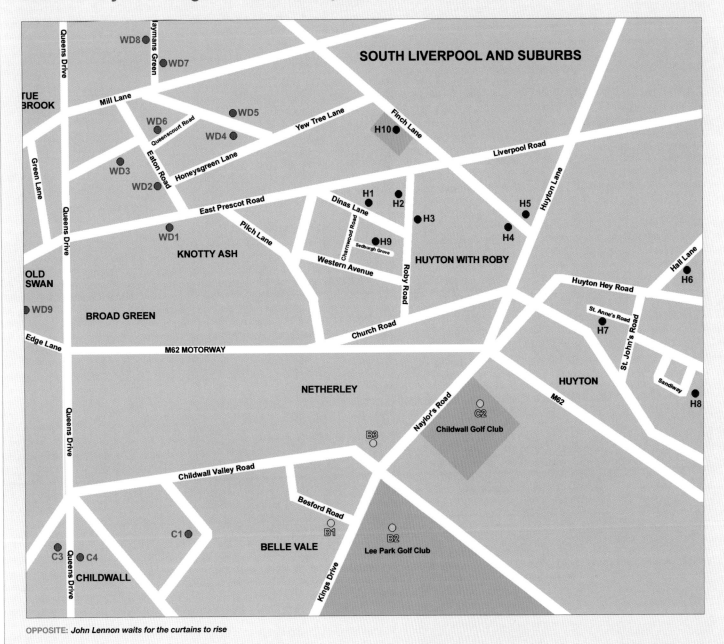

OPPOSITE: *John Lennon waits for the curtains to rise*

Belle Vale, Netherley and Childwall

"The Long And Winding Road"

Belle Vale and Netherley

- *Belle Vale Primary School* - **B1**
- *Joseph Williams School, Netherley* - **B2**
- *Lee Park Golf Club* - **B3**

Childwall

- *Childwall Abbey pub* - **C1**
- *Childwall Golf Club* - **C2**
- *Graham Spencer Studio, Queens Drive* - **C3**
- *197, Queens Drive* - **C4**

Belle Vale and Netherley

Belle Vale and Netherley are small suburbs on the edge of Woolton and Childwall. Previously farmland, Belle Vale sprang out of the little hamlet of Belle Vale Hall, which was swallowed up in the 1950s when the new housing estate of Lee Park was created. Belle Vale and Netherley were established to ease some of the post-war housing crisis that later became areas of unemployment and poverty.

Belle Vale Primary School

Netherley was home to the Joseph Williams School where Paul and his brother Mike attended. They rode their bicycles through Woolton, Belle Vale and Netherley to visit their Auntie Jin, Jim McCartney's sister, who lived in Huyton.

Belle Vale Primary School - B1

Quarrymen guitarist Eric Griffiths briefly attended this primary school.

Joseph Williams School, Netherley - B2

Paul and his brother Mike were moved from Stockton Wood Primary School in Speke to Joseph Williams School, which was a long bus ride away. It was here that Paul took his eleven-plus exam which enabled him to move on to the Liverpool Institute, one of only a few pupils to progress to a grammar school. Paul appeared in a school play here about pirates called *Fatty Fred Protheroe*.

Joseph Williams School, Netherley, which Paul McCartney attended

Lee Park Golf Club

Lee Park Golf Club - B3

This was the venue for The Quarrymen's first engagement. Although they did not receive a fee, they did enjoy a buffet meal in lieu of payment.

Childwall

Childwall first appeared in William the Conqueror's 11th Century Domesday Book as 'Cildeuuelle'. The name was derived from the Norse 'Kelda Vollr' which means 'Spring Field'. The area enjoyed a reputation for its pure water and natural wells.

Childwall Abbey pub - C1

On the hill overlooking Childwall, Gateacre and Netherley and beyond, this was one of John Lennon's favourite drinking establishments in the suburbs.

Childwall Golf Club - C3

Nigel Walley arranged this gig for The Quarrymen in 1957, when they were trying to get themselves established. The local Labour Club was said to be one of many local shows they did, though no date has ever been established.

ABOVE: *Epstein's Artists, from left to right: The Beatles: John Lennon, Ringo Starr, George Harrison and Paul McCartney. Gerry and The Pacemakers: Gerry Marsden, Freddy Marsden, Les Chadwick and Les McGuire. Billy J Kramer and the Dakotas: Robin McDonald, Mike Mansfield, Billy J. Kramer, Ray Jones and Tony Mansfield, with Brian Epstein seated*

Graham Spencer's Photo Studio, Queens Drive - C2

In 1963, just a few hundred yards from Epstein's house on Queens Drive, sat Graham Spencer's photo studio. Epstein engaged Spencer for a photo session with his stable of stars.

197, Queens Drive - C4

When Harry Epstein married Malka Hyman in 1933, her parents gave them this house at 197, Queen's Drive. This was their wedding present. Because of the anti-Semitism that was sweeping across Europe in the 1930s, many Jews had anglicised their names. Malka, which means 'Queen' in Hebrew, decided that she would now be called 'Queenie'. Epstein held meetings here with The Beatles about their bookings and his plans for the group. The Epstein family also held a cocktail party for Paul's 21st birthday.

197, Queens Drive, the Epstein's home from 1933

Huyton and Croxteth

"This Boy"

Huyton

On the outskirts of Liverpool heading east towards Manchester is Huyton, which was a tough suburb in the 1960s. It was where Stuart Sutcliffe grew up before he drifted into Liverpool for study at the Liverpool Art College, and it is also his final resting-place. Map references are shown on page 291

- Air Training Corps, Huyton
- 147, Dinas Lane - **H1**
- Hambleton Hall
- Huyton Parish Cemetery - **H4**
- Huyton Parish Church - **H5**
- Park View Primary School - **H2**
- Prescot Cables Social Club

- Prescot Grammar School
- 22, Sandiway - **H8**
- 17, Sedbergh Grove - **H9**
- St. Aloysius Church - **H3**
- 43, St. Anne's Road - **H7**
- St. Gabriel's Church - **H6**
- Yew Tree Cemetery - **H10**

Croxteth

A suburb near Huyton and West Derby, on the outskirts of Liverpool.

- Mossway Hall, Croxteth

Huyton

Air Training Corps, Huyton
Stuart joined the Air Training Corps in Huyton Village.

147, Dinas Lane - H1
147, Dinas Lane in Huyton was the home of Paul's Auntie Jin. She was close to Paul and Mike and took an active role in raising the boys after their mum had died. The decision was made that they shouldn't attend Mary McCartney's funeral, and so they were sent to Auntie Jin's house.

Jim McCartney took bike rides into the country with his two sons, and sometimes rode through Woolton and Netherley to Huyton to visit Auntie Jin.

The home was also where Cavern DJ Bob Wooler had the infamous fight with John Lennon at Paul's twenty-first birthday party on 18 June 1963.

Hambleton Hall
The Beatles appeared at Hambleton Hall fifteen times from 1961 onwards. The hall has since been demolished.

Pete Best's brother Rory recalled a memorable incident. After The Beatles had finished playing, it was decided to leave as quickly as possible because of its reputation as a rough area. Gigs often ended in fights or all-out brawls. That night, Rory and Neil Aspinall had just finished loading the antiquated van that they used for transporting their gear, when, for no apparent reason, the lads drew the anger of a local gang. Unfortunately, the van was unreliable and even had a crank handle attached to the engine in case the ignition would not turn over. On this particular night, that

Huyton Parish Church, where Stuart is buried in the church's cemetery

is just what happened. Neil continually cranked the handle as the gang drew closer. Rory recalled Neil was able to start the engine in the nick of time, and the gang banged on the sides of the van as they drove away; it was close.

Huyton Parish Cemetery - H4
Stuart's funeral was a small affair and he was buried here in grave 552. The Beatles had just commenced their run at the Star Club in Hamburg and were unable to attend. Stuart's father, Charles, was on his ship bound for Buenos Aires, Argentina, and could not make it back in time. Rod Murray and Stuart's other friends from art college were present as well as George's mother, Louise Harrison.

Park View Primary School

Huyton Parish Church - H5
After the funeral service, Stuart Sutcliffe was buried in the cemetery opposite Huyton Parish Church.

Park View Primary School - H2
Stuart Sutcliffe's primary school was Park View in Huyton, not far from his Sedberg Grove home.

Prescot Cables Social Club
The Quarrymen appeared here in 1959. They were one of many music groups who were booked at this social club.

Prescot Cables Social Club

Prescot Grammar School
Stuart moved to Prescot Grammar School at the age of eleven. He was very mature and did well at school, especially art.

Prescot Grammar School

22, Sandiway - H8
The Sutcliffe family moved here in 1953.

17, Sedbergh Grove - H9
When Stuart's family first moved from Edinburgh, they set up home at Sedbergh Grove in Huyton. Stuart's sister Pauline was born here in 1944. The original houses have been demolished and replaced with new homes.

22, Sandiway

St. Aloysius Church, Huyton - H3
No strangers to Huyton, The Quarrymen appeared at the church's Youth Club in September 1957.

St. Aloysius Church, one of many music venues that The Quarrymen played

43, St. Anne's Road

43, St. Anne's Road - H7
Stuart's family moved to this address in Huyton in 1950.

St. Gabriel's Church - H6
Stuart's family attended St. Gabriel's Church in Huyton Quarry, where nine-year-old Stuart joined the choir. Stuart was the head chorister and sang at three services every Sunday, at weddings and other special occasions. He was also confirmed there into the Church of England. Stuart died in Hamburg, aged twenty-one on 10 April 1962 and his funeral service was held here.

Yew Tree Cemetery, the resting-place of Mary McCartney, with no gravestone, between the front two graves

Yew Tree Cemetery - H10
Yew Tree Cemetery is the final resting place of Paul McCartney's mother, Mary, who died on 31 October 1956. She was buried on 3 November in grave 276, section 3a.

Croxteth

Mossway Hall, Croxteth
The Beatles only appearance in Croxteth took place in Mossway Hall on St. Patrick's Day, 17 March 1961. The venue has since been demolished. The gig didn't earn them any wages, but they could drink as much Guinness as they could manage. Only in Liverpool.

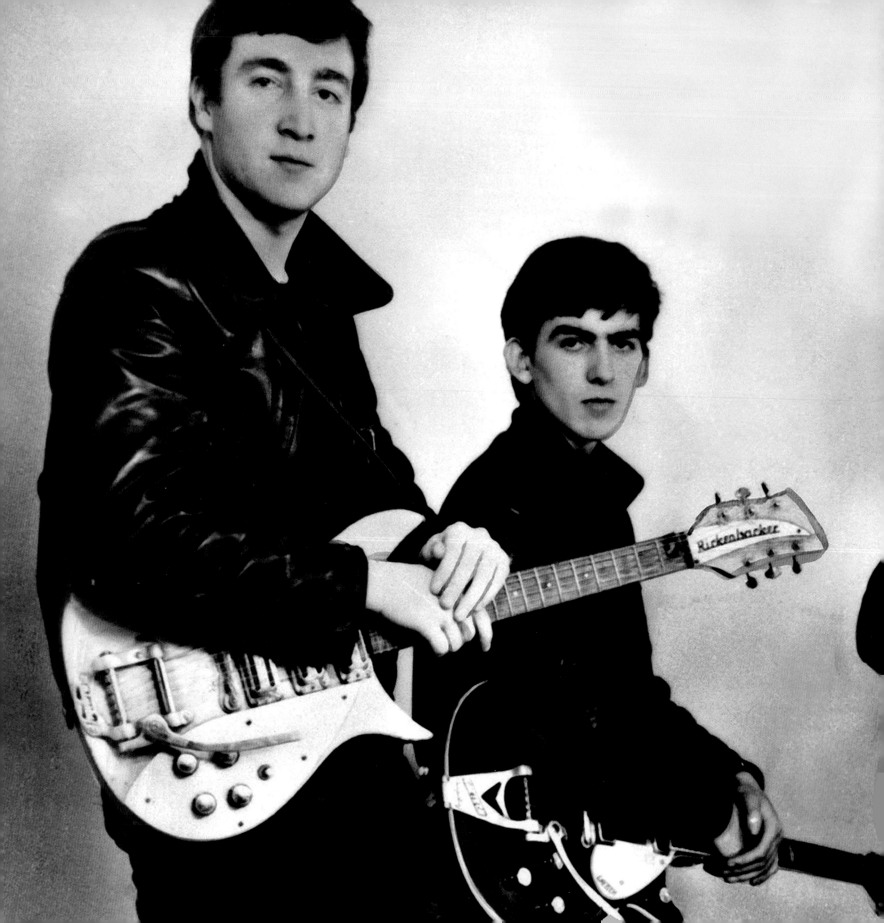

West Derby

"Eight Days A Week"

West Derby

West Derby has been a township for many centuries and was mainly farmland until the mid-20th Century. It was in West Derby that Mona Best set up The Casbah Coffee Club, which played such an important part in The Beatles' history. Map references for **WD1-WD9** are on page 291 and **WD10-WD12** are on page 302.

- Alder Hey Children's Hospital - **WD2**
- Blackmoor Park Infants and Junior School - **WD4: WD5**
- 54, Broad Green Road - **WD9**
- Casbah Coffee Club - **WD7**

- Ellerslie Manor
- Knotty Ash Village Hall - **WD1**
- Lowlands, Haymans Green - **WD8**
- The Morgue
- Princess Drive

- 17, Queenscourt Road - **WD6**
- St. Edward's College - **WD3**
- St. John's Church Hall, Tue Brook - **WD10**
- Stanley Abattoir, Prescot Road - **WD12**
- Tue Brook Bowling Alley - **WD11**

Casbah
Promotions
PRESENT A

Big Beat Dance

ST. JOHNS HALL . SNAEFELL AVENUE
TUEBROOK   LIVERPOOL
On FRIDAY, 17th FEBRUARY 1961
The BEATLES Rock Combo
GENE DAY & JANGO Beats

ADMISSION 3/6   (Doors Open 7-15 p.m.)
The Management Reserve the Right to Refuse Admission

Alder Hey Children's Hospital, Eaton Road

Alder Hey Children's Hospital - WD2
George Harrison spent six weeks in Alder Hey on a special non-protein diet when he was diagnosed with nephritis, inflamed kidneys. He was forced to eat spinach and other 'horrible' food.

Paul's mother, Mary, began training as a nurse here at the age of only fourteen.

Alder Hey is the largest children's hospital in Europe, caring for more than 200,000 young patients each year from all over the North-West of England, including Cumbria, the Isle of Man, North Wales and Shropshire. Founded in 1914, the hospital has led the way in the care of sick children.

PREVIOUS PAGE: *John, George, Paul and Pete, the "savage young" Beatles, pictured in their leathers in 1961*

Alder Hey depends heavily on charitable funding to provide the things that make a difference. In October 2005, a fund-raising appeal named 'Imagine' was launched with the support of Yoko Ono to coincide with what would have been John Lennon's sixty-fifth birthday. The name was chosen because of its existing global awareness and strong Merseyside links. The 'Imagine' logo is made from a drawing created by John Lennon.

Blackmoor Park Infants and Junior School - WD4: WD5
Pete Best attended this primary school until he was eleven, and successfully passed his eleven-plus exam, graduating to The Collegiate, a grammar school.

54, Broad Green Road - WD9
Paul was a regular visitor here during his courtship with Iris Caldwell. Iris' brother was Alan Caldwell, better known as Rory Storm, and 54, Broad Green Road became known as 'Stormsville'. Paul and John met at the house occasionally to write and play songs. It was here that Rory Storm died on 28 September 1972 after taking a fatal dose of whiskey and pills. The following morning, on finding her son dead, Rory's mother took her own life (she had lost her husband only four months before). It was a sad ending to a colourful entertainer who had eluded stardom.

Blackmoor Park Infants School

Blackmoor Park Junior School

54, Broad Green Road, known as 'Stormsville'

imagine

Living for today, giving for tomorrow

The Alder Hey Imagine Appeal, supported by Yoko Ono

Casbah Coffee Club - WD7 *(see page 119)*

Ellerslie Manor former site

Ellerslie Manor
When Pete Best and his family moved from India, they lived in John Best's palatial family home at Ellerslie Manor in West Derby. It has since been demolished and replaced by St. Paul's School.

Knotty Ash Village Hall

Knotty Ash Village Hall - WD1
Mona Best booked The Beatles for many appearances at this local hall, the first being on 15 September 1961. Promoter Sam Leach booked The Beatles plus Rory Storm and the Hurricanes for a St. Patrick's Night Gala on 17 March 1962 to celebrate his engagement.

Lowlands, Haymans Green - WD8
Lowlands was a community hall in Haymans Green in the same road as The Casbah. The Les Stewart Quartet, which featured Ken Brown, George Harrison, Les Stewart on guitar and Geoff Skinner on drums, played several times at Lowlands.

17, Queenscourt Road

The Morgue
The Morgue was a club that was set up and run by Rory Storm, and was established in the basement of a house in Oak Vale Drive-now demolished. The Quarrymen made a couple of appearances here after it opened on 13 March 1958. The Morgue closed soon after on 22 April, because of unsafe conditions.

St Edward's College

Princess Drive
After leaving Cases Street in Liverpool, the Best family moved to a larger house on Princess Drive, West Derby. Soon after they moved to Queenscourt Road. The house is no longer there.

17, Queenscourt Road - WD6
17, Queenscourt Road was the home of Pete Best's family for a while. Mona Best wanted a bigger house and moved her family to 8, Haymans Green, which became the home of The Casbah Club.

St John's Church Hall, Tue Brook

St. Edward's College - WD3
The Beatles made a Sunday evening appearance at a dance on 8 October 1961. St. Edward's is still one of the leading schools in Liverpool.

St. John's Church Hall, Tue Brook - WD10
St. John's Church Hall hosted the first of eleven shows by The Beatles on 17 February 1961. The shows were often promoted by Mona Best's 'Casbah Promotions'.

Tue Brook Bowling Alley

Stanley Abattoir, Prescot Road - WD12
The Quarrymen appeared here in 1957 at the social club and made such a cacophonous noise that they were never invited back.

Tue Brook Bowling Alley - WD11
Many of the Liverpool bands, including The Beatles, went to the Tue Brook Bowling Alley after a gig. They would often bowl into the small hours of the morning.

Lowlands, Haymans Green, where the Les Stewart Quartet, including George Harrison, played

Kensington

"A Day In The Life"

Kensington is one of the more deprived areas of Liverpool. Regeneration plans have long been discussed, but slow in coming to fruition.

Kensington was home to Percy Phillips, whose home studio became the first to record the fledgling Beatles, better known then as The Quarrymen.

38, Kensington, the site of Percy Phillip's studio

- Beatle Streets - **K1**
- The Collegiate, Shaw Street - **K2**
- 1, Elm Vale - **K3**
- The Grafton Rooms, West Derby Road - **K4**
- 38, Kensington - **K5**
- The Locarno Ballroom, West Derby Road - **K6**

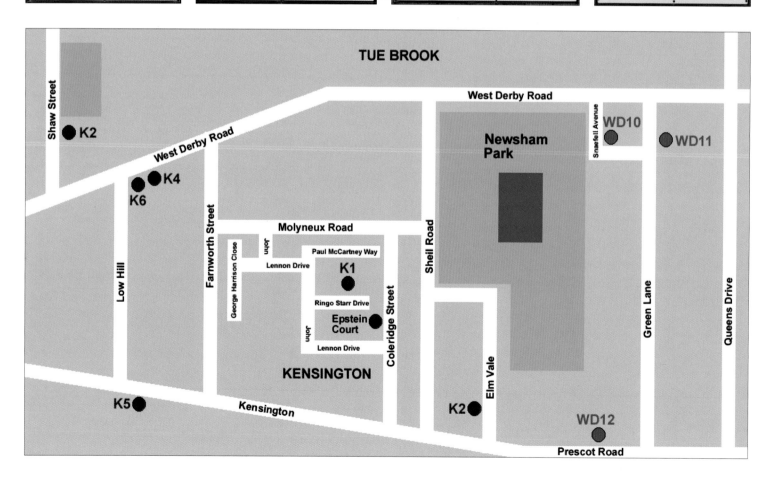

JOHN LENNON DRIVE L6

PAUL MᶜCARTNEY WAY L6

GEORGE HARRISON CLOSE L6

RINGO STARR DRIVE L6

Beatle Streets - K1

In 1981, after campaigning by the Liverpool Beatles Appreciation Society, the city council named these new streets: John Lennon Drive, Paul McCartney Way, George Harrison Close and Ringo Starr Drive. There is also an Epstein Court nearby.

The Collegiate, Shaw Street - K2

The Collegiate, Pete Best's school

Brian Epstein's father had attended The Collegiate, but when Brian was expelled from Liverpool College, his father could hardly approach The Collegiate to admit him—he had to pay for private schools.

Pete Best attended this school from the age of eleven. It was on a par with the Liverpool Institute as one of the best grammar schools in Liverpool. The Black Jacks was the band that Ken Brown formed with Pete's fellow school friends Chas Newby and Bill Barlow, who had formed a skiffle group 'The Barmen' while at school. Pete left here in 1958.

Since then, The Collegiate became a comprehensive school which does not require a test before admission. A fire later destroyed most of the school, and so it has been refurbished as apartments.

1, Elm Vale - K3

Paul's mother, Mary, was so determined that her sons would grow up to become professional people that she sent them to her friend, Mrs. Lewis at 1, Elm Vale in Kensington, Liverpool, for elocution lessons from 1953 to 1955. According to local historian Ray O'Brien, who also attended there, the fact that Mrs. Lewis had an attractive daughter called Heather was just an added incentive. At that time, having a regional accent—especially one as strong as Scouse—was considered a hindrance to a great career. That is why, when you hear Paul speak, he does have a Liverpool accent but it isn't as strong as, for instance, George or Ringo.

The Grafton Rooms

The plaque at 38, Kensington, Percy Phillips' studio, was unveiled in August 2005

The Grafton Rooms, West Derby Road - K4

The Grafton Rooms was one of the biggest dance halls in Liverpool. The Quarrymen entered skiffle contests here in the late 1950s, including one in April 1957.

It was a good night out, according to Colin Hanton. "I used to go there a lot for the dances. They had a strict dress code, and you could only get in if you were a couple, not on your own. So there were no gangs in there, and no spare lads, as you could only go with your girlfriend. They had a big band there and it was a cracking night at The Grafton. But you had to know how to dance".

The Beatles appeared here four times in 1962-63, the last time being on 12 June 1963—an NSPCC charity dance.

38, Kensington - K5

This was the home of Percy Phillips who recorded the Quarrymen here on 14 July 1958.

In August 2005, a plaque was unveiled to commemorate this first recording.

The Locarno Ballroom, West Derby Road - K6

Standing next to The Grafton Rooms, The Quarrymen performed here in skiffle contests in the late 1950s.

The Locarno Ballroom, now The Olympia

It was also where Quarrymen drummer Colin Hanton remembers overhearing a conversation between Paul and John. They had entered one of the many skiffle competitions around the city, but as they went on, Paul noticed the poster, which said it wasn't only for groups, but for male singers too. He mentioned to John that maybe they should consider entering, just the two of them, on their own. John immediately said no, they were a group.

The Beatles made their first appearance here on Valentine's Day, 14 February 1963.

Garston and Speke

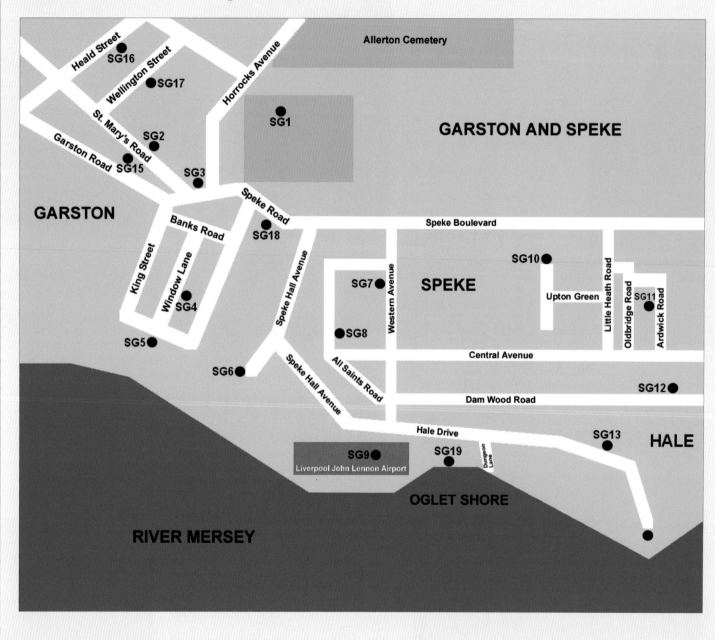

Garston

"What Goes On"

Garston is one of the ancient lost villages of Liverpool along the banks of the Mersey between Speke and Grassendale. The name derives from the Saxon word "Gaerstun", meaning "grazing settlement".

Situated five miles to the south of the City of Liverpool, it had been part of the ancient parish of Childwall. As with many of the rural villages of Liverpool, it changed with the Industrial Revolution. A large dock was built in 1846, and local people not only worked on the docks, but also in new factories. Garston was incorporated into Liverpool in 1902, and a decade later the village was connected to the tramway system.

The post-war economy and industrial decline that affected Liverpool in the 1950s and 1960s was devastating to Garston. Unemployment rocketed as local industries and shipping declined, and by the early 1970s, many of the factories had closed. Unemployment remains high, but the potential for local employment is now much better than it has been for decades.

- *Garston Bottle Works* - **SG5**
- *Garston Job Centre* - **SG3**
- *Garston Stevedores & Dockers Club* - **SG4**
- *Garston Swimming Baths* - **SG2**
- *Riversdale Technical College*
- *St. Mary's School* - **SG1**
- *Wellington pub* - **SG17**
- *Wilson Hall* - **SG15**
- *Winter Gardens* - **SG16**

Garston Bottle Works - SG5
Garston Bottle Works was the place of employment for Tommy Moore, the one-time drummer with The Silver Beatles. He gave the job up to go on a tour of Scotland, with The Silver Beatles backing Johnny Gentle, but went back to his old employment after his girlfriend gave him some earache about getting a proper job.

Garston Job Centre - SG3
After leaving the music scene behind, Pete Best joined the civil service. He eventually became deputy manager at Garston Job Centre, virtually opposite Wilson Hall, the renowned venue in Garston. He was ideally suited to counsel people who were struggling with unemployment, having lost his job with The Beatles on the threshold of stardom.

Garston Stevedores & Dockers Club - SG4
This club was one of the first gigs that George Harrison played with The Quarrymen in June 1958, and that also featured John Duff Lowe, a friend of Paul and George from the Liverpool Institute, who occasionally played piano with them. The original building has since been demolished.

Garston Swimming Baths - SG2
Not much is left of the swimming baths—just the shell, and that

Garston Bottle Works, where drummer Tommy Moore was employed

Garston Job Centre, where Pete Best worked

will be gone soon. This public pool, almost opposite Wilson Hall, would be converted into a dance hall over winter by covering the pool with a wooden dance floor. Bob Wooler famously dubbed it 'The Blood Baths' because of the fights that happened there. These stories became increasingly exaggerated, but it was not quite as bad as some have made out. It has now been demolished.

Riversdale Technical College
Ringo was employed by British Railways and was seconded to the Technical College in Riversdale Road, Grassendale, to complete his formal education before taking up a messenger job with British Railways. The college has since been demolished.

St. Mary's School - SG1
St. Mary's School on Horrocks Avenue was the secondary school that Quarrymen drummer Colin Hanton attended from the age of eleven. It is now St. Benedict's College.

Wellington pub - SG17
The Wellington pub in Garston was one of the places where Ringo's mum Elsie worked to make ends meet.

Wilson Hall - SG15
Paul made his debut appearance with The Quarrymen here, apart from a few unrecorded performances at St. Peter's Church. George Harrison was invited to watch a Quarrymen gig at Wilson Hall on 6 February 1958. Ringo had also appeared here with the Eddie Clayton Skiffle Group. The building is now a carpet warehouse.

Winter Gardens - SG16
The Quarrymen appeared here once in June 1957 at this Co-operative Society-owned hall, tucked away in the back streets of Garston.

TOP LEFT: *Garston Stevedores & Dockers Club*
LEFT: *Winter Gardens, Heald Street, one of the smaller venues played by The Quarrymen*
ABOVE: *Wellington pub, where Elsie Starkey worked behind the bar*
BELOW: *The former St. Mary's School, now St. Benedict's College*

Speke

"Day Tripper"

Speke was laid out by municipal planners between the 1930s and the 1950s. It was a new, self-contained township designed to reduce the housing waiting list. Speke provided homes for both the McCartneys and Harrisons, and Paul once commented that it still looked like a building site with mud everywhere, but was happy to refer to himself as a "scruff from Speke".

The name Speke possibly derives from the Anglo-Saxon word 'Spic', meaning pig. Most likely the land was used for pig farming. For centuries it had been farmland and is still surrounded by woods and farms. Like many parts of modern cities, Speke has struggled with unemployment, poverty and crime. Map references are shown on page 304.

- 12, Ardwick Road - **SG11**
- Bluebell Woods
- British Legion Club, Dam Wood Road - **SG12**
- The Cat pub
- Dam Woods
- Hale Lighthouse, Hale Village - **SG14**
- Hale Village – The Childe of Hale - **SG13**
- Liverpool John Lennon Airport - **SG9**
- Oglet Shore - **SG19**
- Speke Airport - **SG18**
- Speke Hall - **SG6**
- Speke Horticultural Society
- Stockton Wood Primary School - **SG8**
- 25, Upton Green - **SG10**
- 72, Western Avenue - **SG7**

The McCartneys home at 12, Ardwick Road

12, Ardwick Road - SG11
The McCartney family moved from Western Avenue in Speke to the council estate close by at 12, Ardwick Road, in 1950, when Mary became a Health Visitor. The house was very close to George Harrison's home in Upton Green, which enabled them to visit with each other frequently.

Opposite the house in Ardwick Road was a field and what appeared to be a building site. In the corner was a lime pit, which quickly filled with water. The McCartney boys were banned from going into the area by their parents. For kicks one day, they walked the plank across the pit with the obvious result of them falling in. As the water was twice as deep as they were tall, the boys panicked. After grabbing hold of a tree root, they were able to get the attention of a passing workman who fished them out. Jim and Mary McCartney weren't impressed and suitable punishment was meted out.

The McCartneys were the first family on Ardwick Road to purchase a television, and practically the entire neighbourhood watched the coronation of the Queen in 1953 at the McCartney household.

Bluebell Woods
One of the McCartney boys' favourite hangouts was Bluebell Woods. Unfortunately, the site was lost to the Ford Factory in the sixties and is currently producing Jaguars and Land Rovers. Paul and his dog Prince often went into the woods for long walks.

The McCartney boys also stole apples and were caught by the owner, but their dad Jim managed to talk them out of being hauled off to the police station. Another favourite, yet highly dangerous game was called "turnipping". It consisted of standing on the bridge and waiting for the steam train to pass below and attempting to hit the driver with a turnip. They also dropped sticks and bricks and other missiles onto the track.

British Legion Club, Dam Wood Road - SG12
George Harrison formed a group called The Rebels, which included his brother Pete and friend Arthur Kelly. They played one gig at The British Legion Club on Dam Wood Road. The headlining act never turned up and The Rebels covered for them, playing the only two songs they knew. It didn't matter to the audience, who were gracious in their applause.

The Cat pub
It was in a room above this pub where George Harrison and Arthur Kelly received several guitar lessons.

The British Legion Club, Dam Wood Road, where The Rebels played

Hale Beach and Lighthouse

Dam Woods
Paul loved to wander off to the nearby Dam Woods, which were filled with rhododendron bushes. He and his friends made secret dens in the shrubbery.

Hale Lighthouse, Hale Village - SG14
Paul and Mike often cycled the two-mile stretch to Hale Lighthouse where they could see for miles up the River Mersey, or round the bend to Runcorn and Widnes. They also ventured to the beach to swim and play. Paul sometimes went bird watching or hiked on nature trails. He said his love of the outdoors inspired his song "Mother Nature's Son" which he started composing in India in February 1968, and finished a few months later at his father's house in Heswall.

The Childe of Hale's grave

Hale Village - The Childe of Hale - SG13
One of Paul and Mike's favourite stops was in Hale Village where they often visited the grave of the famous Childe of Hale, who was believed to be over nine feet tall. The grave is still there and visited by fascinated schoolchildren.

Liverpool John Lennon Airport

Liverpool John Lennon Airport - SG9
The official renaming of Liverpool Airport was on 2 July 2001, in the presence of Yoko Ono and Cherie Booth, wife of former British Prime Minister, Tony Blair.

Oglet Shore - SG19
George Harrison often visited the shoreline of the River Mersey at Oglet Shore behind what is now Liverpool John Lennon Airport. It was an easy walk or cycle ride to the countryside, and George spent hours walking along the mud cliffs by the sandbanks.

Liverpool honours John Lennon by renaming its airport as 'Liverpool John Lennon Airport'

Liverpool John Lennon Airport media folder for the opening ceremony

Yoko Ono visited Liverpool Airport to announce the renaming and rebranding of the airport, to be called 'Liverpool John Lennon Airport' in honour of her late husband, when its new terminal opened in Spring 2002.

Yoko Ono said; "I was honoured and delighted when I first heard of the proposal to name the airport here in Liverpool after John. As a gateway to the region, this will be seen by millions of passengers and is a fitting tribute to the memory of my late husband. I am proud to be here today to celebrate one of Liverpool's greatest men".

Yoko Ono (left) and Cherie Booth (in red) with children from Dovedale School by the statue of John in Liverpool John Lennon Airport

Sean Lennon, John and Yoko's son, said; "It is a great honour for my dad and for our family. My mom and I are very proud and would like to thank the people of Liverpool for all their warmth and support over the years".

John and Cynthia's son Julian Lennon added the following; "I am happy to see that Liverpool has taken the opportunity to remember one of its most famous citizens in a way that reaches millions of people. It seems that the name 'John Lennon' will be around for a long time. All the best to everybody involved, and I hope everything gets off to a flying start".

Yoko Ono and the former Prime Minister Tony Blair's wife, Cherie Booth QC, unveiled a seven-foot bronze statue of John Lennon, by local sculptor Tom Murphy.

Yoko Ono said: "John would have loved that he is back home in Liverpool".

Yoko at Liverpool John Lennon Airport giving interviews to the press

Oglet Shore, where Paul and George used to walk from their homes in nearby Speke

The original Speke Airport Terminal

Speke Hall, the National Trust property

Paul also frequented Oglet Shore. It was one of the places he and Mike would ride on their bikes. They weren't there to admire the scenery—they looked for coins and jewellery left behind on the beach.

Speke Airport - SG18

As a boy, John Lennon rode his bike to the airport to watch the planes take off and land. John 'Bobby' Dykins, Julia Lennon's partner, worked as the manager at the airport's restaurant. He also managed to secure John a job there.

This is no longer Liverpool's airport since the site has moved a short distance to the edge of Speke. The old airport site is now a hotel, which has won several design awards.

On Friday 10 July 1964, The Beatles returned to a triumphant crowd at Speke Airport where they gave a press conference. That was followed by a drive through the streets of Liverpool flanked by cheering fans to their civic reception at the Liverpool Town Hall.

George Harrison recalled an incident at the airport when The Beatles' plane aborted a take off. As they were taking off again, the emergency door flew off. He was a white-knuckled passenger and hated flying, and this incident did nothing to help.

Speke Hall - SG6

One of Paul and Mike's favourite trips was to the grounds of Speke Hall, which led down to the Mersey where they would go skinny-dipping. Speke Hall is still a very popular tourist attraction and is owned and run by the National Trust. The tours of Mendips and Forthlin Road are run from here.

Speke Horticultural Society

Jim McCartney was a keen gardener and ran the Speke Horticultural Society. He sent young Paul and Mike out to find and collect horse manure for his garden. He also used their help to knock on doors in Western Avenue to recruit new members.

Stockton Wood Primary School - SG8

Built on the new Speke Estate, Stockton Wood Primary School was opened in 1940. Just a short walk from the McCartney's home on Western Avenue, Paul was enrolled into the primary school. However, once the number of pupils reached the 1500, mark, he and many others were moved to Joseph Williams School in Netherley.

The Harrisons lived in 25, Upton Green

The old school was finally demolished in 2005 with a new school building erected on the site of the original playing fields.

25, Upton Green - SG10

The Harrisons moved here from Arnold Grove in January 1950. Instead of the two-up, two-down terraced house of Arnold Grove, Upton Green was not only new, but also much bigger. George had a twenty-minute walk from Upton Green to the bus stop, which was close to Paul's house on Western Avenue, and they became friends, riding on the same bus to school. George's mum was always keen to encourage her son's musical talent. George and Paul often played Lonnie Donegan songs together in the house, and later John and Paul would often call round to practise.

George remembered that the first time he heard "Love Me Do" on Radio Luxembourg, he was in his bedroom at Upton Green. He described it as the best buzz of all time.

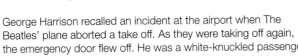

72, Western Avenue, one of two homes in Speke where the McCartneys lived

72, Western Avenue - SG7

The McCartney family moved to this two-bedroom house on Western Avenue when Paul was four, and lived here from 1947 to 1950. They had to move to Ardwick Road when Mary resigned as a midwife.

Stockton Wood Primary School, where Paul and Mike McCartney briefly attended

North Liverpool and Suburbs

Bootle, Crosby, Seaforth and Litherland
Walton, Aintree, Maghull, Everton, Fazakerley and Norris Green

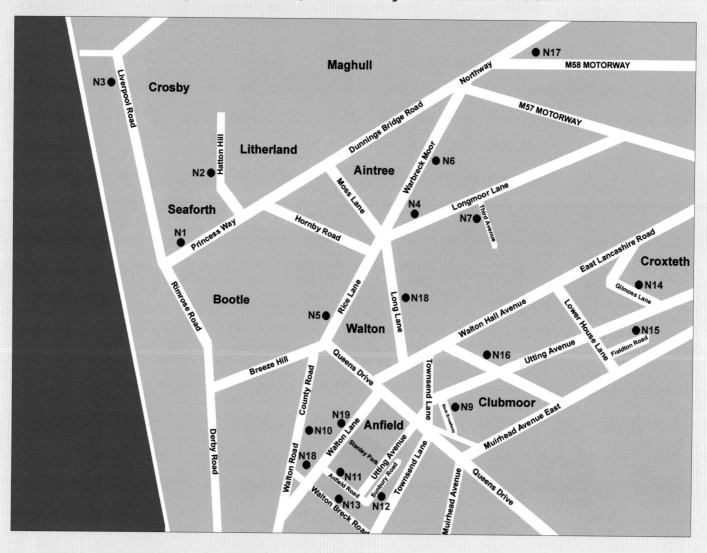

Bootle, Crosby, Seaforth and Litherland
"Yeah, Yeah, Yeah".

Positioned to the north of Liverpool, Bootle was originally called 'Boltelai'. The word came from the Anglo-Saxon 'botl', which means an important settlement or building. Under this name it appeared in the Domesday Book of 1086. Bootle was originally a fishing village and seaside resort, though hard to imagine now. Bootle has changed over the last 150 years, particularly after the dock system expanded this far north.

With the Allies being so reliant on the docks, Bootle became a major target for the Luftwaffe in World War II. In 1939, the population of Bootle was 80,000 people. Within a few years, this was reduced to about 30,000, and it was thought only about 10,000 people stayed in their homes overnight, during the blitz. Bootle lost more than 2,000 houses during the war and only about three dozen houses remained intact.

Scousers have often referred to Bootle as 'Brutal Bootle, where the bugs wear clogs'. One of the better-known Bootle-bucks is Allan Williams, The Beatles' first manager.

Just up the coast from Bootle docks is the suburb of Crosby, situated between Liverpool and Southport. Adjacent to Bootle are the districts of Seaforth and Litherland.

- *Alexandra Hall, Crosby*
- *Ashley Du Pré Hairdressers, Bootle*
- *Lathom Hall, Seaforth* - **N1**
- *Litherland Town Hall, Litherland* - **N2**
- *St. John's Hall, Bootle*
- *St. Luke's Hall, Crosby* - **N3**

A view from Everton over Bootle and Seaforth

Alexandra Hall, Crosby

Alexandra Hall, Crosby
In the heart of Crosby sat Alexandra Hall, which hosted many bands in its day. The Beatles only appeared there once on 19 January 1961. It has since been demolished.

Ashley Du Pré Hairdressers, Bootle
Ringo Starr's girlfriend Maureen Cox (and later his wife) worked as a junior hairdressing assistant at the Ashley Du Pré Beauty Parlour. She was on her way to an evening class when she spotted Ringo getting out of his car and asked for his autograph.

Lathom Hall, Seaforth - N1
This one-time cinema became famous for the advertised gig by The Silver Beats, the only time they used this title for the group. They appeared here on 14 May 1960 under that title with Cliff Roberts on the drums. They were booked to perform again on 21 May 1960, but they did not appear as they were in Scotland on the Johnny Gentle Tour. They later returned as The Beatles ten times.

On one occasion, Stuart was jumped by a gang of thugs. When Pete Best and John Lennon were told about the incident, they quickly ran to Stu's rescue. He had taken quite a battering. John broke a finger in the fight, which resulted in him wearing a splint for a short while.

The hall has been renovated inside and has a nostalgic feel to it.

The renovated stage area in Lathom Hall, where The Beatles appeared ten times

Litherland Town Hall, Litherland - N2
After The Beatles had returned from Hamburg in 1960, they had no immediate gigs lined up. Bob Wooler bumped into Pete and John in Liverpool's Jacaranda and they told Wooler of their adventures in Germany. Bob arranged with Brian Kelly to give them thirty minutes at the Litherland Town Hall concert, between The Del Renas and The Searchers.

Situated in Hatton Hill, Litherland, the famous billing as 'The Beatles direct from Hamburg' made some people think they were a German band. The group was starting to establish their reputation in Liverpool, and weren't known in the northern

Litherland Town Hall, now a health centre

part of the city. On 27 December 1960, Litherland Town Hall saw the birth of a phenomenon later known as Beatlemania. John, Paul, George, Pete Best and Chas Newby were sensational.

On a future gig on 5 January 1961, Paul played bass with The Beatles for the first time while Stuart had remained in Hamburg.

On 19 October 1961, The Beatles and Gerry and The Pacemakers joined forces with Karl Terry at Litherland Town Hall to perform as the Beatmakers. The all-star lineup included George on lead guitar, Paul was on rhythm and the drumming duties were split between Pete Best and Freddie Marsden. Les Chadwick played bass guitar, John Lennon played piano with

Karl Terry joining in the singing. Finally, Gerry Marsden played guitar and sang, with Les Maguire on the saxophone.

Litherland Town Hall is now a health centre.

St. John's Hall, Bootle
The Beatles made five appearances here, the first on 6 January 1961. The hall sat opposite Bootle Town Hall on Oriel Road. It has since been demolished.

St. Luke's Hall, Crosby - N3
The Quarrymen appeared here once in November 1957 at St. Luke's Youth Club, opposite the church. Ringo also appeared here with The Eddie Clayton Skiffle Group. It was a popular venue for the Liverpool bands.

After The Beatles had played here at Lathom Hall, above, Stuart Sutcliffe was beaten up in a fight

Walton, Aintree, Maghull, Everton, Fazakerley and Norris Green

"Let It Be"

Aintree Institute

Walton

Walton is the oldest village in what is now the City of Liverpool. It was 600 to 800 years old by the time the Domesday Book of the 11th Century was published.

Aintree

Aintree is next to Walton and has a history dating back to the 5th Century Anglo-Saxons. However, Aintree is now known the world over for its Grand National horse race. Horse racing started here back in the 17th Century. Aintree also hosted Grand Prix racing, one of George's interests. Map references are shown on page 312.

- Aintree Institute - **N4**
- Aintree Racecourse - **N6**
- Albany Cinema, North Way, Maghull - **N17**
- 27, Anfield Road - **N11**
- Blair Hall, Walton - **N10**
- 58, Fieldton Road - **N15**
- I. Epstein & Sons, Walton - **N18**
- Jewish Cemetery, Aintree - **N8**
- Liverpool Football Club, Anfield - **N13**
- D Napier & Son
- NEMS, Walton Road - **N10**
- New Clubmoor Hall, Back Broadway - **N9**
- Pavilion Theatre, Aintree
- Roach Avenue, Knowsley
- 11, Scargreen Avenue - **N16**
- St. Swithin's Roman Catholic Church - **N14**
- Sir Thomas White Gardens, Everton
- 10, Sunbury Road, Anfield - **N12**
- 2, Third Avenue - **N7**
- Walton Hospital - **N5**

Aintree Institute - N4

The Beatles first appeared here on 7 January 1961 and made approximately thirty more appearances that same year. Aintree Institute was a popular jive club. It was demolished in 2007.

Aintree Racecourse - N6

George loved to visit Aintree, home of the Grand National horse race. He took his box camera there in 1955 to watch the Grand Prix motor racing. Paul bought his dad a horse for his sixty-second birthday on 7 July 1964. It was named Drakes Drum and won the pre-Grand National race here at Aintree. Jim enjoyed betting on the horses.

Albany Cinema, North Way, Maghull - N17

Just outside Aintree is the small town of Maghull. On 15 October 1961, The Beatles made their only appearance here with comedian Ken Dodd, who was the headlining act. After their first of two appearances that night, Dodd made negative remarks towards The Beatles and demanded they be stopped from returning to the stage. The night was a disaster and it was The Beatles first and last appearance at the cinema. The building has been replaced by a supermarket.

Racing car at Aintree, where George Harrison watched the Grand Prix

27, Anfield Road, now Epstein's Guest House

27, Anfield Road - N11

This was the home of Isaac and Dinah Epstein, Brian's grandparents. Brian often visited the home. It is now Epstein's Guest House, a bed and breakfast.

Blair Hall, Walton - N10

The Beatles played five times in 1961. They played for a fee of £12 and asked to be bumped up to £15, but promoter Bob Wooler didn't think they were worth it. He didn't book them there again. The building has since been demolished.

Everton Football Club - N18

Founded in 1878, the "Toffees" are the bitter rivals of Liverpool Football Club, and are separated only by Stanley Park. Jim McCartney took Paul and Mike to games at both stadiums. Paul's support was directed towards Everton, while Mike followed Liverpool.

58, Fieldton Road - N15

This home in Norris Green is where Jim McCartney, Paul's father, was living when he met his future wife, Mary.

I. Epstein & Sons, Walton - N1

This was the furniture business founded by Brian Epstein's grandfather, Isaac. Brian joined the family business on 10 September 1950 at age 15. The family bought the small music shop next door, which was called the 'North End Music Store' (known as NEMS). Jim McCartney purchased a piano from NEMS, which sat in the front room of Forthlin Road, and was used by Paul to learn on.

Jewish Cemetery, Aintree, where Harry and 'Queenie' Epstein were buried

Jewish Cemetery, Aintree - N8

After his funeral service on 27 August 1967, Brian Epstein's body was taken to the Jewish Cemetery at Long Lane, Aintree. He was buried in grave H12, Section A. Brian's parents and brother are also buried there.

Also buried here, near to Brian's grave, is Dr. Joseph Sytner, through whom Nigel Walley secured The Quarrymen's first appearance at The Cavern. The famous club was run by Dr. Sytner's son, Alan.

Liverpool Football Club, Anfield - N13

John Lennon's support of Liverpool Football Club was demonstrated when Liverpool footballer Albert Stubbins appeared on the sleeve of the *Sgt. Pepper* album. When John was with Alistair Taylor in an airport in Dublin, he talked to Manchester United fans and lobbied hard for them to support Liverpool.

D. Napier & Son

As part of the war effort, Jim McCartney's job at the cotton broker was put on hold. He went to work in Napier's aircraft factory during the day and as a firewatcher at night. Napier's factory was located on the East Lancs Road and, classed as part of the Royal Air Force, they made aircraft engines.

NEMS, Walton Road - N10

By the time Epstein took over management of The Beatles, NEMS was the largest record retailer in the North-West of England. They had stores at Whitechapel and Great Charlotte Street in Liverpool city centre; 44, Allerton Road, Allerton; 90, County Road, Walton; 2, Marian Square, Netherton; 37, St. Mary's Road, Garston; 25, High Street, Runcorn; 6, Central Way, Maghull and the original NEMS store at 62–72, Walton Road. Epstein soon opened another City Centre store at 24, Moorfields.

Napier's factory in the distance on the left. On the right, the pre-fab houses, near where the McCartneys lived in Knowsley

New Clubmoor Hall on Back Broadway, where Paul McCartney made his debut with The Quarrymen

New Clubmoor Hall, Back Broadway - N9

Paul McCartney probably made his official, paid debut with The Quarrymen here on 18 October 1957. It was a booking arranged by Nigel Walley via promoter Charlie McBain. It is famous because Paul tried a lead guitar solo on "Guitar Boogie", which he fluffed. Part way through John stopped the song and told the audience; "He's our new boy—he'll be all right given time". The audience laughed and John rescued Paul from an awkward embarrassment.

Generally when performing, The Quarrymen wore whatever they wanted, for example check shirts and jeans. For this evening, Paul suggested they sport white shirts and bootlace ties, and that he and John should wear white suit jackets too. John agreed, and so for the first time, but not the last, John was convinced to wear a suit.

Pavilion Theatre, Aintree

The group played the Pavilion Theatre as The Silver Beatles in 1960. It was mentioned as a venue in a newspaper article about the group's appearance elsewhere, but no date is known for this solitary performance here.

Roach Avenue, Knowsley

The McCartneys moved from Wallasey in 1943 to a small, prefabricated home, on the Knowsley Estate on the outskirts of Liverpool. These homes came in kit form and were made of recycled aluminium and scrap metal from the wartime salvage. Thousands of these temporary houses were erected in the 1940s, since so many homes had been destroyed in the war. They were built to last about ten years, though some have lasted for decades and are only now being demolished.

11, Scargreen Avenue - N16

This was Jim McCartney's family home in Fazakerley, where he lived with his parents Joe and Florrie McCartney. This is where he met Mary Mohin, his future wife. She had been staying temporarily with Jim's sister Jin and her husband. An air raid forced them to spend the night cuddled together in the shelter. Mary was thirty-one and Jim was thirty-nine when they married.

11, Scargreen Avenue, Fazakerley

St. Swithin's Roman Catholic Church - N14

Jim and Mary McCartney's wedding took place at St. Swithin's Roman Catholic Church in Gill Moss on 15 April 1941. Mary had been raised as a Catholic, but married Jim who was a Protestant. As there can be great divisions in Liverpool over conflicting religions within marriage, they agreed between them that their children would be baptised as Catholics.

St. Swithin's Roman Catholic Church

Sir Thomas White Gardens, Everton

After a short stay at the pre-fabricated bungalow on Roach Avenue, Knowsley, the McCartneys moved into Sir Thomas White Gardens in Everton in 1943. This was the first home that came with Mary's new job as a district nurse and midwife. Soon after, the family moved to Western Avenue in Speke.

This estate of high-rise flats has since been demolished.

Sir Thomas White Gardens, centre, with a view over Everton and Anfield

10, Sunbury Road, Anfield - N12

Jim and Mary McCartney moved into 10, Sunbury Road, Anfield, after they exchanged wedding vows in April 1941. It was here in June 1942 that a newborn James Paul McCartney was brought home from the nearby Walton hospital.

2, Third Avenue - N7

Paul's mother, Mary Mohin, was born here at 2, Third Avenue in Fazakerley, on 29 September 1909. Mary's mother died in childbirth

10, Sunbury Road, Paul McCartney's first home

when Mary was only four years old. Her father, Owen, remarried soon after, but Mary didn't get on with her new stepmother, and lived with an aunt.

Walton Hospital - N5

Walton Hospital was originally built in 1868 as a workhouse. James Paul McCartney was born there on 18 June 1942. His mother was given a private ward because she was a nurse at the hospital. Paul had a difficult delivery and he was born with white asphyxia, which is a lack of oxygen, and had to be resuscitated. Paul's brother Mike was also born here on 7 January 1944.

ABOVE: *Walton Hospital, where Mary McCartney worked as a nurse, and gave birth to Paul and Mike*
BELOW: *Paul McCartney returned to Anfield in June 2008 to perform for Liverpool's European Capital of Culture*
OPPOSITE: *Paul and John at The Cavern, February 1963*

Southport

"Sky of blue, and sea of green"

Southport

Southport, home to the world-famous Royal Birkdale Golf Course, was once one of the favourite holiday destinations for many Lancashire families. It is undergoing a renaissance and is still a popular holiday resort.

Now part of Merseyside, it is a great day out for Liverpudlians since it is only twenty miles up the coast. It was therefore a handy place for The Beatles to play, without having to stray too far from home.

- Air Training Corps Club, Upper Aughton Road, Birkdale - **S1**
- Cambridge Hall, Lord Street - **S6**
- The Floral Hall, The Promenade - **S4**
- Glen Park Club, Lord Street - **S5**
- Kingsway Club, The Promenade - **S2**
- Labour Club, Devonshire Road - **S9**
- The Little Theatre, Hoghton Street - **S8**
- Odeon Cinema, Lord Street - **S7**
- Queens Hotel, The Promenade - **S2**

Air Training Corps Club, Upper Aughton Road

Air Training Corps (ATC) Club, Upper Aughton Road, Birkdale - S1
Situated in Birkdale just outside Southport, The Beatles made just the one appearance here on 9 March 1961.

Cambridge Hall, Lord Street - S6
Positioned on Lord Street, Southport, The Beatles appeared here once on 26 July 1962 to support singer Joe Brown.

It is now the Southport Arts Centre.

Southport Arts Centre, formerly Cambridge Hall

The Floral Hall, The Promenade - S4
The Beatles played here four times—twice in 1962 and twice in 1963. It was a popular locale because it had a proper theatre auditorium unlike many of the smaller clubs.

Glen Park Club, Lord Street - S5
The Beatles appeared here once on 5 November 1961.

Kingsway Club, The Promenade - S2
On The Promenade in Southport, The Beatles appeared here eight times in 1962.

They had to play upstairs in the hall as it didn't have a bar. The audience was mainly comprised of teenagers who of course didn't drink alcohol (well, not officially anyway).

The Floral Hall, The Promenade

Kingsway Club, The Promenade

Labour Club, Devonshire Road - S9
The Beatles played here on the same night as they performed at the ATC, which was a few miles away. Now called the "Devonshire", it is still an active club on Devonshire Road in Southport.

The Little Theatre, Hoghton Street - S8
The Beatles didn't perform here, but were filmed at this location for a documentary on 27 August 1963 called 'The Mersey Sound'. It was shown on BBC television on 9 October 1963, which was John Lennon's twenty-third birthday.

ABOVE: *The Little Theatre on Hoghton Street, where The Beatles were filmed for the documentary, 'The Mersey Sound'*

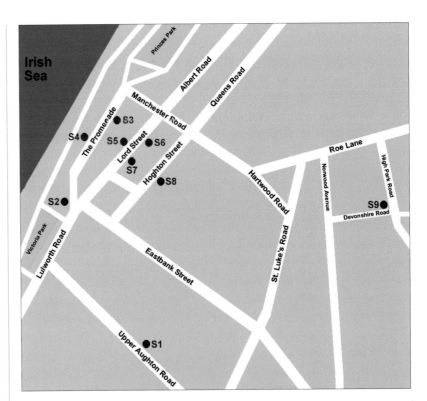

Odeon Cinema, Lord Street - S7

This site, now occupied by a Sainsbury's supermarket, used to be the Odeon Cinema. The Beatles made six consecutive appearances here in August 1963.

Queens Hotel, The Promenade - S2

This used to be a very popular hotel and dance venue. The Beatles made just one appearance here on 6 December 1962 in the Club Django, which was predominantly a jazz club.

The Labour Club, Devonshire Road

St. Helens

"Please Please Me"

In between Liverpool and Manchester sits St. Helens. A great industrial Lancashire town, St. Helens is famous for its Rugby League and glass making. The town is incorporated within Merseyside.

Plaza Ballroom, Duke Street

The Beatles played at the Plaza Ballroom, a popular venue, many times during 1962. It was here that Pete Best remembers having to ask Brian Epstein about his place in the band, after Liverpool promoter Joe Flannery had said to him "Do you want to join my band, oops?", as if Flannery knew something was going on. Flannery was a close friend of Epstein's. Epstein dismissed Pete's fears. "Rest assured, my boy, nothing like that is going to happen to you". It was only a couple of weeks later that he was called into Epstein's office to hear the news that he was sacked.

Town Hall, Newton-le-Willows

This venue is located in Market Street in Earlstown, Newton-le-Willows, near St. Helens. The Beatles made one appearance here on 30 November 1962, in an evening's entertainment billed as "The Big Beat Show 2".

ABOVE: *The Plaza Ballroom in St. Helens* OPPOSITE: *George signs autographs at NEMS, Liverpool, in February 1963*

The Wirral
"Across The Universe"

The Wirral is the name of the peninsula on the opposite side of the River Mersey to Liverpool. There is often great rivalry between the people of Liverpool and their neighbours on the Wirral. However, it features in several significant ways for The Beatles, showing that The Beatles' story is more than just about the City of Liverpool. To explore the sites here, a Beatles guided tour is recommended.

- Albert Marrion's Photo Studio, Wallasey - **WR1**
- Apollo Roller Rink, Moreton - **WR2**
- Barnston Women's Institute, Barnston - **WR3**
- Baskervyle Road, Heswall - **WR4**
- Beno Dorn, Birkenhead - **WR5**
- 92, Broadway Avenue, Wallasey - **WR6**
- Clarendon Furnishing, Hoylake
- The Embassy Club, Wallasey - **WR7**
- The Grosvenor Ballroom, Wallasey - **WR8**

- Haig Dance Club, Moreton
- Hoylake Parish Church, Hoylake
- Hulme Hall, Port Sunlight - **WR9**
- The Institute, Neston - **WR10**
- Irby Village Hall, Irby - **WR11**
- Macdonna Hall, West Kirby - **WR12**
- The Majestic Ballroom, Birkenhead - **WR13**
- Melody Inn, Wallasey
- Moreton Co-operative Hall - **WR14**

- New Brighton Pier
- St. Paul's Presbyterian Hall, Birkenhead
- Technical College, Birkenhead - **WR15**
- Tower Ballroom, New Brighton - **WR16**
- 18, Trinity Road, Hoylake - **WR17**
- Victoria Hall, Bebington - **WR18**
- YMCA, Hoylake
- YMCA, Birkenhead - **WR19**

This pizza shop is the former site of the Albert Marrion Photo Studio.

Apollo Roller Rink

Albert Marrion's Photo Studio, Wallasey - WR1
After Brian Epstein became The Beatles' manager, he set up a photo shoot at Albert Marrion's studio on the Penny Lane roundabout. Unfortunately, there was a mix up and so the session took place at his other studio in Wallasey. It is now a pizza shop.

Apollo Roller Rink, Moreton - WR2
The Beatles made one appearance at the Apollo on 26 March 1962 at one of Tony Booth's famous Rock and Twist Nights. It is currently the Apollo Dance Club.

Barnston Women's Institute, Barnston - WR3
The Beatles played at the Barnston Women's Institute three times on behalf of the Heswall Jazz Club. Their 24 March 1962 appearance was the first time The Beatles had worn their Beno Dorn stage suits. It was also one of the more bizarre venues they played, being a hut in the middle of the

The Barnston Women's Institute

countryside surrounded by cows. It was the hall of the Barnston Women's Institute which still meets there.

Baskervyle Road, Heswall - WR4
Paul persuaded his father Jim to retire in 1964 to this house, overlooking the Dee Estuary and Wales. Jim was sixty-two and had been working since he was fourteen and was more than happy to accept. Paul purchased the house, 'Rembrandt', for £8,750 and spent another £8,000 in furnishings and decorations, and installed a central heating system. Jim had two part-time gardeners and he looked after the vines in a heated greenhouse, studied ornithology whilst watching birds in the garden.

While visiting towards the end of 1966, Paul and Mike invited Guinness heir Tara Browne to stay with them. (Tara was killed in a car crash in December of that year, and was referred to in the song, "A Day In The Life" on the *Sgt. Pepper* album.) The three of them smoked "grass" and then jumped on their motorbikes.

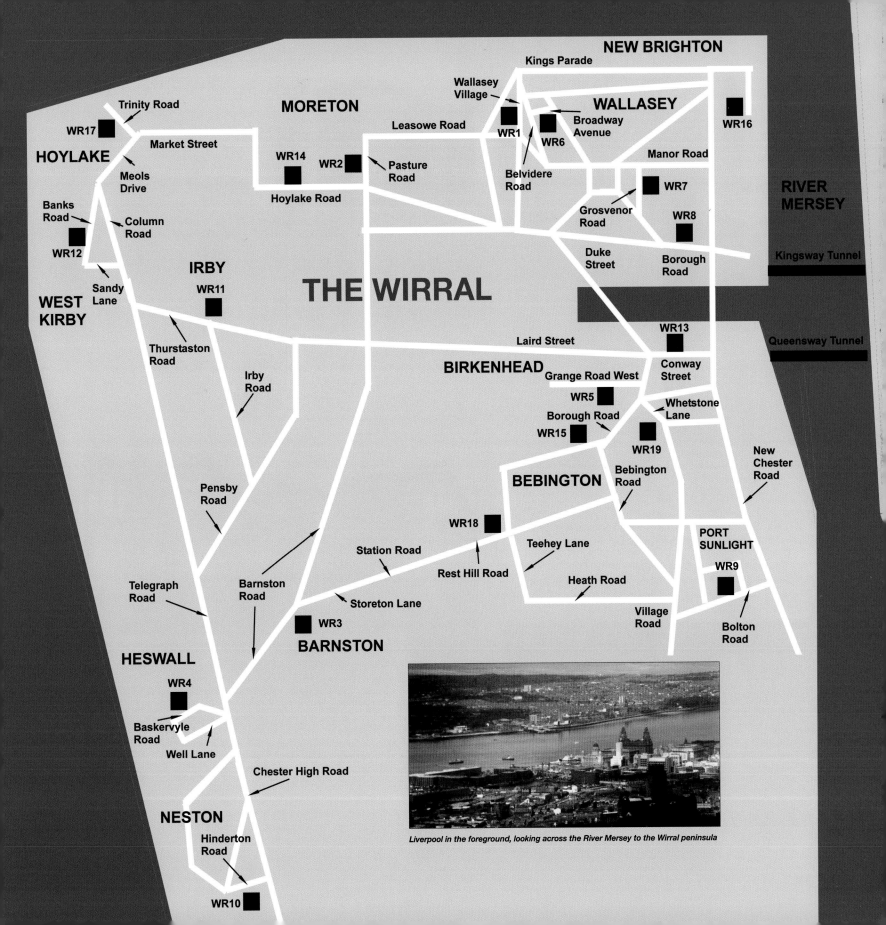

NEW BRIGHTON

Kings Parade

Wallasey Village →

WALLASEY

Leasowe Road

Broadway Avenue

WR16

WR1 **WR6**

Manor Road

Belvidere Road

WR7

Grosvenor Road

WR8

RIVER MERSEY

Duke Street

Borough Road

Kingsway Tunnel

MORETON

Trinity Road

WR17

HOYLAKE

Market Street

Meols Drive

WR14 **WR2**

Pasture Road

Hoylake Road

Banks Road

Column Road

WR12

Sandy Lane

IRBY

WR11

WEST KIRBY

Thurstaston Road

Irby Road

THE WIRRAL

Laird Street

WR13

Queensway Tunnel

BIRKENHEAD

Grange Road West

Conway Street

WR5

Whetstone Lane

Borough Road

WR15

WR19

Pensby Road

Station Road

WR18

Teehey Lane

Rest Hill Road

BEBINGTON

Bebington Road

New Chester Road

PORT SUNLIGHT

WR9

Heath Road

Telegraph Road

Barnston Road

Storeton Lane

Village Road

Bolton Road

WR3

BARNSTON

HESWALL

WR4

Baskervyle Road

Well Lane

Chester High Road

NESTON

Hinderton Road

WR10

Liverpool in the foreground, looking across the River Mersey to the Wirral peninsula

Paul took one bend too fast and parted company with the motorbike, smashing his face. They returned to "Rembrandt" and rounded up the family doctor to put a few stitches in Paul's lip. (Paul's chipped tooth can be seen in the "Paperback Writer" video).

Jim met and quickly married thirty-four-year-old Angela Williams in November 1964. She brought her five-year-old daughter, Ruth, into the marriage. Here they enjoyed a quiet life together until Jim's death in March 1976.

Brian Epstein bought The Beatles their new suits from Beno Dorn's shop

Beno Dorn, Birkenhead - WR5

This master tailor's shop at 5, Grange Road West, produced the finest handmade suits for The Beatles. Beno Dorn was an old friend of Epstein's. The Beatles were fitted with dark blue Mohair suits at a cost of £40 each.

92, Broadway Avenue, Wallasey - WR6

92, Broadway Avenue, the McCartneys home for a short time

The McCartneys moved from Sunbury Road when Paul was very young to 92, Broadway Avenue in Wallasey on the Wirral. They lived here for nearly two years. The area suffered bomb damage during the war and the family moved back to Liverpool.

Clarendon Furnishing, Hoylake

On his return from National Service in 1954, Epstein took up the role of running a new venture of Harry Epstein's in Hoylake. The business was profitable within a year.

The Embassy Club, Wallasey - WR7

The Embassy Club is located in Borough Road, Wallasey, and The Beatles appeared here in July 1960. The club is now a bingo hall.

The Embassy Club

The Grosvenor Ballroom, Wallasey

The Grosvenor Ballroom, Wallasey - WR8

The group first appeared here as The Silver Beatles on 14 June 1960. The line-up was John, Paul, George, Stuart and drummer Tommy Moore. When Tommy Moore failed to turn up, they appeared without a drummer. When John jokingly asked if there was a drummer in the house, an imposing rocker named "Ronnie" jumped up on the stage and began hitting the drums with reckless abandon. No one had the courage to kick him off the stage and the group members went blank when he asked at the end of the gig if he could join them.

The violence at The Grosvenor was so bad that The Beatles eventually stopped playing there.

Haig Dance Club, Moreton

The Quarrymen appeared at the Haig Dance Club four times, the first time in November 1957. It has since been replaced by houses.

Hoylake Parish Church, Hoylake

John and Cynthia's son, Julian Lennon, was christened at Hoylake Parish Church on Trinity Road in 1964. It was very close to Cynthia's childhood home. John was on the road with The Beatles and not present for the christening.

Hulme Hall, Port Sunlight - WR9

Hulme Hall, Port Sunlight, where Ringo made his debut with The Beatles

Hulme Hall in the Wirral's Port Sunlight was the venue for Ringo's first appearance with The Beatles, which occurred on 18 August 1962, and marked the official beginning of the Fab Four. The group was hired by The Horticultural Society, the Golf Club and Recreations Associations amongst others. It was also at this location that Monty Lister, representing hospital Radio Clatterbridge carried out the first radio interview with the Fab Four.

The Institute, Neston - WR10

The Silver Beatles appeared at the Institute six times, commencing on 2 June 1960. The Institute is on Hinderton Road in Neston, and is now a civic hall. The *Heswall and Neston News and Advertiser* covered the event, mentioning that the group had been "pulling in capacity houses on Merseyside". The reporter attributed their names as John Lennon, Paul Ramon, Carl Harrison, Stuart De Stael and Thomas Moore. These were the pseudonyms they used for their Scottish tour.

Irby Village Hall, where George left a suitcase of spare leads and strings, and never returned to collect it

Irby Village Hall, Irby - WR11

Situated on Thingwall Road, The Beatles made one appearance here on 7 September 1962 at a youth club gig in front of eighty teenagers for £35. Also known as the Mary Newton School of Dance, the hall has retained the original stage, and also the bar where they were served their drinks.

After their appearance, the band packed up and left but guitarist George Harrison forgot a suitcase. It was later found by Ernie Irlam whose son had been in one of the other bands appearing that night. He contacted Brian Epstein, who said someone would collect it, but no one ever arrived and the suitcase was put in an attic and forgotten. Local author Ray O'Brien had advised on the historical significance of the suitcase and helped arrange its sale. The case is made of compressed cardboard with plastic trim, and has George Harrison's initials on its sides. A small note on it says: "Mr. George Harrison c/o Beatles Party". It was full of odds and ends such as spare guitar strings and bits of electrical wire. The case was sold at auction in 2006 for just under £2,500.

Regarding the event in 1962, Ray O'Brien commented, "The organisers didn't raise the £35 on the night and held a sale, a bit like a modern car boot sale, on the bowling green opposite the village hall to get the extra money. Brian Epstein came round in his Rolls-Royce to pick up the rest of the cash".

Macdonna Hall, the site of the first Beatles gig under Epstein's management

Macdonna Hall, West Kirby - WR12

This 1 February 1962 appearance was The Beatles' first gig under Brian Epstein's management, arranged through promoter Sam Leach. Panic had set in when Epstein found out that John Lennon had laryngitis. Epstein was ready to cancel the show, billed as 'The Grand Opening of The Beatles Club', but Leach insisted the show must go on. At Leach's recommendation, Epstein picked up Rory Storm, who stood in for John at this concert. And so, Epstein's first line-up as Beatles manager was Paul, George, Pete and Rory Storm. The fee was £18, of which Epstein received 10 per cent, which just about covered his petrol and expenses.

The Majestic Ballroom, now a restaurant

The Majestic Ballroom, Birkenhead - WR13

Owned and run by The Rank Organisation, The Majestic Ballroom was opened in 1962. The Beatles made the first of sixteen appearances here on 28 June 1962. The Majestic was also the venue where Pete Best made his debut with Lee Curtis and the All Stars after being sacked from The Beatles.

Melody Inn, Wallasey

The Melody Inn was on the corner of Grove Road, Wallasey. The Beatles appeared here in 1961. The club burned down in 1969.

Moreton Co-operative Hall

Moreton Co-operative Hall - WR14

The Beatles appeared at the Moreton Co-operative Hall in 1961. The room was on the first floor and was their only appearance here.

New Brighton Pier

Though no dates have been recorded, Pete Best remembers The Beatles playing at the New Brighton Pier in 1960 and 1961. The pier was demolished in 1978.

St. Paul's Presbyterian Hall, Birkenhead

The Beatles made two appearances at St. Paul's Presbyterian Hall, the first being on 10 February 1962. The building has since been demolished.

A short film of The Beatles appearance here was recently unearthed, which can be seen on the *Best Of The Beatles* DVD. It was one the earliest known films of the group and the only time they were filmed wearing their leather suits.

Technical College, Birkenhead - WR15

The Beatles made three appearances here in February 1962. It is located on Borough Road, one of the main thoroughfares leading out of Birkenhead.

The Technical College, Birkenhead

On one occasion, Epstein remembered calling for each of The Beatles to pick them up for the concert, and Paul informed him that he was not ready. They could not wait for him, and so it was the only time a group member refused to play or missed a concert. The college was demolished in 2005.

Tower Ballroom, New Brighton - WR16
'Operation Big Beat' was promoter Sam Leach's rock 'n' roll extravaganza at the Tower Ballroom in New Brighton. Sam booked all the top artists and featured them back-to-back in some of the best Merseybeat shows ever seen. Unfortunately, a 1969 fire destroyed this once great landmark.

18, Trinity Road, Hoylake - WR17
This was Cynthia Powell's family home. Because her marriage to John was kept secret, Cynthia took Julian to her mother's home. Once the press found out where she was living, a throng of journalists and photographers camped outside the home, desperate for a story and photo of Mrs. Lennon and her baby.

Victoria Hall, Bebington - WR18
The Beatles made one appearance here on 4 August 1962. Bebington borders Birkenhead, and the Victoria Hall is on Village Road.

YMCA, Hoylake
This YMCA was near Cynthia Powell's home. The group's only appearance here was on 24 February 1962. It was a bad night for them and they were booed off stage. The building has since been demolished.

YMCA, Birkenhead - WR19
One of the little mentioned dates that The Beatles played was on 8 September 1962 at the YMCA on Whetstone Lane. They performed here and then moved on to The Majestic Ballroom in Birkenhead. Not much is recorded about this event.

This gig was a few weeks after drummer Pete Best had been replaced by Ringo Starr. The stage entrance was not on Whetstone Lane, but on the side street called "Quarry Bank".

The building has since been demolished.

ABOVE: *Victoria Hall, Bebington*
BELOW LEFT: *YMCA, Birkenhead,*
where The Beatles played once
BELOW RIGHT: *18, Trinity Road, Hoylake*

Bibliography

Baird, Julia	*Imagine This*	Hodder & Stoughton 2006
Baird, Julia and Geoffrey Giuliano	*John Lennon—My Brother*	Grafton Books 1988
Barrow, Tony	*John, Paul, George, Ringo and Me—The Real Beatles Story*	Carlton Publishing 2005
Baxter, Lew with Allan Williams	*The Fool On the Hill*	Praxis 2003
Beatles, The	*The Beatles Anthology*	Cassell & Co. 2000
Best, Pete and Patrick Doncaster	*Beatle. The Pete Best Story*	Plexus, London 1985
Best, Pete with Bill Harry	*The Best Years of The Beatles*	Headline Book Publishing Ltd. 1996
Best, Roag with Pete and Rory Best	*The Beatles—The True Beginnings*	Spine 2002
British Beatles Fan Club Magazines		
Clayson, Alan	*The Beatles Box—John Lennon,* *Paul McCartney, George Harrison, Ringo Starr*	Sanctuary Publishing Ltd 2001
Clayson, Alan	*Ringo Starr—A Life*	Sanctuary 2001
Clayson, Alan and Spencer Leigh	*The Walrus was Ringo—101 Beatles Myths Debunked*	Chrome Dreams Publishing 2003
Coleman, Ray	*Lennon*	Harper Perennial 1985 and 1992
Coleman, Ray	*Brian Epstein: The Man who Made The Beatles*	Penguin 1990
Cooper, Jack	*Liverpool Firsts*	Book Clearance Centre 1997
Cross, Craig	*The Beatles: Day by Day, Song by Song, Record by Record*	Iuniverse 2005
Davies, Hunter	*The Quarrymen*	Omnibus Press 2001
Davies, Hunter	*The Beatles—The Authorised Biography*	Granada Publishing Ltd 1979
Epstein, Brian	*A Cellarful of Noise*	Souvenir Press Ltd 1964
Garry, Len	*John, Paul and Me Before The Beatles*	CG Publishing Ltd. 1997
Geller, Deborah	*The Brian Epstein Story*	Faber and Faber 1999
Harrison, George	*I Me Mine*	Phoenix 2002
Harry, Bill	*Encyclopedia of Beatles People*	Blandford 1997
Harry, Bill	*The Ultimate Beatles Encyclopedia*	Virgin Books 1992
Harry, Bill	*The Ringo Starr Encyclopedia*	Virgin Books 2004
Harry, Bill	*The John Lennon Encyclopedia*	Virgin Books 2000
Harry, Bill	*The Paul McCartney Encyclopedia*	Virgin Books 2002
Harry, Bill	*The George Harrison Encyclopedia*	Virgin Books 2003
Henke, James	*Lennon Legend—An Illustrated Life of John Lennon*	Weidenfeld & Nicolson 2003
Jones, Ron	*The Beatles' Liverpool*	Ron Jones Associates
Kane, Larry	*Ticket to Ride*	Running Press 2003

Leach, Sam	*The Rocking City*	Pharaoh Press 1999
Leigh, Spencer	*Drummed Out*	Northdown Publishing 1998
Leigh, Spencer	*The Best of Fellas—The Story of Bob Wooler, Liverpool's First DJ*	Drivegreen Publications 2002
Lennon, Cynthia	*John*	Hodder & Stoughton 2005
Lennon, Cynthia	*A Twist of Lennon*	W.H. Allen & Co. 1978
Lennon, John	*In His Own Write and A Spaniard in The Works*	The Random House Group Ltd.1997
Lennon, Pauline	*Daddy Come Home—The True Story of John and His Father*	Angus & Robertson 1991
Lewisohn, Mark	*The Beatles Live*	Henry Holt 1986
Lewisohn, Mark	*The Complete Beatles Chronicle*	Chancellor Press 2002
Macdonald, Ian	*Revolution in the Head*	Pimlico 1994
Marchbank, *Pearce*	*With The Beatles—The Historic Photographs of Dezo Hoffman*	Omnibus Press 1984
McCartney, Mike	*Thank U Very Much*	Granada Publishing Ltd 1982
McDonnell, Jim	*The Day John met Paul*	Penguin Books
Miles, Barry	*Paul McCartney—Many Years From Now*	Vintage 1998
Mojo	*The Beatles—10 Years That Shook the World*	Dorling Kindersley 2004
National Trust	*Mendips*	National Trust 2003
Nash, Pete	*Paul McCartney—Pics and History*	Tracks Ltd. 2001
Norman, Philip	*Shout—The True Story of The Beatles*	Elm Tree Books 1981
O'Brien, Ray	*There Are Places I'll Remember Vol. 1 and 2*	Ray O'Brien—2001 and 2003
O'Brien, Ray	*There Are Places I'll Remember*	Bluecoat Press 2006
Pang, May	*Loving John—The Untold Story*	Warner Books 1983
Shapiro, Marc	*All Things Must Pass—The Life of George Harrison*	Virgin Books 2002
Shotton, Pete and Nicholas Schaffner	*John Lennon—In My Life*	Stein and Day 1983
Spitz, Bob	*The Beatles—The Biography*	Little Brown & Co. 2005
Sutcliffe, Pauline	*Stuart Sutcliffe—The Beatles Era*	Timeframed Limited
Sutcliffe, Pauline with Douglas Thompson	*The Beatles Shadow: Stuart Sutcliffe and His Lonely Hearts Club*	Sedgwick Pauline and Jackson 2001
Taylor, Alistair	*A Secret History*	John Blake Publishing 2001
Turner, Steve	*A Hard Day's Write*	Carlton Publishing 1994
Turner, Steve	The *Gospel According to The Beatles*	John Knox Press, Kentucky 2006
Wheeler, Scott	*Charlie Lennon—Uncle to a Beatle*	Wheeler Comms 2005
Williams, Allan	*The Man Who Gave The Beatles Away*	Ballantine Books 1975

Image Acknowledgments

Alder Hey Imagine appeal 299

Bagnall, Ann 71

Baird, Julia 50, 52 (top left), 52 (top right), 67

Barnes, Steve 153 (bottom right)

Best, Pete 20, 121 (top left), 121 (left), 122, 124 (top left), 124 (top right), 126, 127, 128, 129 (top right), 129 (bottom right), 130, 131, 132, 142, 143 (top left), 143 (top right), 145, 177

Booth, Tony 184

Chang, Barry 138

City Sightseeing Tours 233

Corbis 96 (top right), 96 (bottom right)

Covington, Bill 167

Dorsey, Don 178

Davis, Rod 98

Fagan, Ged 77, 318

Faron 147

Getty Images 83

Hanton, Colin 39, 108, 288

Holmes, Harry 61, 70

Holmes, Jackie 153, 179

Holmes, Tim 61, 71

Horley, John 27

Leach, Sam 40, 119

LIPA 207

Liverpool Daily Post 196

Liverpool Echo 94, 97

Liverpool Records Office 30, 224, 225, 228, 243, 256, 261, 263

Marsden, Robert 99

Mersey Partnership 230

Milson, Irene 86

Mirrorpix 10, 23, 24, 44, 46, 60, 76, 85, 88, 89, 90, 91, 93, 97, 118, 149, 150, 157, 159, 163, 165, 168, 181, 185, 192, 193, 194, 197, 198, 199, 200, 202, 203, 208, 279, 280, 288, 290, 293, 329

Nash, Pete 38, 80, 87, 226, 227, 264, 287

National Trust 68, 77, 252, 272

National Trust/ Emma Williams (Photographer) 273

Newby, Chas 145

Peacock, Dave 220, 221 (top), 221 (bottom)

The Quarrymen 70, 81, 100, 101, 102 (top left), 105 (top right), 105 (bottom left), 105 (top left), 106

Redferns/ M. Haywood Archives 151

Rex Features/ Everett Collection 296

Rex Features/ Keystone USA 79, 301

Rex Features/ Michael Ward 153 (top), 216

Rex Features/ Sharok Hatami 310

Rhind, Geoff / LFI 111

Rice, Mike 243

Roach, Kevin and Liverpool Records Office 81, 241, 317

Salvation Army 253, 266, 276, 277

Sandells, Mike 35 (bottom right)

St. Peter's Church 109, 113 (top left), 113 (top right)

St. Silas School 288

Sutcliffe, Pauline 132, 134 (top), 134 (bottom), 135, 137

Topfoto 156

Unknown 91, 92, 105, 151, 155, 236, 237

Valentine, Don/ Jones, Ron 187

Ward, Michael 4, 6, 17, 82, 183, 188 (bottom left), 188 (right), 189 (top), 189 (bottom left), 189 (bottom right), 218, 323

Williams, Allan 136, 140

Williams, Stan 104, 258

Young, Roy 42

Other photos and illustrations courtesy David Bedford.

Every effort has been made to correctly acknowledge the source or copyright holder of each illustration and Dalton Watson Fine Books Ltd. apologises for any unintentional errors or omissions, which will be corrected in future editions of this book.

HELP! Visiting Liddypool

If you want to visit the Beatles' Liverpool, then here is a list of useful contact details to help you can plan your trip. It is always advisable to book your tours before you arrive in Liverpool, so that you won't be disappointed. For any other queries not included here, you can find information at www.liddypool.com.

The general tourist information website to research your trip is www.visitliverpool.com, where you can search for Beatles-related information, plus hotels, restaurants and many more activities in Liverpool to plan your trip.

Beatles Attractions

The Beatles Story	www.beatlesstory.com	0044 151 709 1963
The Casbah Coffee Club	www.casbahcoffeeclub.com	0044 151 280 3519
The Cavern	www.cavernclub.org	0044 151 236 8081
City Sightseeing Liverpool Tours	www.city-sightseeing.com	0044 151 203 3920
Homes of John Lennon and Paul McCartney	www.nationaltrust.org.uk	0044 151 427 7231

Beatles Tours

For a one-stop package including transport, hotel and tours, you can visit www.traveltoliverpool.com
For specific Beatles tours, consider the following tours:

Beatles Magical Mystery Tour	www.beatlestour.org	0044 151 236 8081
Liverpool Tour Guide Service	www.visitliverpool.com	0044 7964 515681
Liverpool Beatles Tours	www.beatlestours.co.uk	0044 151 281 7738
Fab Cabs of Liverpool	www.fabcabsofliverpool.com	0044 151 909 1964
Beatles Fab Four Taxi Tours	www.thebeatlesfabfourtaxitour.co.uk	0044 151 601 2111

Beatles Themed Accommodation

Hard Days Night Hotel	www.harddaysnighthotel.com	0044 151 236 1964
Blenheim	www.blenheimlakesidehotel.co.uk	0044 151 727 7380
Eleanor Rigby Hotel	www.theeleanorrigbyhotel.com	0044 151 236 4656
Epstein House	www.brianepsteinhotel.com	0044 7810 100 900

Beatles Gift Shops in Liverpool

Hard Days Night Shop	www.harddaysnightshop.com
The Beatles Shop	www.thebeatleshop.co.uk

Also available in the "Liddypool" series:

Liddypool: Who Put The Beat In The Beatles?: The CD

To accompany *Liddypool: Birthplace of The Beatles,* this music CD tells the story of how The Quarrymen became The Beatles, from skiffle to rock 'n' roll, through the songs and artists that inspired them.

With twenty tracks from Elvis and Buddy Holly, to Lonnie Donegan and The Del-Vikings, the importance of each song is explained in the detailed booklet that accompanies the brand new CD by original artists.

The tracks are:
1. Bill Haley and His Comets - Rock Around The Clock
2. Lonnie Donegan - Rock Island Line
3. Elvis Presley - Heartbreak Hotel
4. Chuck Berry - Roll Over Beethoven
5. Carl Perkins - Be-Bop-A-Lula
6. Eddie Cochran - Twenty Flight Rock
7. The Del-Vikings - Come Go With Me
8. Vipers Skiffle Group - Maggie May
9. Carl Perkins - Matchbox
10. Bill Justis - Raunchy
11. The Crickets - That'll Be The Day
12. Johnny & The Hurricanes - Red River Rock
13. Billy Fury - Maybe Tomorrow
14. Johnny Gentle - Wendy
15. Howie Casey and The Seniors - Double Twist
16. Little Richard - Long Tall Sally
17. Faron's Flamingoes - Do You Love Me
18. Tony Sheridan and the Beat Brothers - My Bonnie
19. The Coasters - Searchin'
20. Kingsize Taylor & The Dominoes - Twist And Shout

More details at **www.whoputthebeatinthebeatles.co.uk**
and you can order the CD from **www.beatlesshop.co.uk**

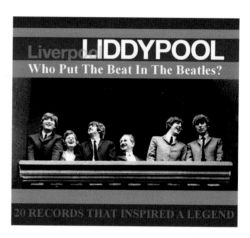

Liddypool: The DVD

Author David Bedford takes you on your own tour of The Beatles' Liverpool through pictures and film to show the Liddypool story. Visit their birthplaces, homes and schools, and your own Magical Mystery Tour around the birthplace of The Beatles.

On the DVD you will find biographies of John, Paul, George, Stuart, Pete, Ringo and Brian, plus visits to The Casbah, The Cavern, Penny Lane and Strawberry Field as he brings the "Liddypool" story to life.

More information at **www.liddypool.com**
and you can order the DVD from **www.beatlesshop.co.uk**

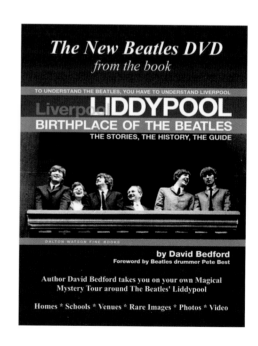